Jack Hinson's
One-Man War

JACK HINSON'S ONE-MAN WAR

TOM C. MCKENNEY

PELICAN PUBLISHING COMPANY
GRETNA 2016

First printing, January 2009
United Kingdom edition, May 2009
Second printing, November 2009
Third printing, October 2010
Fourth printing, April 2012
Fifth printing, May 2014
Sixth printing, September 2016

Library of Congress Cataloging-in-Publication Data

McKenney, Tom C. (Tom Chase)
  Jack Hinson's one-man war / Tom C. McKenney.
    p. cm.
  Includes bibliographical references and index.
  ISBN 978-1-58980-640-5 (hardcover : alk. paper) 1. Hinson, John W., 1807-1874.
2. Hinson, John W., 1807-1874—Family. 3. Landowners—Tennessee—Stewart
County—Biography. 4.   Farmers—Tennessee—Stewart County—Biography.
5.   Bubbling Springs (Tenn. : Farm)—History. 6.   Stewart County (Tenn.)—
Biography. 7. Snipers—Confederate States of America—Biography. 8. Guerrilla
warfare—Tennessee—History—19th century. 9.   Tennessee—History—Civil War,
1861-1865—Underground movements. 10.   United States—History—Civil War,
1861-1865—Underground movements. I. Title.
  F443.S7M35 2009
  976.8'3504092—dc22
  [B]
                                                    2008042121

Printed in the United States of America

Published by Pelican Publishing Company, Inc.
1000 Burmaster Street, Gretna, Louisiana 70053

For all those who did the dying, and those who grieved

Contents

A brother offended is harder to be won than a strong city.

—*Proverbs 18:19*

Preface

Concerning Quotations

Quotation sources throughout the text are as attributed, or explained in the text. Quotations at the beginning of the prologue, each chapter, and the epilogue, not otherwise attributed, are the author's, taken from the text of that portion.

Concerning the Details

This book has been researched, documented, and written as history. It has been an extremely difficult job: first, most of the events occurred more than 140 years ago; and, second, the story has been suppressed, since the war years, by the family. The story's suppression was motivated, in the beginning, by fear of the occupying Union forces' retaliation during Reconstruction. Two generations later, the time of Jack Hinson's grandchildren, some family members considered the old man's exploits to be an embarrassment since he had been, in a sense, an outlaw, a wanted man with a price on his head, a notorious killer. In that locally prominent family, he became a topic not to be discussed, and silence settled over Hinson's story.

As a result, important details, that would otherwise flesh out and enrich the account, were forever lost as many of them were literally taken to the grave. Very few of the details survived the death of Jack Hinson's grandson and namesake, John S. Hinson, in 1963.

When I began the research, almost nothing was known beyond those few words on the historical marker where I began (and part of that was in error). Even the exact location of the Hinson plantation, Bubbling Springs, was not known to the family, nor was the location of their postwar home, Magnolia Hill. The family knew the story of the execution of the Hinson sons, but no one knew where it happened or even which two sons were killed. Nothing was known of the arrest at the time of the surrender of Fort Donelson nor the brief imprisonment of the two sons who were later executed. Nothing was known of Jack's activities during and after the battle or his acquaintance with Grant and the Confederate generals. Nothing was known of the sworn affidavit concerning the surrender of Fort Donelson, which he executed a year later. Nothing was known of Jack's taking of the loyalty oath, his citadel on Graffenreid Bluff, or his postwar status and activities. Camp Lowe, the Fort Heiman satellite and base camp for patrols sent out after Jack Hinson, was forgotten, and its location was unknown.

In the beginning of the work, little was known about Jack Hinson's nearest neighbor, not even his identity, whose plantation home was taken over and used as the Union hospital during the battle. Information on his other neighbor, whose home became Grant's headquarters for the Fort Donelson battle, was also scarce, except for the two oft-repeated words: "Widow Crisp" (and, at the time of the battle, she was not yet a widow). The historical marker, supposedly identifying the location of the Crisp home, is almost a half mile from the actual site. A passing comment by an area librarian led to interviews with a rich secondary source, the granddaughter of Mrs. Crisp's son. He had told her, many times, what he experienced in February of 1862 during the battle. Only through him, do we now know of the sensitivity, kindness, and compassion shown to Mrs. Crisp and her son by General Grant and his staff. Through him, we now also know Martha Crisp's full name, how she became "Widow Crisp," about her life and remarriage after the battle, where she is buried, and how wrong Gen. Lew Wallace's "white trash" characterization was.

Jack's special rifle was found, traced to its current owner in Murfreesboro, Tennessee, and we now know its history and have a chain of possession. A nineteenth century published recollection of Nathan Bedford Forrest's adjutant, Maj. Charles W. Anderson, which told of Hinson's guiding Forrest on at least three raids, confirmed Anderson-Black-McFarlin family tradition concerning Jack's relationship with Forrest.

Most of what we now know about Jack Hinson and his family was dug out the hard way: traveling to pursue the slightest leads, asking thousands of questions, placing newspaper ads, and searching archives. When the research began, four of Hinson's great-grandchildren were still living; they provided the few surviving family traditions, letters, photos, etc. still known to exist.

The Hinson family Bible, letters, photographs, and other records that would have answered so many questions were apparently destroyed when Federal troops burned their home at Bubbling Springs. Few records of that kind have survived, mostly those of Jack's children and grandchildren, and they provide little insight into the heart of the story—Jack's career as a self-appointed Confederate sniper.

The foundational facts of the events are known and documented, recovered in exhaustive research of the records of the National Archives, the Kentucky and Tennessee State Archives, records at Fort Donelson, collections of libraries and historical societies, nineteenth-century newspaper accounts, written reminiscences of contemporaries, and multisource family traditions. We know, for instance, about the armed Union troop transport that, under Hinson's deadly rifle fire, surrendered to that one old man; most of the details, however, are unknown. The same applies to his relationship with Grant, Pillow, Forrest, and others; the burning of the home; the incident in the Hundred Acre Field; his family's tragic exodus in a blizzard; and his citadel on the ridge above the Towhead Chute. We know that they occurred, but, in the writing, many of the details have had to be assumed. In most cases, only God really knows what was said, what people thought and felt, which way the wind was blowing, what Jack ate in the wilderness, or where the slaves stood as the house burned. In every case, the principle followed in assuming such details was this: they were chosen because, in light of the evidence that does survive, local custom, and the historical context, to choose otherwise would have been illogical—flying in the face of reason.

This is a true story, written in its historically accurate context, with its foundational facts extensively researched and authenticated, but it is a story, to the great misfortune of us all, about which many details are unknown. In some places, I fleshed out the story in order to let the reader learn not only what occurred, but also what it was like, in human terms, for the participants. In this way those who suffered and died, both Union and Confederate, soldier and civilian, black and white, young and old, emerge from crumbling, yellowed documents, faded diaries, microfilm, statistical summaries, and footnotes, to take on flesh—to live, laugh, cry, bleed, and die.

The deaths of at least seven of the Hinson children were real. And all those Union soldiers and sailors whom Jack killed were actual boys and men, with parents, families, wives, and children, who grieved at their losses. I very much wish this fact to come to life for the readers, especially those to whom such events seem distant and academic, as impersonal as miles of railroad, tons of supplies, or electoral votes.

I believe that I have rescued a compelling historic and human story from our past, one that was nearly lost forever, and it is my hope that the laughter and the tears, the loving and the hating, the selfless nobility and the venal brutality of that war, the tearing of very human flesh, and the breaking of very human hearts, will become real to the reader.

They happened.

Tom C. McKenney
Long Beach, Mississippi

Acknowledgments

This book could not have been written without Frances Hinson, native of Magnolia, tireless, avid historian, and widow of Charles Dudley Hinson, great-grandson of Jack Hinson. She probably qualifies as coauthor but must not be held responsible for my mistakes.

My wife, Marty, an avid historian, provided ongoing research support, served as a restraint on my excessive zeal for certain aspects of the story, and put up with my extended absences. My historian daughter, Melissa Harris, provided priceless historical review and correction of the early chapters and gave me priceless help in my struggle with the computer, with time she didn't have; and my daughter Sally Mahoney and her husband, Prof. Joe Mahoney, contributed overview editing of the entire manuscript.

Prof. Benjamin Franklin Cooling, of the National Defense University, gave gracious encouragement, tough-minded advice, and critiqued the entire manuscript. His excellent book on the battle for Forts Henry and Donelson was my touchstone for the battle and its aftermath.

Dave and Marian Novak, of Signal Tree Publishing Company, who knew much more about what I was trying to do than I did, suffered long with me, pointing me in right directions at considerable cost to themselves. I owe them a very great deal.

Pam Ford, Stewart County librarian, was supportive from the beginning and my right arm, at times, throughout. Pam's friends, Ruth Mathis and Lynn Stacy at the Stewart County Courthouse, graciously gave priceless assistance in deed research and made available the old courthouse photo.

Scot Danforth, director of the University of Tennessee Press, was generous with his advice and encouragement and played a key role in determining the ultimate form of this book.

Joe McCormick, of Pinson, Tennessee, not only provided the artwork and some of the photographs, but also tramped through the woods and climbed around on Jack's ridge with me, in places where mountain goats would fear to tread.

Susan Hawkins, of the Fort Donelson National Battlefield, graciously and generously provided key help, research guidance, ongoing encouragement, and priceless contemporary newspaper accounts, including that of the arrest and imprisonment of Hinson's sons. Jimmy Jobes, also of the Fort Donelson staff, shared his vast knowledge of the two battles.

Nelda Saunders, Stewart County historian and gifted researcher, was enormously helpful with tax, marriage, and deed research. I owe her much. David Ross, of Dover and Erin, Tennessee, historian, writer, and editor, provided key information and encouragement at an early, critical, discouraging time.

The late Jill Knight Garrett, of Columbia, Tennessee, preeminent historian of the region, encouraged, advised me, and provided me with a key document, never before published. No history of the Twin Rivers area could be written without reference to her work and that of her late mother, Iris Hopkins McClain. The same is true of the many booklets on area history by another tireless area historian, the incomparable Nina Finley.

The late Alvin Crutcher, Bubbling Springs neighbor, patiently provided authentic information on living and farming in that area and led us to the Hundred Acre Field. Frank Cherry, native of the Danville area, who seems to have four generations of river-land history in his head, was a generous source. The Rev. Roy West introduced me to Jack's favorite firing point on Graffenreid Bluff and sent me on the search for it. And Bart Stephenson was an enthusiastic and energetic source on the bluff, where he had made his home, and on the river and flanking creeks.

The late John Stewart Hinson; his late brother, Charles Dudley Hinson; and their niece, Ava Hinson Collett, were zealous for the project and extremely helpful. Betty Jo Hinson Dortch shared valuable family letters and notes, and the late Rosalee Coppage, Thomas Hinson descendant, shared valuable family traditions, photographs, and genealogical information.

The late Fran Swor Abernathy, intrepid historian, tramped through tick-and-chigger-infested woods with me to find long-lost Camp Lowe and contributed key research in Henry County archives.

Cheryl Jameson Smith, of Waverly, enthusiastically provided

crucial information and photographs of Patrick Henry Bateman. Doug Mitchell, also of Waverly, opened his home and provided valuable testimony concerning his grandmother's terrible experience there at the hands of guerrillas.

Gynel Wilson, of Jackson, Tennessee, was generous with vital research assistance there, and Col. James D. Brewer, writer and historian of Elizabethtown, Kentucky, shared his notes on the story.

Mike Silvey, of Clarksville, Tennessee, graciously made available the Reuben R. Ross diaries. Shannon Scott, of Ocean Springs, Mississippi, with his computer graphics, made my hand-drawn maps look respectable. Jane Morrison, faithful friend, was a willing, patient e-mail terminal in Clarksville.

Judge Ben Hall McFarlin, of Murfreesboro, and his family, graciously opened their home and provided access to Jack's rifle (*the* rifle) and vital family history.

And, when I was first searching, blindly, with almost no leads, librarians in area county libraries were generous with their resources and encouragement. I owe special thanks to Kay French and Jenny Rye at Erin and Greta Morton Burnett, formerly of Camden.

Introduction

In the mid 1960s, driving westward across the Land Between the Lakes National Recreation Area, I was thinking about the area as it had been in earlier times. Prior to the building of the dams that created Kentucky Lake on the west and Lake Barkley on the east, flooding the low-lying portions on both sides, the land had been known simply as "Between the Rivers." It was an inland peninsula running north and south, bound by the Tennessee River

The historical marker at Golden Pond.

on the west, the Cumberland River on the east, and the mile-wide Lower Ohio River across the north end. The place and its people were isolated; there were no bridges. In that strip of land, roughly sixty miles long from north to south and ten to fifteen miles across in most parts, there lived some exceptional people. From the time of the earliest settlers in the latter eighteenth century until they were progressively driven from their homes by the federal government in the 1940s, '50s, and '60s to depopulate the area, those people had been independent and self-reliant. They were accustomed to hard work, hardship, and deprivation, complaining to no one, expecting help from no one. They were God-fearing people, and people who feared no one but God. They had asked only to be left alone.

But those people and their homes, farms, stores, churches, and schools were gone, and as I drove, I was thinking of them. In the area where the town of Golden Pond had been, I paused to look around. Only clusters of trees, traces of stone walls, and cemeteries remained of that once vital, proud little town. As I continued westward from the site of Golden Pond, I saw a historical marker, pulled over, and stopped to read it.

The marker was engraved with the brief history of a man named Jack Hinson, whose sons had been executed by Union troops during the Federal occupation in 1862. He had set out to avenge them, becoming a sniper who terrorized the Union army for the rest of the war. Ever since that day, I have longed to know more about the man and his story, but life had taken me elsewhere.

Finally, in the early 1990s, I was able to begin to pursue the story. I went back to Golden Pond, back to that marker, noted the Kentucky archives file number, and there I started my search. Hinson's story was virtually unknown beyond those sixty-five words on the historical marker, and some of that was in error. Except for fragments, the story of Jack Hinson has never before been told. Mentioned only in one small, locally published book and an unpublished manuscript in the Tennessee State Archives, he is not even the subject of a single published chapter, appearing in histories only in brief paragraphs and footnotes.

Nothing has been written of what it was like for the Union occupation troops who pursued him. Now, however, their story is also finally told, woven through the narrative, after extensive research of their unit records, diaries, and letters, in public archives and private collections.

The story of Hinson and his pursuers is true, but it will seem like fiction. It is the story of a responsible family man, prosperous and prominent in his community, with vast land holdings. His plantation home was at times a hospice to travelers and to prominent people. General Grant had been a guest there. Although Hinson owned a large plantation with many slaves, he opposed secession. In most ways, he was a fairly typical man of the South and of his time, but he didn't want to see the nation divided, and he opposed the war.

His attitude was also typical of the people Between the Rivers on the Kentucky-Tennessee border. Their geographical isolation was reflected in their general indifference to political matters beyond those rivers. However, as an unwelcome Civil War crowded into his life, neutrality became increasingly difficult to maintain. By the time of the battle for Fort Donelson, with some of it fought on his land, his neutrality was almost untenable. And, in the Federal occupation that followed, one tragic act of brutality overwhelmed it. The execution and mutilation of two of his sons by the occupying Union army made a deadly enemy of Jack Hinson and plunged the area more deeply into bloody conflict.

He set out to get vengeance, and this he did—spectacularly. He had a rifle specially made for long-range accuracy and began a one-man war against the Union he had previously supported. As a lone sniper, he became a deadly gadfly to the occupying army and to personnel aboard navy boats on the rivers. By the end of the war, he had probably killed more than one hundred. He operated alone, except when making history with Nathan Bedford Forrest as a guide. Elements of nine regiments, both cavalry and infantry, and an amphibious task force of specially built navy boats with a special-operations Marine brigade targeted the elderly man with a growing price on his head. They never got him.

This is the story of one man's reluctant, but savage, war with his country; vengeance; and the high price that it exacts, in not only one life or one family, but a toll that can be levied upon generations yet unborn, with open-ended tragedy.

In pursuit of the man and his story, I have traveled extensively through the area of the events, searched in county libraries, city libraries, university libraries, private collections, the archives of historical societies, the Kentucky and Tennessee State Archives, and the National Archives. I have attended reunions Between the Rivers, sought out living sources, personal papers, and family records. I have climbed Jack Hinson's rugged hills, searched his forests, waded his swampland, and followed him through his creeks and meadows. He has proved as elusive to me as he was to the Union troops who futilely pursued him and the bounties upon his head. Now, at long last, I have found him.

This book is his story.

Prologue

Sudden Death in the Early Morning

"Before the crack of one hundred grains of black powder was heard on the boat below, a spinning, supersonic, .50-caliber projectile slammed the officer to his knees."

As the sun rose above Jack's bluff, climbing steadily higher through the trees, spilling its soft morning light over the bluff and down into the wide valley of the Tennessee River below, morning sounds increasingly invaded the stillness. It was a peaceful early morning between the rivers. The only sounds were those of birds greeting the daybreak, stirring forest animals, and the rising of a warming breeze in the trees.

The bluff was the steep, western end of a high, densely forested ridge. To the north, downstream toward Paducah, Kentucky, was the mouth of Leatherwood Creek; upstream to the south, and much nearer, was the mouth of Hurricane Creek. At the base of the bluff, in the wide river bottom, there were green cornfields and a grove of chestnut trees. A dirt road ran along the river, paralleled by a narrow-gauge railroad. Across the river, near the Benton County shore, was Hurricane Island. On the near side of the river, a short distance offshore, was a smaller island called the Towhead. The islands were landmarks on the Tennessee River, covered with cottonwood, brown birch, maple, and sycamore and fringed with willow and cane, the native bamboo used by the locals for fishing, beanpoles, and pipe stems. The river channel ran close in there, between the near bank and the Towhead, and the narrow passage was called the Towhead Chute.

The chute was a choke point in the river route from Grant's supply depots at Cairo and Paducah to his invading armies in the field to the south and east. All large boats were forced to pass through that narrow channel in order to avoid running aground. Thus, Grant's gunboats, supply boats, and transports were forced to pass nakedly below the gaze of that high bluff, making them predictable and very vulnerable to attack from the shore. That wasn't the only problem. There, in the chute, much of the power of the mighty Tennessee River was concentrated, squeezed through the narrow passage with great force. Northbound boats rushed through the chute at breathtaking speeds, but southbound boats, at full power, could barely make headway against the surging mill-race current that rushed northward. The boats headed south were nearly stationary targets, sitting ducks, in that deadly gauntlet for upwards of an hour. And there was no avoiding it.

From a rock ledge about twenty feet below the crest of the bluff, high above the rushing current of the Towhead Chute, Jack Hinson sat and watched. Downstream, a steamboat was making its way southward from Paducah against the current, visible only in its black smoke, rising above the bluffs in dark, smudgy brushstrokes, against the pale morning sky. Silently and patiently, he watched its progress. There was plenty of time, and it was entirely predictable. He knew that it would continue on its southbound course and would soon pass below him. There was no reason to wonder where on the wide river the boat would pass, for he knew the location of the channel; and there was no reason for anxiety about missing his chance, for he knew that the current in the chute would give him plenty of time. He smoked his pipe contentedly and waited as the big boat appeared and approached at full speed. It was a Union gunboat.

With his heavy rifle barrel resting on a low limb of a small oak, he cocked the hammer, put a cap on the nipple, eased the hammer back down on the nipple, and waited. It was going to be a fine day—pleasant, easy weather, and another opportunity for a kill. Maybe more than one.

Hinson was fifty-seven. By the standards of the day, he was an old man, but he was tough, strong, and agile, and his vision was as keen as his all-business, methodical mind. Some called him "Old Jack." Others, lately, had begun to refer to him as "Captain Jack." Like most Between the Rivers men, he was completely at home in the forested hills and in the cane breaks, cypress bays, and willow thickets of the river and creek bottoms. So this morning he waited, patiently and comfortably, high up on his bluff, watching as the gunboat approached the chute and slowed suddenly as it was struck by the surging current. The gunboat would be in the chute at least forty-five minutes, maybe an hour, a nearly stationary target.

As he looked over the barrel of his rifle, with its growing number of tiny, eighth-of-an-inch circles, each the record of a confirmed kill, he patiently scanned the exposed men on the boat, looking for the epaulet of an officer. Seeing a blue-clad officer leaning on the forward port side rail, smoking his pipe, Jack looked no farther. As his attention closed down on that one man, like the zoom lens of a camera, he no longer saw the others. For that brief moment, Jack and the Yankee officer were alone—the only two people on earth. He pressed his cheek against the curly maple stock of his custom-made, .50-caliber, Kentucky rifle. Looking over the rear sight, he aligned the front sight blade in the rear sight's "V" and, holding his sight picture, moved the rifle until the bright German silver bead of the front sight blade was at the point where the Union officer's neck met his chest. He moved the bead lower, down to the fourth shiny brass button on the blue uniform coat, then eased the bead a little lower still, to allow for the downhill shot. Downhill shots tend to go high, and the six-hundred-yard range was too great to try for a head shot.

Jack cocked the hammer deliberately, one click to half cock, then the second click to full cock.

Unaware that the next few seconds would be his last on earth, the lieutenant puffed contentedly on his pipe and enjoyed the scenery where, just ahead, Hurricane Creek was flowing into the Tennessee River. It was a fine and gentle morning on the river, its watery fragrance was filling the air, and the lieutenant's pipe was the perfect postscript to an excellent breakfast. High above him and unseen, Old Jack held his sight picture tight, his gray eyes as cool as the steel of his rifle barrel, waiting for the breeze to subside. As the gunboat struggled at full power to make headway, the wind fell to a whisper. Jack cocked the set trigger, felt the soft click as it prepared the rear trigger to fire, and tightened his grip on the stock. He took a deep, easy breath, exhaled, then took another deep, easy breath, let half of it out, and held it. After one final check of his sight picture, he touched the trigger.

Before the crack of one hundred grains of exploding black powder reached the boat below, a spinning, supersonic, .50-caliber projectile slammed the officer to his knees as his pipe slipped from unfeeling fingers and fell onto the scrubbed deck in a shower of sparks. He fell slowly over on his back, with his legs awkwardly under him, and rolled gradually onto his side, blood erupting from his chest and flowing more slowly from the exit wound in his lower back. His eyes looked straight ahead, seeing nothing; his face was a grayish mixture of surprise and puzzlement. Without a word, or even a groan, massive bleeding and shock snuffed out the candle of his life. Suddenly he more resembled a crumpled, discarded pile of bloody clothing than the proud naval officer he had been only three seconds before. He didn't move, except for some twitching in his legs. He was dead—another statistic in the grim bookkeeping of that terrible war.

As the sound of the shot reached the boat, the sailors above deck dived for cover, looking in vain confusion for the source of the danger. All they saw was the green sameness of the river bottom and the steep hill rising above it. High up, some of them thought they saw a small cloud of white smoke dissipating in the warming air. Deck guns fired uselessly at the base of the bluff, and sailors fired rifles, impotently, into the cornfield and various places on the bluff beyond.

No fire was returned, and again the only sounds were those of the boat's throbbing engines, its thrashing paddles, the rushing water, and the breeze. As Jack watched, motionless, from above, the surgeon and his orderlies moved quickly to the crumpled remains of the downed officer. He could easily have killed one or two of them, but that was not his way. In his personal protocols for such matters, medical men going to the aid of a downed comrade were off-limits and not to be harmed. All other soldiers and sailors, however, were fair game. Officers were preferred.

He watched as the boat continued its uninterrupted struggle up the chute, finally passing the south end of the Towhead and steering to starboard with the channel, away from the peril of that rushing gauntlet and out into the relative safety of midriver.

As the sun rose ever higher above the bluff and the morning gently warmed, Jack cleaned and reloaded his rifle. Seeing no more boats or smoke downstream and hearing no whistles from that direction, he shouldered his shot bag, picked up his rifle, and, using his free hand to pull himself from tree to tree, climbed to the top of the bluff. He took one more look at the boat as it steamed on toward Danville Crossing, then turned and disappeared into the forest.

Aboard the gunboat, as it picked up speed against the slower current in midstream, the surgeon prepared the lieutenant's body for burial, and bluejackets cleaned the bloody deck and rail. On the quarterdeck, the gunboat's captain began to compose in his mind the condolence letter he would have to write to his lieutenant's family. He was thinking of what a good man the lieutenant had been and was still trying to adjust to the sickening reality of his death. He was also thinking that war is a hellish, nasty business.

Jack Hinson would have agreed had he and the captain been able to discuss the matter. He had been, until recently, a man of peace and one of the leading citizens of Stewart County, Tennessee. His large farm, Bubbling Springs, had been a prosperous, productive plantation and home to his family and a large number of slaves—a place of plenty, happiness, and tranquility. Although surrounded with secessionist friends and family, he had opposed secession and the war. When war had come, he had wanted no part of it; at the time of the Fort Donelson battle, he had been uniquely neutral, a friendly acquaintance of both General Grant and the Confederate commanders. After the battle, Grant had been a guest in his home.

But that was then.

Now he was a deadly enemy, feared and hated by the Union soldiers and sailors who had to pass through his area, and a notorious, most-wanted fugitive hunted by Grant's army and navy, with a growing reward offered for anyone who could kill him.

What had transformed this prominent, prosperous peacemaker into a deadly enemy of his own government, a homeless, shadowy terror of the forest, visiting sudden death upon all in Union blue who had the bad fortune to appear in his sights? What had brought about such tragic transformation? What could have created such a nightmare?

Chapter 1

The Hinsons of Bubbling Springs

"They were, in a very real sense, mountaineers without mountains."

In the western reaches of Kentucky and Tennessee, there is a long slice of land, in effect an inland peninsula, known as the Land Between the Lakes National Recreation Area. It runs approximately north-south, with Kentucky Lake on the west side, and Lake Barkley on the east side. Since 1969, it has been uninhabited except for USDA Forest Service personnel and the hunters, fishermen, boaters, tourists, field trippers, and researchers who constantly come and go. It occupies much of what was once an isolated land surrounded on three sides by great rivers.

Prior to the radical changes brought by the Tennessee Valley Authority, before the flanking rivers became lakes and the people were uprooted and forced to leave their homes, that forested inland peninsula was locally known simply as Between the Rivers. The inhabitants usually pronounced it 'Tween the Rivers.

This land between the rivers consisted of the western portions of four counties and one entire county. In Kentucky, there were the western ends of Livingston, Lyon, and Trigg Counties; in the Tennessee portion, there was most of Stewart County and all of Humphreys County. At Cumberland City the Cumberland River turns off to the southeast toward Nashville, the land between the rivers widens increasingly, and the effects of being bound closely between the flanking rivers diminish imperceptibly. For this reason, it isn't possible to say, precisely, where Between the Rivers ended southward, but it was at some ill-defined point south of a line between Johnsonville and Waverly in Tennessee.

Prior to the mid-twentieth century, Kentucky Lake was the Tennessee River and Lake Barkley was the Cumberland River, unimpeded in their ancient flows, keeping their natural channels. As the two mighty streams neared their mouths, they turned almost due north and ran parallel for sixty miles before emptying into the Lower Ohio River. Paducah, Kentucky, was (and is) at the mouth of the Tennessee, and Smithland, Kentucky, was (and is) at the mouth of the Cumberland. At this point, the Ohio River is a mile wide in its final run to its mouth at the Mississippi River, just thirty-five miles downstream.

This inland peninsula was river country. The lives of the people were woven inextricably into the turns, currents, channels, and the rising and falling of the mighty streams that enclosed their land. The rivers and the associated cane breaks, cypress swamps, and marshes provided abundant fish and waterfowl. It was the rivers that brought what few manufactured goods they had, and it was the rivers that carried away their hides, cotton, tobacco, crossties, barrel staves, and whiskey to markets in Clarksville, Smithland, and Paducah, thence from these markets on to Nashville, Louisville, Memphis, and New Orleans.

As they flow toward the Ohio River, the Tennessee and Cumberland Rivers run from south to north; therefore, the people called south "up" and north "down," so wedded were their lives and thinking to the flow of the streams. Although Paducah and Smithland were at the northern end of the land between the rivers, the people spoke of going "down" to Paducah and Smithland, not "up." Their descendants living in the area still do. This inland peninsula has a geographic crest running north and south, more or less up its center, a "continental divide" in miniature. Rain that falls on its western slopes drains into the Tennessee River, and that which falls on its eastern slopes drains into the Cumberland. Locals called it "the Dividing Ridge;" their descendents living in the area still do.

The People

The typical original settler between the rivers had come from the Carolinas where many had fought at Kings Mountain and in other battles with Brig. Gen. Francis Marion, the "Swamp Fox" of the American Revolution. Many, if not most, of the settlers had come to the Carolinas from Scotland, some by way of Ireland, fleeing persecution (thus the classification, applied to them by some as "Scotch-Irish"). By ancestral nature, these people were fiercely independent, self-reliant, clannish, and suspicious of outsiders.

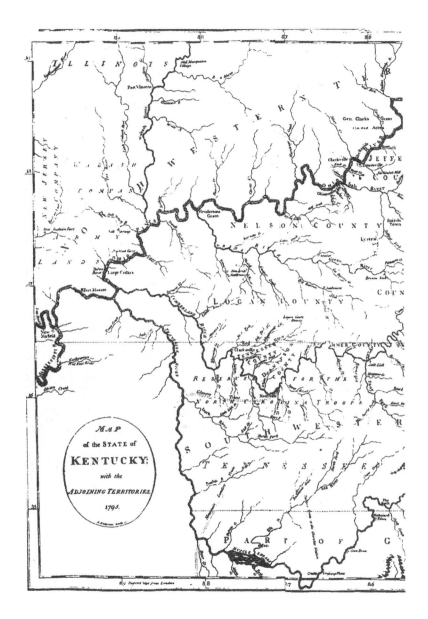

Kentucky and surrounding territories. Note the Land Reserved for the North Carolina Troops. (Courtesy Austin Peay State University, Felix G. Woodward Library)

They were tough, accustomed to hard work, and comfortable with hardship. The raw nature of the frontier and the isolation in which they lived served to intensify these inherent traits. They were, in a very real sense, "mountaineers without mountains," for it is isolation that makes mountaineers what they are—not the mountains. When great political conflicts concerning the area were being debated and resolved, such as the location of the uncertain border between Kentucky and Tennessee, county boundaries, the choices of towns for county seats, and law enforcement jurisdictions, Between the Rivers residents were relatively indifferent. They had little interest in matters of law and government beyond their rivers, including those that could affect them. They were interested primarily in their own very local affairs and wanted most of all to be left alone. And, incidentally, they definitely did consider them to be *their* rivers.

Their attitudes, customs, and bits of the language of many were Scottish Highlands. Like the settlers in the southern Appalachian Mountains, from whence they had come, the people Between the Rivers had brought and retained into the second and third generations some of the customs, values, and traditions of the Scottish clans. Among these was the law of vengeance, a pivotal factor in this story. Such a man was John W. Hinson, whose story this is. Also known, from the Civil War years on, as "Old Jack" and "Captain Jack" Hinson, he settled between the rivers during the first half of the nineteenth century. There is no known record of his middle name. Middle initials were seldom used in the records of the time. Only one known document lists his middle initial, "W." One can only speculate, but since he had a son named William, perhaps that was his own middle name. He married Elisabeth James, established a farm home, and settled down to rear a family. Like the rest of the settlers between the rivers, all he wanted was a chance to work, conduct his business enterprises, support his family, and to be left alone.

The descendants of the original settlers continued to exist in relative isolation, and they lived and thought much like their eighteenth-century ancestors well into the mid-twentieth century, when those proud, independent people "'tween the rivers" were summarily uprooted and driven from their homeland by the federal government. The calamity that had invaded their lives during the War Between the States and the harsh Reconstruction that followed was capped by the depopulation of the area, the final tragedy that forever ended life as it had been known Between the Rivers. The Highland Clearances in Scotland, which had forced Scottish ancestors of Between the Rivers citizens to leave their highland homes and lands to come to the New World in the late eighteenth and early nineteenth centuries, would be repeated for their descendants of the third and fourth generations in the mid-twentieth century.[1]

The Economy

From the beginning, the economy between the rivers was basically one of subsistence farming, augmented by hunting, fishing, and barter. Except for staples, such as sugar and salt, virtually everything consumed on the farm was produced on the farm. Even these items could sometimes be produced locally. Salt of a sort could be had from natural "salt licks," and a form of sugar could be rendered from sorghum cane or honey. Wild honey was abundant, and hives for captured swarms could readily be made from hollow sections of the logs of black gum. Such hives were called "bee gums." Cash crops were cotton and tobacco. Corn could also be sold although most was produced for feeding stock and for grinding into corn meal. Some of the corn was used for making whiskey, a skill the settlers brought with them from the North of Britain, and they took great pride in the quality of their product. Most settlers made whiskey only for home use, but any surplus could be sold or bartered. As commercial contact increased with the markets beyond their rivers, the people produced whiskey in increasing amounts for export and sale. By the turn of the twentieth century, the land between the rivers had become an exporter of whiskey, with Golden Pond in Trigg County, Kentucky, as the industry's center. The best whiskey was made between the rivers; the best of the best came from or through Golden Pond.

In the early decades of the nineteenth century, cotton was a major cash crop for the area, but it quickly depleted the soil. When fields were depleted, farmers either cleared and planted new ground or turned to other cash crops. Less and less cotton was planted for sale. Still, most farms had at least a small cotton patch for home use (spinning, weaving, and quilting). Hemp and flax were also grown for the fibers used in spinning yarn and weaving linen and coarse cloth. Most homes had a loom for weaving and two spinning wheels, a large one for spinning cotton and wool and a smaller one, usually called a flax wheel, for spinning the flax and hemp fibers. Hemp fibers were also used in making rope, a valuable substitute between the rivers for metal chain, which, even when available, was expensive. When cash was in short supply, as it usually was, surplus home products were used for bartering.

Saw mills and gristmills operated throughout the area, with each serving the area immediately around it. As the people Between the Rivers slowly came under the regulation of county governments, mill permits were issued and prices were regulated by the county courts. Inns, where they existed, were likewise regulated by the county courts, including establishment of prices. The people resented all such governmental intrusion into their lives and evaded it when they could. The only heavy industry in the area was the iron industry, utilizing the high-quality native ore. Old stone smelting furnaces, in various states of ruin, still dot the area, bearing silent witness to the once-thriving industry, which reached its peak in the 1850s, but continued through, and after, the War Between the States. On, and in, the ground surrounding the iron furnaces pieces of "blue rock," a glassy biproduct of the iron smelting process, can still be found. Cpl. Eugene Marshall of the occupying Fifth Iowa Cavalry was fascinated with these blue rocks: "The road, and ground, [are] covered with a curious cinder from the iron works. It has every appearance of glass, and [is] a beautiful blue color, many pieces being finely veined and variegated."[2]

The furnaces operated throughout the region between the rivers, both in Kentucky and in Tennessee; however, the majority of the area's furnaces were in Stewart County, Tennessee, where they were concentrated in the Dover area, with most of them on the Cumberland River side of the dividing ridge. During the years from 1815 to 1860, of the three iron-producing counties with portions between the rivers, there were eighteen furnaces operating at various times in Stewart County, Tennessee, compared with only two each in Lyon and Trigg Counties on the Kentucky side of the border.[3] Investors in the iron industry between the rivers were attracted to the deposits of high-quality ore, both brown hematite and limonite, and the limestone, which was used as a flux in the smelting process. In addition, the ore deposits tended to be easily accessed, frequently located just below the surface or exposed in bluffs. The limestone was never far beneath the surface, and much of it was likewise exposed in river bluffs and stream banks. The availability of seemingly inexhaustible supplies of hardwood trees for making charcoal and the great rivers for transportation completed the assets necessary to the industry. In addition to all this, adjacent rich farmland provided ample food for the hard-working crews, many of which were made up of immigrants brought in for that purpose or locally owned slaves. The iron industry, with its furnaces, mills, and cleared "coaling fields," would play a significant role in the coming war, and in the Hinson family's role in it.

"Between the Rivers" was both a geographical entity and a sociological refugium, with their way of life held tenaciously in times past. Because of the isolation between the rivers, it was an area in every way behind the times. In there, by comparison with the surrounding area and its cosmopolitan centers of Paducah, Kentucky, and Clarksville, Tennessee, it was still yesterday. There were no bridges. Except for the boats that came and went and a few ferries, the people were isolated, and few traveled beyond their river boundaries. Like most of the surrounding region, many of the original inhabitants had come in the late eighteenth century to settle on land grants awarded for service in the Revolutionary War. Unlike the surrounding region, however, things "'tween the rivers" hadn't changed much, nearly a century later. And that was not an altogether bad thing.

The Hinson Family

John W. "Jack" Hinson was born in North Carolina in July 1807 and, as a young man, came with his family to Tennessee about 1830. Birth state determinations in Tennessee can be difficult due to the fact that Tennessee was western North Carolina prior to June 1796. In Jack's case, however, his post-1796 birth date establishes his birth state as North Carolina. The year of his birth in some census records can appear to be 1808, depending on the month in which the census was taken.

Like most Hinsons, he was not a tall man. He was about five feet, five inches tall, lean and strong, with unusually long and muscular arms. One local lady, who lived to be 102, vividly remembered descriptions of his long, muscular arms. When asked what he looked like, she replied, "He looked like Popeye."[4]

He was serious and strong-willed. His posture was erect, and his gaze steady. His manners were courtly and genteel for that raw frontier, and his strength of character was apparent. He was a quiet man who spoke sparingly; yet in his manner and countenance there was a suggestion that his relatively small size concealed a combination of great strength and cool courage, if not outright menace. Confederate major Charles W. Anderson, wartime adjutant general to Gen. Nathan Bedford Forrest, knew Jack Hinson and served with him on at least three occasions during the war. He has given us the only known surviving, complete physical description of Jack Hinson. Major Anderson described Hinson's "clear, gray eyes, compressed lips, and massive jaws" and offered his opinion that Hinson's natural appearance "clearly indicated that under no circumstances was he a man to be trifled with, or aroused." His eyes were narrow, above high cheekbones, almost suggesting the oriental, but inclining slightly upward toward the center of his forehead. Known in the family as "Hinson eyes," they are a strong genetic characteristic, which continues to appear in his descendants today.[5]

Jack Hinson before the war. (Painting by Joe McCormick)

Within this quiet, courteous man there lay a depth of character and great inner strength—like a coiled spring of tempered steel, ready at all times for instantaneous action. In a metaphor often used in the rural South to describe such a man, he was "small, but wound up tight." Never boastful, nor even conspicuous, but demonstrably without fear, he was, as Major Anderson put it, indeed a man not to be trifled with or aroused. The same thing, incidentally, could be said of his sons, grandsons, and great-grandsons. These traits seem to have been strong hereditary dominants and carried with them the potential for tragedy.

John Hinson, who came to be called "Jack," first appears as head of a household in the 1840 census in Stewart County, Tennessee. Its county seat was the little village of Dover, on the banks of the Cumberland River. Stewart County, formerly a part of Montgomery County, was named for Duncan Stewart, who in 1793 had come from Scotland by way of North Carolina as one of the first settlers. He had been instrumental in the establishment of Stewart as a separate county in 1803 and was, justifiably, looked upon as the father of the county.

Thomas Hinson, Jack's brother, and wife Eliza (Stanfill), circa 1860.

The identification of Jack Hinson's father is uncertain, but the evidence points strongly to Jacob Hinson of Little Richland Creek in Humphreys County, also born in North Carolina. Humphreys County was the county immediately south of Stewart, and many Hinsons lived in the border area where Stewart, Humphreys, Montgomery, and Dickson Counties met. Jack had a younger brother, Thomas, who lived in the Ellis Mills community, southeast of Dover. Assuming that Jacob was his father, Jack had two other, younger, brothers and a younger sister, whose names are unknown.[6]

Jack's wife, Elisabeth James Hinson was born in 1817. Although her name in later records is spelled with a "z," in the earliest records it is spelled with the British "s," and this spelling will be used here exclusively. Elisabeth was the daughter of John James (1791-1852) and Agnes James (1800-1851), both of whom are buried in the old cemetery in Dover. Wives and children were not named in the 1840 census but were only numbered in categories according to age. Thus, in the 1840 census, she appears only as "female, 20-30." Elisabeth first appears, by name, in the 1850 census, as Jack's wife, with her birth state listed as North Carolina; however, later records consistently state her place of birth as Tennessee. Judging from the age of their oldest child, she and Jack were married about 1835, although the records have not been found.

Jack Hinson today would be called an achiever. He was serious, goal-oriented, and a hard worker. A man of means, he was not only a prosperous farmer, but also bought and sold farm land, timber land, and other properties in the area, sometimes alone and sometimes in partnership with others. His holdings at times included not just rural properties, but also building lots in Dover, and his business dealings were not confined to Stewart County. He bought and sold land and other things across the Tennessee River in Henry County, where he also had relatives. In the 1840 census, he was recorded as owning ten slaves, a number fairly typical of a substantial landowner in that area but fewer than the one hundred or more found on the great plantations of the very rich. In 1840, Jack was thirty-three and Elisabeth was twenty-three; their first-born child, Robert A., was three, and their baby, George, was one.

Jack's holdings became even greater when, in 1847, he acquired four hundred acres on the upper waters of Lick Creek, by a Tennessee land grant. This grant was the beginning of what would become the Hinsons' permanent home, three miles southwest of Dover, which they called "Bubbling Springs." That farm would be enlarged until it eventually included more than 1,200 acres, operated with a growing number of slaves.[7]

By October 1850, Jack and Elisabeth were established at Bubbling Springs and had four more children: William, age eight;

John, age six; Albert F., age four; and Joseph S., age two. Elisabeth had borne at least six sons in fifteen years. There is no way of knowing how many other children may have been born and died in the ten-year periods between censuses. She could have had fifteen babies during those fifteen years. The family Bible, letters, photographs, and other such family records that might have recorded the number have not survived, apparently having been destroyed when Union soldiers burned the house during the war.

In 1853, Jack was issued a tavern-keeper's license. At that time, such licenses were issued to those who had homes large enough to have extra bedrooms and the capacity to serve meals to overnight guests. Such large homes had to be located on or near the existing roads on the stagecoach routes, for there were few hotels in that time, and travelers depended on such places to stay overnight while traveling. Of course, by the unwritten protocols of the rural South, all farm families were expected to take in individual travelers overnight and feed them but not in the numbers of stagecoach loads of passengers.[8]

Jack also found time to build the first toll road in Stewart County, the road passing, of course, through his own land, and he kept a trusted slave at either end to collect the tolls.[9]

By 1860, John and Elisabeth, still at Bubbling Springs, had eight of their ten children at home; the two oldest sons, Robert, twenty-three, and George, twenty, had moved out to make homes of their own. The Hinson sons at home in 1860 were William, eighteen; John, fifteen; Albert F., fourteen; Joseph S., twelve; Charles S., ten; and Thomas W., eight. And, after having borne at least eight sons, Elisabeth had been blessed with two little girls: Mary, three, and (Sarah) Margaret, two. Also living with them in the home was Amanda Nelson, twenty-four. She was probably a live-in teacher for the children, sometimes the only means of formal education for the children of prosperous farm families.

Bubbling Springs, the Hinson home place, sat in a beautiful grassy valley between gently rolling hills, three miles southwest of Dover. The home was one-half mile south of the Dover road that connected Dover, on the Cumberland River, with Paris Landing, on the Tennessee River. That road roughly followed the general line of what is today U.S. Highway 79. What was then the Hinsons' lane to the Dover road is now called Keel Hollow Road.

The Hinson home was characteristic of the homes of prosperous men of that time and place. There was ample room for the large Hinson family and extra room for houseguests and stagecoach travelers. In the front was a nicely furnished parlor used only for entertaining guests and for special family occasions such as Christmas. Guests were a frequent and welcome addition to the family, and visits from relatives and friends were pleasant times, much more important than they are today. There was always room and food for visitors at Bubbling Springs. A large, separate, back kitchen spared the rest of the house the heat of cooking in summer, and in winter, it was a pleasant, warm, good-smelling place to sit. The kitchen was presided over by a slave named Sarah, who also supervised the other house servants. In the peculiar protocols of the old South, a matter largely incomprehensible in the North today, Sarah, although a slave, enjoyed in many ways the status of an elder member of the family and mentor of the children. Although she addressed the children with courtesy ("Mr. Thomas," "Miss Mary," etc.), she spoke with unquestioned authority. The children dared not treat her with disrespect or misbehave in her presence. And, in that kitchen, she was virtually sovereign.

Free-flowing springs, bubbling out of the ground behind the great house, provided a constant supply of cold drinking water. Flowing through the springhouse, they also provided a means of

Bubbling Springs today.

keeping milk, cream, butter, and other perishables cool, and gave the farm its name. The springs were also a major tributary to Hinson Creek, which flowed through the valley, providing water for stock and holes for swimming and fishing. The house sat in a grove of maple trees and faced northward, toward the Dover Road. Clear, cool Hinson Creek ran through the meadow along the west side of the lane, flowing northward.

The Hinson farm was typical of its time and place, except that it was larger than most, and by no means could all the farmers in the area afford to own slaves. Such large farms produced corn, wheat, tobacco, hogs, cattle, plus oxen, mules, and horses for draft and riding stock. Although by 1860 cotton was no longer a significant cash crop in Stewart County, there was usually a patch of cotton for home use. Flax and hemp were also grown to provide fibers for weaving, and hemp fibers were used for rope, made on the place. Sheep were kept for wool and meat, in addition to the usual chickens, guinea fowl, geese, ducks, and turkeys kept for eggs, food, and for mattress and pillow down. Hogs were the primary source of meat. A large "kitchen garden" provided vegetables for family, hired hands, and slaves. Apples, peaches, pears, and plums grew in abundance in an orchard while wild plums, peaches, crabapples, and muscadines grew naturally in the woods. Grapevines on overhead arbors supplied fresh fruit, preserves, and wine. They also provided a shady place to sit in the summer, snap or shell beans, shuck sweet corn, or just rest. Beehives, in the edge of the orchard, produced honey and provided pollination for the fruit tree blossoms. Corn and wheat were carried to gristmills to make corn meal and flour. Unlike at the smaller farms in the county, whiskey was not made at Bubbling Springs. The Hinsons could afford to buy it.

Like most such substantial farm homes in the South, Bubbling Springs was essentially a self-contained little community. There were barns for livestock and hay and for curing tobacco; a smokehouse for preserving and storing hams, bacon, and other meat; stables; a woodshed; and other outbuildings. A root cellar kept such "root" foods as potatoes, sweet potatoes, and turnips through the winter weather. It also stored "keeper" apple varieties and the large, hard Kieffer pears, which softened during the cool fall weather. In its blacksmith shop, horseshoes, mule shoes, hinges, and other hardware were made, and tools were repaired. The blacksmith was either a skilled farm hand or a slave trained to do the work; such a skilled slave took great pride in his work, enjoyed elevated social status, and was worth considerably more, if sold, than a field hand or house servant was.

To the right front of the great house at Bubbling Springs, about three hundred feet to the northeast, there was a row of slave cabins, with their garden plots, chickens, and dogs arranged along a wagon road running eastward off the lane.

The Hinsons were a prominent, respected family. Not merely prosperous, they were also genteel, educated people by the standards of that rough-hewn time and place. They were examples of what Thomas Jefferson called "the natural aristocracy"— those who, regardless of ancestry, were gracious, responsible, productive, and given to learning and self-improvement. These admirable Hinson qualities and values were passed down to future generations. Remembering them, one who knew the family well said that the Hinsons were "different—as if they weren't from here." She also stated that the Hinson men treated ladies with deference, stood in their presence, assisted them in being seated, offered an arm when appropriate, and habitually offered refreshments to all visitors. Such attitudes and customs were a natural part of the family heritage.

In 1851, Elisabeth Hinson's mother, Agnes James, died at age fifty-one and was buried in the old Dover cemetery, next to the Christian Church. Five months later, in January 1852, Elisabeth's father, John James, died at age sixty and was buried beside his wife. His son-in-law, Jack Hinson, was appointed executor of Mr. James's estate. On January 4, 1853, the court allowed him the interesting sum of $3.30 for expenses as executor. Death had begun to arrive in the Hinson family, as it does in every family, but, at that time, they had not yet been visited by tragedy. That kind of magnified pain was still locked in their unknown future.[10]

Life was good at Bubbling Springs in the middle of the nineteenth century. It was an idyllic place for the Hinson children to grow up, fishing, swimming, hunting, and learning to work. In that pleasant, pastoral setting, Jack and Elisabeth passed happily through middle age and into the years beyond, with fulfillment, prosperity, and peace. The future stretched pleasantly before them, seemingly endless and filled with promise.

Elsewhere, however, beyond their rivers, political conflicts were escalating and the winds of war were blowing. In faraway places, pivotal matters were being debated and acted upon. Henry Clay's Whig Party was dying, and the new Republican Party was rising up to take its place. The sovereignty of the individual states was being debated, and secession was discussed. In the background, slavery was becoming a simmering, volatile issue. There were "peace abolitionists," like William Lloyd Garrison, appealing to reason and conscience. There were also radical abolitionists, like John Brown, arming themselves and their followers and calling for the spilling of Southern white blood.

Between the rivers, most of the people knew little of these events and cared about them even less. They asked only to be left alone, to go on with their lives as they had before, but their isolation could not be sustained for long. War, with its multiplied tragedies, would soon arrive, uninvited and unwelcome, between the rivers. And, when it came, it would end life as the Hinsons of Bubbling Springs had known it. Forever.

Regional Conflict Invades the Hinsons' Tranquility

The tranquil, relatively isolated life of the Hinsons, and of their neighbors between the rivers, would soon end in a tragic, bloody conflict, one they did not want. That conflict would change the lives of all the people between the rivers, and it would cost Jack and Elisabeth Hinson their home, the death of at least seven of their children, and their freedom to live out their twilight years in peace. It would be an internecine war of unprecedented savagery, the bloodiest in all of American history. The peaceful isolation there between the rivers would end, shattered and crushed under the tread of massive, outside forces, and, still worse, neighbor would soon be killing neighbor.

How could such horror invade and end the peace and prosperity the Hinsons enjoyed? By the middle of the nineteenth century compelling issues, largely unknown to those living between the rivers, were severely straining the bonds between the states of the North and those of the South. Divisive issues, principally political and economic, accumulated without resolution. Conflicting values and goals, both economic and cultural, produced growing stresses on the nation's political unity. More and more, the citizens of the North and South saw themselves as two distinct and incompatible regions.

Increasingly, politicians demagogued the issues, newspaper editors and pamphleteers editorialized, exhorted, and fanned the flames of controversy. Preachers, in both the North and South, found scriptural basis for their mutually exclusive pronouncements and gave them passionate voice. Among the politicians, there were a few statesmen, such as John J. Crittenden, who strove mightily to find solutions and maintain the peace. When war did come, his two sons were generals, one Union and one Confederate. At the other end of the spectrum, a few radicals, such as the Kansas incendiary, John Brown, took up the sword, figuratively and literally, and actually sought to bring about the war. In Kansas in 1856, he, four of his sons, and two others murdered five unarmed men and boys considered to be proslavery, hacking them to death with broad swords, in what came to be known as the Pottawatomie Massacre. The majority, as always, pragmatically occupied the middle ground.

As the Hinson Family Grew, So Did the Conflict

Between the rivers, however, most people went on with life, largely unaware of the trouble brewing beyond their borders, or essentially disinterested in them. They, as always, just wanted to be left alone. This was the attitude of Jack Hinson. Although he was better informed than most of the citizens between the rivers, he went on with his life and hoped for a peaceful, political resolution.

While trouble was brewing and blood was being shed elsewhere, the Hinsons lived in tranquil isolation and peaceful prosperity. Jack's family continued to grow and flourish, as did his farm and other business ventures. As the Hinson family steadily grew, so did ominous developments outside their rivers, with darkening political skies, growing thunderclouds, and the swirling, sweeping winds of war.

These two growing phenomena, Jack's family and prosperity and the trouble building beyond their rivers, developed in parallel and, in a sense, in mutual isolation. Yet, in time, the parallels would break the rule and intersect with tragic consequences.

South . . . More a Matter of Attitude than of Latitude

Although compelling, hardly anything about the regional conflict in the mid-nineteenth century was simple. For one thing, "North" and "South" were not then, nor are they today, geographic absolutes. "South" was then, and still is, more a matter of attitude than of latitude, more a matter of culture and values than of position on the map. For those seeking a political resolution of North-South conflicts, this was a significant complication.

In 1861, Kentucky was strongly "Southern" and, except for much of the eastern mountains, intensely Confederate. The same was true of Tennessee. There were portions of Missouri and Maryland that were intensely Confederate and identified in every way with the Deep South. The counties in extreme southern Illinois, with its flat, alluvial land, cotton culture, and rivers connecting them with the Gulf, provided many soldiers for the Confederate army. They would probably have seceded had not Cairo, at the confluence of the Ohio and Mississippi Rivers, been quickly occupied by Union forces. At the same time, there were areas of western North Carolina, and of northern Mississippi, Alabama, and Georgia, that leaned toward the Union or, at least, toward neutrality. Even after secession, a faction in one county of Mississippi seceded from the state and organized a fighting company for the Union. Most of the mountainous, western counties of Virginia did secede from Virginia and the Confederacy, with the help of the Lincoln government and Gen. George McClellan's army, and became the Union's new state of West Virginia. No, lines between "North" and "South" were not at all easy to draw in 1861—at least, not on maps.

A Clash of Cultures

Most who considered themselves "Southern," regardless of geographic location, shared a common culture. They might not all have been able to define that culture, but they immediately recognized it, regardless of social class, and they would fight to defend it. That culture was basically agrarian, somewhat feudal, and strongly committed to the values of chivalry, honor, tradition, social graces, consistent (if not always sincere) courtesy, and their strongly held Christian faith. Their commitment to honor, although not always reasonable, was, nevertheless, something for which many were ready to die. Their romantic and cavalier, if somewhat unrealistic, attitudes were sincere; a man without honor, they generally believed, was not fit to live among them.

That distinctive cultural reality bound Southern people together like an adhesive matrix, caused them to see outside intrusion as a threat to their way of life, and made them willing to fight like tigers against whatever threatened it, whether real or perceived. Stephen Vincent Benét, in his epic poem *John Brown's Body,* expressed the complexity of what it was that Southerners were willing to fight for. In the poem, Wingate, an upper-class Southerner on his way to a war to which he was already committed, was still pondering the question: "Why? What is it we are fighting for?"

> *He brooded a moment. It wasn't slavery,*
> *That stale, red herring of Yankee knavery,*
> *Not even states' rights, at least not solely,*
> *But something so dim that it must be holy.* [11]

Because the Union, at the outset, made the first invasive moves, seizing large portions of Kentucky and other border areas of the South, most Southerners saw the issue as defending their homes from invasion. A story is told of one young rebel prisoner who was asked, "Why are you fighting against your country?" The unsophisticated boy, in his ragged, butternut uniform, replied simply and sincerely, "Because you're here."

It is true that many people of the North shared with the South the same Victorian values and attitudes toward matters of honor and chivalry, and yet, as a culture, the differences were significant. Northern culture was more heterogeneous and comparatively multicultural. There was lacking, across the North, a common cultural matrix to bind people in a fundamental similarity. It is oversimplified, but perhaps illustrative, to say that while Southern boys were working in the corn, cotton, and tobacco fields as they always had, or (if sons of the wealthy) were sitting on the veranda, dreaming of glory and writing cavalier poetry, many in the North were desperately trying to learn a new language and find work to feed their wives and children in a strange and ungenerous setting.

In the South, the field hand and the privileged aristocrat, although not mixing much socially, knew one another by name and recognized one another as belonging to the same cultural phenomenon. Each recognized the other as part of his world, both were comfortably "at home" in the South, and would not have felt that way anywhere else. In the North, however, the poor farmer or the working immigrant tended to cling to others of his own situation, and often saw the rest of the culture around him as foreign and threatening. Moreover, in the North, the poor and the privileged sensed little or nothing in common. They lived in separate and very different worlds. This diversity and lack of cultural cohesion was illustrated tragically in the New York City Draft Riots of 1863, in which white immigrant laborers viewed the entire black population as a threat to their jobs and the cause of their being forced into the war.

Race relations were likewise very different. In the South, although definitely subjugated, slaves belonging to the better classes, or more affluent, of whites often enjoyed a mutual affection with their owners, who considered them part of the extended family. Children of the master often had, as best friends, slave children of the same age on the farm and grew up playing, hunting, and working with them. Many slave owners, of course, especially those of the lower class, treated their slaves with cruel abuse, but this was not true of the Hinsons. Family tradition plus the fact that his freed slaves called their new community "Hinson Town" indicate that Jack Hinson's treatment of his slaves was kind and protective. In the Northern states, slavery had existed since colonial times but had been largely abolished by 1861. Although very few of them were slaves, blacks in the North were still generally excluded from white society, lived for the most part in alien separation, and were viewed as an inferior, servant class seldom with any sense of belonging, let alone of familial connection.

State Sovereignty: The Kentucky Resolutions

Although the issue of state sovereignty, and particularly the right of individual states to secede from the Union, can be traced to the Constitutional Convention of 1787, the secession crisis of 1860 and 1861 can be traced significantly to the Kentucky Resolutions of 1798 and 1799. These resolutions of the Kentucky legislature, in reaction to the Federalists' Alien and Sedition Acts,

were secretly written by Thomas Jefferson, who was at the time
John Adams' vice president. They declared that individual states
could not only secede, but could also nullify any federal law of
which they did not approve.

Concentration of financial and industrial power in the North,
what the South saw as unfair import taxes, and the vexing question
of slavery were certainly issues contributing to regional ill-feeling,
but the fundamental issue, still unresolved, was the right of a state
to secede. This issue's resolution would be found in four bloody
years of war.

When the Kentucky Resolutions were adopted in the late
eighteenth century, strengthening the foundation for state
sovereignty and secession, Jack Hinson and Elisabeth James were
not yet born. Their families were living in North Carolina where
most of the people were of Jeffersonian Republican persuasion.
Both families would soon be migrating westward, however, into
the free "lands reserved for the North Carolina Troops." After
the revolution, the North Carolina legislature could not afford to
pay its veterans in cash, so many were paid with land grants in
the largely unsettled western reaches of the state. This payment
accomplished two things: it fulfilled the state's obligation to its
veterans of the revolution, and it accelerated the settlement of
its wild and sparsely populated western area, soon to become the
sixteenth state as Tennessee.[12]

In 1807, when little Jack Hinson was born in North Carolina,
Thomas Jefferson was president and his Kentucky Resolutions
were still being discussed as the rapid expansion of national
borders created many more potential states.

Slavery Was Not the Issue

Jack Hinson and his friend John Bell were perhaps the most
politically aware men in Stewart County, and they followed
developments carefully. They both realized that if a war should
be inevitable, it would be fought to settle the issue of state
sovereignty and secession. It never occurred to either of them
that such a war would be fought over slavery. Although this was
the rallying cry for ardent abolitionists, the war was not entered
into for the purpose of ending slavery. In fact, Lincoln, during the

campaign before the election of 1860 and in his first inaugural speech, went to great lengths to make it clear that he opposed the abolition of slavery in states where it already existed. Like Thomas Jefferson, Lincoln believed that slavery would soon die a natural death.[13]

Actually, African slaves were first imported into New England, not the South, and slavery was fairly common in the Northeast in Colonial times and the early years of the Republic. In 1760, slaves constituted approximately ten percent of the population of Philadelphia. Although he became an abolitionist late in life, for most of his life Benjamin Franklin himself kept one or two slaves who traveled with him as personal servants. In 1804, Vice President Aaron Burr was one of many New Yorkers who owned black slaves.[14]

Providence, Rhode Island, had been the very center of slave importation, dominating the trade from the latter eighteenth century until such importation was ended by Congress in 1808. An illustration of this fact is the life of a slave named Venture Smith. As an African boy, he was captured by other Africans in his coastal homeland and sold into slavery. The African slavers sold him to a white New England slaver who took him to America. Venture grew up in America as a slave. He was abused, sold three times, married, and eventually bought freedom for himself, his wife, and several others. As a free man, he engaged in businesses, bought and sold other black slaves, and left a journal of his long and eventful life. This remarkable man was never in all his life south of Long Island, New York.[15]

Two years into the war, for political reasons, slavery was made the emotional rallying cry in the North. However, despite revisionist contentions to the contrary and the stirring, noble lyrics of the "Battle Hymn of the Republic," the war was not fought primarily over slavery, not in its beginnings or even in its final days. The issue was never that simple. During the war, slavery was legal and common in the nation's capital. As far into the war as 1863, in spite of the Compromise of 1850, which forbade it, a weekly slave auction was conducted one block from the White House in a sale lot behind the Decatur Hotel. Even after the Emancipation Proclamation was signed, slavery legally continued in Washington City (the District of Columbia), for the proclamation applied only to states that had seceded.[16]

And There Were Many Black Slave Owners/Dealers

Also complicating the picture was the fact that there were many blacks who owned, bought, and sold slaves. In New Orleans in 1830, there were 10,689 free blacks, and more than 3,000 of them, nearly one third, owned, bought, rented, and sold black slaves. In 1840 in the city of Charleston, South Carolina, there were 402 black slave owners, with 2,357 black slaves. It appears that these black slave owners were neither more nor less benevolent than the white ones, but were "by and large . . . just darker versions of their white counterparts."[17]

Secession in the North?

In 1860, secession was neither a new nor a bizarre idea. The right to withdraw from the Union had been assumed by the delegates to the Constitutional Convention in Philadelphia in 1787, and they jealously guarded the sovereignty of their individual states. In its vague and pliable form, and with the added safeguard of the Tenth Amendment, the Constitution had long been assumed by many political leaders to allow for secession. Had the delegates from the thirteen founding states not been convinced of this right, it is probable that the Constitution would never have been ratified.

Actually, secession was first seriously considered in the North, not the South. The ink had hardly dried on the Constitution before talk of secession by the New England states and New York began. Northern Federalists distrusted Jefferson's populism and were especially threatened by his authorizing the Louisiana Purchase in 1803. By this time, there was serious talk among such prominent leaders as Vice President Aaron Burr and Massachusetts senator Timothy Pickering, who had been secretary of state under both Washington and Adams, of the secession of New York and the New England states. The plan was to form an independent Northern Confederation, of which Burr would be the likely president. Interestingly, the idea was not without its racial component. In 1803, Pickering's vision for the Northern Confederation was of one with no blacks: "There will be . . . a separation, and the white and black population will be the boundary." Each time the issue rose to a boil, cooler heads prevailed and the idea was eventually abandoned.[18]

Questions of state sovereignty and secession continued to resonate, however, as problems with an increasingly aggressive England led to the War of 1812. There was even serious consideration of another secession, that of the southwestern states and territories, such as Kentucky, Tennessee, and Mississippi, as part of a western empire with Aaron Burr as its emperor. The death of Alexander Hamilton in a duel with Burr, the reelection of Jefferson in a landslide victory in 1804, and the War of 1812, brought an end to these discussions of secession as a serious possibility.[19]

But the idea was not yet buried.

The Hartford Convention

British raids along the New England coast actually created heightened resentment, not of the British, but of the government in Washington, which many blamed for the raids and resulting loss of trading revenue. As a result, in 1814, delegates from Massachusetts, Connecticut, and Rhode Island met in the Hartford (Connecticut) Convention to consider seceding from the Union. Again, cooler heads prevailed, and no fundamental political changes occurred; yet the issue of the constitutionality of secession remained unresolved, a bomb waiting for the right spark to detonate it. That explosion would occur in 1861, but the fuse had been smoldering at least as far back as 1790.[20]

In 1814, when secession was being debated at the Hartford Convention, young Jack Hinson was seven years old, receiving his first schooling on his father's North Carolina farm, learning to ride, fish, and hunt. He dreamed of the day when he could go into the forest by himself with a rifle and knife, like the men and the older boys. He had no idea that he would someday make history with the way he would go into the forest, alone, with rifle and knife, half a century later in Tennessee.

Efforts to Resolve the Slavery Issue
(Not to Abolish It, but to Live With It)

In November of 1820, James Monroe was reelected president. Nicknamed "the Last Cocked Hat," he was the last president from the ranks of the founding fathers with their three-cornered hats, excluding John Quincy Adams, who had been a teenage diplomat during the American Revolution. He was also a staunch Jeffersonian Republican and a defender of state's rights. Jack Hinson was thirteen years old that November and beginning to do the work of a man. He was also beginning to enjoy the freedom of a man who could go into the forest alone with rifle and knife. Far away over the mountains to the west, in the twenty-four-year-old state of Tennessee, Elisabeth James, his future wife, was three years old, walking, climbing, and learning to say, "No!"

The unresolved problem of states' rights versus federal sovereignty, including the right of states to withdraw from the Union, was succinctly expressed in an exchange of toasts in Washington, D.C. at a dinner celebrating Jefferson's birthday on April 13,1830. With meaning as clear as the crystal wine glass he held aloft, Pres. Andrew Jackson stated, "Our Federal Union—it must be preserved." Those present replied, "Hear, hear." Then, with equal clarity, South Carolina's John C. Calhoun countered, "The Union, next to our liberty, most dear!" The eyes of both men must have sparkled like the glasses they lifted to one another, for each knew exactly what the other meant. The problem was that both were right, and, at the same time, both were wrong.

As Jackson and Calhoun crossed philosophical swords over their wine glasses that April, Jack Hinson was approaching his twenty-third birthday, a fully grown man. Elisabeth James was twelve and rapidly approaching womanhood. In five years, they would meet in Jackson's Tennessee and marry.

On March 1, 1845, three days before leaving office, Pres. John Tyler signed a resolution providing for the annexation of the Republic of Texas as a slave state under the provisions of the Missouri Compromise; on December 29, Texas statehood became official.

By that time, Jack Hinson had migrated westward to Stewart County, Tennessee, and married young Elisabeth James. He was then thirty-eight; Elisabeth was twenty-eight, and they already had four sons: Robert, ten; George, six; William, three; and their baby, John, was celebrating his first birthday. Elisabeth was carrying their fifth son, Albert, who would be born the following summer.

As their family grew and prospered, their farm also grew and prospered, and Jack was the owner of about fifteen slaves, a large number by the standards of the day in Stewart County. In May of 1847, he acquired a grant of four hundred acres on the upper waters of Lick Creek and began to build what would be their permanent home.

The following year a sixth son, Joseph, was born to the Hinsons, followed by Charles, two years later.[21] Jack and Elisabeth had now been married fifteen years, had six sons, and their extended family at Bubbling Springs included an ever-growing number of slaves.

State Sovereignty Could Not Be Separated from the Slavery Issue

The year that Charles Hinson was born, Congress in far-off Washington struggled to effect a compromise that would keep the Union from splitting. The principal issue at that time was the vexing matter of the extension of slavery into the new territories of the West, recently acquired as a result of the war with Mexico. The Compromise of 1850, adopted after extended political debate, failed to stop the relentless drift toward division and war. It had postponed the inevitable clash by applying the concept of "popular sovereignty" to the issue of slavery in the southwestern territories ceded by Mexico. Rather than resolving the fundamental issue of states' rights, it seemed to have made it more divisive. The vexing, emotional issue, which continued to cast sparks into an already volatile situation, was slavery.

Making bad matters worse, the Compromise of 1850 strengthened the Fugitive Slave Act. This was a law in which abolitionists in the North already took particular pleasure in violating, and its strengthening only resulted in increasingly strong feelings on both sides of the issue.

During this volatile period, Harriet Beecher Stowe, of the prominent abolitionist Beecher family, was living in Cincinnati, where her husband was a seminary professor. She had seven preacher brothers, the most famous of whom was abolitionist Henry Ward Beecher. His support for arming antislavery forces in Kansas with state-of-the-art Sharpe's rifles and saying that the rifles might be "a greater moral agency" in Kansas than Bibles caused the Sharpe's rifles to be called "Beecher's Bibles." Already a dedicated abolitionist, Mrs. Stowe crossed the Ohio River into Northern Kentucky, and witnessed a small slave sale at the courthouse in the village of Washington in Mason County. She also made at least one visit to the plantation home of friends in Central

Kentucky, the Thomas Kennedys of Garrard County. On the basis of this brief experience with slavery, she wrote the imaginative and highly emotional book *Uncle Tom's Cabin.* Published in 1852, the book was an instant sensation. It did little to clarify thinking, but it mightily fueled antislavery emotions in the North, where the popular perception was that every slaveholder in the South was a cruel Simon Legree. In the South, her book was just as vehemently hated as it was lionized in the North, and it was viewed as abolitionist propaganda (a position not without basis in fact). The book was an immediate success, more and more people read it, and sectional divisions grew yet wider.[22]

Also in 1852, at Bubbling Springs, the eighth son, Thomas, was born to Jack and Elisabeth Hinson.

The new law not only fanned the flames of regional tension, but also led to an undeclared border war between proslavery men in Missouri and antislavery men in Kansas Territory. Raids and counterraids, atrocities and counteratrocities drenched the border area in blood and created new animosities that would not only hasten the war, but would long outlive it.

In March 1857, Chief Justice Roger B. Taney handed down the *Dred Scott* v *Sanford* decision, which declared that any person of African ancestry was simply property and runaway slaves could be pursued and recovered from a free state or territory. Taney went even farther, stating that blacks could not sue or be sued in court because they were not, and could never be, citizens. Further, he said that Congress had no power to forbid slavery in new territories, once and for all nullifying the Missouri Compromise. There was fury in the North and general rejoicing in the South.

In Stewart County, most people were not aware of the Dred Scott decision, let alone what it would mean. That year, after having eight sons, Elisabeth Hinson gave birth to a girl and named her Mary.

In October 1859, John Brown, the fanatical, unbalanced abolitionist who was a fugitive from Kansas for multiple murders, attacked the U. S. Arsenal at Harper's Ferry, Virginia. With eighteen followers, he seized the virtually undefended arsenal, and the next day fought an all-day battle with local militia, killing several local blacks who declined to join his "slave revolt." United States Army colonel Robert E. Lee, on leave at his Arlington, Virginia, home, was sent with a detachment of twenty Marines, led by Lt. Israel Green, to retake the arsenal and capture Brown, who was fortified in a brick firehouse. Lee was assisted by a young officer, Lt. J. E. B. "Jeb" Stuart, whose negotiation for a surrender failed. Leading his twenty Marines in a bayonet assault through a hail of rifle fire, Lieutenant Green brought his sword down on Brown's head, stunning him, and his Marines seized the building. Green's sword, identical to the one worn by Marine officers today, was a ceremonial sword, not a saber; otherwise, it would have split Brown's head in two. The blow brought Brown down but ended the career of the sword; still bent in the general shape of John Brown's head, it is today in the collection of the National Museum of the Marine Corps. One Marine was killed, ten of Brown's men lay dead, and four escaped. Brown, stunned and bleeding but intact, was captured with four of his men. They were all subsequently hanged for treason.

By the time of the John Brown insurrection, a second daughter had been born to Jack and Elisabeth Hinson, and little Sarah Margaret was one year old.

The Catalytic Election of 1860

In the profoundly pivotal election of 1860, the Democratic Party split along sectional lines. The southern Democrats nominated John C. Breckinridge of Kentucky, who was at the time Buchanan's sitting vice president. The northern Democrats nominated the "little giant," Illinois senator Stephen A. Douglas.

The Democratic Party had been the only national institution still holding the North and South together, and with the party thus divided, that uniting cord was severed.

The new Republican Party, concentrated in the North, nominated Abraham Lincoln of Illinois. A third party (actually, with the Democrats split into north and south, it was a fourth party) met in May and nominated Jack Hinson's friend, John Bell of Stewart County, Tennessee. Calling itself the Constitutional Union Party, it attracted those in the South, largely the remnants of the Whig Party, who wanted to preserve the Union and their way of life, but without war. Bell carried three states: Kentucky, Virginia, and Tennessee. Douglas carried only Illinois and part of New Jersey. The result was to elect Lincoln with only forty percent of the vote.

Lincoln did dismally in Kentucky, the state of his birth and early childhood, where the vote was divided between Breckinridge and Bell. In fact, in strongly "old South" Fayette County, Kentucky, where he had been married and where his wife's family, the Todds, was still one of the most prominent, Lincoln received only five votes! One is tempted to believe that all five of the voters were named Todd.[23]

In that pivotal year of 1860, the Hinsons were living peacefully and prosperously at Bubbling Springs. They had ten children, ages two to eighteen, and a young lady named Amanda Nelson in the household, probably a tutor for the younger children. In addition, to operate the large and expanding farm, there was a growing number of slaves.

It is unknown how Jack Hinson cast his vote that fateful November, but it would be difficult to believe that he did not vote for John Bell, whose political position he shared. Bell, a wealthy émigré from Nashville, was at the time the leading citizen of Stewart County, and one of the most prominent men in the entire South. After Bell, who occupied a category of prominence all his own, Jack Hinson was perhaps the second most prosperous and prominent man in the county. However Hinson cast his vote in the election of 1860, he could not have imagined how the election of Lincoln would eventually change his life.

Secession Becomes Reality

With Lincoln's election, mechanisms for secession, already in place, were immediately set in motion in South Carolina. On December 20, the South Carolina legislature met in Columbia and voted unanimously to secede. The entire student body of the University of South Carolina enlisted in the army of a Confederacy that did not yet exist.

President Buchanan called upon the nation to pray for peace and proclaimed Friday, January 5, 1861, to be a national day of fasting and prayer for a peaceful solution to the growing conflict.

During January 1861, Mississippi, Florida, Alabama, Georgia, and Louisiana followed South Carolina out of the Union. On February 1, Texas seceded, and eight days later Virginia followed. In March, the Crittenden Compromise, the frail, last political hope for holding the Union together, failed in Congress.

Meanwhile, Between the Rivers . . .

The winds of war were blowing with gathering force, and peaceful isolation between the rivers could not continue. As historian B. F. Cooling observed, "the tranquil days of packet whistles sounding around the bend, and waters gently lapping against the soft clay banks" were numbered. War was coming. Some visionary leaders saw its awful potential and went on struggling against it. Perhaps only God knew just how terrible it would actually be.[24]

At Bubbling Springs, Jack Hinson followed these events and was deeply troubled. Like his friend, John Bell, he favored life in the South as he had always known it. He viewed the ardent abolitionists as radical meddlers who understood nothing of life in the South, but he did not want the Union divided, and he was strongly opposed to the war. Like John Bell, Jack thought that war, if it did come, would be fought over the right of states to secede. He believed that once the issue had been settled, his life could go on as he had known it before. He was right about the former point; about the latter, however, he could not have been more wrong.

Chapter 2

War Comes to Bubbling Springs

"The Federal troops have occupied Paducah . . . neutrality, I assume, is at an end."
> —J.W. McGaughey's diary, September 14, 1861

Between the Rivers in 1861, spring came as it always had. The pine groves brightened and seemed to fluff up from their winter droop. The cedar thickets began to soften with subtle changes of color, from the dreary dark green of winter to their brighter summer shades. Self-heal sprang up indifferent to chilly soil and became acres of lavender in warming sunshine. The leafless, gray-brown deciduous forests began to light up with the scattered, off-white masses of sarviceberry blossoms, followed by the burgundy of the redbuds and the brilliant whites of the dogwoods. Here and there in the brown hillsides appeared surprising splashes of pink—the wild peach trees, making their presence known. Spring beauties carpeted meadows in palest pinks and whites, as bluebells brightened the creek banks. May apples spread up the hills in islands of green with their lemon-scented flowers. Honeybees made their sluggish, cool-weather rounds, and the willows in the bottoms turned yellow, then green, as stems took on color, buds opened, and leaves emerged. Pasture grass greened and began to grow. In farm orchards, pear trees turned white, to be followed by the pink of peaches, the pink-white of apples, and the clean white of cherry blossoms. The sweet blossom scents mingled with the earthy scent of fresh-turned soil. The Stewart County air was rich with the aromas of new life.

The Beginning of Sorrows

Spring was mild and gentle in 1861. In April and May, corn was being planted and tobacco plants were being pulled from their beds and set out in the fields. It was a pleasant, warming springtime after a bleak, cold winter. Nevertheless, in that gentle spring of 1861, passionate war fever was sweeping the country. Although the Hinsons of Bubbling Springs, didn't know it, that gentle spring was the beginning of sorrows.

Leaders, both in the North and South, abandoned the conference table for the parade ground, the encampment, and the battlefield. Volunteer companies began to be raised all across the South. From Stewart and the adjacent counties of Montgomery and Robertson, eleven companies were soon raised and organized into the Fourteenth Tennessee Infantry Regiment. Excitement mounted, and martial sentiment ran high. In nearby Beverly, Kentucky, a compelling speech was delivered by one Henry Barnett, and a Confederate company was raised in a single day. Newly organized companies drilled in the streets and meadows. Speeches were made, bands played, and citizens and volunteer units paraded through their towns. Idealism and patriotic passions prevailed as martial songs were sung; battlefield honor was glorified in speeches, sermons, and editorials; and patriotic poems were written. Ladies knitted socks, sewed uniforms, and stitched beautiful battle flags. It had not yet occurred to them that there would soon be a greater need for cutting and rolling bandages for the wounded, knitting stump socks for the amputees, and for cutting flowers to decorate the graves of the dead.[1]

Except for old soldiers like Winfield Scott, in neither the North nor the South did soldiers have any realistic sense of how terrible the war would actually be.

Opening Shots and Secession

In April, Lincoln sent supplies and additional troops to strengthen Fort Sumter, at Charleston, South Carolina. On the twelfth of that month, in response to Lincoln's provocation, Confederate batteries at the Citadel opened fire on Sumter.

Three days later, on the fifteenth, Lincoln declared a state of insurrection and called for the raising of seventy-five thousand volunteer troops to be enlisted for a period of three months. The brevity of Lincoln's period of enlistment in his call to arms is illustrative of the generally accepted and completely unrealistic opinion concerning how long the conflict would last. Lincoln's proclamation shook the hopes of those who were trying to remain neutral, and it pushed many, who had avoided a choice until then, to move into one camp or the other. It was clear, at last, that hope for a peaceful resolution was leaning on a bruised reed. When Confederate batteries fired on Fort Sumter, the die was cast and the Rubicon had been crossed. All remaining hope for peacefully preserving the Union was swallowed up in the flame and thunder of all-out war.

On May 7, the Tennessee legislature passed a resolution in favor of military support for the seceding states, and Gov. Isham G. Harris issued a call for volunteers to defend the South. Patriotic feelings for the South and enthusiasm for the war were running high in the area, and volunteer companies were springing up around local leaders in Stewart County and neighboring Montgomery County.

Jack Hinson still opposed secession and held quietly to his conviction. His young son William, however, caught the war fever and responded. On May 18, eleven days after Governor Harris's call for volunteers, William Hinson said goodbye to his family, rode off to Dover, and enlisted for one year in Company E, Fourteenth Tennessee Infantry Regiment, commanded by Capt. Clay Roberts. With only rare exceptions, recruits were sworn in by their captains (company or battery commanders) or their colonels (regimental commanders). William had the unusual distinction of being sworn in by Brig. Gen. Daniel S. Donelson, for whom Fort Donelson would later be named, who was in Dover at that time.[2]

This was the first disruption of life at Bubbling Springs, the first of what would become an accelerating cascade of events that would break the hearts of Jack and Elisabeth, tear asunder the Hinson family, and end life as they had known it. It would be almost a month before Tennessee would officially secede, but the war had already come to Bubbling Springs.

On June 8, a referendum for secession was presented to the voters of Tennessee. In Stewart County, the referendum results were 1,883 for secession and 99 opposed. It is safe to assume that Jack Hinson and John Bell cast two of those "nay" votes. Statewide, the vote was two-thirds "yea" and one-third "nay," with most of the "nay" votes cast in the mountains of east Tennessee. That June, as the Confederate government scrambled to find its form and get itself organized, Tennessee, Arkansas, and North Carolina seceded.

While the Fourteenth Tennessee Infantry Regiment was traveling by train toward Virginia, word reached them of the Confederate victory at Manassas, and they fretted that the war might end before they had a chance to fight in it. They could not have been more wrong. They would fight there in Virginia, and in Maryland and Pennsylvania, in every bloody battle for the remainder of the war, thirty-three of them all told. They would fight until, in 1865, nothing would remain of the regiment but a ragged, exhausted, nearly starved remnant weeping on an April morning at Appomattox.

July passed and August came with no word from William, and Jack and Elisabeth worried about their boy. However, there was much work to be done at Bubbling Springs, and it went on as it had before, in the ageless seasonal rhythms of crops, gardens, orchards, livestock, and haying. Life between the rivers was changing, and most of the talk in Dover was of the war. Even talk of weather, business, crops, markets, and river traffic were discussed in terms of the war and of the changes it was bringing. It had already brought an accelerated demand for the county's iron and salted sides of bacon. There was also much talk of threats to commerce on their rivers, and they wondered how much longer they would be able to ship their valuable tobacco from the landing at Dover.

In early September Maj. Gen. Leonidas Polk, the Confederacy's "Bishop General," occupied the high bluffs at Columbus and Hickman in Kentucky, on the Mississippi River. The bluffs at Columbus, which came to be called, "the Gibraltar of the Confederacy," commanded an unobstructed view of the Mississippi for several miles upstream and downstream. Immediately across the river from Columbus, Polk established an outpost at Belmont, in southeast Missouri. He stretched a massive chain across the Mississippi, from Columbus to Belmont, anchored at Columbus with a twelve-thousand-pound naval anchor to prevent passage of Union boats below that point. The son of a Revolutionary War officer and the Episcopal bishop of the Diocese of Louisiana, Polk would later be promoted to lieutenant general for bravery at Perryville, Kentucky, and would be killed in action in 1864 at Pine Mountain in Georgia. That six-ton anchor and part of the chain can be seen today at Columbus-Belmont State Park, on the site of the Confederate position at Columbus, Kentucky.[3]

Also in September, Lincoln was convinced that if Kentucky seceded so would Missouri and Maryland. In Kentucky, Gov. Beriah Magoffin favored secession but feared an immediate invasion from the North if Kentucky should secede. He vowed to fight any such invasion by the Federals and walked a narrow line of fragile "armed neutrality." It could be argued that, for a short time, the United States had become three nations: the Union, the Confederacy, and Kentucky. But before Magoffin could bring about secession, the issue was overtaken by events. Large Union forces invaded the Commonwealth and quickly occupied Louisville, then the capitol at Frankfort, and then Lexington. By mid-November, Magoffin no longer controlled a vast portion of his state.

On November 18, a convention representing sixty-seven Kentucky counties met in Russellville, quickly voted to secede, and selected Bowling Green as the Confederate capital. On December 10, by act of the Confederate Congress, Kentucky was unanimously accepted as the twelfth Confederate state. But by then, it was too late to matter much. The man elected Confederate governor, George W. Johnson of Scott County, was soon a governor without a state to govern, and within sixteen months, he would be dead, mortally wounded on the battlefield at Shiloh. The Kentucky Confederate government would then select Richard Hawes, a prominent Bourbon County lawyer, to succeed Johnson as governor. For Hawes, the position would have even less practical meaning than it had held for Johnson.

Defensive fortifications were being constructed on the Cumberland River near Dover, to be called Fort Donelson, and twelve miles to the west on the Tennessee, at what would be called Fort Henry. In addition to the soldiers working on the two strongholds, there was a call for civilian laborers. Some of the farmers and iron furnaces sent laborers to work for hire, both free men and slaves. It was the patriotic thing to do, and it was also good business. Besides, Between the Rivers people were more and more aware of the threat of invasion from the north that their rivers provided, and there were already rumors of Federal gunboats sighted on the Tennessee and the Cumberland, downstream toward Paducah and Smithland. Jack Hinson declined to hire some of his slaves out for the work, as others were doing. He needed all the hands he had on the farm, and he didn't need the money.

The Union Army Invades Western Kentucky

On September 6, Grant invaded Kentucky and seized Paducah at the mouth of the Tennessee River and Smithland at the mouth of the Cumberland. On the fourteenth, Kentucky plantation owner J. W. McGaughey, of nearby Christian County noted in his diary, "Federal troops have occupied Paducah, Ky. Neutrality for Ky., I assume, is at an end." The diarist was correct. Governor Magoffin's difficult policy of "armed neutrality," already gasping its last after the Union's seizure of Louisville, Frankfort, and Lexington, collapsed and died under the weight of Polk's and Grant's bold moves into western Kentucky.[4]

In Kentucky, occupying Federal forces had begun arresting many leading citizens. Without ceremony or due process, such distinguished citizens as former governor Charles Morehead were peremptorily arrested and shipped off to prisons in the North. Some, such as John Hunt Morgan and John C. Breckinridge, both of distinguished central Kentucky families, managed to escape

The Western Theater, 1861-1865

and make their way to Confederate lines in Kentucky to serve the Confederacy with distinction. Morgan became a cavalry general, the dashing "thunderbolt of the Confederacy," and a favorite of Nathan Bedford Forrest. Breckinridge had been a United States senator, vice president under Buchanan, and Democratic Party (Southern) candidate for president in 1860. He became a respected general and at the end of the war would be Jefferson Davis's secretary of war.

In Christian County, McGaughey noted in his diary that Breckinridge had been in the area, speaking and raising troops. He noted, "Mr. Breckinridge delivered a long and able speech . . . he advocated secession at once . . . Kentucky is in a blaze of excitement."[5]

While work on Fort Donelson continued in spurts and sputters, carried on largely by mill hands and slaves, Col. Adolphus Heiman and his Tenth Tennessee Infantry Regiment proceeded with work on Forts Henry and Heiman (a smaller fortification, high on a bluff across the Tennessee River from Fort Henry, in Calloway County, Kentucky).

While the work on the river forts progressed slowly, the Hinsons and their neighbors began to cut and house their valuable tobacco crop. They carried on the hot, hard, dirty work of taking the tobacco from the field to the barn as they always had. They cut it and hung it on individual oak and hickory sticks worn smooth from long use and blackened with the sticky tars in the sap. This black, sticky "tobacco gum" made their fingers bond together as they handled the tobacco. Having neither time nor the means of washing it off, they periodically stopped and rubbed their hands in the dry dirt of the field, temporarily freeing their sticky fingers to continue the work. It was hard, hot work, and it was also dangerous. Climbing high in the tobacco barn, standing with smooth-sole shoes (or bare feet) on smooth, round tier poles that spanned the interior of the barn, they passed the heavily loaded sticks upward, from hand to hand, with no pausing, and hung them there on the poles above them to cure. Falls from high on the tier poles were not rare, and they meant certain injury—sometimes death.

Jack missed William, but he had little time to worry about him, for that kind of intense, hard work consumed everyone's time and strength. There were times when they could talk, following the loaded wagons to the barn and riding the empty wagons back to the field for another load, and the talk was mostly about the war. That war was becoming **their** war, whether they wanted it or not. And, although they couldn't know it, some of it would be fought on their land, beginning soon.

As the night air cooled and leaves took on autumn colors, there was much talk among the people of the threats from Paducah and Smithland. Rumors flew freely through the area; the people went on with their work but with an increasing anxiety about the future. Although the Hinson family lived with the general uncertainty and tensions that pervaded the area, they at least had the security of the Confederate presence in Stewart County. Their neighbors between the rivers in the Kentucky counties of Livingston, Lyon, and Trigg, however, had no such protection. The nearest Confederate units, except for neighboring Stewart County, were with General Polk at Columbus, and they were already experiencing the threatening presence of Union gunboats on their rivers.

In October, as thoughts between the rivers turned to killing and curing hogs, the gunboat *USS Conestoga* began making incursions deeply into Twin Rivers country, confirming the fears of the people and giving substance to the rumors. Lt. S. L. Phelps, the *Conestoga's* captain, pressed his mission aggressively, patrolling the rivers, seizing all watercraft and cargo that he suspected of doing anything to help the Confederate cause, and issuing dire threats to the increasingly pro-Confederate populace. They, in response, were thinking of places to hide their livestock, boats, curing pork, and other foods being stored for winter.

Grant's Fumbling First Attacks

In November, Grant embarked a force at Cairo, Illinois, the Union stronghold and operating base, landed them below the small Confederate outpost at Belmont, and attacked it. After a stubborn Confederate defense in which a horse was shot from under Grant, the outnumbered Confederates retreated to positions behind the riverbank, and Grant's troops briefly occupied the encampment. The undisciplined Union troops, however, disintegrated into a looting mob and didn't press the attack. From across the river at Columbus, Polk immediately sent reinforcements, the Belmont Confederates counterattacked, and Grant barely escaped with some of his men, leaving behind his dead, his wounded, and a large number of prisoners in the hands of Polk's Confederates. It was not a pretty sight, and Grant's superiors at St. Louis took note of the dismal performance, strengthening their already low opinion of him.

On November 18, the Federals attacked Polk's position at Columbus without success. The cannonading could be heard in Christian County, on the east side of the Cumberland, where J. W. McGaughey recorded in his diary, "A short time since there was a fight at Columbus, Ky . . . Many were killed. The Federals repulsed."[6]

As fresh leaf mulch deepened in the forest and trees became increasingly bare, chill autumn winds began to whisper warnings of winter. When the air grew cold, Jack had the Hinson hogs killed and cured. Pork was their foundational meat, and the custom was to kill one hog for each member of the family, at least one for company, and all that was needed for the slaves. In his case, more hogs were required for the stagecoach travelers who stayed there overnight. Hog-killing time was an annual event that had become a mixture of concentrated, nonstop hard work and a festive occasion. Almost everyone, black and white, was involved, from the building of the fires long before daylight to boiling the water required for scalding to the final cleaning up at the end of the day. Work was organized, and plenty of food was prepared in advance. It was an exciting time for the children, and grownups talked and visited as they worked. With the mix of relatives, friends, and neighbors gathered there to help, it was a pleasant social occasion. Hog-killing time in 1861 was the mix of hard work, good food, and pleasant socializing that it had always been, but this year the conversation was dominated by the war. Jack and Elisabeth thought of their William, who had so enjoyed this time the year before. They wondered if he were able to stay warm and had enough to eat. They wondered aloud how many more hog-killing times he would have to miss, and, although they gave no voice to an inescapable thought, they both wondered if he were still alive.

Although pleased to have his hay loft full of excess hay stacked for the winter, his tobacco housed and curing, and his pork curing in a full smokehouse, Jack was pensive as the first cold, gray rains arrived. They spoke to him, as they always had, of the coming of winter, unwelcome but irresistible; he didn't like it, but he couldn't keep it away. In the same way, he felt a different kind of chill as the war was closing in on Bubbling Springs, unwelcome but irresistible. Within a few weeks, in bitter winter, the war, like a lowering, black, off-season thundercloud, would roll in and explode with irresistible force all around him.

The Union War Machine Crowds In

In the fall of 1861, the ordinary people Between the Rivers were as concerned about the Union invasion of their rivers as were the Confederate strategists but for a much more personal reason— they were beginning to experience it. They were seeing those boats right off their own river banks with their guns, their crews, and embarked Union soldiers. In addition, some were suffering from the depredations of Union raiding parties that came ashore in the Kentucky counties between the rivers. Col. Randall MacGavock was sent by Polk to take charge of the defenses at Dover. In addition to the pressure of finishing the work on Fort Donelson, he was also the one who received the complaints of area citizens asking for

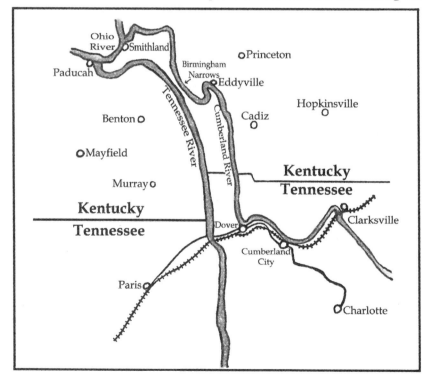

The Twin Rivers Area, 1861-1865

protection. He was sympathetic but could do little to help them. He confided to his journal, "The people in the counties of Trigg and Lyon, in Kentucky, are calling on us every day for protection, and I think we are losing ground in that region simply because they are overawed by gunboats and small parties that come out from Smithland and steal everything that they can lay their hands upon." The days of peaceful isolation between the rivers were numbered. Indeed, they were already past, swallowed up in the ugly intrusion of war. Now, the steamboats heard and seen on their rivers would not be the welcome Paducah packets or boats coming to haul away their crops. They were, instead, almost certain to be hostile agents of unwelcome change.[7]

The Union gunboat, *Conestoga*, continued its pressure on the builders and defenders of Fort Henry, creating such anxiety among the citizens along the Tennessee River that they began to fire on her with their Kentucky rifles, old flint lock muskets, and shotguns. Their scattered shots made a statement but were more emotional relief to the citizens than any real threat to the *Conestoga*. At the end of October, Lieutenant Phelps and his *Conestoga* led an attack on a Confederate encampment on the Cumberland River near Eddyville, Kentucky, and local anxiety levels rose still higher.[8]

Between the rivers, there were strategic targets whose importance was becoming increasingly clear to both Union and Confederate planners. The iron furnaces, forges, and foundries were already beginning to produce critically needed war materials for the Confederacy and were at that time its leading source. The railroad bridge at Danville Crossing, in Stewart County, was the only Tennessee River crossing in the entire area. In terms of planning and preparation, conduct of the war had essentially "just happened." In the west, especially, it had been a scene of haste, confusion, and blunders, with both sides tripping over their own feet. As autumn gave way to winter, however, matters were beginning to shake down and find their form. In the clear, cold air of early winter, the strategic picture was coming into ever clearer focus, and priorities were being established.

Today, as one considers the Confederate situation, a fundamental strategic error appears to be clear. It seems obvious that a much better place to have built fortifications to interdict Union use of the Twin Rivers would have been at the Birmingham Narrows in Lyon County, Kentucky, where the rivers were only three miles apart, which is now the location of the canal connecting Kentucky and Barkley lakes. Two such forts there could have been mutually supporting, more easily resupplied, and would have allowed for much easier communication. In addition, strategically, this would have presented a cohesive, unified Confederate front, from Columbus-Belmont on the Mississippi through the Birmingham Narrows on the Tennessee and Cumberland to Hopkinsville and Bowling Green in Kentucky, north of Nashville, and eastward to the mountains. But it seems that with the Confederacy still trying to find its form, and in the hasty and confused efforts to organize and prepare defenses in late 1861, there was no cool, decisive, strategic planning for such a cohesive, defensible frontier. Now, anyway, it was too late.

A Mellow Prelude to Horror and the Opening Shots

December was mild, as it often is Between the Rivers, and the builder/defenders of Forts Henry and Donelson were in a mellow mood. Living quarters were comfortable by soldiers' standards, and the food provided by the Confederate supply system was good. Local soldiers were free to hunt deer, squirrels, and turkey in favorite places where they had hunted as civilians only a few months before. This not only enriched their diets, but also did good things for their morale. In addition, area families visited soldiers, bringing food, clothing, books, and other items of comfort from home. It was, all told, a pleasant early winter. On December 20, McGaughey recorded in his journal, "I do not think I have ever seen a prettier spell of weather for Winter as the last six or eight days have been. The nights frosty, and the days warm as Spring."[9]

As Christmas of 1861 approached, many of the soldiers whose families were in the area were granted leave to go home for the holidays; others, who couldn't get leave, were visited by their families who "brought Christmas to them." Those who did get leave at home would return to a rapidly deteriorating situation, and those who survived the battles of the early weeks of 1862, to fight on for the next three years, would carry with them only the warm memories of

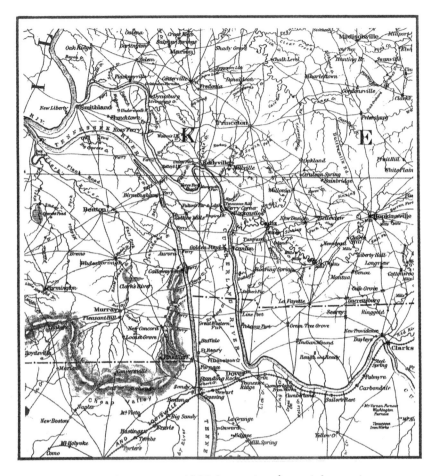

The Twin Rivers Area, circa 1862 (a portion from *Atlas to Accompany the Official Records of the Union and Confederate Armies, 1861-1865;* courtesy the U.S. National Archives and Records Administration)

that December's comfort, pleasures, and plentiful food. They would live and fight without their realities.

The year 1862 arrived wet, cold, and gray. On January 9, Grant left Cairo to move south into the Jackson Purchase of Kentucky, between Columbus and the Tennessee River, in a reconnaissance in force. He directed his men to remain disciplined and orderly and not to harm or plunder the local people. However, his order also declared all the local Kentuckians to be their enemies, a decidedly mixed message, especially for his undisciplined troops. The weather continued wet and cold, the men were miserable and frustrated, and they ravaged the countryside between the Mississippi and Tennessee Rivers. They found mostly women and children, as most of the men had enlisted in the Confederate army. At every stop in the march, they stole anything useful and destroyed the rest. The Grant force returned to its muddy encampment at Cairo wet and miserable, in disorder, and in increased disrepute.

In November, Gen. Lloyd Tilghman, a Kentuckian from Paducah, had been sent from Hopkinsville to take command at Fort Henry. A West Point graduate, veteran of the Mexican War, and a stern disciplinarian, he had continued the work begun by Colonel Heiman, who became his deputy commander. In January, Flag Officer Andrew H. Foote's gunboats conducted intermittent shelling of Fort Henry. Tilghman paid little attention to the shelling, but it was a significant milestone— for the first time, exploding shells were falling on Stewart County. War—real war—had arrived with a roar Between the Rivers. Although Tilghman was indifferent to the harassment of Foote's gunboats on the Tennessee, the people in the area were not. They heard each explosion and felt the shock. In northwest Stewart County and southwest Trigg County, houses were shaken and windows broken.

At Bubbling Springs, only seven miles away, the war was finally at their doorstep. They went about their late-winter work on tobacco, fences, and equipment as usual but with a somber preoccupation. The Hinsons felt each explosion viscerally, and they all wondered about William, and what shot and shell he might be facing, over in far-off Virginia.

General Tilghman continued work at Fort Henry and pressed ahead with work on Fort Heiman, on the bluff across the river in Calloway County, Kentucky. Winter rains had the Twin Rivers rising, as they had always done, and the bottoms along the Tennessee and the Cumberland began to disappear under cold, muddy water. At Fort Henry, it became increasingly apparent that the fort had been located too low, and the water was rising faster and higher than usual. As the river continued to rise, parapets were built higher and higher with sandbags, but there seemed to be no end to it.

On the last day of January, Grant received guarded permission from Gen. Henry Halleck to advance on Forts Henry and Donelson, with the support of Foote's gunboats and transports. Halleck remembered Grant from years gone by when, as a captain of infantry, Grant had been forced to resign from the army as unfit because of excessive drinking. Halleck didn't like Grant, he didn't trust him, and he made no attempt to hide either.

Grant and Flag Officer Foote, the navy commander, however, got along fine. They organized men and supplies, and on February 4, Grant's force assembled on the levee at Paducah and embarked for the short trip up the Tennessee to Fort Henry. The troops went ashore that afternoon at the Bailey's Ferry Landing, and for the first time, invading blue-clad soldiers had arrived in Stewart County. It would be fifteen years before the last ones would leave.

About noon on the next day, February 5, Grant's leading units, under Brig. Gen. John McClernand, encountered Confederate pickets at Panther Creek Ford and were driven back. The firing was heard for miles around as, for the first time, the sound of musketry crackled out across Panther Hollow and echoed through the surrounding hills. It was another milestone on the road to bloody tragedy.

After a night of drenching rain, February 6 dawned clear and mild, one of those springlike days that can soften February in the upper South. The river continued to rise, and inside some parts of Fort Henry, the water was waist deep. With the rising water, Tilghman realized that his position was probably untenable. He made an on-the-spot decision to evacuate the bulk of his troops to Fort Donelson that morning to avoid their capture. Colonel Heiman hastily set out for Dover with two brigades, and Tilghman remained, with only about one hundred men, to man his guns and fight as long as possible. A little after noon on that Thursday, Foote's gunboats opened fire, and Tilghman's big guns, for the first time, replied. The battle was on.

The Opening Round: Fort Henry

At noon on Thursday, February 6, the roar of the guns was heard and felt at Bubbling Springs, and it was nothing like the sporadic cannonading during January. This, by comparison, was like continuous thunder, rolling down from the northwest, and all work at the farm stopped. Twenty miles to the east, plantation owner McGaughey recorded in his diary, "Between twelve and one O'clock a tremendous cannonading began. . . . For one hour the roar was like the distant thunder." He also recorded the other matters most on the minds of people in the area: the weather and sickness. He wrote that a heavy rain had fallen the night before, and he was greatly worried about one of his slaves: "Trat has the measles, and is very sick."[10]

The battle was ferocious but short-lived. Foote's ironclad flagship was quickly disabled by Tilghman's guns, Foote was wounded, and he withdrew with heavy casualties. The remaining gunboats, taking heavy damage and fatalities, were on the verge of retreating when one of Tilghman's cannons exploded, killing the entire crew. Then his largest gun, a Columbiad, which had been demolishing Foote's gunboats, was accidentally spiked and rendered useless. Frantic efforts to repair it on the spot failed. Tilghman himself sprang forward and manned a gun, but it quickly became obvious that his situation was hopeless.

With Foote's gunboats taking a pounding, they could not survive. Quite suddenly, the tide of battle turned, unexpectedly and completely. At the very moment of defeat, himself wounded and his flagship disabled and drifting helplessly back toward Paducah, Foote was unexpectedly handed a stunning victory! When a white flag was reported on the Confederate parapet, he refused to believe it until, through the smoke, he saw the Confederate flag being lowered. Among the shattered pieces of disabled guns and the scattered bodies of his dead and wounded, standing in bloody backwater, General Tilghman surrendered himself, his flooded fort, and seventy-six survivors.

Foote was under no illusions about what had nearly befallen him and his battered gunboats. He wrote to his wife, "We have made the narrowest escape possible, with our Boats and our lives." Tilghman and his tiny force, fighting from the flooded fort, had shattered Foote's gunboats; unbelievably, the small, out-gunned Confederate garrison had the battle won when their big gun was spiked. To wounded Calvinist Foote, his costly, unforeseen victory, at the very moment of defeat, was an act of God. Maybe it was.[11]

This seemingly minor turn of events amounted to the loss of a flooded, nearly worthless river fort, a brigadier general with seventy-six men captured, and about twenty-four dead. Yet the loss would have enormous eventual consequences—perhaps even the ultimate defeat of the Confederacy. When the cannon exploded and the Columbiad was accidentally spiked, it was one of those tiny turning points in history, which later prove to have been of enormous significance. Such pivotal moments were called by Winston Churchill, "the agate points, on which the wheels of destiny turn."[12] This was certainly one such moment.

Grant's troops, trudging through the mud, had not yet reached the scene of battle. They would arrive later that afternoon to occupy the surrendered, flooded, muddy fort and enjoy the food and personal effects hastily abandoned by the departing Confederates.

Tilghman's small force across the river at Fort Heiman, with its contingent of Kentucky scouts, had played no role in the battle for, from the high bluff, their guns could not be depressed low enough to fire downward on Foote's gunboats. Observing the outcome, they wisely abandoned the works and headed south into Henry County with everything they could carry. They would be the last Confederates to occupy Fort Heiman until 1864 when Jack Hinson would occupy it, alone.

Six miles to the southeast, at Bubbling Springs, after two hours of continuous martial thunder, the Hinsons heard the guns at Fort Henry fall silent and wondered what had happened. They couldn't know that a week from that day, the gathering storm would arrive at Bubbling Springs and sweep them into its vortex.

On to Fort Donelson

While the fall of Forts Henry and Heiman was being celebrated in the North, Grant was actually in an extremely vulnerable position at Fort Henry, with his back to the flooded Tennessee River and far from being ready to move against Fort Donelson. Flag Officer Foote's gunboats, which had suffered heavy casualties and were severely damaged, were back down river at Paducah for repair, or off on other missions. Grant had no protection or support from the river. He had no knowledge of Confederate strength or intentions at Dover. He had not a single piece of artillery to support his infantry, and at that point, he was outnumbered by Confederate forces at Dover. While the North celebrated his victory (actually, it was Foote's victory, not Grant's), Grant, in the mud at Fort Henry, was in a very bad spot.

Contrary to orders, Grant's undisciplined volunteers were looting the Stewart County countryside around Fort Henry. Some, under command of Grant's subordinate General McClernand, were so out of control that Grant sent them back to Cairo. This victimization of the farm families in northwest Stewart County was a first taste of the embattled existence the locals would experience for the rest of the war.

In the second week of February, although the Hinsons and others around Dover no longer heard and felt the thunder of artillery from Fort Henry, they were beginning to hear a more ominous scattering of musketry, and it was much closer. Grant sent scouting parties out the two parallel roads to Dover, and they were skirmishing with Confederate patrols sent out from Donelson.

Grant grew more restless that week, and on the eighth, he traveled by boat upriver to Danville Crossing to have a look at the vital railroad bridge. Grant, in his personal reconnaissance of the Danville Bridge, passed through the Towhead Chute at the mouth of Hurricane Creek. He, of course, couldn't know it, but he passed through what would later become Jack Hinson's favorite death trap for Union boats.

He also sent small infantry units southward through western Stewart County that week, toward the Danville Bridge, where they were driven back by the Confederate defenders. Halleck directed Grant to destroy the bridge altogether, and a raiding force from the Thirty-second Illinois Infantry Regiment was sent to seize and dismantle it. They were only partially successful and were forced to withdraw.

By Monday, February 10, there was heavy gunboat traffic on the river, continuous skirmishing along the roads between Forts Henry and Donelson, and brief engagements southward toward Danville Bridge, which had already changed hands three times. The people of Stewart County, west of the Dividing Ridge, were having their first close experience with a shooting war, and the tempo was increasing daily.

What was a matter of conjecture and debate among the generals, politicians, and newspapermen of the North was settled and obvious to even the most indifferent farmer in Jack Hinson's neighborhood. There was a battle coming for Fort Donelson and Dover—and it was coming very soon!

About noon on Tuesday the eleventh, the skies cleared, and the breeze turned warm from the south, and Grant ordered McClernand, who had returned with his brigade, to clear Fort Henry before dark and move out onto Dover Road. Foote was reluctantly moving his damaged gunboats back around to the Cumberland at Smithland, then upstream toward Fort Donelson. The fast gunboat *Carondelet,* far ahead, was to be in position to fire on Fort Donelson the next morning. Grant expected a quick strike, which would, with the help from the gunboats, make short work of Fort Donelson. He was wrong. The battle for Fort Donelson would be bloody, hard, and an even worse disaster for the gunboats than Fort Henry had been.

Wednesday, February 12, dawned clear and mild with a warm south breeze. It was one of those balmy, springtime-like spells of pleasant weather that often interrupt winter in February Between the Rivers. In such times, crocuses open to the sunshine; daffodils pressing through the leaf mulch take on a brighter yellow; self-heal appears as lavender carpets on south-facing slopes; the frogs sing in a cacophonous celebration of life; and the birds wax romantic. The locals knew that more cold weather always follows, but the soldiers from the North didn't.

The Union volunteers set out in the warming sunshine, on the march toward Fort Donelson, in high spirits. Pvt. B. F. Thomas of the Fourteenth Iowa Infantry wrote, "The air was as balmy as a May morning." His chaplain, the Reverend F. F. Kiner, observed, "The day was beautiful and warm, and the distance about 15 miles." As the sun rose higher and they began to sweat, the soldiers began to discard their heavy blue overcoats and blankets. How could they need such things, they thought, when they were going to fight in "the sunny South?" As such encumbrances were left behind along the roadsides, their spirits soared ever higher. They would make short work of Johnny Reb here, they thought, and then head farther south. Those blankets and blue overcoats quickly found their way into the hands of local citizens and many, eventually, to poorly clad Confederate soldiers. This explains at least some of the Union reports, later on, of Confederate soldiers and guerrillas operating in the area in Union uniforms and, thus, worthy of immediate death if captured. In fact, such would be reported concerning George and Robert Hinson, Jack's sons. In most cases those ragged Confederates weren't spies impersonating Yankees; they were just cold and underfed, and those blue coats were to them a godsend. This practice continued and became ever more common. In fact, by the last year of the war, the blue uniforms of escaping Union prisoners were not a handicap to escape for many of the Confederate guards were wearing Union uniforms.[13]

Commander Henry Walke and his gunboat *Carondelet* appeared as promised off Fort Donelson, just before noon on the twelfth, and fired a few rounds from his bow guns into the fort to draw fire and locate the fort's guns. It was also his prearranged signal to announce to Grant that he had arrived. The river batteries returned fire, and after about forty minutes, *Carondelet* withdrew. Grant did not hear the canons' reports, but the people of Stewart County definitely heard them—and those around Dover also felt them.

The rest of Foote's flotilla was delayed. The repair and resupply of his gunboats had taken longer than expected, and his boats were undermanned for many of his sailors had deserted after the bloody battle at Fort Henry. Finally, however, he had to sail for Donelson with what he had. There, on the Cumberland, his sailors who had survived Fort Henry would experience combat even more bloody and more devastating under Donelson's guns.

The Union columns moved along the two, roughly parallel dirt roads leading to Dover, with cavalry screening their advance. As the blue columns approached, the locals disappeared, hiding, giving the advancing soldiers eerie feelings as they passed empty, silent farmhouses and abandoned ironworks and charcoal fields. Still, with the brightening sunshine and musicians filling the balmy air with martial music, all of them, including the usually morose Grant, moved along in the highest of spirits.

At Fort Donelson: High Spirits and Command Confusion

Spirits were also high among the Confederates at Fort Donelson. Reinforcements were arriving at the Upper Landing below the Dover Hotel. They were confident, had a bring-them-on attitude, and were anxious to "give those Yanks a whoopin'." After the next three days, attitudes would change; both Union and Confederate survivors would be bloodied veterans, sobered and traumatized out of all such unrealistic enthusiasm for battle. Although most sources describe the Confederate defenders as being in high spirits, expecting victory, and working with alacrity to prepare, when Brig. Gen. Gideon Pillow arrived, he perceived gloom hanging over the troops as a result of defeat at Fort Henry and sensed that they were apprehensive. Most likely, he was wrongly attributing to his men what he, himself, was feeling.

While the high-spirited Confederates continued preparations for the defense of Fort Donelson and reinforcements continued to arrive at the landing below the Dover Hotel, confusion and indecision reigned among their ranking generals at Bowling Green, Kentucky. Nine months into the war, the Confederate government still had not formed a decisive strategy for Kentucky, Tennessee, and the river country of the west. Generals in Bowling Green watched, waited, and worried as the war in the west largely found its own form.

While their superiors watched and worried, warrior generals like Simon Bolivar Buckner and Bushrod Johnson at Dover chaffed and waited for direction, with their hands tied by matters of rank. The audacious Forrest was already skirmishing with Grant's advance forces, but he was only a colonel, and his hands were similarly tied. The warriors could only prepare as best they could and wait for the political generals to make decisions. Clear, determined, overall command was needed by the Confederates as Grant approached

The Dover Inn (Dover Hotel) today from the Upper River Landing.

Fort Donelson. Its absence was expressed in eloquent silence.[14]

While Forrest skirmished with Grant's lead elements almost within sight of the Confederate outer perimeter, junior officers and enlisted men at Fort Donelson worked to perfect their defensive positions and to master the artillery pieces they were just learning to use.

Brigadier General Pillow arrived and was invited by his friend and ad hoc aide, Dover resident Maj. J. E. Rice, to make the Rice home his quarters, an invitation Pillow accepted.

Because the Rice house became the de facto command post for Fort Donelson, there has been considerable controversy concerning its location. The matter now seems to be settled by deed record of January 29, 1879, stating that J. W. Rice sold to G. C. Robertson, lot number 109 on the southeast corner of Petty Street and what is now called Pillow Street, *"it being the lot upon which J. E. Rice resided up to February 16th 1862"* [emphasis added]. This seems to make it clear that Major Rice's wartime home was on lot number 109, between the Robertson Hotel, "previously operated by Judson Horn," and the Dover Hotel (Surrender House). Major Rice fled with Pillow at the time of the surrender; he moved to Clarksville after the war and did not return to Dover.[15]

Pillow visited the river batteries and other units at work on fortifications to give speeches that would have been more appropriate at a political rally. Commendably, he organized the growing number of independent regiments into brigades, and the brigades into divisions, as a stream of regiments continued to be carried by steamboat from the railhead at Cumberland City to the landing below the Dover Hotel. Among these was Colonel Hylan B. Lyon's Eighth Kentucky Infantry Regiment. Colonel Lyon was a grandson of Revolutionary leader Matthew Lyon, for whom one of the Kentucky counties Between the Rivers was named. He was operating in home territory and would do so, effectively, for most of the war.

Pillow placed Bushrod Johnson in command of one division, and when General Buckner, with his well-trained troops from Kentucky, arrived on the eleventh, Pillow placed him in command of a second division. It rankled Buckner, a professional soldier, to be subordinated to Pillow, whom he considered merely a politician and not a soldier. Gideon Pillow was indeed a prominent Tennessee politician, a close friend of Governor Harris, and of former president James K. Polk, who was his law partner in Columbia. He seems to have been a strange mix of personal courage on the battlefield, instability, confusion under pressure, and shameless, self-serving, political bombast. His friend, Governor Harris, had recently made him a Confederate brigadier general.

On that warm Wednesday in February, the battle was only hours away, yet Pillow seemed not to realize it. Today it is difficult to imagine how he could have known so little about an area of conflict so small, considering the fact that his army was operating in home territory with the sympathy and support of the populace in the countryside, and with Forrest aggressively scouting and skirmishing.

A flurry of telegrams flew back and forth from one general to another during the day. Brig. Gen. John Floyd and more of his Virginians would be arriving that night at the Dover landing, and he would be senior to Pillow, who would be senior to the other brigadiers. Meanwhile, those at Dover were to do what they deemed prudent and appropriate. In other words, they were to "play it by ear."

In the West, the Union had Grant, with a simple vision and clear intentions; however, in that theater, the Confederacy had no Jackson or Lee. Tilghman was a prisoner of war, and matters of rank tied the hands of Buckner and Johnson, the only remaining professionals among the generals there. As Grant advanced toward Dover, the Confederates, with their superior fighting potential, only waited, like Prometheus bound, as their advantage dissipated and their opportunity for a decisive victory passed.

Grant's Headquarters: The Crisp Farm

For his headquarters, Grant commandeered the farm home of John and Martha Crisp, Jack Hinson's good neighbors to the north, which was situated just west of Fort Donelson, on Hickman Creek, immediately to the rear of the deploying Union regiments. As news of the Yankees' approach swept across the county, so did panic. Such an invasion had never happened there—not only within living memory, but never in all of history! Fear that the invading soldiers would kill or arrest all men had sent most of them into hiding. John Crisp, caught up in the panic, had swum across the cold, flooded backwaters of Hickman Creek, seeking a safe place to hide. Unwilling to endanger their six-year-old son, Hiram, Martha had remained, trusting that the soldiers would not harm women and children. Martha and Hiram stayed there throughout the battle, and Mrs. Crisp later said that they "were treated decently" by Grant and his staff. Grant and his officers were thoughtful and very kind to little Hiram, realizing that he was frightened by the presence of so many strange, armed men in his home, and upset by the absence of his father. Hiram recalled in later years that, from time to time, Grant and his staff officers would give him coins to comfort, reassure, and please him.[16]

It was a humble home, very small for the headquarters of an army in the field but ideally located. Brig. Gen. Lewis "Lew" Wallace, who was later governor of New Mexico Territory and author of the classic Christian novel *Ben Hur: A Tale of the Christ,* ungraciously described it later as "a poor, little, unpainted, clap-boarded affair of the 'white trash' variety, of logs, and a story and a half, with a lean-to on the side . . . half-room and half-porch."[17] Dr. John Brinton, Grant's chief medical officer, recalled, "The kitchen had in it a double feather-bed and this was occupied by the general, some small rooms in the other parts of the house were crowded by other members of his staff."[18]

By way of personal effects and comfort items, the spartan Grant had only a toothbrush, which he kept in his waistcoat pocket. Contrary to much that has been written on the subject of Grant's drinking, there was, by his order, no alcohol of any kind in his headquarters, except that kept by Dr. Brinton. The doctor recalled:

> Of whiskey or liquor, of which so much has been said, there was not one drop in the possession of any member of the staff, except that in my pocket, an eight-ounce flask, which I [kept] only for medical purposes, and I was further instructed [by Grant] not to furnish a drink under any pretext to any member of the staff, except when [medically] necessary in my professional judgment.[19]

For the soldiers involved, Wednesday night was not a night of rest. As units continued to be moved into position, the digging, chopping, and carrying went on all night. Pvt. Wilbur F. Crummer of the Forty-fifth Illinois Infantry was cold and wished that he had not left his blanket behind on the approach march. He recalled, "The night was very chilly and cold . . . Cold, hungry and disappointed, we shivered during that long, dreary night . . . We were forbidden to leave the lines, hence could not go back for our blankets." Crummer and his friends would miss them even more the next night.[20]

The sun rose on a cloudless Thursday morning, warming the soldiers after a clear, cold night. Except for scattered musketry, the night had been tense but quiet. Pvt. B. F. Thomas of the Fourteenth Iowa Infantry wrote of that balmy day: "February 13th was equal to a June day in Iowa." Yankee spirits rose with the warming sun that Thursday, with one notable exception: General Grant arose to meet the pleasant day, deeply troubled.[21]

Grant Has Sobering Thoughts

Grant woke to Thursday's bright dawn feeling insecure. As he breakfasted in Martha Crisp's warm kitchen, he considered his grim situation. He was facing an enemy he believed to be twice his strength, dug in, well supplied, and with a massive artillery advantage; and he had no idea where Foote and his gunboats were. Although he had ridden over from Fort Henry in almost holiday spirits the day before, he was so sobered by these thoughts that he even issued an uncharacteristic order to his commanders, directing them to avoid initiating heavy contact and forbidding any attacks toward the fort.

Meanwhile, unknown to both Grant and the Confederate generals, Foote's gunboats were moving slowly upstream from Smithland, laboring against the strong current in the flooded Cumberland River. Although Floyd and Pillow were also in the dark about this, the people between the rivers on the Cumberland side of the Dividing Ridge knew exactly where the gunboats were. In fact, they could have, had they been asked, accurately predicted Foote's arrival time. Somehow that information, like so much other useful information about the enemy, failed to reach the generals in the fort.

General Floyd had arrived at the Dover landing at daybreak on Thursday, bringing more Virginians with him, and had immediately assumed command. He astutely observed some shortcomings in the works, but it was too late to do anything about them. The battle was beginning.

Sharpshooters and Cannon: The Battle Begins

Sharpshooters had been firing at targets of opportunity since the leading elements of Grant's army had arrived the afternoon before. With little else to occupy him at the time, even Colonel Forrest had climbed a tree with a Maynard rifle and killed one of Grant's sharpshooters; it was a strange portent of his future partnership with the sniper Jack Hinson. This exchange of sniping began in earnest at first light, which came early on that cloudless Thursday morning. Then the cannon began to speak.

During the morning, Union cannon fire largely passed overhead and caused few casualties along the dug-in Confederate lines. At the Confederate extreme left flank, however, along Wynn's Ferry Road, direct artillery fire was a rude welcome to the war for reinforcing Confederate units moving into Dover from the river landing. They were subjected to direct, flanking, canister fire as they marched into town. They climbed the hill above the landing, up what is now Petty Street, past the Dover Hotel, Major Rice's home, and the Robertson Hotel, and turned right onto Charlotte Road (what is now Spring Street and State Route 49), toward the courthouse. At that point, they were exposed to the Union gunners on their left. Pvt. S. A. Cunningham recalled:

> We marched up the street to the perpendicular [intersection], leading to the court house. Here the head of the column . . . was exposed to the cannon shot of the enemy. . . . A piece struck Captain Thomas B. McNaughton, killing him instantly. . . . When the orders "Forward; file right" were given, the regiment started up the main street toward the court house . . . McNaughton's body lay by the line of march as the command hurried by. The cape of his overcoat, thrown over his head, hid from view the awful mutilation of his shoulders and chest.[22]

With Foote's other gunboats still several miles downriver, struggling against the flood current, Commander Walke's fast Carondelet reappeared below the fort that morning and opened fire with her long-range guns. The Confederates returned fire, and the exchange lasted for two hours. Serious damage was done to the *Carondelet,* and she withdrew downriver, out of sight around the bend, with a number of casualties. One of the few Confederate casualties was Captain Dixon, killed in the first hour, leaving Capt. Reuben Ross in overall command at the crucial river batteries. The real battle with Grant's navy would come the next day, after the rest of Foote's boats arrived, and Captain Ross would be more than adequate for the challenge.[23]

As the battle lines were drawn in the hills and hollows around Dover, farm homes were commandeered by Union forces for use as headquarters and hospitals. The dispossessed families in those homes crowded either into their own cellars, lofts, attics, or barns, or they moved in with neighbors and relatives. Chief among these was the large plantation home of Albert Rougement, a Swiss immigrant; his wife, Rebecca; and their children. They were Jack Hinson's nearest neighbors to the north. Their large home, a mansion by local standards and very similar to the Hinson home, was seized for use as a hospital. The Rougement home was situated in the meadow of Hinson Creek, a half-mile north of Bubbling Springs, on Dover Road. An abundant supply of clean, cold water was supplied by the same bubbling, underground stream that gave the Hinson home its name. In front of the house, there was a large pool of this clear, cold water and a large springhouse for homespun refrigeration. By the standards of the day, the place was ideal for a battlefield hospital, and it would see heavy use in the coming days that would leave its wooden floors deeply stained with blood—stains still visible today.[24]

Despite Grant's orders to the contrary, the first day saw three bloody, unsuccessful, infantry assaults on Confederate positions. The assaults were uncoordinated and resulted only in the death of hundreds of Union soldiers. Confederate private Louis Douglas Payne, of the Second Kentucky Infantry, took note of the bravery of Brig. Gen. C. F. Smith's soldiers and of their slaughter: "Three times they advanced . . . but without success. The ground was literally strewn with their dead." One memorable display of courage and grace occurred during the afternoon. The leaves on the ground were dry and deep, and the artillery fire set them ablaze, creating a roaring brush fire. A large number of Union wounded lay, helpless, in its path. Spontaneously, Confederate soldiers rushed forward, braving both the brush fire and continuing Union rifle fire to rescue the men they had been trying to kill only moments before. Those rescued Union soldiers never forgot that humane interlude in an otherwise savage afternoon.[25]

Thursday ended as a succession of indecisive, bloody Union

failures. Confederate spirits soared, and Grant grew still more pensive; this was definitely not going to be another Fort Henry walk-in.

Battle Thunder Shakes Bubbling Springs

The citizens of Stewart County heard it all and saw some of it. The occasional crack of the pickets' rifles which had punctuated the night, increased at dawn and continued through the morning, a backdrop to daily chores. The eruptions of musketry, and the thunder of cannon that followed, brought work at Bubbling Springs to a standstill. Only the preparation of meals and other essentials went on as usual, as units moved over their land, the sounds of killing filled the Stewart County air, and the explosions shook the ground. The younger children chattered excitedly; Elisabeth, the older children, and the servants were mostly silent, wondering; and Jack Hinson was on the move. He was on his big saddle mare early and on the go much of the day, moving among the Federal units, watching, listening, inquiring, analyzing—his countenance grave, his gray eyes as serious and shiny as pieces of rain-wet slate beneath his wide-brimmed felt hat. Many of the Federals were encamped on his land, others were moving through his land, and some of the fighting took place on his land. He stopped at Grant's headquarters; greeted his neighbors, Martha Crisp and little Hiram; spoke briefly with Grant; and rode on. At the end of that day, he probably had as good a grasp of the overall situation as any of Grant's brigade commanders—maybe better.

He was not acting as a spy or as an advocate of either side. He had come to know many of the Confederate officers, including Pillow, as Grant's army was arriving. Since their arrival, he had met Grant and some of his subordinate commanders. One venerable source, published thirty-seven years after the battle, states that Grant made his headquarters at Hinson's home during the battle. This cannot be true, however, in light of the eyewitness accounts of Lew Wallace, Dr. Brinton, and others, including Mrs. Crisp and her son, Hiram, concerning the Crisp house. This error probably arose from Grant having been a guest at Bubbling Springs in the weeks following the surrender.[26]

Jack had no agenda to promote; it was just that he was not the kind of man to stay at home, wondering what was happening. He was a man of action, and he had responsibilities. He was not only responsible for the protection of his wife and children, but also of the wider group, his extended family, which included his slaves.

In the complex sociology of the old South, a good man of that time considered his slaves to be part of his family, and spoke of them in that way. When they celebrated a wedding or the birth of a baby, he shared their joy; when they were sick, he sent for a doctor and watched over them; when there was a death, he grieved with them. This peculiar relationship between slaves and the better class of owners is illustrated in a diary entry by J. W. McGaughey, plantation owner in nearby Christian County, Kentucky. On March 16, 1861, he wrote, "Tonight we have a wedding in the family. Esther (servant girl) marries a good-looking man belonging to Col. Jas. Wallace. There is general rejoicing."[27]

Such a slave owner also didn't call them his slaves—he called them servants, as was the common practice among slave owners, except for those of the lower classes. So, in this way, Jack Hinson was responsible for the welfare of a very large family. This battle was erupting among his family and neighbors, and he made it his business to know what was happening.

Oh, What a Long and Cheerless Night!

Those who fought, those who marched back and forth, and those who simply waited that Thursday carried with them different memories of that first day. But no one who was there ever forgot the night that followed.

As the sun went down in the southwest, the wind turned and came out of the north, chilling the men in exposed positions (and that was most of them). Then a cold rain began to fall, gentle at first, then harder and harder. As the temperature plummeted, the rain turned to freezing rain, and then to sleet, which pelted men, horses, and mules with icy bullets from the sky. As darkness gathered, the temperature continued to plunge and snow began to fall, soon becoming ankle deep. The temperature dropped below ten degrees, and the wind blew with such a lacerating force that it was difficult to stand. Conditions for field soldiers, who are accustomed to misery, don't get much worse than that. Making it worse, many Union soldiers had abandoned their topcoats and blankets on the approach march, and many Confederate late arrivals had been separated from theirs by logistic inefficiency.

Pvt. D. L. Ambrose of the Seventh Illinois Infantry summarized in soldierly understatement, "Oh! What a long and cheerless night." Pvt. Dabney S. Wier of the Fourteenth Mississippi recalled, "I don't think in all my life I ever spent a more horrible night. It was so extremely cold that our clothes froze stiff upon us and it was almost impossible to keep the men on watch. They were so worn out that many of them dropped down and slept in the snow and water."[28]

"Snow and water?" One may wonder how the men could have been standing in water, with the temperature well below freezing. Unfortunately, this was the case, because the earth was still relatively warm. In low places, and in the trenches where the Confederate soldiers stood that night in frozen uniforms, they stood in ever-deepening ice water. Many of those who succumbed to exhaustion and lay down in it died from hypothermia. The wounded who fell in it during the next thirty-six hours had little chance of survival. Pvt. Wilbur F. Crummer of the Forty-fifth Illinois expressed it all in a few compelling words: "The cold was intense and the men suffered much; some perished."[29]

Flag Officer Foote and his flotilla arrived that night but were ill-prepared for the battle. Understrength, himself wounded, and with two of his gunboats still damaged beyond functioning, he had headed, reluctantly, up the Ohio to Smithland, and then up the swollen Cumberland toward Dover. It was past midnight, in snow, sleet, and high winds, when the flotilla finally joined the damaged *Carondelet* in its protected mooring, four miles below the fort.

With relatively little firing, those at the Hinson farm passed a comfortable and peaceful night at Bubbling Springs. Although the cold wind whistled around the houses and penetrated cracks, they had gone to bed warmed by the fires. They were dry and comfortable in their beds of feather and corn shuck mattresses. Their sleep was disturbed somewhat by anxious thoughts and the occasional firing, but compared with the soldiers out in the open, they enjoyed luxurious comfort. The Hinsons' horses, mules, cows, hogs, geese, and chickens were much more comfortable that night than were those shivering soldiers on both sides of the battle lines.

With dawn, the Hinson family arose as usual to coffee, warm clothes, and a hot breakfast. Only a few hundred yards away, the half-frozen soldiers, some of whom were on Hinson land, arose stiffly in the snow and icy wind to their individual rations of hard crackers (hardtack) and raw salt pork that had frozen in their knapsacks and pockets during the night.

By sunrise on Friday, the temperature rose some to hover around the freezing mark, and the snow was replaced with more mixed rain and sleet, followed by clearing skies. It was Saint Valentine's Day, February 14, but romance was the farthest thing from those shivering, miserable soldiers' minds.

The Dreadnoughts Versus the River Batteries

The action Friday morning was limited to artillery duels and sniping. The main event that second day was to be the battle between the river batteries and Foote's powerful flotilla of gunboats. Capt. Reuben Ross and his novice artillerists would be put to their severest test and would present the generals with what would be, by far, the most decisive, and significant, Confederate victory of the entire battle. Something that makes the stunning performance of Captain Ross and the river batteries even more amazing is the fact that most of the men were not artillerymen. They were infantrymen, just beginning on-the-job training with the artillery pieces when the battle began.

In the early afternoon, Flag Officer Foote's six gunboats started slowly upstream, unable to make more than three or four knots against the strong current. They rounded the bend and came into view of the river batteries at 2:35 P.M. The main event was about to begin.

The gunboats slowly drew into battle line and advanced, with the four ironclads in the lead and the two wooden gunboats trailing. The shore batteries drew first blood as both sides opened up. Captain Ross confided to his journal that the air "was filled with shot, solid case, and shell, and the river below was almost a continuous spray."[30]

Foote, undaunted, advanced on the shore batteries, firing as he came. Those four ironclad dreadnoughts, moving steadily in, cannons roaring, were an awesome, heart-stopping sight, a vision of invincibility that gave even the intrepid Nathan Bedford Forrest pause. Observing their approach from a hillside above the river batteries, Forrest ordered his chaplain to pray, saying, "Parson, for God's sake, pray; nothing but God Almighty can save that fort!"[31]

The damage to the boats was massive, and the carnage aboard them was terrible. What happened to Foote and his flagship *St. Louis* was essentially the fate of all four ironclads. The *St. Louis* took a total of fifty-nine hits, including four at the waterline and one that penetrated the heavily armored wheel house, shot away the wheel, killed the pilot, and wounded Foote again. The old warrior attempted to steer the boat himself despite his wounds and the damaged wheel, but *St. Louis* was finished. More shots tore through her, and she drifted helplessly downstream, out of control. The other three dreadnoughts suffered similar damage and dreadful casualties and drifted helplessly away. Meanwhile, the wooden-clad gunboats were firing airbursts, which were falling short, "friendly fire" that was killing and wounding their fellow sailors on the crippled ironclads.

The mighty *Carondelet,* high-speed pride of Foote's fleet, had taken thirty-five hits, including waterline hits that had her leaking fore and aft. Her life boats were shot away, the pilothouse shattered by six hits, a pilot killed, another wounded, and the wheel knocked out. Her smokestacks were shot off; her anchor shattered into deadly shrapnel; and her armor plate ripped off "as lightning tears the bark from a tree," recalled Commander Walke. There was so much blood on her decks that the crew couldn't stay on their feet without pouring deep sand over the blood. To make things still worse, *Pittsburg,* trying to escape, crashed into *Carondelet,* destroying her starboard rudder. *Carondelet* was finished and so was the naval assault on Fort Donelson. It was a bloody debacle, an amazing Union disaster.[32]

Friday Night: Celebration and Soul-searching

As the defeated gunboats drifted helplessly back down the river, gathering darkness closed out the second day. The Confederates cheered and celebrated far into the night. In Mrs. Crisp's house, however, Grant absorbed this major reversal grimly and pondered his dismal situation. Those few Confederate amateur cannoneers had denied him the decisive stroke from the river that he believed he must have, and victory for him now seemed unlikely. He need not have worried for the committee of generals at the Rice house would hand him his victory at the end of the next day as an amazing, irrational gift.

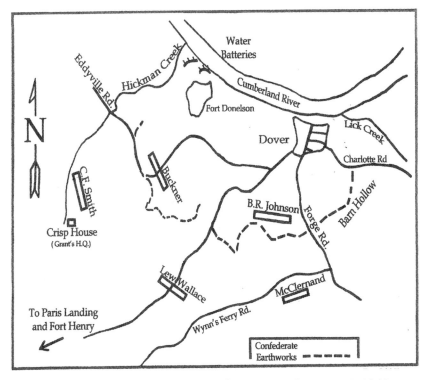

The Battle of Fort Donelson, Friday afternoon, February 14, 1862

Friday night Col. Charles Whittlesey of the Twentieth Ohio came ashore at the crowded landing downriver and sought out Grant at the Crisp house. Colonel Whittlesey left us a more complete, and much more gracious, description of Martha Crisp's home than did Lew Wallace. He noted that the house was "comfortable," on the bank of a small stream, two stories of hewn logs, and had a garden and orchard. He also noted that the fences were gone, having been used by the Union soldiers for firewood.

Whittlesey had personal messages for Grant from his father and his sister in Ohio, which Grant received "without remarks." Grant had never enjoyed a good relationship with his father, who had disapproved of his son since childhood, and considered him hopelessly incompetent and an all-around failure. Grant didn't open the messages; his prospects were gloomy enough already.[33]

Preparing for the Saturday Battle

While Grant sat in Martha Crisp's kitchen pondering his dismal situation, the committee of Confederate generals was meeting in Dover, at the home of Major Rice, to decide what to do next. Apparently, following the thinking of their superiors in Bowling Green, Buckner recommended to Floyd that they break out and offered to provide the rear guard; his plan was agreed to. According to Pillow later, the agreement was "unanimous," and yet Pillow apparently misunderstood Buckner's plan, which he had just endorsed. The generals seem to have left the meeting with different ideas of what was to be done. It was a deadly leadership failure on the part of Floyd, and one that would cost him everything.

Early Saturday morning, Grant rode off in the predawn darkness to the Union boat landing, to confer with the again-wounded Flag Officer Foote. The very last thing Grant expected was that the Confederates would attack. Actually, it was also the last thing on the Confederates' minds. Except for Pillow, the rest thought they were going to break out and leave the battlefield. Grant later remembered, "I had no idea that there would be any engagement on land unless I brought it on myself."[34]

After the Confederate generals' conference, Bushrod Johnson's troops shuffled through the mud and snow in the icy darkness, assembling on the extreme left. In fact, finding no Union troops there in front of him, Johnson moved forward two hundred yards beyond the outer works, with Forrest and his cavalry in the lead. The enemy situation was perfect. There were no Federals along the river, and the Confederates were ideally positioned for a breakout to the southeast, toward Charlotte, Cumberland City, and Nashville. All was ready, but confusion, Floyd's failure to take effective command, plus Pillow's excited bad judgment, would snatch tragic defeat that day from the jaws of blood-bought victory.

The Confederate Defenders Attack

As dawn broke, rebel yells split the predawn half-light, and Forrest leapt forward with Johnson's division following in brigade column. Out of Barn Hollow rushed ten thousand cold, hungry boys, howling like Indians, energized by the excitement of getting underway. They headed for Dudley's Hill, occupied the day before by Col. John McArthur's Illinois brigade. Pillow and Bushrod Johnson headed for McArthur's right flank, with Forrest ranging back and forth ahead of them. Buckner was to their right, moving toward Wynn's Ferry Road to establish a blocking position to hold the Federals back while the rest escaped. The Confederate artillery within the fort was providing supporting fire, moving it ahead of Forrest.

The Confederates struck the Union right flank as Colonel McArthur's cold, sleepy pickets began to rouse themselves. With his infantry component, Forrest swept around the south side of Dudley's Hill and completely outflanked McArthur's position. Somehow, at this point, Floyd's breakout became a full-scale attack on the Union right, and it rolled on like a juggernaut.

By eight o'clock, General McClernand's entire division was crumbling. His soldiers fell back; then they broke and began to run to the rear. Officers began to see their situation as hopeless. McClernand's division disintegrated.

The peripatetic Pillow seemed to be all over the field, berating officers for not moving faster and urging the weary, hungry soldiers to greater effort. At one point, he rode up to Buckner and accused him of being a coward for not rushing forward. So caught up was he in the excitement of the moment that he seemed to have forgotten that Buckner was supposed to be holding the Union forces away, not attacking them.

Adjusting to the new orders, Buckner and his brigades attacked, reaching Wynn's Ferry Road and completing the rout of McClernand's division. By late morning, Bushrod Johnson held Forge Road and the entrance to Wynn's Ferry Road, this in spite of command confusion, communication problems, and his men's difficulties with priming their old flintlocks in the wet conditions. Both Forge Road and River Road were wide open to a Confederate withdrawal.

Pillow, beside himself with excitement, found time to gallop back to Dover and dash off a telegram to the theatre commander, Gen. Albert Sidney Johnston, saying, "On the honor of a soldier, the day is ours!" He still seemed not to remember the overall objective but didn't pass up an opportunity to send a self-serving, histrionic message to his commander.

Lew Wallace Saves the Day—and Much More—for Grant

When McClernand's messengers discovered that Grant was not at the Crisp house, they were sent to Lew Wallace for help. Without waiting for orders, the audacious Wallace immediately began to move to his right, toward McClernand's sector. He arrived on the ridge just in time to save the day, not only for the Union troops, but, almost certainly, for Grant's entire future. Wallace's initiative prevented what otherwise would almost certainly have been a complete rout of Grant's army and a disastrous defeat. Had that occurred, Halleck would have taken great pleasure in banishing Grant to permanent home guard status in Illinois (or worse) and the eventual outcome of the war could have been very different.

Wallace placed howitzers astride Wynn's Ferry Road with infantry on either side and an infantry reserve to the rear. It was an ideal position to defend. Scrub oak and dense brush covered the flanks, funneling the attackers onto the road, where the howitzers waited with grape shot and canister.

The Confederates hit Wallace's position on Wynn's Ferry Road at full speed and were stopped in their tracks. Forrest had his horse shot out from under him and made his way off the field on foot. Unable to break through, Johnson stopped to reorganize, and the battlefield briefly grew quiet. It was the Confederate high water mark at Fort Donelson. Both sides caught their breath, reorganized their scrambled units, waited, and watched. It was a standoff.

Grant, in spite of his outwardly calm demeanor, was aware that he could lose the entire battle. At some point that day, he penned a revealing note to Flag Officer Foote, asking for support to stave off defeat. Grant was definitely entertaining thoughts that he might lose the entire battle and be forced to retreat back toward Cairo. Without the support of Foote's gunboats, he knew that he might not even be able to escape. Complete disaster was a distinct possibility, and it was very much on his mind.[35]

General Floyd's whereabouts during all this are unclear. He seems not to have known exactly what Pillow was doing—but then, maybe no one else did either. Floyd seemed to be moving about but more as an observer than as the overall commander.

In early afternoon, with a stand-off in place at Lew Wallace's roadblock and with Grant wondering if he might lose it all, Pillow made a pivotal, amazing decision: he ordered Buckner to return to the fort and reoccupy the trenches. Buckner, incredulous, refused, but Pillow repeated the order. Floyd, at first furious at Pillow, acquiesced, and Buckner reluctantly led his troops back into the fortifications.[36]

And Jack Hinson Was There

Jack Hinson was on that deadly battlefield, and he conferred that day with Pillow. A year later, he stated under oath that he was on the battlefield Saturday morning and afternoon, had spoken with General Pillow, and had provided him with information as to the enemy's situation. He had "heard General Pillow direct our forces to be withdrawn, saying that we were out of ammunition and could not meet Smith's fresh forces of twenty thousand men." Even now, more than 140 years later, Pillow's words of that day have a distinctly hollow ring.[37]

Only God knows what might have happened had those muddy, hungry, half-frozen Confederates been blessed with competent leadership on that long, heartbreaking Saturday. We are left, however, with only the knowledge of what did happen, and even that knowledge is somewhat clouded with uncertainties that remain to this day. What we do know, very clearly, is the result. Pillow (and Floyd, for Floyd's weakness cannot be divorced from Pillow's incompetence) delivered up to the enemy a significant victory, one that their cold, hungry, exhausted soldiers had won at so great a cost. The Federals were handed the day, which they had clearly lost on the battlefield, as an amazing, irrational, blood-drenched gift.

And the day wasn't over yet.

The Attack of the Second Iowa

During the lull after the standoff at Lew Wallace's roadblock on Wynn's Ferry Road, Grant rode back around toward his left flank and C. F. Smith's division. There, he ordered an immediate attack, saying, "General Smith, all has failed on our right, you [on the left] must take Fort Donelson."

Smith rode over to his favorite unit, the Second Iowa Infantry, and ordered them to fix bayonets and follow him. They moved down the snowy slope, struggled through the brush and abatis (sharpened stakes, or the sharpened limbs of downed trees, pointed at the attackers), and up the steep, slippery slope toward the outer Confederate trenches. Pvt. John T. Bell of the Second Iowa summarized the intensity of the struggle and the valor of the officers and men in that bloody attack:

> The first lieutenant drops with a dreadful wound in the leg; the second lieutenant is wounded; Harry Doolittle, the color-bearer, receives four wounds . . . and the flag is stretched upon the ground; it is raised by Corporal Paige, who is shot dead; Corporal Churcher then takes the colors and has his arm broken and is succeeded by Corporal Twombly, who is knocked down by a spent ball but jumps up and carries the colors.

Cpl. Voltaire Twombly survived the battle and the war, and thirty-five years later, he received the Medal of Honor for his heroism that day.[38]

Defending the entire sector were only three thin battalions of the Thirtieth Tennessee armed with flintlock shotguns. They were definitely no match for Smith's regiment with rifles and bayonets. The Iowans pressed on with their bayonets, and the outnumbered Tennesseans withdrew up the slope with their empty shotguns, many falling to the rifle fire now opened on them from the rear. With the air buzzing and cracking with bullets, Buckner arrived from the battlefield and quickly reinforced the retreating defenders.[39]

The Second Iowa, having breached the outer line and captured the rifle pits, couldn't advance beyond them for the intensity of the Confederate fire from the ridge above. Then they withdrew from the position they had gained for artillery began to find them. They had to climb back out of the captured works and take refuge in the defilade below them. Little had been accomplished by their amazingly heroic attack.

As night fell, the firing sputtered and died; both sides were completely spent.[40]

At the Other End of the Battlefield

Meanwhile, back at the other end of the battlefield, to his right along Wynn's Ferry Road, Grant had ordered General McClernand to retake the ground lost in the morning. McClernand had declined, saying that his shattered division could not be reassembled, but Lew Wallace, who had already saved the day with his initiative, said that he would do it.

Wallace's counterattack proceeded slowly; nevertheless, his superior numbers, superior firepower (some of his men were armed with breech-loading Sharp's carbines, state-of-the-art weaponry at the time), and fresher troops slowly forced Bushrod Johnson's men with their ancient flintlocks back. With Forrest's help, Johnson's exhausted soldiers conducted a fighting withdrawal all the way back into the muddy Fort Donelson earthworks from which they had sallied forth at first light.[41]

It had been a long and terrible Saturday. Grant ended his day before the fireplace in the Crisp house, worrying silently and wishing he had the support of Foote and his gunboats. Out on the battlefield, his men sought something to eat and a way to get warm enough to sleep. Across the valley at Fort Donelson, cold, muddy, exhausted Confederates sought food—any kind of food—and sleep. For most of them, it was their fourth day and night of strenuous—at times desperate—effort, with little food and almost no sleep. Most fell to the ground where they halted and slept as if dead.

As February's early darkness flooded the valleys and the battlefield at last grew quiet, both Grant's and Floyd's armies occupied essentially the same positions that they had held when those first rebel yells had erupted out of Barn Hollow at daybreak. Only there were far fewer of them on both sides now; nearly three thousand men had fallen that day.

On the battlefield, the dead and wounded nearly covered the ground. It was a scene of horror not to be forgotten. Union major James A. Connoly recalled dead horses, pools of blood, and many hats containing pieces of skull with hair, brain tissue, and blood. The mutilated dead were lying in every conceivable position, and he recalled bloody equipment, blankets, packs, canteens, weapons, clothing, and, everywhere, bloody snow and mud.

Major Connoly's recollections were not unique. All survivors of such battles, in all centuries, have seen and remembered what the prophet Isaiah succinctly summarized 2,700 years ago: "For every battle of the warrior is with confused noise, and garments rolled in blood." It never really changes, and it isn't easy to forget.[42]

Having been on the battlefield all day, Jack Hinson stayed in Dover that night. For one thing, it would have been extremely dangerous to try to pass through the confusion and promiscuous gunfire that prevailed between himself and his home. For another, he realized that the momentous things happening were far from being settled. In the morning, he would again play a unique role in those momentous things. Of course, he didn't know that and settled for dinner and a relatively warm bed in the Dover hotel.

About midnight, Generals Floyd and Pillow were in the home of Major Rice, just south of the Dover Hotel. While their men suffered in freezing, bloody mud, the two politicians-turned-generals drank hot toddies before a roaring fire, discussed events of the day, and composed dispatches to be sent to General Johnston, the theater commander. Soon after midnight, General Buckner arrived. As usual, Bushrod Johnson, the other brigadier general, was not included in their deliberations.

The Committee of Generals Decides on a Breakout (Again)

About 1:00 A.M., Floyd summoned all division and brigade commanders to a conference at the Rice house. Like so much else that was vague concerning Floyd's command, the location of his headquarters seems never to have been made clear in that dismal week of leadership failures.

All units were to prepare for a breakout before dawn; the jump-off time was set at 4:00 A.M. The subordinate commanders, knowing what was expected of them, went back to their units to prepare for the breakout and the evacuation of the fort. All, it seemed to them, was settled, but they could not have been more wrong.

At about 2:00 A.M., Major Rice told the generals that high water had flooded the roads leading out of town and opined that their chances of crossing Lick Creek were "decidedly unfavorable." Rice did, however, recommend that they send for Dr. J .W. Smith, who lived in Dover but owned the farm land that included the ford where River Road crossed Lick Creek, one mile southeast of Dover.[43]

Dr. Smith had been born and reared on Lick Creek where he and his father before him had owned the land for forty years. The crossing was called Smith Ford. He got up, dressed, saddled his horse, and rode out River Road to the ford. He returned to report "that the road was open and that the creek could be crossed"; furthermore, and equally important, he reported, "There were no federals in that locality."[44]

Forrest reported that he had ridden over the battlefield several times in the evening and had not seen a single enemy soldier. He then rode out to check the crossing personally, accompanied by the courageous and helpful Dr. Smith, who was making the trip a second time. When they reached Lick Creek, Dr. Smith left Forrest and rode three hundred yards upstream to another ford called Hay Ford, where he found the creek only eighteen inches deep. In addition, he reported that there were no Federals within a mile of Smith's Ford on the main road. The crossing was wide open.[45]

Other scouts rode out Forge road and found that fires that were being mistaken for federal units closing in were actually just small groups of the Union wounded, trying to keep warm.

The way out was unprotected. Jack Hinson would confirm this within the first two hours after sunrise and testify to the fact under oath a year later. As the wounded who were left on the battlefield did what they could to survive the cold night, and as the midnight deliberations continued in the Rice home, Jack Hinson slept in the Dover Hotel. What dreams he had may have been troubled ones for what he had seen so far was horrific suffering and death, and it appeared to have accomplished nothing.

Cheers and Tears in the Mud—A Shameful Surrender

As Jack Hinson slept that night in the Dover Hotel, up the street in the Rice home, a shameful scene of fear, irresolute weakness, and betrayal was being played out.

In spite of the accurate road reports by Forrest, Dr. Smith, and others, Floyd and Pillow increasingly embraced the belief that they were surrounded. We will probably never know exactly what happened for the surviving accounts of what was said next are mostly written by Pillow, a man deeply given to self-justification, or by his aides, who were loyal to him and to his version of the events. For the rest of his life, Pillow tried to justify his actions of that morning; his and his aides' statements concerning what took place must be read with this in mind. According to Lt. Hunter Nicholson, Pillow's aide, General Floyd made a pronouncement: "Then, gentlemen, a capitulation is all that is left to us." Pillow concurred, saying, "There is only one alternative, that is capitulation."

Forrest, returned, saw their gloomy faces, and sensed surrender. Amazed and enraged, he stomped out of the room shouting that "those soldiers have a lot more fight left in them than you all suppose." In the snowy darkness, he gathered his officers around him and snorted, "Boys, these people are talking about surrendering, and I'm going out of this place before they [do it], or bust Hell wide open!"[46]

With the committee of generals having come to the conclusion that there would be a surrender and not a fighting withdrawal, a bizarre and shameful scene unfolded. Floyd and Pillow began speaking of the need for them to escape across the river. Floyd said that since he had been accused of moving military supplies southward just before the war when he was Pres. James Buchanan's secretary of war, he would most likely be hanged as a criminal. It is true that Floyd was under indictment in Washington, D.C. at the time.

Pillow's argument for abandoning his troops was extremely vague, but he somehow linked his case to Floyd's, stating that there were no two men in the Confederacy that the Federals would rather get their hands on than Floyd and himself.[47]

Seeing what was taking place before him, Buckner asked, "Am I to consider the command as turned over to me?" Floyd replied, "General Pillow, I turn over my command." Pillow quickly replied, "I pass it." Buckner then responded simply, "I assume it." In a period of no more than five seconds and with the utterance of only thirteen terse words, overall command had passed from Floyd to Pillow to Buckner. He was now the commanding general, and Floyd and Pillow were unattached bystanders free to flee their responsibilities. Buckner might as well have been appointed captain of the *Titanic* after she struck the iceberg.

Pillow then asked Floyd if he agreed that he should leave with him. Floyd, who did have his limits, reacted angrily. According to Buckner's recollections, Pillow hesitated briefly, then said,

"Well—General Floyd, it will be far more pleasant to be at home in a comfortable bed than to be in a Yankee prison, and I will go with you."[48]

Meanwhile, Gen. Bushrod Johnson, without the slightest idea that any of this was going on, was standing in the cold predawn with his division, ready to lead the breakout. The same was true of all the other unit commanders and their fourteen thousand troops; it was one of the most flagrant examples of incompetent, self-serving leadership failure in our history—and, perhaps, one of the most costly in its ultimate outworkings.

At about this time, two steamboats arrived at the landing below the Dover Hotel, bringing the Twentieth Mississippi's fresh troops and a large amount of food and ammunition. By the time the troops began unloading, General Floyd was there making preparations to put his Virginians aboard. Using his rank, he commandeered the Mississippi infantrymen to guard it for him, keeping all others away until he could get himself and his regiments aboard. Obediently, aware of nothing amiss, they did so.

Floyd embarked, and the boats sailed with Floyd waving his sword, shouting, "Come on, my brave Virginia boys." He left the Mississippians standing there; they didn't know it, but they had arrived just in time to become prisoners of war. Floyd's Virginia artillery and a good many more of his "brave Virginia boys" were standing with them.[49]

Pillow escaped across the river on a barge, which was somehow provided by his friend Major Rice, leaving his mounted servant behind. His staff joined him on the far side of the river, whence they traveled overland to Clarksville, to safety, comfort, and a hero's welcome.

Forrest Leads His Men Out, as the Amazing Surrender Begins

At 4:00 A.M., the time previously set by the generals for the breakout, Colonel Forrest started out on River Road toward the Lick Creek crossing (Smith's Ford), followed by five hundred cavalrymen and approximately three hundred shivering infantrymen, including Companies A and H of the Fiftieth Virginia. These two companies, abandoned by Floyd, walked, fought, and made their way back to Virginia, where they joined Lee's Army of Northern Virginia and fought under Stonewall

Jackson. A large number of Virginia artillerymen unhitched their draft horses and also followed, riding bareback.[50]

Grant, when writing of it later, estimated the total number of Confederates Forrest led to safety to be one thousand.[51]

Buckner, in an extremely angry mood, called for paper and pen with which to send a note to Grant and for a bugler to sound the call for "Parley." He also ordered the display of white flags along the Confederate front. It was a moment of painful turmoil for everyone, including Buckner. His distaste for the odious surrender was expressed in one notable exception to his order: he specifically forbade the display of white flags at the river batteries. Because of their great heroism and the victories they had won, he would not have them suffer that disgrace. Then the order for a bugler presented a problem. No one present had ever before been involved in a surrender so no one knew how to play "Parley." The frustration was intense. Since the bugler didn't know how to blow "Parley," he had been told by an angry colonel to "blow everything you know, and if that won't do, blow your damned brains out." It was a bad day for everyone.

Convincing the Federals: The Ordeal of Major Cheairs

Maj. Nathaniel F. Cheairs was chosen to head the parley party, to find Grant, and deliver Buckner's letter. However, there was a problem. The Union troops were as unprepared to believe the fact of the Confederate surrender as were the Confederates themselves. Cheairs recalled, "We reached the Federal lines about daylight. . . . We commenced waving our [white] flag and blowing the bugle, and kept it up for an hour or more before they paid any attention to us."[52]

In the Union positions, across from Major Cheairs and his party, the soldiers of the Fourteenth Iowa heard the strange medley of bugle calls and assumed that it meant that the Confederates were preparing for an attack. The possibility of surrender had not entered their minds. Lt. Richard Channing, of the Thirteenth Missouri (Union) Volunteer Infantry, was amazed. He wrote that on that Sunday morning he and the rest of his unit were still depressed over their having been "thoroughly defeated" the day before and found it unbelievable that the Confederates were surrendering.[53]

Major Cheairs and his party were finally taken to General Smith, who led them to Grant at the Crisp house. Grant read Buckner's request for terms of surrender and conferred with Smith, who snorted, "No terms to the damned rebels." Grant chuckled, sat down, and penned his now-famous "unconditional surrender" letter. With Grant's letter in hand, Major Cheairs and his party rode back toward Dover.

Meanwhile, at the Lick Creek crossing, Forrest led his men safely across and settled into a steady march, as the unnecessary surrender of some fourteen thousand men and a vast store of supplies began behind him at the fort. He later recalled that after two hours on the road, "Not a gun had been fired at us, not an enemy had been seen or heard." When night fell on that tragic day, he was twenty miles from Dover and had seen no Federal units. A day and a half later, Forrest arrived in Nashville, having lost not a single man.[54]

At Fort Donelson, as word of the surrender spread through the command, the reaction was the same everywhere: first, disbelief, followed by anger, which then gave way to grief. Pvt. T. A. Turner of the Forty-second Tennessee expressed what they were all feeling: "There never was a greater surprise . . . that the troops that had fought so bravely were to 'pass under the yoke,' not whipped, but surrendered." Pvt. Sam C. Mitchell of the Third Tennessee remembered: "We felt that we had [won] a glorious victory, but . . . to our utter surprise and humiliation, we were surrendered on Sunday morning."[55]

Discovering the Surrender, Many Simply Walked Out

Realizing the situation, many men simply exercised initiative and left—alone or in small groups of two or three, with most moving out on foot. Some men like Pvt. James Woodard left on horseback. "Passing up the bank [from the landing] I saw a Negro man dismount from a horse, which he left standing in the road as he rushed down to try to get aboard the boat. . . . I got on the horse and started out of Dover along the road leading up the river." He never looked back. This was very likely the horse of General Pillow's abandoned servant.[56]

If only the committee of generals had believed Forrest and Dr. Smith or had possessed the boldness and initiative of Private

Woodard that morning, the tragedy of surrender could have been avoided. It was too late. The bugle had sounded, its strange, sad medley echoing through the freezing air up and down the blood-soaked hills and hollows. The surrender was a fact—*a fait accompli*—and it was irreversible. The fleeing generals had voluntarily forfeited a game that had already been won.

A Strange State of Affairs: Where is Everyone?

Jack Hinson, up before daylight, was aware that something momentous was happening; however, like almost everyone else in Dover, he didn't yet know what it was, let alone that he would play a role in it. He breakfasted hurriedly at the hotel and questioned the officers he found nearby about the situation. Forrest had just left Dover, leading his command toward safety. General Pillow was not at the home of Major Rice where he expected to find him, and General Floyd was not at the Robertson Hotel. General Buckner took his quarters on the second floor of the Dover Hotel but was not available. General Floyd made his quarters during the battle in the Robertson Hotel, next door to the Rice house, up the hill toward Spring Street. The location of Floyd's operational headquarters remains a mystery today as it appears to have been then, but decisions seem to have come from the Rice house, where Pillow stayed. During the battle, Petty Street could be thought of as "Generals' Row"; now they were gone and something strange was going on.[57]

Soon Jack was hearing talk of surrender.

Jack's Ride Around the Battlefield

Jack had his horse fed and saddled, and at daylight, as Major Cheairs was making his reluctant and difficult way to Grant's headquarters, Hinson rode out of Dover on his own reconnaissance. Following the riverbank downstream, he slowly and carefully made his way northward. At the river batteries, he spoke with the indomitable Captain Ross. Riding on, he left the Confederate lines and continued northward along the river until he had passed the Federal left flank. To his relief, there were no Federals there along the river. For had there been, he would have been fair game.

He rode far enough down river to be well clear of C. F. Smith's left flank and turned back to the southwest along Hickman Creek and the Union rear. He stopped at the Crisp house, but Grant was not there. Continuing along the Union rear, he found him, conferring with his staff on horseback.

Hinson greeted Grant, whom he had already met, and informed him of the surrender decision. Grant and his staff were waiting for a return message from Buckner and were preparing for the battle to resume if Grant's demand was rejected. Characteristically, Grant said nothing but fixed his eyes on Hinson, chewing on his unlighted cigar. His staff officers were skeptical; some of them thought it "was a trick." Hinson insisted, saying that he had just come from Dover, had spoken with several officers there, and "the white flag was out." The staff officers were still suspicious. They still had vivid memories of the surprise attack the day before, which had disintegrated their right flank and sent McClernand's division fleeing in chaotic retreat. In addition, Grant had apparently ordered them the night before to be prepared to retreat to Fort Henry. This was later confirmed when a Union officer told Major Cheairs that Grant had issued a warning order on Saturday night to be prepared for a retreat to Fort Henry on Sunday morning.[58]

Characteristically, Grant listened. When he did speak, he asked Hinson if he had any reason to doubt the Confederates' apparent intention. Hinson assured him that Floyd's and Pillow's headquarters and quarters were strangely unoccupied, that he had spoken with several Confederate officers, and that he had seen some of the flags himself. He also told Grant that the way out for the Confederate command along the river was unguarded with nothing to stop them. Grant expressed the need for this news to reach his entire command, and Hinson was asked if he would be willing to ride on along the Union rear and inform the unit commanders of the surrender. He said that he would, touched his hat brim as a parting courtesy to Grant, and rode on. Turning southeast, he disappeared from sight.

Riding slowly and carefully, stopping to inform each Union commander along the way, Hinson rode on into the pale, early morning sun until he reached Lew Wallace's extreme right flank along Wynn's Ferry Road. Then he rode northeastward across Forge Road and back toward Dover, scanning the slopes fought over on the previous day. He found not a single Union soldier,

Jack Hinson conferring with Grant on the battlefield, Sunday morning, February 16, 1862. (Drawing by Joe McCormick)

except for the dead and the wounded east of the point on Wynn's Ferry Road where Lew Wallace had made his stand and stopped the Confederate attack the day before ("near where their battery was on the previous day"). As he rode slowly on, growing daylight revealed that reports of the Federals "reoccupying the battlefield and cutting off all avenues of escape" were merely phantoms of the imaginations and fears of incompetent scouts, fears of the committee of generals in the Rice house, or both. Testifying to all this under oath a year later in Columbia, Tennessee, Jack would state plainly that no Union forces had moved to reoccupy the previous day's battlefield as of two hours after sunrise ("two hours by sun") on Sunday morning. He would testify very precisely that even two hours after sunrise from the extreme right flank of the Union Forces on the Wynn's Ferry Road, it was "about one mile and a half east to the Charlotte Road [River Road], and about two miles to the River Bluff." He would conclude, "I know that the whole of the intervening space was open and free from Federal troops Sunday morning, and that there was nothing to have prevented our forces marching out and retreating towards Charlotte or Nashville." The way out had indeed been clear.[59]

Grant would return to Stewart County upon being relieved by Halleck and replaced with C. F. Smith. It is almost certain that it was during this period of exile to Fort Henry, that Grant was a guest at Bubbling Springs. After Grant finally left Stewart County to direct the rest of the war, restored to his command by Lincoln, the two men would never meet again. Grant, however, almost certainly heard of Jack Hinson after he became a notorious Confederate sniper, and he must have wondered what had made an enemy of the man who had helped him and in whose home he had been graciously received as a guest.

Old Friends in Strange Roles

As the sun rose higher and the air warmed a little, Buckner sat in his gloomy, de facto headquarters in the Dover Hotel thinking of his old friend Sam Grant. Because of Grant's initials (U. S.), his fellow cadets at West Point had called him "Uncle Sam," and to his friends, he had become just "Sam." Like so many of the opposing commanders in that war, Buckner and Grant had been friends since their days together at West Point. They had both been members of a fraternal group of twelve cadets, which they had called the Twelve in One. As young lieutenants, they had served together in Mexico. Eight years before the Fort Donelson battle, when a penniless Grant had been stranded in New York after being forced to resign from the army in disgrace, Buckner had rescued his old friend. He had paid for Grant's lodging and food and raised money from other officers in New York for a cash gift to help him. They had indeed been very close. Until receiving the "unconditional surrender" letter, Buckner had had every reason to expect that Grant would give him generous terms for the surrender; the shock of the demand deepened his gloom.[60]

Buckner and his staff, running low on food, had a sad and simple breakfast, attended to final preparations for the surrender, and waited for Grant to arrive. When Grant finally arrived, his friendly manner put Buckner at ease, and the two briefly discussed the situation. In speaking of Pillow's escape, Buckner said that Grant was probably anxious to capture him. In a rare display of humor, and a wry comment on Pillow's flawed generalship, Grant replied that had he captured Pillow, he would then have turned him loose, stating, "For I would rather have him in command of you fellows, than as a prisoner."

Grant and Buckner spoke pleasantly of old times, the Twelve in One club, the war in Mexico, and their climbing of Mount Popocatépetl together in the snow. They then discussed specific matters concerning the surrendered force, and Grant was gracious.[61]

With these matters settled, Buckner started to go upstairs to his living quarters. As he left the hotel dining room, Grant followed and took him aside. Undoubtedly remembering how Buckner had rescued him in New York eight years earlier, Grant took out his wallet and said, "Buckner, you are, I know, separated from your people, and perhaps you need funds. My purse is at your disposal." Buckner thanked him, declined his help, and went upstairs to prepare for the trip to a northern prison. It was, as historian Stephen Ambrose observed, "a strange war." It was indeed a strange war. Twenty years later, when former president Grant was again in financial difficulty, it was Buckner who offered to help him out of his crisis a second time. And when, a few years after that, Grant lay dying, Buckner visited him on his deathbed and was, with Sherman, a pallbearer at his funeral.[62]

Having moved out of the Crisp house, Grant settled into Buckner's chair, and the hotel temporarily became his headquarters. Positions of command and the locations of headquarters had been changing with dizzying speed on Petty Street that morning.

Meanwhile, Martha Crisp had to rearrange her home after Grant's departure and adjust to the changes. She knew nothing of her husband's situation, but the shock of swimming the cold backwaters of Hickman Creek and the subsequent exposure to severe cold had weakened John Crisp, leading to the pneumonia that killed him. After the battle, Martha was unable to operate the farm alone, a problem made worse by the fact that Union soldiers had burned her fences as firewood. She and her son, Hiram, went to live with her brother, Dave Jones, and his family, on the Cumberland River north of Dover. She never returned to the home that Grant made famous.[63]

Grant began to organize the chaos of surrender. The battle was over, and the victory that would propel him ultimately to the White House was his. The irony for Grant, although unknown to him, was that at this moment of pivotal victory and on his way to becoming the commander of the entire Union army and the North's greatest hero, his immediate superiors, Generals Halleck in St. Louis and McClellan in Washington, were plotting to have him relieved and court-martialed.[64]

The Beginning of the End: Had the Committee of Generals Doomed the Confederate Cause?

It is most unlikely that Grant was thinking that morning of the part his victory would play in the Union's ultimate triumph for he had immediate, compelling things on his mind. Perhaps he and Jack Hinson speculated about the question days later when Grant was a guest at Bubbling Springs—we shall probably never know. It was indeed a pivotal victory.

Meanwhile, Lincoln, preoccupied with the fact that his son, Willy, was dying, had nevertheless been following the news from Fort Donelson with considerable anxiety. In a message to Halleck, he wrote, "Our success or failure at Fort Donelson is vastly important, and I beg you to put your soul into the effort." Lincoln needed a victory—any victory—but it is doubtful that even he realized fully the strategic importance of a victory there.[65]

As historians do today, politicians then tended to view Fort Donelson as a minor engagement in the backwaters of the war, and attention was focused on Virginia, Maryland, Pennsylvania, and Washington, D.C. A strong case can be made, however, for the argument that with the surrender of Forts Henry and Donelson, an enormously significant turning point in the war was reached. The mighty Twin Rivers were opened into the Confederate heartland, and the Mississippi River and its outlet to the sea were as good as lost. Actually, Anna E. Carroll, a woman with access to Lincoln and his cabinet, had urged this strategy in a written plan in 1861. She cited, perhaps prophetically, the advantage of the Cumberland and Tennessee Rivers' northward flow. The disabled navy boats would drift northward to safety, rather than southward into Confederate hands. In the battles for Forts Henry and Donelson, they had indeed done exactly that.[66]

The anchors of the Confederate defense in the west, at Columbus-Belmont and Bowling Green, were left exposed and would be quickly abandoned. Kentucky would never be regained; Nashville would quickly become a permanent Union stronghold; and the ultimate outcome of the war may already have been determined. Simply put, it is likely that when the unnecessary surrender was decided upon in the Rice House in the early hours of that fateful Sunday morning in February 1862, the war was lost for the Confederacy. It would just require three more bloody years to play it out.[67]

At any rate, one thing is certain: for Jack Hinson and his family, life would go steadily, tragically, and irreversibly downhill from that day on.

Chapter 3

Occupation and the Rise of Guerrilla Warfare

"Death to bushwhackers is the order. . . . Execute [them] immediately if they are unfortunately taken alive."
—Maj. Gen. S. R. Curtis, March 30, 1863

C. F. Smith's division was given the honor of advancing directly into the Confederate positions to possess the fort. Smith chose the Second Iowa, which had fought so valiantly against Buckner's Kentuckians and Tennesseans the afternoon before, to lead the way in.[1]

The other regiments followed, bands playing and colors flying. The betrayed Confederates stood with their rifles lying at their feet, arms folded across their chests, glaring at the entering Federals. Forrest, as usual, had been right: there was plenty of "fight" left in them yet. An interesting manifestation of the fact that the Rebel soldiers didn't consider themselves "whipped" is that not a single Confederate battle flag was surrendered to the Federals. When the triumphant Federals entered the fort, there was not one to be found. All had been removed from their staffs and hidden.[2]

The Stewart County Seat Was a Shambles

Dover had suffered great damage during the battle. Charles Coffin, a correspondent for the *Boston Journal*, described Dover as he saw it that Sunday morning:

> "The town of Dover . . . is a straggling village on uneven ground, and contains perhaps five hundred inhabitants. There are a few buildings formerly used for stores, a doctor's office, a dilapidated church, a two-story square brick courthouse, and a half dozen decent dwellings. . . . Nearly every building was [an improvised] hospital. Trees had been cut down, [wooden rail] fences burned, windows broken, and old buildings demolished for fuel."[3]

Private Thomas, of the Fourteenth Iowa Infantry, described the grim scene he found there:

"We hastened through the mud and water, for the ground was thawed again by this time, to the town of Dover. . . . There were broken vehicles and crippled horses scattered about the streets. In many of the houses were dead men who had been carried in from the battlefield by their friends. Some wounded men and many prisoners. Nearly all the houses were abandoned by their owners."[4]

The Rice house and the two hotels were in a relatively protected position on Petty Street, in defilade below the crest of the central hill, and were intact. The brick courthouse in the central square, standing two stories high with a central cupola, still dominated the scene. As McClernand's division entered the town from the south, one of his soldiers seized the initiative and ran into the courthouse and up the stairs to the second floor, climbed up into the cupola, and hung a Federal flag. Reporter Charles Coffin observed the event: "A private ran into the courthouse and threw the flag of the Union to the breeze from the belfry."[5]

Was the Courthouse Destroyed in 1862?

Goodspeed's History of Stewart County is one of a statewide series of nineteenth-century, commercial, county histories with a questionable reputation for accuracy and scholarship. Goodspeed states that the two-story, square, brick courthouse with square cupola was "destroyed by the Federals during the year 1862." This cannot be true. For to have been destroyed in 1862, the destruction would have had to occur during the battle that lasted from February 13 to 16. Yet here is the firsthand testimony of the reporter that it still existed after the battle. As further evidence, a drawing of Dover was made for *Frank Leslie's Illustrated Newspaper* in March 1862, a month after the battle, and it clearly shows the courthouse dominating the skyline, square, two stories, complete with cupola.

There is no record or trace of a tradition to suggest that the Federal army destroyed the courthouse later in the year 1862. In fact, after the surrender of Fort Donelson and Dover, the town and its courthouse were under Federal control until the end of the war. It would have been insane for them to have destroyed such

Dover from the river a month after the battle. Note the intact courthouse dominating the skyline. (From *Frank Leslie's Illustrated Newspaper,* March 15, 1862)

a vital building. The preponderance of evidence declares that the Stewart County Courthouse survived the war.[6]

Grant Moved His Headquarters (Briefly) to the Dover Hotel

By noon, rain had begun to fall, making the muddy conditions worse. The little town, normally home to about five hundred citizens, was being trampled into a muddy morass under the feet of forty thousand soldiers.

A large but never completely known number of Confederates continued to escape as the confusion of that Sunday drew on. Most of them simply walked out through the loosely organized Federal lines. The most distinguished escapee was Brig. Gen. Bushrod Johnson. Discovering the betrayal of Floyd and Pillow and accompanied by Captain J. H. Anderson of the Tenth Tennessee Infantry, he walked forward through what had been Colonel Heiman's defensive sector and kept going. He related later that he had not heard of even one Confederate soldier who tried to escape who was not successful.[7]

In the afternoon, Grant moved his headquarters from the Dover Hotel to the boat *New Uncle Sam*; Buckner accompanied him, and the formal surrender took place there. Then Buckner, Tilghman, and approximately twelve thousand of their soldiers were shipped northward to Yankee prisons.

The frozen bodies of Confederate soldiers still unburied on the battlefield would be thrown into mass graves by their Union conquerors, a process witnessed by Capt. R. L. McClung of the Fifteenth Arkansas, who was left behind in a makeshift hospital in Dover. Some of those mass graves remain unmarked, a lingering and controversial footnote to the tragedy of the battle.[8]

The little village was reduced to a shambles. The county's center of social order and seat of law was a muddy scene of destruction, disorder, and chaos with many of its trees cut down or shot to pieces, its streets littered with the wreckage and jetsam of war, and many of its homes and store buildings damaged or destroyed, occupied only by dead and dying soldiers.

Shocking News Waited at Bubbling Springs

As the sun began to settle in the direction of Bubbling Springs and order began to prevail over the disorder and confusion of that Sunday, Jack mounted his saddle mare, reined her around toward the road to Paris Landing and set off pensively for home at a steady, deliberate walk. Riding slowly through what had been his neat little hometown, Jack saw its streets littered with a churned mixture of red clay mud, dirty snow, and deep puddles of bloody water. It was like a slow-motion sequence from a nightmare. In the descending quiet, he picked his way around wrecked wagons and the bodies of dead horses and mules. On the rising westerly breeze floated the pitiful sounds of those not yet dead. Among the pleading, whimpering animal sounds, he also heard the voices of men still clinging to life, calling for help to friends, God, and their mothers. Even for cool, tough-minded Jack Hinson, the sight was disorienting, like a scene from Dante, Goya, or Armageddon. He had been away from home for more than three days, and passing out of town, he thought and wondered what he would find there.

Already sickened by the battle and its aftermath, he was shocked by what he found at home. His young namesake, John, and John's older brother George were prisoners at Fort Donelson! They had been arrested during the surrender that day, accused of being Confederate spies. The battle and its prelude were by far the most exciting things that had ever happened in the area. They, like others among the bolder citizens in the Dover area, had been in the woods and fields on previous days as near to the battlefield as they could safely be, trying to see what was happening. On that Sunday morning, they had gotten too close to the Union troops.

In the confusion that prevailed during the surrender, they had been seized, and despite their protestations to the contrary, they were accused of spying for the Confederates.

It was completely irrational to think that a surrendering army would employ spies during the surrender process, but that Sunday was a day of chaos and confusion when many irrational things took place. George and John would be shipped north with the rest of the prisoners and held in a prison boat on Bloody Island, near St. Louis, for slightly over a month before the mistake in their case was revealed and they were returned.

Up from Abject Failure: The Amazing New Grant

In spite of the fact that General Halleck and others were scrambling to claim the credit for the swift victories at Forts Henry and Donelson for themselves (or to ascribe it to General Smith), and in spite of Grant's natural modesty and unwillingness to promote himself, the reporters on the scene at Dover quickly made him the hero of the hour. He became an instant national celebrity when the northern newspapers published a stream of stories about the triumphs of "Unconditional Surrender Grant." Through these stories, the people in the North learned of Grant's fondness for cigars, and thousands of boxes arrived for him, gifts from an adoring public. These cigars, gifts of love and appreciation, were probably the eventual cause of Grant's untimely death. Whereas he had before kept cigars with him and frequently had one in his mouth, he had not smoked them. After Donelson, he began to smoke them and was seldom without one until his painful death in 1885 from throat cancer.

In Grant, Lincoln had finally found the fighting general he had been praying for, and Sam Grant suddenly had a most important friend in the very highest of places. Although Grant wasn't yet aware of his favor with Lincoln, he would never need it more, for the public's adoration of Grant didn't stop the anti-Grant scheming of Halleck and McClellan. Their plans to have Grant removed and sent back into the obscurity from which he had emerged, and where they both devoutly believed he belonged, were rendered moot by Lincoln's approval and appreciation of the nation's new, cigar-smoking hero.

The magnitude of Grant's amazing change of status from abject failure to national hero can hardly be exaggerated. Following his forced resignation from the army for drunkenness, he had failed dismally at everything he tried to do. He was reduced to selling firewood cut from his father-in-law's woods on the streets of St. Louis, wearing his faded blue uniform coat with the rank insignia removed. With the outbreak of the war, he sought to return to the army, but no one wanted him. After being repeatedly snubbed by McClellan and other former army acquaintances, he finally obtained an appointment by the governor as a colonel of Illinois volunteers. He was the better-than-nothing replacement for the commander of a regiment of undisciplined, untrained volunteers, a position no one else wanted. From there, needs of the rapidly expanding army moved him to Cairo, command of a brigade, and then as a brigadier general feeling his way toward Columbus-Belmont. He pressed on to Forts Henry and Donelson, where he was handed the victory that propelled him to national prominence and favor with Lincoln. People who had known him before the war could not believe they were reading about the same man.[9]

On the brink of a disastrous and almost certainly final defeat, Grant was handed a momentous victory at a time when Lincoln badly needed one. They would become an inseparable team.

Grant Moves on to Clarksville and Nashville

Following the surrender of Fort Donelson, Grant had to untangle the administrative and logistical problems that naturally followed, organize the preliminary occupation of Dover and the surrounding area, and get more than twelve thousand Confederate prisoners on their way to prisons in the North. He made short work of those matters and looked eastward.

Although he might have been expected to sit in pleasant bewilderment, enjoying his newly found status of stunning success, Grant seemed rather to be lifted to a new and positive vision. With an apparent sense of destiny, he immediately pressed forward toward Clarksville and Nashville. Moreover, according to his superiors, Generals Halleck and McClellan, he had done it without their authority; they still intended to have him arrested, court-martialed, and cashiered from their army, in spite of his sudden favor with Lincoln, whom they also viewed with contempt, as inferior, and incompetent.[10]

Confederate military garrisons and public officials fled before Grant's advance and so did a great many of the private citizens, who fled from what they viewed as a rapacious horde of invading barbarians.

Largely unaware of most of the posturing and political maneuvering by powerful men going on above him (even Secretary of War Stanton was involved), Grant wasted no time in following up on his victory. Three days after the surrender, he sent Flag Officer Foote upstream with two gunboats to occupy Clarksville. On February 19, within hours of shoving off from Dover Landing, Foote and his sailors took possession of Clarksville for the Union, without a fight, as Generals Pillow and Floyd again took flight— this time to Nashville.[11]

From his "flag steamer," the aggressive Lieutenant Phelps's *Conestoga*, Foote reported on the twentieth that he found Clarksville virtually deserted, with streets largely empty, except for wandering, bewildered slaves. The fearful citizens who had not fled the city remained indoors. Fort Defiance, as Clarksville's river front fortifications were called, was deserted; its spiked cannon never fired a shot in anger. Foote issued a proclamation reassuring the citizens of their safety, if military stores would be surrendered and "no secession flag . . . or feeling be exhibited." That same day, Grant ordered C. F. Smith and his division to proceed overland to occupy Clarksville. Four days later, when Smith's division moved out for Clarksville, Grant accompanied them. Exactly a week after the surrender, he moved his own headquarters from Dover to Clarksville, taking possession of a vacant mansion on Second Cross Street. (Today, this street is called simply Second Street. A few large homes remain there, but the identity of the one where Grant made his headquarters is not known.)[12]

The gallant old Gen. C. F. Smith, Grant's right arm, would soon be injured in a fall, sicken from dysentery and an infection resulting from the fall, and die two months later. His battlefield leadership would be sorely missed at the Battle of Shiloh in April, which took place eighteen days before his death.

As the Union dead were collected and buried, casualty lists were prepared and released to the press. As the lists were published in hometown newspapers, family members began to arrive at Fort Donelson to claim the bodies of their loved ones. This added to the confusion there. Pvt. John Metzger of the Seventy-sixth Ohio Volunteer Infantry was surprised to see his uncle, John G. Weeks, arrive at Fort Donelson. Mr. Weeks was there to claim the body of his son, Metzger's cousin, who had been killed in the gallant charge of the Second Iowa on Saturday afternoon. Metzger described his uncle's grief as "unconsolable." Multiply this tragic scene by the hundreds and we get a fuller idea of what those muddy, chaotic postbattle days were like. Except for local families who received word directly from friends about their loved ones, almost no relatives could come for their Confederate dead. There was no Confederate presence in attendance, and the surviving friends and commanders who knew of their deaths had already been shipped north to prisons. Most of the Confederate dead had been merely dumped into unmarked, mass graves.[13]

The Confederate Strategic Position Unravels

Meanwhile, the Confederate presence in Kentucky and west and middle Tennessee quickly began to unravel. Albert Sidney Johnston and his Confederate force evacuated their stronghold (and Kentucky's Confederate Capital) at Bowling Green, Kentucky. Johnston's withdrawing army was accompanied by Kentucky's Confederate governor, George W. Johnson, and what was left of his state government. Johnston's withdrawing columns were also followed by many of Bowling Green's private citizens, a number of whom had set fire to their own homes as they left rather than leave them behind for use by the hated Yankees. Kentucky was lost to the Confederate cause. Although one major battle would be fought for the state in October and raids by John Hunt Morgan, Nathan Bedford Forrest, and Hylan Lyon, as well as guerrilla warfare, would continue in all parts of the Commonwealth until the end of the war, Kentucky would not be regained. In little more than a month, both General Johnston and Governor Johnson would be mortally wounded at the Battle of Shiloh.

Upon arrival in Nashville from Bowling Green, Johnston almost immediately abandoned Nashville also, burned its bridges, and moved his army southward to Murfreesboro. Governor Harris and

his Tennessee government would be exiles for the remainder of
the war. The Confederates would never again possess Nashville.
However, the last and most costly major battle of the Army of
Tennessee in the west would be fought in a futile and bloody
attempt to recapture it at the end of November in 1864.

By the end of February, Leonidas Polk, the "Bishop General,"
left alone and exposed on all sides, abandoned his stronghold
overlooking the Mississippi at Columbus, Kentucky, and withdrew
southward. The Confederates' "Gibraltar of the West" was in
Union hands, occupied by Halleck's forces without firing a shot.
The Union was now in complete possession of what had been the
Confederate strategic line of defense, from Columbus-Belmont
on the Mississippi through the Twin Rivers of the Tennessee and
Cumberland to Hopkinsville and Bowling Green. Nashville, which
had been the Confederate command and logistics center in the
west, quickly become a major center of Union command and
logistics, continuing as such until the end of the war.

Adjustment in Stewart County

In Stewart County, life began to return to its normal rhythms
after the surrender. There was still the considerable damage to
be cleaned up and repaired in Dover and on the farms-turned-
battlefields around Dover, and this included Bubbling Springs.
The northeast part of Hinson land was bivouac and battlefield
area, near what later became known as Hinson Town. The Union
occupation forces would become a permanent presence, but
faced with the necessities for living, the people returned as well
as they could to their former lives. Beneath it all, there was a
discernable tension in the county, an ongoing uncertainty. Jack
Hinson hoped that life there could again be the same as it had
been before the battle, but it was a decidedly vain hope. Those
halcyon days before the war would never return for the Hinsons.

Occupation Becomes a Grim Reality

The Union presence was spreading outward from Dover into
all parts of the area, with soldiers seizing the property of those
suspected of Confederate sympathies and arresting some of them.
Jack was also hearing quiet talk of small groups of guerrillas

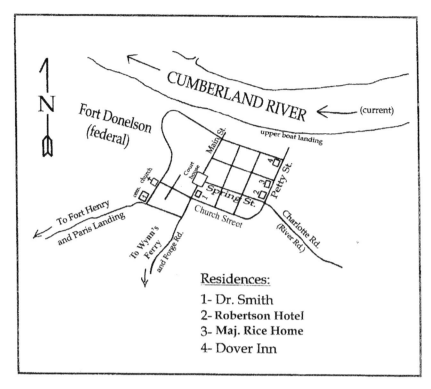

Occupied Dover

organizing in the backcountry to oppose the Yankee invaders, but he wanted nothing to do with such things. There seemed nothing for him to do but to get back to the operation of the farm at Bubbling Springs and take care of his growing family, black and white, as he had before.

Some of his neighbors, who had hired out slaves to work on the fortifications at Fort Donelson, lost their slaves; they had been confiscated without compensation by the Federals. In the chaos following the surrender, other slaves had left in the confused rabble of unwelcome "contraband" blacks that followed the Union army. Some local slaves were pressed into forced labor gangs for the Union troops, some were confiscated to become personal servants for Union officers, and others simply milled about, expecting to be cared for. Still others were confiscated without ceremony by Union patrols and taken away, never to be seen again. In Jack's case, however, he had provided no slaves for the Confederate works, was known as a man of peace and a friend of Grant, and he, for the time being, was left alone. The Bubbling Springs slaves stayed in the only home most had ever known, discussing the awesome events taking place around them.

Occupying Union troops wasted no time in punishing local citizens whom they suspected of having given support of any kind to the Confederates, or for having perceived Confederate sympathies. Within three days of the surrender, Flag Officer Foote on his way to occupy Clarksville stopped off at Cumberland Iron Works and burned it. Although Mr. Lewis, one of the owners, proclaimed himself to be a loyal Unionist and pleaded that he had not sent his slaves to work on the Confederate fortifications at Donelson, his plant was destroyed because he had sold iron to the Confederacy, and he was imprisoned without a trial.[14]

As the war moved eastward to Clarksville, Nashville, and beyond, a relative quiet settled over Stewart County as people tried to reorder their lives and reestablish normal commerce. It wasn't easy. River traffic was greatly disrupted since the Twin Rivers were crowded with transports filled with troops and supplies, and many civilian boats had been "pressed" into service for the Union and not returned. The citizens who had suffered property damage set about rebuilding. Houses and barns damaged or destroyed in the fighting had to be repaired or replaced. Rail fences burned by the soldiers for firewood had to be rebuilt. At the Rougement home, just north of Bubbling Springs, the challenge was enormous. Horses, mules, ambulances, and hospital wagons had churned the yards into a muddy, bloody morass. The vast amounts of scattered, overlooked, and abandoned arms, legs, and other human body parts, all beginning to decompose, combined to create an overwhelming, noisome presence. By early summer, the cleanup would be finished, the spring branch would have flushed itself clean, and grass would again grow around the house. However, the family would never forget that pervading smell, nor would they ever get the blood stains scrubbed out of the floors. The presence of death would seem to hang over the great house for a very long time.

In the aftermath of war's devastation, the people of Stewart County went about early spring planting as well as they could.

Although the early springtime was one such as they had never known, there were things that had to be done—things that they had always done in early spring. And, as well as they could, they set about doing them.

By late February, most of the dead soldiers had been located and buried. As February gave way to March and longer periods of warm, sunny days accompanied the arrival of spring, the multitudes of dead horses, mules, and cattle as well as yet-unburied soldiers, made their putrid presence powerfully known. As late as the end of March, an Indiana soldier wrote to his family of the terrible stench that remained there.[15]

The Rise of Guerrilla Warfare

As the war and public attention moved away from Between the Rivers, peace did not flood in to take its place. Instead of peace, another kind of war arose, one widespread and much more personal; it touched almost everyone. Guerrilla warfare began to break out Between the Rivers almost as soon as the guns of Fort Donelson fell silent. It began slowly in those early months of 1862, erupting in scattered places, from Paducah and Smithland southward to Waverly and Charlotte. Wherever Confederate forces had given way and left the area to the Federals, guerrilla bands began to appear. Gen. William T. Sherman, who commanded in the western rear areas for most of the war, lived with this kind of warfare, understood it, and expressed it eloquently: "Though our armies pass across and through the land, the war closes in behind [us], and leaves the same enemy behind."[16]

This new kind of war wasn't breaking out just between the rivers. In fact, although the Confederacy would never again occupy and control parts of Missouri, Kentucky, Virginia, and Maryland and vast areas of Tennessee and Arkansas, those states would be bloody battlegrounds for the remainder of the war. Worse, this new kind of war would involve savagery and barbaric atrocities unknown on the regular battlefields. Although the war had supposedly moved away from them, the people of those border areas would bleed terribly for the rest of the war. The ongoing suffering and manifold tragedy in the rear areas would go virtually unnoticed by the press, overshadowed by the clashes of major armies to the east and south. However, it would become a central fact of life for those involved—Union soldiers, Southern partisans, self-serving hoodlums, and a great many innocent civilian victims in the area.

The Confederacy had abandoned the Twin Rivers, and Union forces now occupied it, but they would never really control it and would definitely never pacify it. For the rest of the war, the Union occupation troops would not only be unable to exercise true control of the area, but would also find themselves, much of the time, unable to move freely about the area with safety. At times, occupation troops would pass through an area with no difficulty; at other times, they would find themselves in the very same place, fighting or fleeing for their lives.

For the most part, guerrilla warfare arose spontaneously. Throughout the upper South, this resistance to Union occupation appeared like scattered grassfires, and as the local Union troops would seem to stamp out the fire in one place, it would appear in several others. The might of the Union army and navy in the occupied territories of the upper South would never succeed in stamping out the fires nor would they ever feel completely safe in their own jurisdictions. Many a partisan would be shot where he was encountered, his body put on display as an example or left for his family to find and bury. Many a blue-clad soldier would be buried at small encampments, major fortifications, or sent home to grieving families in the North. Many an innocent farmer or merchant, his wife or his children, would fall victim to the violence of both sides. One Tennessee lady in her latter years remembered the occupation as she had experienced it on White Oak Creek in Stewart County. Her succinct summary was: "The Yankees were bad, but them old guerrillas were worse!"[17]

Interdicting the River Fleet

One way in which guerrillas and small bands of Confederate raiders were effective against the occupation forces was in small-scale attacks on the Union navy. Boat traffic was heavy on both rivers, carrying supplies and troops south and east to the Union field armies. The boats were vulnerable to attack by brief hit-and-run maneuvers and deliberate ambush by substantial forces, and they were never safe from sniping attacks. Such attacks were so effective that by October 1862 Rear Adm. David Dixon Porter issued orders from his headquarters at Cairo for boats never to tie up to the banks, to keep deck guns loaded and trained on the banks, and to keep small arms loaded and ready to repel boarders. They were directed to shell and destroy any houses near the source of sniping or other attack from the banks "with spirit," regardless of casualties among innocent civilians ("it is their own fault").[18]

By January 1863, Union secretary of the navy Gideon Wells wrote to the senior naval officer at Cairo, "It is imperative that more gunboats should be sent in the Cumberland and Tennessee Rivers to protect the transports." But what Secretary Wells didn't know was that the gunboats were in many ways as vulnerable to attack from the banks as were the transports. The gunboats were designed to attack other boats. Although their crews were exposed to rifle and cannon fire from the banks, their guns could not be elevated enough to fire uphill to the bluffs, or depressed enough to fire on lower, near banks. Thus, they were largely useless against small arms and artillery firing from low riverbanks or high bluffs.[19]

General Sherman's policies concerning guerrillas were particularly harsh. In December 1863, he wrote to Gen. John A. Logan about retaliation: "For every bullet shot at a steamboat, I would shoot a thousand 30-pounder Parrots [rifled cannon shells] into even helpless towns." Sherman's reactions did tend to run to irrational extremes, but he seems never to have been reprimanded for them, and he maintained their rightness until he died. Although the fact was still locked in the unknown future, Jack Hinson would become a one-man nightmare for officers, crews, and embarked troops on those boats of the Union navy. Single-handedly, he would make such hazards much greater on both rivers.[20]

The Confederate government would be accused of organizing, supporting, and directing the guerrilla warfare, but such charges were almost entirely without basis. The Davis government had more than it could handle in trying just to direct and support its regular army and navy units. In the nearly one and one-half centuries that have elapsed since that war ended, and with the thousands of historians who have studied its every facet, there has never surfaced any record of a Confederate governmental bureau in charge of organizing and supporting guerrilla bands. Perhaps there should have been one. These bands of irregulars impacted the Union forces committed against them far out of proportion to their numbers and assets. The increasingly harsh policies on the part of Union commanders in dealing with these irregulars are an eloquent testimony to their effectiveness against Union freedom of operation, success, and morale.

Most guerrilla bands were small, consisting of five to ten men organized around a natural leader. A few were of company size or larger. The leader was often called "Captain" although he may have had no actual rank. Only a few of the leaders, who were deemed legitimate and reliable, actually carried commissions from the Davis government. For the most part, they operated on their own, subsisting on what the countryside could provide. The smallest groups usually operated near their homes, returning there periodically for rest and resupply. The larger ones operated over greater areas, depending on local farmers wherever they were for food and horses. Sometimes they took what they needed, raiding smokehouses, root cellars, and stables, whether the farmers were supportive or not. Some degenerated into outlaw bands, victimizing Union and Confederate sympathizers alike; others were merely criminals from the start, taking advantage of the opportunities to pillage that the war provided but calling themselves guerrilla soldiers. The worst of these criminal opportunists terrorized the rural areas until run down and killed, either by Union soldiers, Confederate soldiers, or by groups of local citizens. Stewart County would have its share of all these types, from patriotic Confederate irregulars to brutal, self-serving criminals.[21]

At times, even Union army units, home guards, and the more legitimate guerrilla units, otherwise orthodox in their behavior, took the opportunity to pillage and expand their attacks to include those whom they disliked or with whom they had previous grievances unrelated to the war. Such personalized expansion of attacks was difficult to control but was definitely not a new phenomenon. Flavius Josephus, preeminent historian of the first century, complained of this practice when he was governor of Galilee. Some Jewish rebels, with his approval, burned a palace of Herod the Tetrarch, then expanded the attack for their own purposes. In his autobiography, Josephus wrote, "These incendiaries also plundered much furniture; then they slew all the Greeks who dwelt in Tiberias, and as many others as were their enemies before the war began."[22]

The Vexing Nature of Guerrilla Warfare

At all levels in Union occupation forces, from Texas and New Mexico to Kentucky, Tennessee, and Virginia, aggravation with the growing problem of guerillas operating in their midst quickly became acute. It was extremely frustrating for the occupation forces to have their telegraph wires cut, their railroad tracks torn up, and their bridges burned on an ongoing basis. To make matters much worse, the repair parties sent out to repair the damage were routinely ambushed along the way. Union soldiers were dying daily, and seldom were their friends able to confront the guerillas in open combat to get even the dark satisfaction of revenge for their dead comrades. When the Union patrols attacked in strength, the Confederate irregulars seemed to melt into the forest and vanish. The military principle is eternal; since the misty days of prehistory, such guerrilla attacks have been extremely disruptive for invading armies.

The Confederate guerillas would attack a Union unit in direct combat only when they had equal or greater strength than the unit and a high probability of success. It is axiomatic that such irregular units should never engage a regular military force in direct, deliberate combat, unless they have a clear advantage in numbers, firepower, or position. The guerrilla's primary modus operandi was always, and is today, to harass, ambush, hit and run, and interdict and destroy facilities in the enemy's rear areas. Effective guerilla action not only hurts an occupying regular force in terms of destroyed facilities and casualties, but it also becomes, in a word, maddening.

This has been true at least since Caesar's campaigns in Gaul and Britain, and thus it was from 1861 to 1865 throughout the occupied South. It very definitely was the case Between the Rivers in Kentucky and Tennessee.

One complicating factor, which exacerbated the guerrilla problem for the occupying Union commanders, was the difficulty of knowing just who, and what, was a guerrilla. Some irregular units were little different from regular Confederate army units. They were well organized, wore uniforms (if they had them to wear), were disciplined, and functioned under responsible leaders. Some of these units proudly called themselves "partisan rangers," stayed together, and cooperated closely with higher Confederate command. Below these "nearly regular" units, there was every degree of organization and orthodoxy, from guerrilla bands, which functioned under leaders over a large area in an organized way but dispersed and disappeared when confronted with a superior Union force, down to very small groups consisting of only a few men, who operated only near their homes.

Jack Hinson would become a guerrilla who operated alone, but such lone guerrillas were extremely rare. In fact, in the Twin Rivers area, if not the entire South, he was probably unique.

Because regular Confederate soldiers were themselves often in unorthodox uniforms, it was difficult at times for Union commanders to know whether they were fighting them or guerrillas. One Union commander, operating out of Fort Heiman, after a number of skirmishes with small groups of Confederates, reported killing one and wounding five, "either guerrillas or soldiers"; he didn't know which they were.[23]

The lowest class of irregulars consisted of the small groups of criminal opportunists who robbed, raped, and murdered for their own selfish purposes, often calling themselves guerrillas, both Union and Confederate. The fact that in the South these thugs sometimes attacked Union troops in order to rob them of weapons, horses, and personal possessions added to the blurring of distinctions between the self-serving criminals and legitimate Confederate guerrillas.

As a result of the difficulty of clearly knowing who were legitimate Confederate irregulars and who were simply opportunistic outlaws, Union commanders ceased trying to differentiate and lumped them all into one hated category—"bushwhackers," criminals not entitled to traditional protocols for the treatment of prisoners of war.

Dealing with Guerrillas

With the increasing frustration on the part of Union commanders, there came in response increasingly harsh policies for dealing with the guerilla problem. Since 1861, local commanders had been asking their superiors for guidance in dealing with guerrillas. By

1863, attitudes had hardened and policies had become simple and harsh. The overall policy could be summarized in three words: "Take no prisoners!"[24]

Such became the policy Between the Rivers, and by the time of the arrival in October 1863 of Maj. Gen. William Starke Rosecrans to assume command of area occupation forces, the policy had crystallized. Rosecrans, who had commanded the Army of the Cumberland, had committed a major blunder at Chickamauga for which he was relieved. He was removed from command on the fighting front and transferred to St. Louis to command the Department of the Missouri, which included the Twin Rivers area. Banished to occupation duty in the backwaters of the war, he would remain there until the war's end.

Rosecrans, however, was not new to the problem or the area. In January 1863, while still in fighting command, he had sent troops to Clarksville with orders to take ten days' rations and sweep the entire area between the Tennessee River, the Cumberland River, Murfreesboro, and the Duck River. This was a completely unrealistic assignment. They could not have effectively "swept" one county in ten days. If they had, the guerrillas would simply have disappeared and reemerged after the soldiers were gone. At that time, General Rosecrans still had much to learn.[25]

Guerrilla Policies in the Department of the Missouri

Illustrative of the vexing problem of guerrillas in Rosecrans's new occupation duty command, and the attitudes toward dealing with it, was the situation in Missouri. Although Missouri was west of Stewart County across the Mississippi River, that area was within the Department of the Missouri, which also included Stewart County and the surrounding region. Although the Twin Rivers area was at the eastern end of Rosecrans's command and Missouri in its western end, the following dispatches have been chosen because they do reflect occupation policies throughout the Department of the Missouri and because they are the most complete such records known to have survived.

Brig. Gen. Clinton B. Fisk commanded the District of North Missouri, with headquarters at Saint Joseph. To a subordinate commander, Lt. Col. Daniel M. Draper in Macon, Missouri, he wired on April 18, 1864, the following message: "Try the bushwhacker by drumhead court-martial tonight, and *let every soldier in Macon shoot him if guilty, as he doubtless is.*" At this point, General Fisk closed his telegram with his wish that the man had not been brought in at all: "*Don't allow (in the future) such prisoners to be brought in*" [emphasis added].

The same day, General Fisk telegraphed another subordinate, Col. J. T. K. Hayward in Brookfield, Missouri, who seems to have needed reassurance that he had not misunderstood the policy: "Tell the party who have [sic] the bushwhacker at Hunnewell that *I want no such prisoners.* Your orders are correct. *Let that be the rule henceforth*" [emphasis added].

The following day, April 19, Lieutenant Colonel Draper at Macon City, Missouri, seems also to have needed reassurance about the "take-no-prisoners" policy. This time, General Fisk forwarded to Lieutenant Colonel Draper a copy of a dispatch he had just received from Major General Rosecrans, his own superior. General Rosecrans, from his headquarters in St. Louis, had wired General Fisk:

> Jackman, the bushwhacker, is at the house of the ex-sheriff of Howard County, 20 miles northwest of Glasgow, with 15 or 20 desperado companions. You must with all dispatch and secrecy and with ample force *fall upon them; let none escape.* Sharp and secret must be your motto [emphasis added].

On the April 30, General Fisk reported to General Rosecrans, "All quiet in the northwest. The militia are mustering in great numbers. I hope to do the country good service with them by producing large crops of corn, wheat, hemp, and tobacco, *and shooting every bushwhacker we can find*" [emphasis added].[26]

Two days later, he reassured one "A. Allen, Esq." in Crab Orchard, Missouri, apparently a concerned lawyer and local official, that the policy was legal and indeed that of General Rosecrans. With considerably more deference than he used in addressing his subordinate commanders, Fisk's assistant adjutant general wrote that killing guerrillas was Department of the Missouri policy, quoting Rosecrans who had written, "I . . . acknowledge the receipt of your favor of the 30th instant (ultimo), and to authorize you to *kill any bushwhacker you can find engaged in his hellish work"* [emphasis added].

On June 3, 1864, General Fisk wired a subordinate in Plattsburg, Missouri, Capt. Benjamin F. Poe:

> Captain: You will order one of your lieutenants with a squad, say 15 men, to Ridgeley, where they will remain until the loyal men of that section can organize. You had better not weaken your force at Plattsburg, but call in additional men of your company. Keep safe, be cautious, preserve good order and discipline, *and exterminate every bushwhacker you can find* [emphasis added].

Three weeks later, on June 23, General Fisk wired his subordinate, Colonel Hayward in Hannibal, Missouri, to reassure him that the actions of one of his officers, apparently zealous for killing guerrillas, were orthodox and in keeping with the existing policies. He expanded the policy to include family, friends, and anyone else even suspected of helping the guerrillas. He wrote:

> You may be assured that Captain Crandall's policy, so far as I know anything about it, meets with my entire approval. . . . Tell him to go ahead. He must expect the snakes will hiss when they are stirred up. I am quite sure that I have no better officer in the district than Captain Crandall. When complaints are made against him [by the local citizens], they will be placed before the captain, that he may better understand who is flanking him [who his enemies are]. *Tell Captain Crandall to kill every bushwhacker he can put his hands upon, and to make the feeders, aiders and abettors of the villains sorry for what they have done to help.* . . . No gloves on now [emphasis added].[27]

On August 15, Fisk wired General Rosecrans to affirm the policy of treating those who support the guerrillas with the same ferocity as the guerrillas themselves and to complain about the widespread support of the guerrillas by the local populace. He wrote:

> I am now at this end of the district [Macon City] to do all I can by my personal presence to organize a sufficient force *to exterminate the fiends;* but this is a very difficult task, when in all the Missouri River counties from Buchanon to Saint Charles the guerrillas have three times the number of friends we have. *Nothing short of holding the bushwhacker aiders and abettors responsible with*

their own lives and property for these barbarous acts will ever
drive out the murdering villains [emphasis added].[28]

The harsh policies toward guerrillas did not change as the
war neared its end. On January 10, 1865, when Maj. Samuel A.
Garth was assigned to command the subdistrict of Howard, his
instructions for dealing with guerrillas upon assuming command
were clear. General Fisk wrote to him:

> We must, during the winter and spring *kill these disturbers of
> the peace, and in your sub-district I trust the work will begin
> at once and continue until the last imp expires. . . . Hesitate not
> to burn down every house where it can be demonstrated that
> the occupants harbor and conceal the murdering fiends . . . and
> destroy everything on the premises.* Deal summarily with the
> parties who harbor and conceal. *They are equally guilty with the
> bushwhacker and must share his fate* [emphasis added].[29]

As violence begat still greater violence, this policy that had
evolved in the Department of the Missouri was approved by
General Rosecrans when he assumed command in the fall of
1863, and the policy prevailed until the end of the war.

Guerrilla Warfare and Atrocities

Inseparable from the guerrilla phenomenon and the policies for
dealing with it was the ugly reality of atrocity in the backwaters
of the war. War seems to bring out the best and noblest in man
but also the worst and most depraved. Things that were never
known on the major battlefields of the war became commonplace
in the occupied areas. Some incidents were the result of long-held
animosities that had found their opportunity for expression in
the war; some were acts of rage, taking vengeance for an earlier
outrage; and some were simply sadistic brutality rising from the
ugly depths of unredeemed human nature.

Such acts of cruelty began with the rise of guerrilla warfare
almost as soon as the field armies finished their major battles and
moved on, and as time passed, they became more common and
more brutal.

The self-serving criminals who used a thin cloak of false
patriotism to cover their crimes committed most such atrocities.

However, sad to relate, some were committed by legitimate Union army units. Sometimes Union soldiers committed such acts while on official business. At other times, they made raiding a "second job," moonlighting in uniform after hours. From time to time, Federal soldiers from Clarksville, disguised as Confederates to conceal their identity, came into the Stewart County area to rob and discredit the Confederate cause. Often the Union soldiers were local militia (Home Guards), or from detached regular Union units, operating independently Between the Rivers with less than adequate discipline and supervision.

Such was the case in what befell Phillip Redd, of Redd Hollow, Between the Rivers in Trigg County, Kentucky. He was a law-abiding businessman, who had signed a loyalty oath at Fort Henry on September 29, 1862. Redd was one of the wealthiest men Between the Rivers, operating a complex of prosperous businesses on the Tennessee River side of the Dividing Ridge, including a tannery, sawmill, gristmill, and blacksmith shop. He was reputed to keep a large amount of cash hidden somewhere on his property. One evening Union soldiers arrived, called him out, and demanded that he tell them the location of his money. He refused; they threatened to hang him, and he still refused. Strung up with a rope around his neck, drawn ever higher over an apple tree limb in his orchard, they continued to warn him as the rope was drawn higher. After being given one last chance and telling the soldiers to "hang and be damned," they gave up on him, dragged him up in the air, tied off the rope, and rode away, leaving him swinging. As soon as the soldiers disappeared up the road, a dark form dashed out from hiding, cut him down, and saved his life. It was Bill Miller, one of Redd's slaves. Redd freed his slave and gave him a home on the place. Bill Miller lived there as a hero the rest of his life.[30]

Although Phillip Redd was badly abused, he at least escaped with his life. The same can't be said for young Joe Bogard, who, with his widowed mother, also lived Between the Rivers in Trigg County near Golden Pond. Union soldiers took him from his home, ignoring the pleas of his mother. The day before his twentieth birthday, he was taken to Egner's Ferry Landing across the Tennessee River in Marshall County, Kentucky, hanged, and castrated (the order of those two events is not known). He was left there until word reached his mother, who took a team, a wagon, and a faithful slave to recover his body. It was later said in Golden Pond that when Mrs. Bogard reached the scene and saw her son hanging there, she gripped a small willow tree for support and wept so hard that the tree shook. She brought her son home for burial, and his grave can still be seen in the Bogard Cemetery. Carved into the top of his handmade headstone is a weeping willow, symbolic of his mother's weeping and the supporting willow tree that shook. Why was such a cruel, barbaric thing done? Only God knows, but it may have been because he had two older brothers, William and Taylor Bogard, who were Confederate guerrillas.[31]

As terrible as this was, it was often even uglier than that. A common technique was to hang a man over a fire or tie him to a plank and "put his feet to the fire," moving his feet progressively into the flames until he would tell where his valuables were. In 1863, James Gray, an elderly, prominent Stewart County farmer, was visited by Jayhawkers, the name applied in the South to pro-Union guerrillas. The Reverend Mr. Gray was a man of distinguished English ancestry, had commanded a company at the Battle of New Orleans, had served in the State Assembly, and was a framer of the Tennessee Constitution. He was also a Baptist minister. The Jayhawkers demanded his money, but he protested that he had none. They hanged him by the neck, slowly, three times. Still he repeatedly disputed their claims. They then tied him to a board, built a fire, and roasted his feet "until the flesh dropped off," but there was no money. The Jayhawkers left him in agony and rode away. Although badly crippled, Gray survived the incident.[32]

On a quiet summer evening in 1864, Edward Barnes was sitting peacefully on his front porch in what is now known as Mitchell Hollow, east of Waverly, Tennessee. His youngest child, seven-year-old Almary Barnes, was sitting on his lap. The place was, and still is, a beautiful, green, creek bottom place, an idyllic setting. Despite the presence of a detachment of Union Colored Infantry guarding a bridge nearby, guerrillas rode arrogantly into his yard and shot him to death, blowing away part of his face, with his daughter, blood-spattered and terrified, still clinging to him. Little Almary lived to be one hundred, and she never forgot the horror

Mrs. Bogard discovering her son's body. (Drawing by Joe McCormick)

of that moment. The gold and silver that Mr. Barnes had buried in the back yard was never found.[33]

At least one general took a dim view of this. Gen. Nathan Bedford Forrest not only complained officially to both Union and Confederate authorities about Union atrocities, but was himself an exemplar of just and impartial treatment of murderers and thieves, whether Confederate or Union. A case in point is one Howell Edmonds, a notorious murderer who was supposedly a Confederate partisan operating in and out of Stewart County. In one day and night in September of 1864, he beat a small boy

named Brandon and took his team of mules, killed two men
named Brandon, murdered two wounded Union soldiers, crossed
the Tennessee River into Calloway County, Kentucky, and killed
another man named Brandon. Edmonds, who was obviously a
self-serving guerrilla of the thug class and had a grudge against
the Brandon family, was captured the following day by Forrest's
men. By Forrest's order, he was duly tried after several weeks,
convicted, and executed. Forrest's administration of justice was
not a drumhead execution. It was legal, deliberate, and impartial
for Edmonds claimed to be a Confederate partisan.[34]

Atrocities Committed by the Union Army as a Matter of Policy

Not all atrocities were the work of guerrillas and unattached
criminals. At times, the Union army was also guilty of such things
as a matter of official acts and the carrying out of policy. The
Union officer most remembered for carnage against civilians is
undoubtedly Gen. William Tecumseh Sherman, notorious for his
path of rapine devastation across Georgia and the Carolinas in
1865. Along with his policy of deliberate destruction of homes,
livestock, and crops as he advanced, there was toleration of murder
and widespread rape. Some of the victims were white women,
but most were helpless black women in the countryside. One of
his own soldiers, while loyal to the Union cause, thought that
Sherman's policy was criminal. Harvey Reid wrote to his uncle,
"When general officers allow their men to pillage helpless women
and children of [everything they have] and then burn their houses
over their heads . . . our country has a great crime to answer for."
Although best remembered for his "march to the sea," Sherman,
for most of the war, commanded in the Western Theater, where
his counterguerrilla policies, which urged devastation of innocent
villages by artillery fire in retaliation for a single sniper's bullet
fired at Union boats, were particularly brutal.[35]

Sherman's subordinate and protégé, Bvt. Maj. Gen. Stephen G.
Burbridge, practiced a brutal form of retaliation, which he called
"atonement," while he commanded the Department of Kentucky.
Under his policy, when a Union soldier (or a citizen assumed to
be a Union sympathizer) was killed, four Confederate prisoners
of war were to be taken from prison to the site of the killing and
"publicly shot to death." It mattered not that the prisoners had no

involvement in the incident for which they were executed, or that they were supposedly under Burbridge's protection as prisoners of war. Sherman praised Burbridge and defended his policy of atonement, just as he defended his own brutal wartime policies.[36]

In middle and west Tennessee, however, the regular Union army unit by far the most notorious for violence was the Sixth Tennessee Cavalry Regiment (Union), commanded by Col. Fielding Hurst. Colonel Hurst, a man remarkable for his autocratic audacity and cruelty, was a "homegrown Yankee," as others in the area called him. He was a wealthy and locally powerful man before the war, a virtual ruler in his hometown of Purdy in McNairy County, Tennessee. In fact, due to its population of Hurst families and domination by Fielding Hurst, locals referred to that part of McNairy County as "the Hurst Nation." In the midst of an intensely Confederate area, the Hursts were Unionist, and from that area, Hurst raised a regiment, declared himself its colonel, and was taken into the Union army. Operating primarily between Memphis and the Tennessee River, Hurst devoted much of his energies to stopping Forrest, an enterprise in which he was consistently unsuccessful.

In September of 1863, Hurst's regiment participated in the looting of Jackson, Tennessee. Although he blamed the misbehavior on other units, the Union army's investigation placed the blame on him and his regiment and levied a fine of $5,139.25, the amount of damages the government had paid the owner of a looted millenary store. The money was to be withheld from his regiment's payrolls until all was repaid to the government. The following February, on his own, Hurst seized Jackson and demanded payment of the amount his regiment had been fined, threatening to burn the downtown area if the money was not paid. The town's leading citizens raised the money and delivered it as promised, but Hurst, still angry with his innocent victims, had the downtown burned anyway and cut the well ropes so the citizens couldn't fight the fire. He was definitely one of a kind. Capt. Albert Cook of Hurst's regiment said Hurst had "a heart as tender as a woman if you approach him right—if you don't, he is the damndest, meanest man that God ever made."[37]

Two examples of mayhem committed by Hurst's men, outrageous but true, will suffice. On one occasion, in July 1863, Hurst's regiment captured six Confederate soldiers. He had them march along Purdy-Pocahontas Road, and at each mile, one was shot and buried upright, head above the ground. They were left as mile markers.

One of the most horrendous of all Hurst's savagery, however, was the murder of Lt. Willis Dodds of Newsom's Regiment, Forrest's command. Captured on leave at his father's home, Lieutenant Dodds was tortured to death. An eyewitness reported to his commander that Dodds had been "most horribly mutilated, the face having been skinned, the nose cut off, and the body otherwise barbarously lacerated and most wantonly injured, and his death was brought about by the most inhumane process of torture."[38]

Hurst ordered or approved such atrocities, claiming they were merely quid pro quo. Because of their behavior, Hurst and his cavalry were often at odds with Generals Grant and Grenville Dodge and other superiors, and were rebuked; however, with the exception of the fine resulting from the looting of Jackson, they were never punished for their terrible crimes. After unsuccessful attempts to get Union authorities to reprimand and restrain him, General Forrest himself publicly declared Hurst and his regiment to be outlaws, who were to be treated as criminals, not soldiers, if captured.

Hurst's Sixth Tennessee Cavalry Regiment came to be despised by all but the most ardent Unionists in the area, and the locals referred to them as "Hurst's Worst." One old man came upon Confederate cavalrymen who were burying some of Hurst's men, whom they had killed in a skirmish. He strenuously objected to giving the dead Union soldiers a decent burial. He exclaimed in disbelief, "But them thar belongs to Hurst's Worst," and he demanded they be buried in the middle of the road, where they would be trod upon and driven over by wagons.[39]

Indiscriminate Killing

Increasingly harsh policies on the part of the occupation forces and lack of direct oversight of detached Union units ranging over the area led at times to what can only be described as indiscriminate killing by Union forces. This was especially common in the areas of southern Stewart County and northern Humphreys County, involving small Union detachments. It was an area far from the supervision of superiors at Dover, active with guerrillas, and supportive of those guerrillas. One Sunday in the summer of 1863, a group of Union soldiers entered a church northeast of Erin and took James Rushing and Hub Edmunson from a Sunday School class. The two young men were marched about a half mile up the road and ordered to kneel and say their prayers. While they were still praying, they were shot. The soldiers then walked "up the road a piece," accused Frank Warden of being a guerrilla, and shot him dead.[40]

Such was the background to events in Stewart County that spring of 1862. During this period, Jack and Elisabeth Hinson attempted to go on with their lives as they had done before the battle. This was a time of turmoil and adjustment, and everyone, military and civilian, Union and Confederate, was trying to find his place in the overwhelming developments and radical changes of all-out war. It was a time of establishing values and policies, foreign to most of those involved, and the lessons in reality were coming fast and hard. This was the stage and the setting for the prolonged tragedy that would be played out in the lives of Jack Hinson and his family and in the lives of the soldiers of the occupation forces around them.

The battle had been the prelude. The first act was about to begin.

Chapter 4

Death Comes to Bubbling Springs

"The dream had ended. The nightmare had begun."

In February, at the time of the battle for Fort Donelson, Col. William W. Lowe and his Curtis Horse, United States Volunteers (later redesignated as the Fifth Iowa Cavalry Regiment) had reached Fort Henry as reinforcements. Actually, very few of the men in the Fifth Iowa Cavalry were from Iowa. Most of them were from Nebraska for it was from a Nebraska unit that the Curtis Horse was first organized, one battalion was from Minnesota, and a great many of the men were Germans, with recorded hometowns such as Berlin, Hamburg, and Dresden. Some, especially the battalion from Minnesota, resented the "Iowa" designation.

The regiment had arrived still not fully organized, poorly trained, and only partially equipped. In December, Cpl. Eugene Marshall had had to borrow a pistol and saber in order to have the traditional "warrior" photo taken since he had as yet been issued no weapon. As late as the following July, five months after the battle, many of Lowe's men still had no weapons, except for sabers. There were serious disciplinary problems, and the unit was not well thought of by some of Grant's staff. As a result, Colonel Lowe and his regiment had waited in the mud at Fort Henry as a better-than-nothing reserve and, with the exception of one officer, missed the battle.[1]

The one man who did participate in the battle did so by accident. He was Capt. Charles C. Nott, a New Yorker, who had been left behind in St. Louis to participate in a court-martial. When he caught a ride on a southbound steamboat, it was a transport carrying part of the Second Iowa Infantry. He went ashore at Fort Donelson and fought with them in some of the most bitter parts of the battle, rejoining his own regiment after the surrender. His experiences were later published in a series of letters titled "Sketches of the War."[2]

Strange Bedfellows: Adjusting to Occupation

The men of Colonel Lowe's regiment were undisciplined, and even as they waited at Fort Henry during the battle, they had helped themselves to corn, sweet potatoes, chickens, and sheep belonging to the local farmers. After the surrender of Fort Donelson, this behavior continued, uncontrolled. Corporal Marshall described the muddy conditions at Fort Henry as "terrible to endure" and wrote that twelve mules could not pull one empty wagon through the deep mud. The Fifth Iowa Cavalry, confirming its bad reputation, was in a miserable situation.

Colonel Lowe complained to his superiors that the wet, muddy conditions there ("a swampy piece of ground") were debilitating for both men and horses, and he asked to be relocated to higher ground. Part of the regiment was then moved to the bluffs across the river to occupy the Confederates' abandoned works at Fort Heiman in Calloway County, Kentucky. In developing Fort Heiman, Lowe soon established a new satellite installation south of Heiman, a fortified encampment three miles upstream in Henry County, Tennessee, which his officers named Camp Lowe. With his headquarters for the time still at Fort Henry, he spent much of his time at Fort Heiman, and he had plenty of problems to keep him busy, on both sides of the river. Except for depredations around Fort Henry, his presence had not yet been felt in Stewart County, but that was soon to change.[3]

After the capture of Nashville, Grant was removed from combat command, replaced with C. F. Smith, and under investigation, threatened with arrest. He was sent back to Stewart County and given a new command, the District of West Tennessee, with his headquarters at muddy Fort Henry (a facility no one else wanted). It was probably during this troubling but relatively undemanding period that he was a guest of the Hinsons in their Bubbling Springs home.

By the time Grant returned to Stewart County, he was aware of what Halleck and McClellan were trying to do to him, and he knew that he was a victim of malicious rumor and prejudiced animosity. "There is such a disposition to find fault with me," he wrote to Halleck. He knew what was being done to him, and he was demanding a fair hearing. He had not forgotten what had happened to him eight years earlier as a captain in California when loneliness, depression, and drunkenness had combined to bring about his disgraced dismissal from the army. Nor had he forgotten that McClellan, a captain at the time and a highly favored rising star, had been a scornful, disapproving witness to his downfall back then. The cards were definitely stacked against Grant, but he held the ace of spades. He had no need to worry about McClellan and Halleck. He now had almost limitless favor with the president of the United States. His status with Lincoln would do nothing but improve with the passing of time.[4]

For a short while, Lowe's regiment operated under Grant's direct command, located together in misery at Fort Henry. Grant was at least pleased with their reporting. Soon, however, Grant assumed a new command, the Department of the Tennessee, and moved his headquarters to Jackson, Tennessee, leaving Colonel Lowe to have Fort Henry to himself.[5]

Colonel Lowe remained at Forts Henry and Heiman, and settled in to occupy the area, suppress guerrillas, and pacify the occupied territories around the forts. With the onset of summer, the rivers receded and the mud dried. However, problems of inadequate supplies continued, made more complicated by the fact that parts of Lowe's regiment were supplied by the governors of three different states: Minnesota, Nebraska, and Iowa. Morale was hindered by the reality that the junior officers were political appointees with no military training, and most were not respected. Relative inactivity also aggravated morale problems. Soldier bad behavior included drunkenness, refusal to obey orders, and depredating the surrounding countryside. In April, Corporal Marshall wrote in his diary that he had no respect for most of the officers: "The only thing in which they are proficient is in drinking whiskey." Nevertheless, problems with Lowe's officers were not confined to drinking. Corporal Marshall recorded on May 5, 1862: "Found Lieut. Neely about to ride out with a lady, known as the Provost Marshall's wife. He appears more attentive to whiskey and women than to his business. I am sick of such proceedings." In addition to all his other problems, Colonel Lowe's assignment was a largely thankless one. It was one at which he would never succeed, nor would any of his successors.[6]

With George and John Arrested, Suspicion Grew

Watching, listening, and pondering, Jack went on with the

business at hand. His family remained unmolested but was increasingly viewed with suspicion. William Hinson was a Confederate soldier in Virginia, so the family was automatically suspect. To make their status even more questionable, two of Jack's other sons, his young namesake, John, and his older son George, had been arrested on charges of being Confederate spies on the day of the surrender and held briefly in prison before being "paroled" and released.

"Parole" was not a word in the Stewart County lexicon in early 1862, but it would soon be added and used with increasing frequency. In that war, it meant the release of a prisoner upon his verbal or written promise to do the opposing forces no harm after release. It was merely a formalizing of the giving of one's word. Also, in that war, "parole" was sometimes used as a synonym for "password."

John's release was reported in the *St. Louis Democrat* as being due to lack of evidence of being a combatant, and he was returned to Dover on the steamer *John J. Roe*. It is likely, however, that his father's friendly acquaintance with Grant was a factor in his favor. George was likewise released on March 19 after being held for slightly over a month. The article in the *St. Louis Democrat* speaks only of John being taken to Bloody Island Prison and later returned to Dover. However, since the brothers were captured together and paroled together and, at the time, there were no facilities for imprisoning captives at Fort Donelson, it is only reasonable to assume that both George and John were interned at Bloody Island and subsequently returned to Dover.[7]

George and John, although innocent, would be remembered by the occupation force. Further undermining the image of the Hinsons as loyal citizens, Jack's eldest son, Robert Hinson, who was married and had a family of his own, was becoming involved with a guerrilla group in the Stewart County/Humphreys County border area. Jack was trying to hold on to peace and a tenuous status of neutrality while protecting his family and businesses. Despite his best efforts, that status was slipping away. Increasingly, Bubbling Springs was becoming an embattled island of peace and normality surrounded by a rising, dark and stormy sea of conflict and suspicion.

When Colonel Lowe arrived in Stewart County that February, it is likely doubtful that neither Jack Hinson nor Colonel Lowe was aware of the other's existence. The time would soon come when they would not only be aware of one another, but would inhabit one another's dreams. Their paths would intersect, culminating in tragic results that neither could have foreseen. Not even in their nightmares.

As the occupation force became established in its new situation, no one really knew what to expect. The troops had to establish new quarters and settle into a new routine in new surroundings. The people of the Twin Rivers watched and wondered as the strange soldiers from far away moved in and took charge of their lives. They had never before lived under the control of armed strangers, and the Union troops had never before occupied someone else's home territory. Like a man in remote country meeting for the first time his mail-order bride, each had a vague idea of what this new situation would be like, but neither could really know. There were going to be some major adjustments for them to make, and, almost immediately, those adjustments proved to be painful.

Soon, the local people began being victimized by Union occupiers and civilian criminals, especially in the rural areas. At the same time, the soldiers of the Fifth Iowa Cavalry began to learn how difficult, frustrating, and dangerous their new duty would be. The occupation quickly became a time of increasing terror and suffering for the defenseless people in the countryside. Colonel Lowe and his troops suffered casualities and increasing aggravation. The locals and Colonel Lowe's regiment were somewhat like the man who had never before ridden a horse trying to ride a horse that had never been ridden. They were "learning together," but it was a painful process.

Occupation policies in the Department of the Missouri were harsh, and Colonel Lowe's local policies would be in perfect harmony with those of his commanders. The situation was becoming grim in Stewart County and the other counties Between the Rivers, and it would only get worse.

Troubles for Colonel Lowe on the West Bank

Although his area of responsibility included both sides of the

Tennessee River, Colonel Lowe's attention was at first focused primarily on the west side of the river. On the west bank in early May, he sent a force of 125 cavalrymen under his friend, Maj. Shaeffer de Boernstein, to intercept Confederate supplies reportedly moving south from Paducah. Instead of the reported supply train, the Confederate column was Col. Thomas Claiborne and his Sixth Confederate Cavalry Regiment. Learning of the presence of the Union force, Claiborne sent a detachment under a Captain Ballentine in pursuit. Shaeffer de Boernstein's force was overtaken and immediately attacked. In hand-to-hand combat with sabers, pistols, and rifle butts, the Iowa cavalrymen were scattered, leaving behind seven dead (including Major de Boernstein, mortally wounded by Captain Ballentine), ten wounded, and seventy-one prisoners. The Confederates suffered no casualties. It was the first real combat for the Fifth Iowa Cavalry, and it was a disaster for Colonel Lowe.[8]

The tragic failure was a hard thing for Colonel Lowe to report to his superiors, and he greatly inflated Confederate strength to make his heavy losses look less culpable.[9] Although Colonel Lowe had full responsibility for the area around Forts Heiman and Henry, his regiment, not fully equipped or armed, was still trying to find its form and was beset with disciplinary problems. His men were galloping around the countryside pillaging and looting. In February, in response to his men's ongoing attacks in the surrounding area, he had been forced to issue a "no depredating" order. In November, Colonel Lowe issued a similar order forbidding pillaging. Corporal Marshall observed, "It was much needed, as the men are in the habit of taking whatever they wanted from houses."[10]

On June 26, twenty-two men (two corporals, one artificer, and nineteen privates) were dishonorably discharged and drummed out of the camp. On July 17, Colonel Lowe complained that many of his men were still armed only with sabers. A month later, on August 18, he complained to the Iowa adjutant general that his regiment "was hurried into the field without being properly armed and before organization was complete." Still, he carped, less than half his men had pistols and carbines, and the ones they had "were of poor quality." Desertion was an ongoing problem. His troops called deserting "a French furlough."[11]

"Scarecrow Duty" and a New Fort Donelson

One of Colonel Lowe's responsibilities was protecting and maintaining the telegraph lines. This was a particularly vexing problem because they were so vulnerable and were a favorite target for guerrilla attack. Men of the Fifth Iowa were periodically assigned to detached duty away from base camps to protect the lines, but the soldiers so assigned knew that their job was impossible to accomplish. They were really a token presence that was supposed to make the Confederates afraid to attack the lines. They knew that what they were doing looked good on paper, but in reality, they could not stop the Confederate attacks. Therefore, they named the assignment "scarecrow duty." Scarecrow duty had the disadvantage of inherent futility but also had the advantage of relative comfort and freedom of action. When assigned to distant sections of lines, the soldiers boarded with local families. On the line between Fort Donelson and Smithland, the soldiers assigned to the northern portion of the line lived with a Smithland family. Friendly relationships with the host family and other civilians in Smithland often developed, at least on the surface. Romances sometimes blossomed, resulting in at least one marriage.[12]

This duty continued to the end of the war. In December 1864, Sergeant H. A. Revelle of the Thirty-fourth New Jersey Volunteer Infantry, wrote home from Smithland. He spoke of the same wild rumors of expected Confederate attacks as had Corporal Marshall nearly three years earlier and complained that the "damned Rebel citizens" would lie to protect the guerrillas.[13]

In late July of 1862, Colonel Lowe was asked to deal with a Confederate force threatening Eddyville, Kentucky, and the telegraph stations in the area. He sent part of his command toward Eddyville as directed, but they made no contact, and all that was accomplished was additional frustration.[14]

That summer a new and smaller fortification was being built at Fort Donelson, upstream from the old Confederate positions and closer to Dover, approximately where the Fort Donelson National Cemetery is today. By midsummer, the new fortifications were completed and manned by four companies of the Seventy-first Regiment Ohio Volunteer Infantry commanded by Maj. James H. Hart.

A second significant event took place that summer: Jack Hinson freed all of his slaves.

The Freeing of the Hinson Slaves

That summer of 1862 Jack's keen instincts for business and his awareness of changes in the political winds had convinced him that the status of slave owner under the occupation was extremely precarious, and it was increasingly obvious that the war was not going to end soon. He had already seen his neighbors lose their slaves to confiscation by the Union troops, and they seldom knew afterwards anything of the well-being, or suffering, of their slaves. There was no way for Jack to know when the Union might seize his slaves and send them off into places and situations that might be harmful to them and their families. If, however, they were legally freed, they would have a much more secure status and a better chance of being left unmolested. Without them, of course, it would be extremely difficult for him to operate the plantation, so he needed to consider his own family's welfare. After much deliberation, he decided to begin the process of freeing his slaves, legally giving them the status of free blacks.

He gathered the family heads and explained to them what he had decided to do. They were asked to stay where they were and work for him as before; but they would be given their freedom documents and had the option of leaving if they wished to do so. If they stayed, he would take care of them as he had before and pay them a reasonable salary. Then, as the postwar system found its form, they could make adjustments as necessary. Only God really knew what the future would hold. But he was sure that whatever the new way of living would be in this way his servants would be less likely to have their lives disrupted. At first, they felt threatened and fearful at the thought of such a radical change. He let them ask questions and gave time to think about it and discuss it with their families. When he gathered them again for decisions, they thanked him and said they all wanted to stay right there.

Jack Hinson's remarkable move was made only a few months ahead of Lincoln's September executive order in which he declared emancipation of all slaves in the seceded states, beginning January 1, 1863. One might suspect that Jack had advance knowledge of the emancipation proclamation and was making a meaningless, cynical gesture, but that would have been virtually impossible. Lincoln's decision to issue the proclamation was a closely held secret. There were government officials high up in Lincoln's administration as well as most members of the Federal Congress who had no advance knowledge of what Lincoln would announce in September. It would be absurdly irrational to believe that an unknown farmer in an obscure county in the backwoods of occupied Tennessee would be privy to advance information of such a paradigm change in federal policy. No, Jack Hinson was merely following his business and political instincts and acting on his commitment to the welfare of the black members of his family.

The exact number, classifications, and value of Hinson's slaves at that time are unknown. A healthy field hand was worth about one thousand dollars, house servants and children somewhat less (between five hundred and eight hundred dollars), and skilled workers such as blacksmiths, farriers, and stonemasons were worth much more. He had approximately fifty slaves on the farm and owned others, whom he leased to the local iron industry, including one named Anderson Gray, who was called in his obituary "a skilled iron worker." Such skilled men were worth several thousands of dollars each. All things considered, it is reasonable to assume that when he gave his slaves their freedom, Jack Hinson presented them with a gift worth approximately fifty thousand dollars, a very considerable fortune in that day.[15]

Colonel Lowe's Problems with Confederate Units Get Worse

As summer wore on, Colonel Lowe's situation became increasingly threatening. On August 18, the Federal garrison at Clarksville surrendered to a mixed Confederate cavalry force of regulars and partisans under Kentuckians Col. Adam "Stovepipe" Johnson and Col. T. G. Woodward. Learning of this and fearing that Confederate forces would immediately turn west and recapture Fort Donelson and Dover, Major Hart telegraphed Colonel Lowe for immediate reinforcements.

On the nineteenth, Colonel Lowe reported the news to his commanding general, stating his intention to reinforce Major Hart's Donelson garrison. He asked for more troops and accurately observed, "guerrillas are organizing everywhere."[16]

Three days later on August 22, on General Grant's order, he assumed command of Fort Donelson, and the command structure was clarified to some extent. Major Hart now commanded Forts Heiman, Henry, and Donelson and all their troops. He now had complete responsibility from the west bank of the Tennessee River to Dover and the surrounding areas.[17]

On the twenty-fourth, Colonel Lowe informed his commander that a detachment from one of his companies out of Donelson had been scouting Between the Rivers for several days and had encountered a Confederate force, "whether regulars or guerrillas is not known."[18] He added that another Confederate unit—a large one—was also reported to be in that area. The next day, Major Hart's fear became fact when Fort Donelson itself was attacked by a cavalry force under Colonel Woodward, who demanded the surrender of the fort. Major Hart discussed the demand directly with Colonel Woodward, and Hart refused to surrender. Woodward's cavalry attacked the Union defenses, but they had no artillery, and after about thirty minutes of indecisive combat, the Confederates withdrew.

Major Hart, who had ordered several buildings in Dover to be set afire, later expressed the belief that the fire and smoke had greatly contributed to his being able to hold the fort. Corp. Eugene Marshall, who arrived in the dark with reenforcements after the battle ended, described what was left of Dover as "a miserable little hamlet" and reported that "about two-thirds of the town were burnt," including the courthouse. Soldiers tend to believe and repeat rumors and exaggerations about things they haven't seen. If a "courthouse" burned, it could only have been the old, log courthouse. The brick courthouse, surrounded by its wide grass lawn and wide adjacent streets, was in protective isolation from other (burning) buildings. Major Hart would never have set fire to the brick courthouse as its lawn was the location of his big naval siege gun, which was mounted on a permanent swivel track, and the key to the defense of Dover from the south and east. This big gun would be the instrument of the slaughter of Forrest's men the following February, and the key to the Union's successful defense when under serious attack. In keeping with the chivalrous manner of that day, Major Hart stated in his after-action report that Colonel Woodward "bore himself like a gentleman."[19]

Colonel Lowe took reinforcements to Donelson, but arrived after the battle had ended and Woodward's force had vanished. The next morning, he set out to locate the Confederate force. He found them at Cumberland Iron Works and attacked. Again,

Lowe was defeated; he withdrew and retreated to Fort Donelson, leaving behind four dead and eleven captured, six of whom were wounded. Colonel Lowe was taking it on the chin, and things were far from being under control Between the Rivers.[20]

Recapturing Clarksville

By September 5, Colonel Lowe had received requested reinforcements, and he moved out of Donelson with a much larger force consisting of parts of three infantry regiments, part of his Fifth Iowa Cavalry, and artillery. He headed for Clarksville. On the seventh, he again met Colonel Woodward's force, forced their withdrawal, and reoccupied Clarksville for the Union. He burned some Confederate supplies, brought out others, and the following day turned back toward Dover, leaving behind offended and aggrieved Clarksvillians who would never forget his ill treatment of them.[21]

It had been a long and difficult summer, and the fall promised to be no easier. As Colonel Lowe had put it, guerrillas were organizing everywhere, and he wasn't faced just with guerrillas. There were also fast-moving regular units like those of Woodward, Forrest, Morgan, and Hylan Lyon that seemed to be everywhere, yet nowhere, until they struck. Lowe even had spies in the field. In one mysterious message to his commanding general on September 2, he wrote, "Am almost ready. Can I be furnished with a small amount of secret-service money? I have some valuable spies who ought to be paid." With surprising audacity, he demanded, "Answer at once."[22]

Autumn brought Colonel Lowe no relief from Confederate pressure in the Twin Rivers area. On October 5, he reported that one of his scouting parties operating out of Fort Henry was subjected to a hit-and-run attack that killed one soldier before the attackers disappeared into dense fog. Patrol size had been necessarily increased for their own safety, often in company strength, sometimes in multicompany strength. Patrols on the west bank were going as far south as Camden. Between the rivers, they patrolled as far north as Cadiz and Eddyville in Kentucky and as far south as Waverly in Tennessee. By this time, Lowe was reporting to Grant, who was his commanding general. Constant command reorganization, redesignation, and the resulting conflicts and confusion added to the difficulty of Colonel Lowe's situation.[23]

In mid-October, a representative group of the leading citizens of Clarksville met and drew up a formal statement of grievance to be delivered to Pres. Jefferson Davis. Their complaint was concerning the "savage and brutal" mistreatment of innocent citizens by Union troops, including the arrest and imprisonment of ministers during church services and confiscation of the horses and buggies of the parishioners. Many homes, the complaint went on, were invaded, women insulted, their clothing seized, and the men put into "a loathsome dungeon." The complaint mentioned, "Two or three regiments of these thieves and robbers . . . stationed at Forts Henry, on the Tennessee, and Donelson, on the Cumberland, who are daily visiting and destroying everything that comes in their way." Singled out were Col. William W. Lowe and Col. A. C. Harding.[24]

On October 25, Confederate secretary of war G. W. Randolph, in response to the complaints, recommended to President Davis that all possible be done to protect the citizens of Clarksville. He further recommended that Colonels Lowe and Harding be denied the treatment normally accorded to officers if captured and that they be treated as felons instead. On November 1, President Davis responded by promising to do what he could to protect the loyal citizens and directed that Gen. Braxton Bragg be made aware that Colonels Lowe and Harding, if captured, were to be denied the treatment normally accorded to captured officers. Davis stopped short of directing that they be treated as felons.

Winston Churchill observed that our 1861 to 1865 war was "the last war fought between gentlemen." By this time, however, the chivalry and civility of the gentlemen on both sides were wearing increasingly thin.[25]

While the Union Troops "Beat the Air," the Local People Suffered

In late October, a patrol from Fort Heiman marched fifteen miles south to Sulfur Wells, thence to Camden and Wagoner's Landing, and then twenty-seven miles back to Heiman with no enemy contact and with only the destruction of some boats to report after five days. On October 29, John Hunt Morgan was reported to be at Hopkinsville, Kentucky, with a large force. Grant ordered troops from Paducah and Cairo under command of Brig. Gen. T. E. G. Ransom to form at Eddyville for an attack on Morgan. He ordered Colonel Lowe to take available forces from Forts Henry and Donelson to support Ransom in his attack on Morgan, and Lowe's weary force was stretched even farther, but the expedition accomplished nothing. On November 26, General Rosecrans telegraphed Lowe from Nashville: "Twelve hundred rebel cavalry crossed the Cumberland at Harpeth Shoals yesterday." Lowe was directed to cut them off, but he made no contact. Once more, they were exhausting themselves, but they were only beating the air.[26]

As is always the case in such situations, it was the local people who suffered most; the war and its aftermath had turned a beautiful, prosperous countryside into wasteland and reduced its people to destitution. Corp. Eugene Marshall of Colonel Lowe's regiment described the area around Dover as desolate and its citizens as hungry and ragged. "The war has made a desert of this part of Tennessee," he wrote. "Never a garden, it is now desolate in the extreme. Miserable, half-starved women and children, old men and cripples, make up the mass of what people are left here."[27]

The Situation Was Reversed in the Eastern Mountains

The situation in east Tennessee and western North Carolina was an interesting reverse of Colonel Lowe's situation. In those areas, the guerrillas were largely Unionist, and the pursuing army units Confederate. The difference was that in the Confederate-controlled areas of the mountains, the conflict was more personal. Often guerrillas and their Confederate pursuers were natives of the area and knew one another. The Confederate army units had little more success in their areas than did Colonel Lowe in his, and the Confederates' countermeasures were just as brutal as those of the Union soldiers were. In fact, at times they were more brutal. The Unionist guerrillas sometimes brutalized the families of the Confederate soldiers who pursued them, and the desire for vengeance exacerbated the violence. To make things still worse, in those areas there were often both Unionist and Confederate guerrilla bands, and the local citizens suffered much at the hands of both.[28]

For Colonel Lowe and his men at Forts Heiman, Henry, and Donelson, it was a stressful, frustrating autumn with very little rest for the weary.

A Mellow Autumn at Bubbling Springs

It was not a stressful autumn at Bubbling Springs. It was, in fact, just the opposite. Autumn had always been a pleasant time at Bubbling Springs, a gentle time of mild, sunny weather as the heat of summer released its grip and the breezes began to blow cool and refreshing. It was a fulfilling time of barn lofts full of sweet-smelling hay, tobacco safely curing in the barn, and corncribs overflowing with "yellow gold." It was a time of hickory smoke in the air, a pleasant reminder of a smokehouse filled with meat for the next year, and watermelons in the field. The apple-scented breeze from the orchard meant that it was time for fresh apple pies, fresh cider, and the unique smell of apple slices drying on shed roofs in the autumn sun. The cellar would soon be filled with baskets of apples, potatoes, and carrots—and with turnips, the last product of the season from the garden. The hard work of summer was finished for another year, and most of the remaining work was done sitting down in the shade of porches, grape arbors, or the large, old maple trees. There was still work to be done, but the work was done in a time of easing off and in a pleasant setting.

In spite of the war with its disruptions, worries, and fears, the fall of 1862 was a mellow time for the Hinsons, a succession of soft, warm days and cooler nights, which made for better sleeping. It was as if the whole Bubbling Springs family, both black and white, was quietly heaving a shared sigh of relief after another hot, hard summer and smiling with satisfaction and security.

They did worry, however, about young William fighting far away in Virginia, and they waited, anxiously and prayerfully, for his infrequent letters. In mid-September, he had been captured in the bloody battle at Antietam Creek near Sharpsburg, Maryland, but they didn't know that.

As the days eased toward winter, the night air took on a decided chill and autumn began to paint the woods with extravagant color. The black gum trees, always the first to change, turned burgundy. Then the sumacs burst into scarlet flame; the sweet gums took on their surprising variety of yellows, reds, and purples; and the Southern sugar maples slowly turned to translucent gold. In the creek bottoms, the red maples earned their name. Even the unspectacular browns of the oaks and the sickly, spotted yellows of the leaves of apples, pears, hickories, and wild pecans didn't spoil it. They were just an understated counterpoint to the awesome beauty of the rest. It was the time of "the turnin'," and it was a cool, refreshing, and beautiful time.

Fall was a special time for a number of things, and chief among them for boys and men was hunting squirrels, turkeys, and deer. Still, midwinter was the best time for hunting rabbits, a time when they believed rabbit fever wasn't a danger. Actually, any of these could be hunted at any time of the year (and at times were), but in autumn and early winter, when harvesting of crops was finished and there was a time of relative leisure, was when hunting was done in earnest. It was this part of their well-ordered lives that brought on the opening tragedy in what would become a succession of tragedies that would eventually decimate the Hinson family. Very soon, all the years of work, achievement, and fulfillment at Bubbling Springs would end—unbelievably, horribly, and permanently.

Death on a Bright Cold Morning

Author's Note: What follows is a description of the atrocity that made an enemy of Jack Hinson. It was the genesis, the sine qua non, of the cascading tragedy that ended, forever, life as the Hinson family had known it, launched Jack's campaign as a one-man special operation against the Union, and broke hearts in more than one hundred homes of men in Union blue. I have carefully inspected the geography and details of the terrain of this pivotal event. Although the exact point of the capture of George and John is not known, the general location is known, and it is near the documented place of their execution and mutilation, which immediately followed. Details have been added to flesh out the framework of documented facts, but the following is the essence of what actually took place.

It happened on a bright, cold morning as autumn was giving way to winter. It promised to be a beautiful day, and the woods were calling. Fresh venison, squirrel, or turkey would be good on the table. Regardless, it would be pleasant just to be out there, in the woods, in *their* woods, on such a day. It was that pleasant time of year when work on the farm was slack. George Hinson and his younger brother, John, were going hunting in the woods northwest of the house between Wynn's Ferry Road and Dover Road.

George was twenty-two and could already have enlisted in the Fourteenth Tennessee, but he had not caught the war fever as his brother William had. John was seventeen; he likewise felt that his place was at home, helping his family on the farm. There was plenty of cured meat in the smokehouse, and they didn't really need the meat for the table, but they had time on their hands, and fresh meat was always a treat for the family. Besides, the weather was just too nice to stay out of the woods.

They rose early, ate a hasty breakfast in the warmth of the old kitchen, and moved out into the chilly darkness. With their long rifles, shot bags, powder horns, and game bags, as they had done many times before, they crossed the yard, crossed Hinson Creek on a riffle, and passed through the frosty grass of the meadow beyond. Then they eased into the forest, climbing northwest up the ridge. They knew those woods as well as men today know their own backyards. These were their woods—they had grown up in them. They were at home there.

Well before daylight, the boys were far into the woods, moving almost silently in spite of the deep leaf mulch on the ground. The deer and squirrels would be up and about with the first predawn twilight, and they would be ready. They would be sitting still and inconspicuous in their favorite stands, places they knew were likely to produce fresh meat for the kitchen table, spots in the woods they knew as well as they knew their places at that table.

As gray morning twilight began to take on pale pastels in the southeast, the birds began to move about, scratching for their breakfast. A chilly breeze began to stir, and crows began their early morning complaining. Behind the boys, back at the house, they could faintly hear the bells on the milk cows as they began to move about, with their calves bawling for attention. Roosters in all directions began to claim credit for the new day. It was a deliciously peaceful moment in what promised to be an unusually pleasant day. They sat silently, enjoying the moment. Around them in the forest no deer stirred and no squirrels scolded until the silence was finally broken—strangely broken. Instead of the quiet, tentative rustling of deer hooves lightly touching the ground, they heard the heavy thudding impact of larger hooves. The sounds of horses and riders disturbed the stillness. It was a patrol of the Fifth Iowa Cavalry making its way through the woods—their woods—and coming their way.

They had seen such patrols a number of times before, and they always perceived them as an uninvited intrusion onto Bubbling Springs land, a violation of their homeplace. They hadn't liked seeing them with their guns, clanking swords, and hostile looks. In the past, the blue-coated soldiers had arrested them and held them as prisoners for a month on the absurd charge that they were Confederate spies observing the Fort Donelson surrender. The soldiers were a decidedly unwelcome, unsettling presence, and the early morning hunt was off to a bad start. Thanks to those foreigners, there would be no game in that spot today.

When the soldiers spotted the boys sitting motionless near the trail, the lieutenant held up his hand and stopped. It was as if he had been out searching for George and John for when he saw them sitting there, waiting with rifles in their hands, his total attention was fixed upon them. He turned his horse toward them as they sat there, barely visible in the faint, gray light. His face turned dark and threatening, a thought was forming in his mind, and something terribly wrong was about to take place. He leveled his carbine at the boys, and the members of the patrol followed suit, turning their horses toward the boys, coming into line, and bringing up their carbines. Without one question being asked, a deadly assumption was made in the mind of the patrol leader: these boys were rebel guerrillas, bushwhackers—just like those others who had been ambushing his men and disappearing into the forest. He had finally caught two of them with weapons in their hands, and he had seen these two before, being paroled at Fort Donelson. These were two of those troublemaking Hinsons he had been told to watch for, and he had the drop on them. They were enemies. They were caught in the act. They were under arrest.

Quickly and easily disarmed, the boys were tied and led northward to Dover Road as the sun rose higher and daylight spilled over the hilltops and into the dark hollows. It was the last sunrise George and John would ever see. Thinking it was all a misunderstanding, the boys complained but did not struggle. They had been arrested before, then released. They were annoyed. Their beautiful day of hunting was now spoiled. However, they expected to be back home in time for the noon meal. Although these meddling Yankees had spoiled their hunt before it began, they consoled themselves with the thought that they could hunt tomorrow.

But there would be no tomorrow. In fact, they wouldn't even see the rest of that morning. They would not return home for dinner or ever again sit at their familiar places around the old kitchen table. In the Department of the Missouri, such rebels, if they unfortunately survived being captured, were expected to be executed without the complication of a trial and preferably on the spot. Under this policy, Colonel Lowe concurred, suspicion of wrongdoing was sufficient justification for execution. No such prisoners were to be brought in.

George and John were apparently innocent victims of overactive suspicion and negative assumptions. Nevertheless, suspicion was sufficient basis for a guilty finding, and after all, they had been arrested nine months earlier. It was decidedly injudicious and tragically unfair, but it was the way things were done.

Thus, the stage was set for a pivotal tragedy of enormous significance.

Roadside Execution

As the sun rose above the hills toward Dover, the boys were tied to a tree on the north side of Dover Road, 350 yards east of Model Road, less than a mile from their home at Bubbling Springs. With the soldiers turning deaf ears to their protests of innocence, an unceremonious, ragged crash of carbines silenced George and John forever. While the anger within the breasts of their executioners was still hot, the spirits of the boys had taken flight, and the warmth was leaving their bodies.[29]

It was all a mistake—a horrible, irreversible mistake. An assumption made in one emotional second and acted upon in unreasoned anger had snuffed out the lives of two of Jack and Elisabeth's sons for no valid reason. But more than just two killings had occurred that morning—much, much more. What the soldiers had done would set in motion a bloody cascade of killing that would take many more lives before it ended and bring heartbreak into homes in the North.

There would be many more deaths, producing more grieving families and friends, a major disruption in Union operations in the Twin Rivers area, and the brutal end of the Hinsons' tranquil Bubbling Springs existence. Jack Hinson, formerly the determined friend of the Union, opponent of secession, the friendly acquaintance and helper of Grant, would become a brother offended, one who had been wounded in the house of his friends. He would never again be a friend to the Union. Instead, he would become an implacable enemy, a fire-breathing avenger, an ongoing nightmare for Colonel Lowe, his successors, and all other Union forces in the area. He would exact a particularly heavy toll on the officers and crews of Federal shipping on the Twin Rivers, contributing to a problem so severe as to significantly affect the Union Navy Department's policies in far-off Washington City. He would become a deadly Confederate sniper, a terrifying phantom of the forest, killing and disappearing for the rest of the war. He would also become a friend and scout for Nathan Bedford Forrest with spectacular results.

Shooting the boys didn't satisfy the cumulative anger in the patrol leader. He had seen too much killing of his men, and he wasn't yet finished. With his heavy, razor-edged saber, he severed the heads of the Hinson sons and took the bodies to Dover for public display.

One persistent version of the story that has come down through the family and others in the area is that the soldiers dragged the bodies of the boys to Dover and circled the courthouse square with them before leaving them there and heading for Bubbling Springs with their heads to arrest their father. There seems no way to verify this, but the variety of consistent, unrelated sources lends to this scenario a significant degree of probability.

Whatever the details, the Federals had sown the wind, and for the rest of the war, they would reap the whirlwind.[30]

The Beginning of Sorrows

That crisp late-autumn day that began so peacefully had become a nightmare before the sun was an hour into the southeastern sky. By the time the sun was at its midday zenith, George and John, so recently alive and filled with promise, were lying dead in Dover, their mutilated bodies a grim display. Early afternoon would bring to the Hinsons knowledge of their sons' tragic deaths, an accusation of sedition, and threats to their lives and property. Moreover, before the sun completed its low orbit and set again into the pale pastels of the southwestern sky, lines would be drawn and decisions made that would deepen and perpetuate the nightmare that had only just begun. That day was truly the "beginning of sorrows" for the Hinsons—sorrows that would reach down into a generation not yet born.

Although the citizens of Dover had become somewhat accustomed to violence and death since the bloody battle for Fort Donelson and Colonel Woodward's brief attack in August, the execution and mutilation of the two Hinsons was shocking. The news was electrifying not only because of the savage nature of the killings, but also because the victims were the sons of one of Stewart County's leading citizens, a man of peace. The first to know of the killings were those who saw the procession from the killing tree to Dover as the soldiers returned with the bodies. Then, within minutes of their arrival in Dover, all those around the Courthouse Square were aware of what had happened, and from the Courthouse Square the news raced across the battered little village like sheet lightning, spreading outward in all directions. Soon, there was almost no one in Dover who wasn't aware of what had been done to the Hinson boys.

Dr. Smith Intervenes

One of the first civilians to know of the tragedy was the local physician who rushed to inform and aid the Hinson family. Although his identity is uncertain, all evidence points to Dr. J. W. Smith, the man who twice had ridden selflessly out in the freezing rain to examine the Lick Creek crossing on the morning of the Donelson surrender. The records mention only one other physician in the Dover area, a Dr. Williams, and he was located five miles north. It is unlikely, if not impossible, that news of the killings could have reached him in time to travel to Dover, southwest for another four miles to Bubbling Springs, and arrive there ahead of the soldiers.

Dr. Smith, on the other hand, with his home and medical office in the first block south of the square, was the only physician in Dover. He may even have seen the grisly procession pass his door. He was also a neighbor of the Hinsons. His farm on Lick Creek, where he was born and reared, joined the Hinson land. They had been neighbors for more than twenty years. He is almost certainly the local physician and friend who rushed to the aid of the Hinson family that terrible day.[31]

Realizing that the elder Hinsons were probably unaware of the death of their sons and knowing that soldiers would surely soon be going to Bubbling Springs to threaten or arrest his Lick Creek neighbors, Dr. Smith made haste to have his horse saddled and hurried toward Bubbling Springs.

At Bubbling Springs, the doctor pulled Jack aside and as gently as he could broke the terrible news. Before Jack could accept the reality of what he was hearing, his friend urged him to listen carefully concerning the danger in which he and his family had suddenly been placed.

The policy of the occupying Federals was to assume that all members of the family of those believed to be guerrillas were equally guilty and were to be similarly punished. The policy even extended to the assumption that the neighbors of a suspected guerrilla must be supporting him or, at the very least, they were aware of his activities and had failed to report him. They too were presumed to be guilty. Due to this policy, many innocent family members and neighbors were shot, imprisoned, or deported, and their property confiscated or burned during those terrible years in the backwaters of the war.

Colonel Lowe expected his soldiers to have no mercy on suspected guerrillas, their families, or their neighbors. The Hinsons, guilty of no wrongdoing and having just suffered the tragic loss of two sons, were themselves now in very grave danger—and with very little time to prepare. Like all such families in that day, the Hinsons had several rifles, shotguns, and pistols for various purposes. At Smith's urging, all their weapons were collected. Behind the house, there was a large silver-leaf maple tree with a hollow trunk. There were undoubtedly better hiding places, but with so little time, Jack and Dr. Smith quickly hid the weapons in the old tree. Once in place within the hollow tree, they were further concealed by the piling of pieces of scrap iron and old farm implements over the base of the tree. With that done, Dr. Smith took Jack and Elisabeth into the parlor and broke the news to Elisabeth. She was aware that something was very wrong, watching the concealment of the guns and her husband's stricken face, but she had not even imagined how terrible the situation really was. Dr. Smith did what he could to comfort them while urgently trying to make them understand the danger they were in. The children were called in and told about their brothers. Once Sarah had been told, she sent a house servant to inform the other servants, who also told them to know nothing about family guns and to hide their own.

Dr. Smith, their good neighbor and friend, had evaluated the situation correctly. For even as he had pushed his horse toward Bubbling Springs, the leader of the patrol had returned to his Donelson headquarters and reported what had been done. Within minutes, the patrol leader, a lieutenant, and three enlisted men had been sent back on the road at a steady trot toward Bubbling Springs. They were going to deal swiftly with the rest of the Hinson family.

As the doctor sat in the parlor with Jack, Elisabeth, and the children, the soldiers rode down the Hinsons' lane, clomped and rattled past the slave quarters, and dismounted at the front yard gate. One of the soldiers carried the heads of George and John in a blood-soaked burlap sack.

Leaving Elisabeth in the parlor with Sarah and the stunned and weeping children, Dr. Smith walked with Jack to the front door to meet the soldiers. They arrived at the door and opened it just in time to see the soldier with the bloody burlap sack reach into it, withdraw the heads, and place them on the posts of Jack's front yard gate. Jack was staggered by what his unbelieving eyes beheld; so was Dr. Smith.

As the heads were being placed on the gateposts, the lieutenant walked up the brick path to the porch with his pistol drawn, mounted the steps onto the porch, and demanded to see Mr. Hinson. Dr. Smith introduced himself and Jack. Jack's mind was reeling, his knees ready to buckle, assaulted by the surreal sight of his sons' heads. That predictable conflict between denial and acceptance when learning of the death of a loved one had been struggling within Jack since Dr. Smith's arrival, but the sight of his

The lieutenant approaching the Hinson house after the killing of the boys. (Drawing by Joe McCormick)

boys' lifeless heads washed away everything except the horrible reality.

Within Jack Hinson, there now swirled a rising mixture of grief and fury, which choked him, released every restraint within him, and yet sickened and immobilized him as if he were frozen in place. Elisabeth sat behind them in the parlor with her younger children and Sarah, hearing it all and weeping as she had not wept since the day she had clung to those same gateposts watching her boy William ride away to be a soldier more than a year before.

The lieutenant, who knew who the doctor was, barely gave him a nod and fixed his accusing eyes on Jack. Again, Jack's understanding friend spoke as his mediator and asked the lieutenant what he wanted. Roughly and rudely, the officer stated that the Hinson boys had been caught bushwhacking with rifles in their hands that morning and executed on the spot. Now, he said, he was there to accuse the rest of the family of complicit guilt in the boys' criminal behavior, confiscate their weapons, and arrest them all.

Dr. Smith asked the lieutenant to be reasonable. He pointed out the obvious fact that Jack and Elisabeth were overwhelmed with grief. He further explained that Jack was known throughout the area to be an opponent of secession and a man of peace. He recited Jack's history before and during the battle for Fort Donelson, how he personally had taken information to Grant at risk of his life the morning of the surrender. After the battle, Grant had been a guest in Hinson's home, Dr. Smith pointed out. This man was no secessionist criminal and whatever was done to him would soon be made known to Grant. Jack, detached from the conversation as if in a dream, silently tried to come to grips with the horrible reality as Elisabeth sobbed and the children and Sarah wailed behind him.

Becoming a little less hostile but still in a decidedly rude and adversarial manner, the lieutenant demanded their weapons. Smith said that he didn't think they would find any other than the rifles the boys had taken hunting that day, but invited the soldiers to search the house, which they immediately commenced to do.

They moved and overturned furniture, emptied pie safes and kitchen cabinets, even dumped the cream from Sarah's churn, despite her angry protests. They emptied the standing clothes cabinets and the trunks, pulled blankets, quilts, and feather mattresses off the beds.

Unable to find any weapons in the house, the soldiers made a cursory search of the outbuildings without results. They questioned the adult slaves about the Hinsons, their actions, and their attitudes. Very much afraid of the soldiers and already aware of the boys' deaths, the Hinson servants defended their master, said that he had never mistreated them, had cared for them when they were sick, and had even given them their freedom. Amidst the wailing, which was spreading down into the slave quarters, the servants proclaimed that he was a good man and were proud to bear his name and be a part of the Bubbling Springs family.

Not having found the hotbed of secession and sedition that he expected to find and hearing what he did not want to hear, the lieutenant assembled his men, mounted, and with a last dire warning to the Hinsons that they would be watched turned back northward and led his patrol at a trot past the slave quarters, disappearing down the lane toward Dover Road.[32]

As the sound of the horses faded to silence, darkening blood from lifeless heads continued to run slowly down the gateposts, the gateposts that had for so many years welcomed friend and stranger alike into the warm hospitality of Bubbling Springs. The departing soldiers left behind them a grieving family, a home ransacked, and the genesis of a new and terrible chapter in the war Between the Rivers.

With the soldiers finally gone, there was much to accomplish. Prayers were made for the souls of the boys and the comfort of the family and thanks offered to God that no weapons had been found. Sarah oversaw the reordering of the house by the house servants and the weeping girls, and the leading field hands saw to the straightening of things outside. The weapons were left, for the time being, in the old maple tree. The grim trophies on the gateposts were gently removed, washed, wrapped in linen cloths, and placed in the springhouse to await the recovery of their bodies. The dark, drying blood was washed from the gateposts, and there was again at least the appearance of normality.

Such barbarous actions were not bizarre events. They became increasingly commonplace in the backwaters of the war, with one atrocity begetting still worse ones in retaliation. In this case, the beheading and placing of the heads on the gateposts is affirmed not only by redundant documentation of similarly barbarous practices in that time and place, but by identical accounts handed down in two widely separated families unknown to one another. In addition to the Hinson family account, there is that of Mrs. Frances Love Black of Murfreesboro, Tennessee. Mrs. Black heard the story from her great uncle, Maj. Charles W. Anderson, adjutant general to Forrest, whom she knew as "Uncle Charley." Anderson knew Jack Hinson well, served with him on at least three of Forrest's raids, and heard the story from him. The Love-Black-McFarland family is a prominent, respected old family in Murfreesboro, one in which family traditions are taken as seriously and preserved as carefully as is family honor. The validity of this account is highly credible if not unassailable.[33]

The Law of Vengeance

Within Jack Hinson's bosom, a smoky, dark fury was quickly overriding his grief. This fury rising within him was oddly strengthening him and turning the softness of his pale gray eyes into the hardness of Stewart County flint. His Scottish ancestry was speaking to him from the heather hillsides of the misty past, and thoughts of vengeance must have taken form in his embattled mind.

> They dealt in blood, did they? They killed my innocent boys merely on suspicion of wrongdoing, did they? Had those Yankee thugs never lived in the country? Did they know nothing about bringing home fresh meat from the forest for the table? Maybe they just enjoy shedding innocent blood; after all, these boy soldiers from the North had missed the real blood letting of the big battles. And had they no civility? No feelings? How cruelly they have treated my Elisabeth, the children, and the servants. They're not civilized, not even human; they are blue-coated brute beasts. Well, they will learn the error of their ways; they will remember this day; they will have cause to remember and regret what they have done to my sons and to my family. *Their* blood will flow, and *their* mothers will weep. It will be blood for blood, an eye for an eye, and a tooth for a tooth.

These thoughts might have arisen within him quite naturally, a manifestation of his cultural heredity, reaching back through unbroken, unremembered generations to his remote, ancestral roots. Faithfully did his ancestry speak to him of blood for blood, eye for eye, and tooth for tooth. Those ancient laws of the Scottish Highlands would become bloody reality, there, Between the Rivers. Colonel Lowe, his soldiers, and their successors would be subjected to a hard lesson over the next two years in the law of sowing and reaping.

A plan was already taking form in Jack's mind, and for it, he would need a special kind of rifle—accurate at long range and of such a large caliber that it would inflict a fatal wound almost anywhere above the thighs. He knew just where to get such a weapon—not an inaccurate, smoothbore musket, but what he called a "rifle gun."

These dark and pivotal thoughts took place in Jack's mind in mere seconds. Just now, however, he realized that he needed to get control of his emotions and comfort his wife. He held her and let her cry, as the small children formed a clinging, grieving mass around them. Within his own emotional limitations, he tried to console her. Such affection and comforting did not come easily for iron-souled Hinson men, but his beloved wife was shattered, and she needed his strong arms.

Soon relatives and neighbors would be coming, bringing food, and condolences. Dr. Smith would see to the recovering of the boys' bodies at Dover, and a Hinson team and wagon would return them to Bubbling Springs. The relatives would help with the painful work of preparing the bodies for burial, lifting such burdens from Jack, Elisabeth, and the children. As people did in that time and place, and still do, necessities would be provided for, including the compassionate sharing of the weight of the pain.

In Jack's mind, thoughts of avenging his sons had begun to form at some unremembered point in the visit of the soldiers— somewhere in that foggy blur of unreality, shock, and grief. Now, with the shock passing and the grief subsiding to an aching throb, definite thoughts began to take form in his mind. In time, his burning grief would be replaced by an unwavering resolve and an icy pragmatism. His heart would cool and harden progressively each time he sent a blue-clad invader into eternity. Before the war ended, his heart would be as hard and cold as the long barrel of his rifle on a winter's night, his emotions as steady and fixed as his stony, gray eyes. Yes, it would change him—such acts of violence always do—and some of the change would be irreversible.

When the sun had risen on that chilly, clear morning, a horrible day began, the most painful day ever in the lives of the Hinson family. As the sun set on that blood-stained day, it was also setting on the life that the Hinson family, black and white, had known for so long at Bubbling Springs. That life of love, hope, work, play, birthing, growing, learning, peace, and security was over. All that was gone, and it would never be regained.

The dream had ended. The nightmare had begun.

Friends and Family Gather

The day was one of those crystalline, early-winter days with the pale blue sky cloudless. The slight breeze that did stir from the north was warmed some by the sun, its soft rays slanting onto the scene from the south. The sunlight danced like an explosion of diamonds on the bubbling, crystal-clear water of the springs and the tumbling, cold headwaters of Hinson Creek.

The boys were buried behind the house, beyond the kitchen garden near the springs. The graves had been easy to dig in that deep, creek bottom soil, and the day was just warm enough that the servants doing the digging had beads of sweat glowing on their faces, coalescing now and then with their tears. They loved those two young men and had known them all their too-short lives. They had taught them to drive a team and plow a straight furrow; they were family. Truly, they were young men, but to Jack, they were still his "boys." At any rate, they were much too young to die.

When all was ready, the entire family gathered for the commitment. Due to the mutilation of their bodies, they were not laid out in the parlor for viewing as would normally have been done. The homemade caskets were already nailed shut when family and friends had begun to gather. Hinson and James relatives had come, neighbors had come, along with sympathetic citizens from the area. Dr. Smith's presence ministered a special comfort.

Scriptures were read, prayers were prayed, and the slaves sang their songs of sadness and hope, songs from their aching hearts, handed down from generations long forgotten. With a final prayer committing the spirits of the boys into the hands of God, the graves were filled and covered with the mounded-up, raw, red dirt blanketed with Christmas fern, holly, pine, and cedar branches from the woods. Having the graves swathed with greenery, fresh and alive, softened the visual blow and whispered a comforting promise of life beyond the grave.

As was the custom in rural areas of the South, friends and

relatives brought an abundance of food. Sarah and the other house servants arranged it all on tables under the big shade trees, along with the food they had themselves prepared. Groups gathered, eating and socializing, weeping mixed with laughing as stories, new and old, were told and news exchanged. The children in their own naturally sorted age groups played from the parlor to the yard, the barns, and the surrounding woods. Some of the younger white Hinson children wandered off with their black Hinson friends and played in familiar settings.

At the end of the day, saddle horses were brought around from stables and paddock; friends and relatives climbed into wagons and buggies; goodbyes were said; final weeping, laughing, and hugging concluded; and most of the visitors headed for home. Some stayed longer to help with the work, continue to comfort, or do what they could to ease the burden of the loss. When the last of them finally disappeared down the lane, the ache settled quietly over Bubbling Springs, and reality was to be faced and lived with. The absence of the two Hinson sons seemed to shout at the rest of the family from empty chairs, empty beds, and coats hanging on familiar pegs. Yes, the pain of losing them would go on for now, for only God can heal that kind of pain. Life would go on; it, too, had to be faced and dealt with.

Life did go on, naturally following the cycles and rhythms of old, if in decidedly muted tones.

A Gentle, Peaceful Interlude

With crops in and the tobacco curing in the barn, it was a slack time in the work at Bubbling Springs. It would be weeks before it was time to strip and sort the tobacco and pack it for market. Life was relatively easy. The servants, with a luxury of time, were making final preparations for the cold of hard winter, visiting and enjoying their pipes and porches in the warmth of a softened midday sun. Their children, with the white Hinson children, played the easy days away, fished the local ponds, and caught crawdads and small fish out of Hinson Creek. However, the children were not allowed to roam out of earshot of the house now; the deaths of George and John had changed all that. No one at Bubbling Springs would ever again think as he had before, about safety in everyday things. No longer could the children roam freely in the woods. Those pleasant and innocent days were gone, not to return until long in the future. Fear and caution would dominate each day and qualify decisions that once neither required thought nor brought anxiety.

In this slack period, Jack had considerable time to think, and think, he did. He had vowed to take vengeance on the Yankee soldiers and the commander whose policy had directed the killing, Colonel Lowe. But what would that actually mean? What would he do? How would he do it? He couldn't enlist in the Confederate army—he was too old, and, anyway, that would take him far away from Stewart County. No, it would have to happen there, in the county and the surrounding area. It was a local matter. Moreover, it was a private matter. He would have to do it alone. As he thought of Colonel Lowe's responsibility for the death of his sons, his anger grew and spread, slowly and darkly, to include all officers, especially that lieutenant who had presided over the brutal killing of his sons, the rude and cruel treatment of his family, and the ransacking of his home. Ordinary soldiers had to follow orders, but their officers issued those orders.

Preparation for Vengeance

Jack was completely at home in the forest, where those invaders from the North were strangers. He would meet them in his home terrain, where he was familiar with every hog path and deer trail and where they knew nothing. He could wait in the forest, unseen, and pick them off if it came to that. He had to think ahead of them and continue to think ahead of them. He would need a plan for only a fool would act without a plan, and he would also need a special weapon to carry out his plan.

His old flintlock and caplock Kentucky rifles, of which he had several, were accurate. They were excellent for squirrels, turkeys, deer, and other such game, but with their relatively small caliber balls, a killing shot on a man at long range would almost require a center hit in the head. To be reasonably sure of a long-range kill would require a heavier projectile—something in the neighborhood of .50 caliber. The rifle to fire such large projectile would need a long barrel for accuracy, one heavy enough to sustain the chamber pressure of one hundred grains or more of black powder and hold steady when fired.

As he thought about it, the weapon in his mind became increasingly clear. He would need a .50-caliber for long-range accuracy, with a long, very heavy barrel. The rifle should have a caplock mechanism, not a flintlock, for ease and efficiency in loading and reliability in wet weather. The rifle he would need would have a full stock and octagonal barrel. There was only one place to get such a rifle. He would have it made—custom made. Some of the best blacksmiths and gunsmiths were in the, area and the very best iron in all of America was made right there in Stewart County from Stewart County ore, limestone, and charcoal. He enjoyed the thought that his instrument of justice would be a local product—a custom-made instrument of death, springing entirely from his mind and made from local resources. Yes, out of the Stewart County soil those foreigners had soaked with his sons' blood would arise the instrument of their punishment.

It takes time to make a rifle that way, especially one of the quality Jack demanded, and he would not rush the process. While the rifle was being made, he used the time to think, to plan, and to purchase necessary supplies. He couldn't be seen buying large amounts of caps and powder. He would have to spread the acquisition over several purchases and from different sources. And he would need a quantity of .50-caliber lead bullets of the conical Minié ball shape with pointed nose for greater accuracy than the ordinary, spherical musket balls. Such Minié balls (so called for their developer, French Captain Claude Etienne Minié) were as common as horseshoe nails in the Union army, but Hinson would have to find a source for himself without attracting attention. Yes, he needed time, and that was alright for it wasn't his nature to hurry things.

Watching and Learning

On his big saddle mare, he ranged about the county, watching, learning, remembering. He arranged to be in Dover, where he often had business to conduct, learning the patterns of Union presence in the village. He visited friends near the Union headquarters at the new Fort Donelson for the same reason, but only he knew that.

The pattern of the soldiers' activities would determine the future pattern of his own activities, and he observed them a great deal more than he allowed them to observe him. When he had occasion to meet them on a trail or road or in the village as they left and returned, he greeted them with a taciturn nod of the head, his cool gray eyes revealing neither hostility nor affirmation. Most of those blue-clad soldiers ignored the small old man, unaware of his identity. Of those who did take notice of him, the more perceptive ones experienced a sensation hard to identify. There was something about his cool inscrutability that made them wary and a little bit uncomfortable. What, the perceptive ones wondered, almost viscerally, was he thinking? What was his purpose? He allowed them to wonder; he suggested no answers.

Jack observed the Union patrols, their sizes, their armaments, and their schedules. Ranging over the county, he observed repeatedly used patrol routes, creating well-trodden paths. He observed the behavior of the men, noting relative relaxation and carelessness when returning to the fort. He carefully analyzed different patrol leaders, their individual practices, and qualities of leadership. He seemed never to hurry or meander. He was a man with a mission known only to him, and a man completely sure of what he was doing and where he was going.

Jack spent a lot of time scouting out firing positions. Pine Bluff, overlooking the Tennessee downstream from Fort Henry, provided observation of the river for miles in both directions; however, it was periodically occupied as a base camp by Federal units from Forts Henry and Donelson. Also, the Confederates, in establishing a strong point there, had cleared the timber for some distance around it, making concealment poor. Pine Bluff had possibilities but was not promising.

Across the Dividing Ridge, on the Cumberland River side, he found vantage points to cover trails and boats on the river. The bluffs on that side tended not to be so high above the river, but there were numerous thickets along the banks that would provide concealment; it was good duck blind country. That area, both upstream and downstream from Dover, had definite possibilities.

South of Dover, the county was more thinly settled, there was much less of a Yankee presence, and the forest was generally denser, especially on the Tennessee River side. There, below

Leatherwood Creek, far from the Union base camps and away from most of the iron furnaces with their cleared "coaling field" areas, there were excellent vantage points, fewer Yankee patrols, and heavily wooded, hilly terrain into which he could more easily disappear. And, there, he was among family and friends.

From there on the Tennessee River, he could also cross the river and operate in Henry and Benton Counties in Tennessee and in Calloway and Marshall Counties in Kentucky. On the west bank, there were high bluffs overlooking the river as well as vast stretches of low, marshy bottoms ideal for duck blind concealment and water-level shooting. There, on the west bank, he could vex the soldiers who operated out of Fort Heiman in Kentucky and Camp Lowe to the south and punish the Yankee boats effectively.

But his favorite vantage point and primary base of operations would be in southwest Stewart County, a high and rugged bluff overlooking the Tennessee River at the mouth of Hurricane Creek. From there, on a rock ledge high above Towhead Island, he would exact a terrible toll on men and morale aboard Grant's gunboats and transports. In that region of rugged, forested hills, shady creek bottoms, and the long miles of the Tennessee River bottoms, Jack could move easily and almost invisibly from place to place, appear, strike, and disappear. There were some Union sympathizers in that area but not many; to the rest, he would be a hero, one to be protected and supplied. When he wished, he could strike the invaders almost anywhere in the area, from Golden Pond to Waverly, but in his "Sherwood Forest," he could do it with the greatest advantage.[34]

Jack realized that he might soon become a hunted fugitive. He also realized that a fugitive status might involve more killing. His speculation was only a pale suggestion of what would eventually take place. Although Jack could not have imagined such a thing, by the end of the war the Union would have committed against him the assets of at least two cavalry regiments, seven infantry regiments, and a specially equipped amphibious task force of sailors and Marines, both infantry and mounted. With his custom-made rifle, Hinson would kill more than one hundred members of Grant's army and navy.

At that moment, however, as he planned and watched, he really had only one kill in mind—that lieutenant.

His Rifle Takes Form

Between scouting trips, Jack took care of business and oversaw the making of his rifle. The maple wood for the full stock had to be a single piece, flawless, well cured, clear of knots, and tight grained. Jack bought the lock assembly with its hammer, triggers, and springs already made. The best ones were manufactured far from Dover and would have to be imported. On occasion, an area gunsmith would make his own, but Jack wanted the very best. A local blacksmith would make the heavy barrel, or the gunsmith would make it himself, slowly and patiently, protecting its temper and strength. Afterwards, the gunsmith would bore it to a rifled .50 caliber, put the sights on it, brown finish it with vinegar, and assemble the completed rifle: lock, stock, and barrel. The barrel had to be seated perfectly in the full maple stock, carefully carved and chiseled to an exact fit. Otherwise, some accuracy would be lost. After the finished rifle was assembled, the gunsmith would test fire it until he was satisfied that it was perfect. There could be no gas leak around the breach plug or the nipple, the hammer must be tight and the trigger function soft and smooth, and, most importantly, the firearm needed to be accurate, consistently accurate at ranges beyond a half mile. This rifle had a job to do, and it had to be right.

Finally, Jack had a plan, and soon he would have the means to carry out that plan. Things were coming together nicely.

And he was not in a hurry.

Chapter 5

A Time to Kill

"And in that soft and pungent stirring of new life, death waited."

As the winter of 1862 and 1863 settled in with cold, gray days, raw winds blew the remaining leaves from the deciduous trees, except for the beeches, Southern sugar maples, and some of the oaks. The leaves that did not fall clung as dreary remnants, defying wind, rain, and snow until spring. Jack's plan, as persistent as those tenacious, brown leaves, was taking final form and was ever more clear in his mind. His supplies were being laid in, and his special rifle was nearing completion. He continued to take occasional scouting trips through the county, and he did so without arousing suspicion because he was well known as a large landowner and speculator who frequently bought and sold farm and timberland, as well as building lots in Dover. It was a perfect cover for his visits to places that would fit into his plan. Winter provided additional cover for these scouting trips because it was duck- and goose-hunting time. He could build duck blinds along the rivers, concealed firing points camouflaged with brush and driftwood, and he could build them without arousing any suspicion. To make such activity appear even more legitimate, he actually used the blinds to shoot ducks and geese and brought them home for the family table. No one among the Union occupying force seems to have guessed at the duck blinds' more sinister purpose.

Although things were going smoothly, further preparations for vengeance would have to wait for a while; there was work to be done at home.

Stripping the Tobacco Crop

In December and January, the fully cured tobacco hanging in the tobacco barn was taken down and stripped. This meant repeating the dangerous process of housing the tobacco, only in reverse. Again, the field hands climbed up into the tier rails, the heavy poles on which the sticks of tobacco had been hung in late summer, only this time each stick was handed down, from tier to tier, until the man on the barn's dirt floor took it. The process was just as dangerous as had been the housing of the crop but slower for the tobacco was now cured, dried, and somewhat brittle. Handing the heavy hickory and oak sticks that December, each with a full load of stalks of tobacco, was easier in that the tobacco didn't weigh as much as when it was housed green. However, moving it was more tedious because it was breakable. Although the leaves were somewhat moistened by the rainy winter weather, they could still be crushed and ruined in the handling.

Once down from the tier rails, the leaves were stripped from the stalks under Jack's supervision, sorted, and tied into bundles called "hands." A good crop could be ruined in the stripping. If it wasn't sorted and tied carefully, the results could range from a reduced value at the market to a nearly worthless crop. The labor of stripping the crop was just as cold as that of housing it had been hot. The tobacco was stripped in the stripping shed attached to the barn. The shed was "chinked and daubed" to close the spaces between the logs so the field hands were out of the wind. Storytelling, singing, and laughter made the work lighter, and wood fires in a pot-bellied stove took the edge off the cold.

Once the leaves were tied into hands, they were "bulked down" and packed carefully into low, wide, split hickory baskets for carrying to the market in Dover. Some or all of the crop, depending on sale prices, would be loaded on steamboats and taken upriver to the market in Clarksville or downriver to Paducah. All of this was cold, midwinter work.

Meanwhile, at Fort Donelson, the new year of 1863 was off to a bad start.

The Earp Brothers of Fort Donelson

Fort Donelson was manned by Col. A. C. Harding and his Eighty-third Illinois Volunteer Infantry under the overall command of

Colonel Lowe, who was by then responsible for everything from Fort Heiman, Kentucky, to Clarksville. At times, other units, including those of the Fifth Iowa Cavalry, operated in and out of Fort Donelson, but in January 1863, it was primarily the responsibility of Colonel Harding and his Eighty-third Illinois Infantry.

Disciplinary problems continued, especially the misbehavior of the troops off base, galloping their horses, terrorizing the citizens, and pillaging. Courts-martial continued to consume much time and energy. A remarkable manifestation of the morale and discipline problem occurred on January 7 not outside among the citizens, but inside the compound, at the very center of the disciplinary system. Someone set the guardhouse (the fort's jail) on fire, and, amazingly, it burned to the ground as the guards watched; they made no effort to fight the blaze. ("The guard allowed the guard house to burn down.")[1]

Virgil Earp, of the Eighty-third Illinois Infantry, after the war.

Among the soldiers of the Eighty-third Illinois were two whose surname would become prominent in western American history: Virgil and Francis Earp. The brothers enlisted when the regiment was formed and served in no other unit. Eighteen years later Virgil would make history as city marshall of Tombstone, Arizona. In October 1881, along with his younger brothers Wyatt, Morgan, and James, whom he had deputized, and their friend Dr. John Henry "Doc" Holliday, Virgil would walk into the realm of legend in the gunfight at the O.K. Corral.[2]

During his time at Fort Donelson, Virgil was seriously wounded in the torso by a twelve-gauge shotgun at close range—very possibly by Robert Hinson, or one of his "shotgun cavalrymen." Virgil was wounded at close enough range that the buckshot pellets entered the front of his body and passed out through his back, and he carried the scars the rest of his life. During the bloody battle for Fort Donelson and Dover in February 1863, there is evidence to strongly suggest that Virgil played a key role in the Union's successful defense.[3]

The Political Aftermath of Surrender

Meanwhile, in Confederate circles, the unnecessary surrender of Fort Donelson was still an unresolved issue. After the tobacco was packed and ready to ship to the market, Jack had a trip to make. He had been asked to go to Columbia to testify under oath about the surrender of Fort Donelson the previous February.

In the winter of 1862 and 1863, the disastrous surrender of Fort Donelson the previous February was still a hot topic of conversation, from the farmers swapping pocketknives at the courthouse in Dover to the Confederate Congress and Jefferson Davis himself. Extremely sensitive to the issue were the principal parties to the surrender, especially General Pillow. Generals Floyd, Pillow, Buckner, and Tilghman had all submitted reports (in the case of Buckner and Tilghman, after their release from Union prisons) along with those of lower-ranking commanders involved in the battle and surrender. Only Pillow had been tardy in submitting his report, and to magnify his offense, before submitting his report to President Davis, who had made repeated requests for it, he gave his version of the story to a newspaper reporter. While Davis still waited impatiently for the report in Richmond, General Sherman in Paducah had already read it in the *Memphis Appeal* and sent it on to Halleck! Pillow had gone public with the defense of his actions, which infuriated his superiors and failed to convince the public.[4]

Having been relieved of duty and suspended from the army until the following August (1862), Pillow continued to make statements defending himself and accomplishing little more than the further offending of Pres. Jefferson Davis and the secretary of war, Judah P. Benjamin. From that day until the present, he is remembered primarily as the politician-general who snatched defeat out of the jaws of hard-fought victory.[5]

General Floyd was likewise dismissed from the army, but he

remained publicly silent about the entire affair. He went back to southwestern Virginia, his home district, where the governor made him a major general of Virginia state forces. He served adequately, but he was not to live long. Under the weight of it all, he died, a sad and broken man in August 1862, the month that Pillow was reinstated in the Confederate army. The epitaph on his gravestone includes a sad paraphrase from the Book of Job: "Why was I ever born?"[6]

Pillow was reinstated and fought as a brigade commander at Stone's River, where he infuriated General Breckenridge who found him cowering behind a tree. It was his last combat command. Subsequently, he served, always with controversy, in the Confederate Conscript Service. His last command was as a cavalry commander in an embarrassing failure in Georgia, and he finished the war as commissary general of prisoners of war. Both Pillow and Floyd demonstrated at times personal courage and incompetence as fighting generals. They were both successful politicians, but neither had the training nor natural abilities to be a battlefield commander. Pillow was especially given to seeking glory and blaming others for his failures as far back as his conflicts with Winfield Scott during and after the Mexican War.

The Confederate government conducted an investigation into what President Davis had been calling a "disaster" since immediately after the surrender but with unspectacular results. That winter, the issue was still unresolved and being discussed all across the South. Additional depositions continued to be submitted to the Davis government in Richmond by such prominent witnesses as generals Bushrod Johnson and Nathan Bedford Forrest. Testimony was also solicited from Stewart County private citizens who had personal knowledge of the battle and the conditions of the surrender. Chief among these was Jack Hinson.[7]

Because of his first-hand knowledge concerning the Fort Donelson battle and surrender, knowledge, not only of the Confederate forces, but also of Grant and the Union forces, Jack traveled to Columbia to testify. With the tobacco crop packed and shipped, he arrived there as January gave way to February, one year after the battle. On February 2, 1863, he gave sworn testimony. His testimony was in perfect harmony with that of Forrest, Bushrod Johnson, Dr. Smith, and others. He testified that the road to evacuation was wide open on the morning of the surrender, and his testimony was particularly powerful in that he had seen the situation from both the Confederate and Union positions. He could establish that Grant had been still cautious that morning about the reported surrender and that his staff at first refused to believe it, thinking that it was a trick and expecting the Confederates to attack. His testimony was unique; there was not another living soul who was in a position to know what Jack Hinson knew about that pivotal Sunday morning in February 1862.

It is interesting to note that by early February 1863, although he had taken no overt action against the occupation force, Jack was no longer neutral. In his testimony, he referred to the Union forces as "the enemy" and the Confederates as "our forces." There had been a change in his heart. Jack Hinson had at last taken a side, and it was the obvious one. The killing of his sons had made him a convinced Confederate.[8]

The Second (or Third) Battle for Dover

While Jack was in Columbia to testify, cavalry generals Joe Wheeler, Nathan Bedford Forrest, and John Wharton moved from their base at Columbia against Dover and Fort Donelson, with Wheeler in command. In what would become the tragic second battle for Dover and Fort Donelson (or the third such battle if we count Colonel Woodward's attack the previous August), they attacked Dover on February 3, the day following Jack's testimony.

The attack seemed ill fated from the start. They had been sent by Gen. Braxton Bragg to interdict Union supply traffic on the Cumberland on Bragg's western flank, but word reached the Federals, and they simply suspended all shipping on the river. Frustrated, Wheeler decided to attack Dover and recapture Fort Donelson. Forrest objected and predicted a disaster, but Wheeler was senior, and they pressed on.

At Cumberland Iron Works, eight miles south of Dover, the Confederates encountered Company G of Colonel Lowe's Fifth Iowa Cavalry, commanded by Captain Von Minden. The Confederates quickly overwhelmed them, capturing Von Minden and twenty-eight of his men. They released Von Minden and his men on parole but kept their forty-six horses and sixteen mules, and the humiliated remnant of Company G returned to Dover on foot. This was the second time the unfortunate Von Minden was captured. He had been captured in the disastrous expedition of Major de Bernstein and had been released only two months before being recaptured here.[9]

A few of Von Minden's men escaped, however, and carried the alarm to Donelson. Col. A. C. Harding, in command there, telegraphed his immediate superior, Colonel Lowe at Fort Henry, for reinforcements. Most of Lowe's force was on the west side of the Tennessee River at Camp Lowe and Fort Heiman. With the Confederates only a few miles away, Colonel Harding did the best he could with what he had. With no more than an hour to prepare, he organized defensive positions around the village with one artillery battery. In addition, there was a large siege gun, which had been moved from the river batteries, in the courthouse square.[10] Permanently mounted on a pivot track, the gun could be aimed at any angle from the south to the east, the directions from which the Confederates were about to attack.[11]

The Confederates drove into the town with Forrest attacking up Spring Street (Charlotte Road) from the east. When almost to the square, his men were decimated by canister fire from the huge gun; his leading men, almost within reach of the gun, were literally blown to pieces. He attacked again and was again stopped by the devastating fire of the big gun. Forrest was wounded and had two horses shot out from under him. It is almost certain that this siege gun, the key to Colonel Harding's successful defense of Dover, was manned by Virgil Earp. His company muster rolls record his duty for the spring and summer of 1863 as "manning siege guns and batteries" and "manning gun." By far the most important gun at the new Fort Donelson was the siege gun in the courthouse square.[12]

Wharton's Confederates broke through Union defenses from the south and seized the old cemetery where Elisabeth Hinson's parents were buried. They captured one artillery piece and advanced into the edge of the village but stopped there when they ran out of ammunition. The murderous cannon fire, Wharton's running out of ammunition, and the dogged defense by Harding's smaller force ended the attack within the village.

That night, with Union reinforcements from Fort Henry pressing toward Dover against Wheeler's blocking force and gunboats coming upstream to Harding's aid, the Confederates withdrew. They bivouacked that night four miles from Dover and counted their casualties. It had been a costly failure, with Forrest's brigade losing approximately 250 men compared to Wharton who lost only seventeen. Wheeler accepted the blame for the disaster, but Forrest's relationship with Wheeler would never again be the same. After a year, the disastrous loss of Fort Donelson had only been made worse.[13]

Colonel Harding, who was a businessman, a political appointee colonel, and not a professional soldier, conducted his defense brilliantly. He was later brevetted brigadier general for his performance on February 3.

Jack Hinson left Columbia and started back toward Dover as the bloodied Confederates withdrew southward back to their base in Columbia. He met them along the way, learned what had happened, and his mood darkened.

Passing through Dover on his way home, Jack was sickened by the fresh destruction caused by the cannon fire and the hideous carnage of man and beast. Men, horses, and their pieces were still scattered along Charlotte Road and Spring Street, from which Forrest had attacked, and on the south side of town, including the cemetery. There, the graves of Elisabeth's dear parents had become part of a bloody battlefield. He passed through it all as he rode through Dover and onward to Bubbling Springs, and he was heavy with the knowledge that Dover had again been soaked with the blood of brave men, and it had again accomplished nothing. Absolutely nothing.

The Rifle

Jack's rifle held by the author.

Jack returned home to find a message awaiting him. His special rifle was ready. The rifle was a marvel of beauty, a masterwork of the gunsmith's art. It had a full stock from butt to muzzle made of a single piece of carefully selected, air-cured maple with vertical, dark stripes in the grain, wood known to the gunsmiths as "tiger maple." With its peculiar grain pattern, tiger maple was the most desirable wood for a rifle stock. The unusually heavy, octagonal barrel was 41 inches long from muzzle to tang, nearly 1.5 inches in outside diameter, and bored to .50 caliber. The rear sight was set into the top surface of the barrel and had a graded "V" notch, with a wide, upper level for hasty aiming and a deeper, narrower "V" at the bottom for deliberate, accurate, long-range firing. The front sight was also set into the flat, upper surface of the barrel. Set into the top of the front sight, there was a narrow "blade" of shiny German silver, the rear end of which appeared in the sight picture as a shiny, silver dot and provided the "bead" for precision aiming, thus the expression to "draw a bead."

On the left side of the rear of the barrel, the gunsmith, William E. Goodman of Lewis County, had carefully imprinted his initials, "W. E. G"; this was his hallmark, declaring permanently that he was proud of his creation. The manufactured lock plate had the maker's name and "Warranted" engraved on it; it was the best lock assembly available between the rivers. The name of the lock maker, now partially worn away, appears to be John Archer.

Aside from its heavy bore and weight, it was a classic Kentucky rifle, except for one remarkable feature: it was so plain. In the stock, there were no imbedded silver or brass decorations and no fancy, inset patch box. Its butt plate, trigger guard, ramrod guide, and muzzle band were all of plain iron rather than the shiny brass expected on such a fine rifle.

The rifle's plainness was unique but entirely in keeping with the nature of its owner. Jack Hinson was a plain, serious, unpretentious, businesslike man, and his special-purpose, custom-made rifle was a plain, serious, unpretentious, businesslike weapon. With no decorations or frills, it was a deadly precision instrument of violent death just as its owner would come to be. It could not be spotted at a distance by sunlight reflected from a shiny surface for it had none.

Jack's new rifle weighed eighteen pounds, too heavy for accurate offhand firing. It would need to be rested on a tree limb or other support for long-range accuracy. The unusually heavy barrel was intentional. It would provide the stability required for long-range accuracy with the necessarily heavy load of powder. Competition rifles and sniper rifles today are often made the same way.

The gunsmith also made a bullet mold to match the rifle's bore. The mold made the conical Minié ball projectile with a banded, concave base that would expand into the grooves upon being fired, causing it to spiral up the barrel and on to its target like a tightly thrown football. The rifled barrel with its spiraling lands and grooves,

The rifle's heavy barrel.

and the spiraling, pointed Minié ball projectile were state of the art and provided by far the greatest accuracy of any rifle and projectile design of that day. These features enabled an ordinary rifleman to hit a target at five hundred yards, one that could be hit with a smoothbore musket and spherical ball at no more than fifty yards. And, Jack Hinson was no ordinary rifleman; he was an expert.

The unique weapon Jack Hinson would use to avenge the deaths of his sons was ready.

Clinging to a Crumbling Neutral Image

Back home from Columbia, the February work began. The seedbeds for the 1863 tobacco crop were prepared on new ground. The soil was worked very fine, and a fire of brush and tops from the clearing was prepared to cover the entire bed. The fire was burned carefully in order for the intense heat to be applied to the entire bed, killing the weed and grass seeds in the soil and enriching it with the ashes. Once the fire burned itself out, the ashes were worked into the soil, tobacco seed was sown, and the bed was covered with "tobacco canvass," a sheer, white, loosely woven cotton fabric similar to cheese cloth. This tobacco cloth, stretched over poles to hold it a few inches above the soil, allowed considerable light to penetrate, creating a hotbed while protecting the young plants from late frosts as they sprouted and grew. Early garden plants, such as radishes and lettuce, were planted in one end of the bed to give Sarah's kitchen garden an early start.

Jack Takes the Oath of Allegiance

With suspicion of him and his family growing steadily stronger in the minds of the officers at Fort Donelson, Jack took a step to allay their suspicions and minimize the problem. On February 21, 1863, he saddled his big mare and rode up to Fort Donelson. At the gate, he asked to see the provost marshal, 1st Lt. James Moore of the Eighty-third Illinois Volunteer Infantry. It was a quiet day at Fort Donelson, and Jack was escorted to the provost marshal's office. There, he introduced himself and said that he would like to take the oath of allegiance. Lieutenant Moore asked him a few routine questions about his place of residence, family, etc. Then he had Jack read the oath he was about to take. The oath was very similar to oaths administered today, including a statement supporting and defending the Constitution of the United States against all enemies, foreign and domestic, and a statement acknowledging the oath was taken freely and voluntarily, without mental reservation or evasion, etc. What was different was the last section, in which the one taking the oath swears not to "go beyond the military lines of the United States," and the penalty statement, that "death, or other punishment . . . will be the penalty for the violation of this, my solemn oath and parole of honor."

After Jack read the oath carefully and said he had no questions, the oath was administered, and with Lieutenant Moore as a witness, he signed it simply, "John Hinson" (signatures of that day, like those of the eighteenth century, seldom included the middle initial). He was the only one to take the oath that day; there had been none administered in the previous two days or the succeeding two days. Perhaps he hoped to be the only one in a slack period in order to make a more conspicuous statement of his peaceful intentions. We will never know whether he had that in mind; however, what we can know is that it definitely would have made him conspicuous for it was not unusual for as many as fifty men to take the oath in a single day. Thirty-six had taken the oath at Fort Donelson the previous Christmas Eve, a day when most men would have preferred to be at home. Jack was the only one to take the oath in a five-day period. He would be remembered.

Jack knew that in taking vengeance for the killing of his sons he would be violating the oath he had just taken, but he was doing all that he could to head off trouble for his family. His oath taking was not deceitful for he was not yet at war with the Union—only with that lieutenant.[14]

With the tobacco crop sold and the tobacco beds for the new crop prepared and planted, the hands turned to spring plowing. The garden and the cotton patch for home use had to be broken and harrowed, and after that came the same in the growing acreage of corn, wheat, flax, and hemp. For more than one reason, Jack knew that all this work must be done, and that it was his responsibility to oversee it carefully. Life must go on at Bubbling Springs for when he struck, he would have to do so within the context of ongoing, normal, farm and home activities. No matter what happened, he would be a suspect. The continuation of normal work and family life would mitigate the suspicion. His mission of retribution would have to be woven inconspicuously into that matrix of ongoing, normal routine.

There was so much midwinter and early spring work to be done at Bubbling Springs that one season almost phased imperceptibly into the next. This was especially true when tobacco was grown, giving rise to the country proverb that if you grew tobacco, "there was something to be done thirteen months out of the year." That one slack period on the farm, in late fall and early winter, had come at a perfect time for Jack, and he had used it well, planning and preparing.

Preparations for a Different Kind of Harvest

The plowing, harrowing, and planting of corn and other crops didn't require Jack's constant oversight, allowing him relative latitude in his personal schedule. At irregular times, he carefully test-fired his new rifle, taking note of the drop of the bullet at various ranges, variations in trajectory caused by crosswinds of different velocities, and adjustments required for firing down from the bluffs and upward from the bottoms. He had to know exactly where his bullet would strike at all ranges and in all situations. He would normally get only one shot, and that one shot must kill. In time, he came to know his new rifle perfectly—knew exactly what to expect of it and exactly what it required of him. The rifle became almost a part of him.

As spring returned to Stewart County in 1863, Jack assembled his essential kit, watched, and waited. He especially watched the Yankee patrol route just over the ridge to the northwest, where his sons had been seized. That route, and the soldiers who traveled it, were often on his mind, and unknown to them, they were often under his steady gaze.

Those soldiers were, like all men, creatures of habit, and they were accustomed to repetitive, military routine. Unfamiliar with the county, except for the main roads and their customary patrol routes, operating under orders and on a schedule, they were largely predictable. In addition, once settled into their routine, they tended to become comfortable and careless, especially on the return leg of a patrol. On the way in, their minds tended to wander to more pleasant thoughts of the relative comfort of the fort, of free time in the village, mail, and, ever and always, of home. Thus-minded, they were somewhat given to daydreams on patrol, to conversations concerning these and other distracting subjects, and their thoughts and their eyes often wandered far from the deadly matters of war. Jack learned these things about them as he watched and listened, and they were aware of his presence only when he wanted them to be.

As the enemy soldiers plodded along on their repetitious patrol routes, sabers clanking, saddles squeaking, and horses snorting, Jack moved into, and out of, their presence like a sinister shadow, silent and unnoticed. As they rode along and talked, he watched and listened, measuring and evaluating his adversary. At times, he was far above them on bluffs, looking down, able to see the rank insignia of the officers who would be his targets of choice. At other times, he watched from duck blinds on the riverbanks as boats passed, following the channel close in to the bank, close enough to hear the commands of the officers and petty officers and the conversations of the crew and passengers. When the cavalry patrols passed by on their assigned routes, he was sometimes close enough to smell their horses, their sweaty uniforms, and their tobacco smoke—close enough to hear clearly every word they spoke. He was sometimes almost close enough to touch them although they never knew it.

Soon, they would know it.

Robert Hinson's Arrest and Escape

In March 1863, Colonel Lowe abandoned Fort Heiman and Camp Lowe and moved his operations across the river to Forts Henry and Donelson. Fort Heiman and Camp Lowe would stand empty, except when used as temporary bases for Union patrolling units, or when, unknown to the Federals, they would be used by Jack Hinson for the same purpose.[15]

At the end of March, Robert Hinson was arrested by a Union patrol on suspicion of guerrilla activity and taken to Fort Donelson to be held for interrogation, execution, or shipment north to a permanent prison camp. Most such suspects were simply shot when captured. Perhaps he was treated more gently because he was Jack's son and the brother of George and John; there was still strong feeling in the county against the soldiers for what they had recently done to Jack's sons. Robert's family was allowed to

The old Stewart County Courthouse—Robert Hinson jumped from the second-story window and escaped.

visit him with food and necessary items. He was subsequently taken to the courthouse and locked temporarily in a room on the second floor. Seizing the opportunity, he leapt through a window, survived the fall with no broken bones, and escaped. After hiding briefly in town, he disappeared into the Stewart County wilderness and returned to his unit near Waverly. Many years later, Mrs. Ollie Richardson Hinson, widow of Jack Hinson's grandson, pointed out to her son, John S. Hinson, Jr., the window in the old courthouse from which her husband's Uncle Robert had jumped to escape.[16]

Word of this quickly spread over the area, and on April 7, a woman wrote from Waverly to her sister about his escape:

> I suppose you have heard about Bob Hindson [sic] making his escape. Mrs. Hindson has got back from the fort. Amanda White has

been to the fort. She said the boys was so glad that Bob Hindson got away. Harris said, before the Yankees, that Bob Hindson did not run away to get away from the Yankees, [but] he run away because he was in their debt. He owed them their dinner. Harris said that they had plenty to eat, but it came out of their own pockets.

Apparently, the Confederate prisoners there had to pay for their food.[17]

Now, with Robert an escaped prisoner and a hunted fugitive, Jack and his family would be under immediate suspicion and scrutiny. He knew that on any day the Union soldiers could again come riding up his lane to arrest him and his family and burn or confiscate everything he owned. He would have to be careful. Extremely careful.

A Time to Kill

Rising in the darkness of an early springtime morning and dressing without disturbing Elisabeth, Jack went to the kitchen, made a fire in the old wood stove, and brewed a pot of coffee. He had told no one, not even his family, what he was about to do. They would be safer that way, and so would he. The night before, he had carefully checked his rifle, his shot bag, and its contents and laid them out on the old kitchen table, the scene of so many happy times, of so much family living. He thought of that cold, clear, winter morning when George and John had enjoyed an early breakfast at that same table before venturing out into the promise of an early morning that would prove to be the last few hours of their lives.

He enjoyed his hot coffee with a snack of cold biscuits, butter, and sorghum molasses. There was always an abundance of such food in that comfortable, good-smelling kitchen, where some food was left on the table between meals, covered with tablecloths, and the setting of one meal phased into the next. As he sipped his coffee and ate his biscuits and sorghum in the predawn stillness of the big house, he was thinking. One more time, he ran a mental checklist of the preparations he had made. He thought again of his preselected firing point, its field of fire and visibility, and his route from there back to the house. Since he had been watching them, he knew the Union patrol would be coming along the same trail they had been following on that terrible morning. He knew they would have ridden about three miles already and would have settled into the ride they had taken so many times before. On the out-bound leg of their patrol route, they would be relatively alert and watchful; it would be essential that he not move at all once they were near, except to touch the trigger.

When the boys had been spotted on that awful winter morning, the trees and shrubs, except for the hollies, pines, and cedars, had been leafless and bare, providing no concealment. On this morning, however, the forest was in full, new leaf. It would give him perfect concealment unless a soldier should happen to look right at him from the kill zone.

He thought of all these things as he sat in the quiet comfort of his kitchen. Finishing his coffee and biscuits, he moved the coffee pot off the heat and banked the fire in the stove with ashes to save it for Sarah when she came to prepare the family's breakfast. The coffee would not be boiled away and a settled bed of hot coals would need only a few sticks of stove wood to be ready for her cooking. He left his coffee cup, plate, and silverware at his customary place on the table. He planned to be back in a few hours and would have a real breakfast then. His family would know only that he had been "out."

Jack stood silently for a moment, looking at his custom-made rifle, shot bag, and hunting knife without picking them up. This was not a small thing he was about to do. Hinson men were easily moved to fighting anger; it ran in the family. Some would say they "went through life on half-cock," not looking for a fight but always ready for one should the situation arise. Jack was "pure Hinson," but he had never before killed a man or even contemplated such a thing until that cold winter morning when Dr. Smith had come to his door with the terrible news. This would not be an act of passion, the result of a hasty, emotional decision; there would be no "heat of the moment" at play here. No, those emotions that had once raged within him had long since subsided and settled into cool, clear-headed intent. What he was about to do was not only right in his orderly mind, but any other course would have been wrong. It was justice rightly executed. It was the only thing to do. It was in his cultural genes.

With his thoughts clear and focused, and with a quiet, settled certainty that he was now ready, he put on his coat and slouch hat, strapped on his hunting knife, draped his shot bag across his chest, picked up his rifle, stepped quietly out into the chilly darkness, and gently closed the kitchen door behind him.

As he walked through the yard behind the house, rounded the southwest corner of the house, and turned toward the front, he sensed what would come with a mixture of satisfaction and a vague, visceral dread. However, he could not have imagined then the horrors that would actually follow.

His dogs followed him silently, wagging their tails, happily wondering where he would take them, but he "shooshed" them quietly and waved them back. The dogs couldn't go along on this trip into the forest; it was something he had to do alone. He passed soundlessly through the front gate, where the soldier had placed the heads of his sons, closed and latched it. With the dogs watching him, sitting in obedient disappointment in the yard, he turned down the lane and disappeared into the darkness.

Jack walked northward for a few minutes toward Dover Road, then turned off to the left into the meadow, crossed Hinson Creek on a riffle, and continued to the northwest into the forest and up the hill. In the deeper darkness of the forest, he depended on his sense of direction and familiarity with the terrain as the moon was down, and the starlight seldom penetrated the tree canopy. Following a familiar draw, he climbed quickly, easily and almost silently, up to the crest of the ridge.

The ridge, which ran roughly north and south, was an approximate parallel to Hinson Creek and its meadow. At the top, Jack paused to rest and listen. The faintest gray light was beginning to spread in the east, turning the black night sky into pale gray-blue at the horizon. The sun would be appearing in about thirty minutes, and the patrol would be mounting up at Fort Donelson. Ahead of him, down the long slope to his firing point above the trail, the darkness prevailed, and into that darkness, he moved, sure-footed and calm.

Down the western slope, he followed a shallow draw to his preselected firing point. It was slow going down the draw, but Jack was not in a hurry. Getting there was what mattered and not just getting there, but getting there without turning an ankle, without noise, or leaving obvious evidence of his passing. It was still quite dark on the lower slope when he reached his goal, a shallow, brushy depression overlooking the trail. Just on the downhill side of the depression there was a large deadfall—an old oak tree that had fallen years before, its trunk covered with deep, dark green moss. The mossy log provided a perfect rest for his heavy rifle and almost-perfect concealment for the rifleman. The shallow depression was filled with leaf mulch, making it a comfortable, if damp, place for a rifleman in the prone position. The place couldn't have been much better had it been designed for the purpose. Below it, the hill dropped steeply down to the trail below.

From the trail, with the climb, the rocky surface, and the density of the forest, the cavalrymen would be hindered in a rush uphill should they pursue. That same draw he had followed down from the crest to his firing position would lead him away from it after the kill. There was no effective way the patrol could rush him, mounted, because of the terrain and the trees, and it would be difficult for them to see him or the direction he took in withdrawal because of the dense foliage.

Faint morning twilight was diluting the darkness along the trail as Jack sat down on the log to rest and look back uphill, examining the way he had come and the way he would leave. He was tempted to light his old pipe as he waited, but he knew the smell of the tobacco smoke might linger, warning the soldiers of an unseen presence. He laid his heavy rifle across the log and opened his shot bag. Deliberately, carefully, he situated his powder flask, patch, Minié ball, and cap box on the log beside him. He would make only one shot that morning—just one careful shot and a quick, equally careful, withdrawal.

The patrol would be somewhere on Dover Road about then, he

thought, probably about to the Rougement home, where his lane met the road, and they would soon be at the place where they had killed his boys. Even now, that thought pierced his heart with pain.

The growing light made the trail increasingly visible, and the new day began to stir. From several directions, roosters greeted the dawn. Forest birds began quietly to skitter about, and the squirrels fussed and scolded in the treetops. A slight mist began to rise from the water in the small, wet-weather branch that trickled and gurgled along the trail. It wouldn't be long now.

Picking up his rifle, created for just this moment, he carefully measured out one hundred grains of powder, poured it carefully down the muzzle, and replaced the flask in his shot bag. He took a small, thin patch, wrapped it around the base of a Minié ball, punched it into the muzzle with his starter (a short, wooden rod), and then rammed the shot home to the bottom of the barrel. With two or three taps of the hickory ramrod against the Minié ball, to make sure it was snugly seated against the patch and powder, he withdrew the ramrod and carefully returned it to its place below the barrel. Taking a percussion cap from its tin box, he cocked the hammer, placed the cap snugly on the nipple, lowered the hammer gently onto the cap, put the cap box back in his shot bag, and then closed and fastened the bag. His rifle was ready.

Resting the rifle on the log, he sat facing downward toward the trail. The light was brightening now, as the first low rays of the sun reached the treetops high above him. The patrol must be off Dover Road and on the trail now, moving south toward the opening below him. Recently, that same lieutenant had led the patrol that he would meet this morning. It was he whom Jack wanted. If someone else should lead the patrol today, he decided, he would wait for another day.

The air was damp and slightly chilly but alive with the smells of the forest. The trees and leafy shrubs surrounded the spot with a shadowy cloud of green. Wildflowers and mushrooms were breaking through the mulch on the forest floor. Animals were stirring, digging, investigating, releasing the muted, earthy aromas of new life. Birds were announcing their presence and staking out territorial claims.

In that soft and pungent stirring of new life, death waited.

Rendezvous with Death

Increasingly, the woods came to life. Birds began to sing and flitted back and forth through the trees. Somewhere, back up the hill, a mockingbird proudly performed his amazing repertoire at the top of his lungs. Not far off to the right, crows suddenly squawked, fussed, and flapped irritably away from an unwelcome intrusion. The patrol was approaching. Then he heard a faint metallic clank of a saber in its scabbard, then another; up the trail, he heard a horse whinny out a complaint. They were coming, and although they didn't know it, they had a rendezvous with death.

Jack eased himself down into the shallow depression behind the log, settled into the deep leaf mulch, and got comfortable behind his rifle. As he looked over the barrel, he pointed it into the open spot on the trail below. He pulled the brim of his old slouch hat down over his eyes to shield out any glare from the sunlight beginning to slant in over his right shoulder. From down on the trail, all that was visible above the mossy log, to anyone who might look that way, was a muzzle view of the rifle and Jack's steady gray eyes under the soft brim of his hat. He was ready.

He could hear the patrol clearly now—clanking equipment, squeaking leather, the heavy plodding of the horses hooves on the trail. He could hear voices but couldn't yet make out the words. That didn't matter anyway. As long as they were making such comfortable sounds, they were not alert, and they were not expecting trouble. That would make everything much easier for the one who waited and watched.

Around the small opening, he had cut in the foliage ahead of him, the opening through which he would fire; the leaves rustled and shook. It was a beautiful, male brown thrasher pursuing an equally beautiful female in the low shrubs. He flew across in front of Jack's face, and she flew the other direction, back across the opening. They were earning their name, thrashing about in the shrubbery between Jack and the trail. Now the patrol was near enough for him to hear the breathing and snorting of the horses.

He didn't want the disturbance in the shrubs to draw attention his way, and he was relieved when they both flew away.

He aligned the rifle at the spot where the first soldier would soon appear and checked his sight picture. The shiny, silver front sight bead rested snugly at the bottom of the notch in the rear sight. He might have to make a quick, minor adjustment in his aim as the soldier appeared, but for the moment, he was on target. The range was exactly fifty yards. He knew this because he had paced it off several times on past visits.

Jack could hear them plainly now although he still couldn't see them, and he figured that the first man was only seconds from the small clearing. He could hear every word, every creak of the leather. He even heard one of them spit a mouthful of tobacco juice into the branch along the trail, laugh, and say he thought he might have killed a frog.

Jack was breathing slowly, easily holding his aim at a rock he had chosen on the far side of the trail several days before, an aiming point that would automatically make his shot chest high on a mounted man. Slowly, he cocked the hammer, one click to half cock, then the second click to full cock.

As the first horse's head appeared in the clearing, he cocked the set trigger, the front one of two, which prepares the rear trigger for firing. Once the rear trigger is set, it requires only a touch to fire. He took a deep breath, let half of it out, and held the rest. He would have only three seconds to recognize the lead soldier's uniform and face before he passed from sight to the left. The first man's right hand appeared, resting on the pommel and holding the reigns—then the blue sleeve—then the left shoulder. The man had turned his head and shoulders to his left, listening to the man behind him, and on his shoulder, Jack saw the officer's epaulet. Then he saw his face; the lieutenant, *that* lieutenant, turned his head back to speak to the man behind him. He was looking right at Jack! In the fraction of a second that the lieutenant looked directly toward Jack, his expression seemed to change, as if he realized what he was seeing through the opening in the foliage. Jack touched the trigger.

*"The lieutenant—**that** lieutenant—was looking right at Jack."* (Drawing by Joe McCormick)

The heavy rifle cracked, and the big, spinning, projectile reached the trail just ahead of the sound. It struck the lieutenant at the base of his throat, and he disappeared over his horse's right flank, with his boots still in the stirrups, as if snatched away by a huge, invisible hand. The horse reared in terror in a mist of blood as the rest of the soldiers looked on, momentarily frozen in amazement. Then they dismounted frantically, seeking what cover they could find as the loud report of the rifle seemed to roll around in the valley.

As the sergeant's commands brought order to the tumult on the trail, the patrol formed and moved as dismounted skirmishers up the slope in the direction from which they had heard the shot, but there was no one there. Except for the dead lieutenant's body and his bloody, trembling horse, there was no evidence that the attack had taken place. The soldiers had no idea who had been there, or where he had gone. The only trace of Jack Hinson remaining on that once-more tranquil hillside was the lingering smell of gun smoke.

With the lieutenant's body tied to his horse and on its way back to the fort with an escort, the sergeant led the remainder of the patrol away, continuing on its assigned route. Far up the rocky draw, Jack sat, unseen, and listened. When he discerned the dead lieutenant was on his way back to the fort and the remainder of the patrol had continued up the trail, he made his way, carefully and quietly, to the crest. Again, he stopped, sat, and listened; he listened for footsteps, and he listened to the birds. Apart from the sighing of the rising breeze, the forest was silent, and the birds were again happily going about their normal morning business, undisturbed. Sure now that he was not being pursued, he stood and headed back toward the house.

Jack felt relieved—he had succeeded; his preparations and his plan had worked perfectly. In fact, it had gone even more perfectly than he could have hoped. That bloody-handed Yankee lieutenant had turned and looked right at him just as he was touching the trigger! It even appeared, in that fraction of a second before the bullet struck him, that he had seen Jack, recognized him, and realized he was about to die and knew his helplessness to prevent it. That must have been the way his sons had felt as the carbines were raised and that lieutenant gave the command to fire.

Jack walked through the meadow's wet grass, crossed the creek at the riffle, and turned south up the lane toward the house. He was quietly excited; it had gone perfectly; he had left no evidence at the scene; and there had been no real pursuit. Yet there was a bit of heaviness within him, something troubling, whispering and stirring—deep inside. What he had just done had settled an emotion that had burned within him for nearly half a year. He had fulfilled the thing he had thought of and planned for—even dreamed about. It was right. So what was wrong?

He had never before killed a man. Perhaps that was all it was. He knew that there would be terrible trouble for him and his family should he be discovered. Justice had been served. Nonetheless, as he approached his front gate, he wondered, was it settled? Did full justice require the death of yet others? It was others who had killed his boys, after all, on the lieutenant's order. These men had torn the hearts out of Elisabeth and the children with the unthinkable cruelty of confronting them with the boys' heads. His first killing was not sitting easy within him, but the lieutenant was not the only guilty party.

As he passed through the gate to the excited welcome of the dogs, the matter was turning over in his mind. With his shoes wet from the dew-soaked grass in the meadow and his coat and trousers damp from lying in the wet leaf mulch, he walked silently around to the back door, ignoring the happy greetings of the dogs, and stepped into the kitchen. The family had already finished breakfast and gone to the morning's work, but Sarah had kept his plate warm on the stove. He cleaned his rifle, then took it and his kit out to the barn and hid them. Returning to the kitchen, he sat down to eat and think.

As he sat, wrapped in the warmth and pleasant-smelling tranquility of his kitchen, eating his breakfast and reflecting, Jack knew a significant milestone had been reached and what he had done could not be undone. Only God knew exactly what the future would bring, but deep within him there was a whispered thought that this killing would not be the last.

The Last Springtime at Bubbling Springs

The passing of April to May brought that climatic paradox of the upper South called "Blackberry Winter," the last cold spell of the New Year, which normally occurs when the blackberries are in full bloom. The days seem to be self-contradictions, with the new grass emerald green, daffodils blooming in carpets of bright yellow, the forest in new, tender green leaf, and the air cold enough to make a fire in the fireplace feel good. On such gray, windy days, the horses, mules, and cows, strangely subdued, turn their backs to the wind and seem to be depressed, waiting for it to end. Once Blackberry Winter passed, as it always had, the wind turned and came out of the south, and warm springtime returned to stay. Honeybees busied themselves everywhere as new blooms appeared, grass grew green and rank in the meadows, and the cultivated earth grew warm to the touch. Growing time was setting in with permanence, and both crops and weeds seemed to spring upward in the cultivated fields. Horses, mules, and cows grew frisky again, prospered, and put on smooth flesh. It was a fine time to be alive on a farm in the South.

As the Earth tilted southward and the sun moved ever higher in the sky, the protective cloth was removed from the tobacco bed, and the plants began to adjust to the direct light of the sun, growing and toughening in preparation for transplantation into the field.

The spring garden sprang forth and flourished at the hands of Sarah and her selected subordinates. That garden was her domain. No men were permitted in it, except for the plowing and harrowing, and she allowed only selected women servants there. Under her supervision, the garden began to bear its early food: radishes, lettuce, green onions, and peas. As they bore, planting was done for the later, more substantial foods of summer.

In late April the tobacco field, already broken and harrowed smoothly into loose and fine condition, was laid off in furrows three feet apart. Then furrows were dug across the first set, perpendicular to them, also three feet apart, with each intersection of the crossing furrows marking the place to set one plant. After the first good rain in May, the tobacco plants were pulled from the bed and taken to the field. At each intersection of the crossing furrows, a shovel of barn manure was dropped, worked into the soil, and a hole was made with a pointed, sweat-stained, whittled wooden peg. Then one plant was set in the hole, and the moist soil carefully pressed in around it. There would be plenty of work to be done as the tobacco plants grew, from suckering, worming, and topping each plant by hand, repeatedly, as needed, to hoeing out the grass and weeds, but the growing from that point onward depended on the right amount of rain and was entirely in the hands of God.

In the fields, spring crops appeared in their orderly rows of refreshing green against the background of well-worked, red Stewart County clay. In the barns and the fields, the rich aroma of freshly worked soil was mixed with the smell of sweating horses and mules and the unique scent of well-used work harnesses. All about were the sights and smells of recurring life. The pear, peach, plum, and apple trees transitioned into heavenly blossom and filled the warm air with nature's perfume. Except for the servants, this would be the last blooming that the Hinsons would enjoy, and the last fruit crop they would ever gather at Bubbling Springs.

Under Increasing Suspicion

As the warm days of spring transitioned imperceptibly into the hot days of summer, the Hinson family's status found form, ever more clearly, as clandestine Confederates. In that spring of 1863, Robert had become, after his escape from Fort Donelson, a "most wanted" guerrilla leader and was operating openly Between the Rivers. Jack himself was the special object of increasing suspicion. His persona as a harmless old man, understandably converted to Confederate sympathies as a result of the killing of his sons, was beginning to unravel.

Since the killing of the lieutenant, patrols were much more alert, and Colonel Lowe aggressively cast about over his territory for suspects to be arrested and eliminated. Jack continued his normal activities as conspicuously as possible, and his special rifle remained in its hiding place in the barn. He and the servants were questioned but not arrested. There were many guerrillas operating in the area, and they had been there for more than a year; so there was an abundance of suspects to diffuse and dissipate the attention otherwise directed at the Hinsons. The family was allowed to go on about the business of living—for the time being.

Since the killing of the young Hinsons, Union forces had been going into the field in increasing numbers. Patrols grew from platoon-size to company-size, and in the spring of 1863, multicompany forces were not unusual. At times, they went out in numbers approaching regimental strength. Operations were concentrated in the home area of Robert's guerrilla band, on Hurricane, White Oak, and Wells Creeks. For four days in April, a force of five companies from the Fifth Iowa and the Eightieth Illinois camped on Hurricane Creek and scoured the area. No contact was made, and they returned to Donelson with nothing but chigger and mosquito bites and eighty-four horses confiscated from the local farmers.[18]

Robert Hinson's Rise to Prominence and a New Alias

By that spring, Robert had emerged as the leader of his band of guerrillas, and they came to be known to the Union authorities as "Hinson's Raiders" or "Hinson's Guerrillas." Their primary theater of operations was the area from Hurricane Creek, southward, through Cane Creek, White Oak Creek, Magnolia, and Wells Creek to Waverly. There, the local population was almost entirely supportive, and Robert's band operated throughout the area with relative impunity. One might say they virtually owned this area, but they were mounted and could strike almost anywhere, from the Tennessee to the Cumberland, from Smithland to Waverly.

On May 8, while riding alone along Wells Creek, Robert was surprised by a Union patrol and captured a second time. It was only two months since his first capture and bold escape from the courthouse, but the soldiers apparently did not recognize him, and he identified himself as a Confederate soldier on leave from Company H of the Fourteenth Tennessee Infantry Regiment. He was taken to Fort Donelson, where he was charged with having participated in attacks on Union forces. In the capture report filed at Fort Donelson, an ominous note was added: "It can be proven that he has worn the US uniform in attacks on the Federal forces."[19]

For Confederates to be found wearing blue Union uniform items was not at all unusual for many Confederates had nothing else to wear. As the war wore on, this became so common that it made escape for Union prisoners much easier. Their blue uniforms blended in with their Confederate surroundings. At about the same time that Robert was recaptured, Lt. James M. Wells of a Michigan cavalry regiment was captured and confined in Richmond, Virginia's Libby Prison. He later wrote that after his escape, his blue uniform attracted no attention since most of the Confederates in Richmond, including the prison guards, were also wearing Union blue. Nevertheless, this annotation made the charge against Robert much more serious.[20]

His situation was indeed serious, and the outlook grim, but once more he escaped trailside execution. Perhaps his position as leader made him an important catch with useful information, or maybe the army wanted to bring him before a tribunal in a show trial; we can only speculate. At any rate, he was held overnight at Fort Donelson; on May 9, he was transferred to the custody of the provost marshal general, Department of the Cumberland in Nashville. When interrogated in Nashville, he was recorded as being a member of Company D, Fourteenth Regiment Tennessee Cavalry, with the notation, "See report from Fort Donelson, May 9, '63."[21]

His apparent claim to a new unit identity may simply have been a clerk's error. It may also have been deliberately evasive testimony on his part. If Robert did claim a different unit, he was using his head. The Fourteenth Tennessee Cavalry, a unit with the same numerical designation as the Fourteenth Tennessee Infantry, operated at times in neighboring Henry and Benton Counties. Such a claim would have been strengthened by the fact that there actually were several men named Hinson serving in the Fourteenth Tennessee Cavalry at the time, including some of Robert's relatives.

Another Escape and Merged Identities: Robert and George

Robert deceived the Union authorities in Nashville either to the extent that he was paroled or he escaped for a second time. We can only wonder, but it is much more likely that he escaped as the charges against him carried the death penalty. No matter how he did it, he again escaped almost certain death and made his way from Nashville back to Stewart County to rejoin his unit. During this period, the authorities apparently began to believe that his name was George. Robert may have allowed federal clerical confusion to turn to his advantage, or he may have created that confusion deliberately as an evasion by using the name of his dead brother. If the Federals created the confusion by mistake, Robert probably enjoyed the irony of seeing his dead brother, in a sense, come to life to help him harass the enemy. If Robert created the alias deliberately, he may have done so to confuse the Union authorities, to honor his dead brother, or—what is more likely—both.

There is, in the records of Fort Donelson at the National

Archives, a charge sheet in the name of "George F. Hinson of the County of Stewart." The document is what today would be called a "rough" or a "worksheet," not a finished document. It contains line-outs and strikeovers, definitely a working document, in which charges and specifications were accumulated over a period of time. It reaches back to the date of the surrender on February 16, 1862, when George and John were arrested for being too close to the battlefield and accused of spying, and it carries forward to include deeds that were clearly the work of Robert, documented elsewhere. The last entry is May 8, 1863, the day of Robert's capture on Wells Creek and five months after the real George's death in 1862. The open-ended document has no closing date, no authentication, no name of a convening authority, or any signature. After being held briefly in June and escaping for a third time, it seems clear that when Robert was killed as "the notorious guerrilla George Hinson" three months later, the case was closed, and the finished version of the charge sheet was never made.[22]

However it began, the federal authorities definitely seem to have been merging the identities of George and Robert Hinson in their records. The date of Robert's second capture on May 8, 1863, in the Union capture document is the same as the closing date in the preliminary charge sheet the provost marshal had been preparing concerning George. Also very suggestive of the merged identities is the fact that "George" was accused of wearing articles of Union uniform while operating against Union forces, the ominous charge appended to Robert's capture document of May 8. On that day in May when "George" Hinson was charged with his last offense, the real George Hinson had been dead for nearly half a year.

At any rate, it is clear from the records that by May 8, the provost marshal at Fort Donelson was completely convinced of the guilt of one "George F. Hinson of the County of Stewart." The charge sheet he was developing began with the charge of spying, with which the real George had actually been charged on February 16, 1862. The sheet continued with subsequent offenses, actually committed by Robert, after George's execution. The last entry on

"George's" charge sheet is for engaging in guerrilla activities, the very same charge for which Robert was actually arrested on May 8, 1863. One can now see clearly that in the spring and summer of 1863, the Fort Donelson provost marshal was not seeing anything clearly concerning the "two" Hinson guerrillas. In June, Robert would be captured again and taken to Fort Donelson. A sergeant of the Seventy-first Ohio, reporting the capture to his hometown newspaper, spoke of being harassed by "Hinson's Guerrillas" and Federal troops having captured "his [the leader's] brother."[23]

During this time of captures, escapes, and federal confusion about Robert's identity, Hinson's Guerrillas continued to harass and interdict Union operations in Stewart and Humphreys Counties, raiding, cutting telegraph lines, ambushing the units sent out to repair them, and, when the situation was favorable, attacking Union units in open battle. They were operating freely from Dover to Waverly with consistent success, and with Robert, now alias "George," at their head.

Colonel Lowe: "Take No Prisoners"

On May 23, Colonel Lowe reported still more skirmishes with guerrilla cavalry on Yellow Creek and informed the assistant adjutant general at Murfreesboro that he had issued "orders to take no more prisoners." Colonel Lowe's reporting of "skirmishes" here may have been an exaggeration for Cpl. Eugene Marshall of Brackett's Battalion in Lowe's regiment recorded in his diary for May 23: "Met colonel Lowe and detachment, coming from Yellow Creek—had been following guerrillas with orders to take no prisoners. No contact."[24]

There was in Colonel Lowe's regiment one exceptional asset in countering the guerrilla threat: a remarkable man in Brackett's Battalion, Corporal Marshall's close friend, Sgt. George W. Northrup. Northrup had been a famed frontiersman and scout on the Minnesota-Dakota frontier, and he was motivated to find and kill guerrillas. He was so good, in fact, that General Crook sent him on detached service, leading a handpicked team for special operations behind Confederate lines in the fall and winter of 1863.

However, not even George Northrup was successful in stopping Robert Hinson's guerrillas.[25]

As that warm and fragrant spring gave way to hot Tennessee summer, the cloud of suspicion surrounding old Jack Hinson deepened and darkened, bringing ever-more stormy political weather. By that time, the Federal authorities, because they confused the identities of Robert and George, believed that Jack had two sons who were guerrillas, not just the one. With increasing frequency, small units came to Bubbling Springs to question Jack about guerrilla activities in the area, and with similarly increasing frequency, he was not there to be questioned.

Robert's Third Escape

This growing suspicion was greatly accelerated when, in late June, Robert was arrested for the third time! A fifth sergeant of Company B, Seventy-first Ohio Volunteer Infantry, reporting from Fort Donelson to his hometown newspaper the *Troy (Ohio) Times,* wrote,

> We are troubled but little at present. Sometimes Hinson's little band of shotgun cavalry trouble [sic] our pickets, but [they] have not done us much damage yet. His brother is here in jail—this being the third time that he has been in our possession and this time I suppose will prove his last stay with us. He has had his trial; the sentence I know not.[26]

Robert was again in very deep trouble, and here again, we see that the Federal authorities still believed that there were two of him. It is fascinating to see that the Federals not only thought that there were two such Hinsons, but that they believed that their most-wanted guerrilla was still loose in the countryside when they actually had him in their custody. Astonishingly, he had once more escaped trailside execution to be brought for the third time to the Fort Donelson guardhouse. Still more astonishingly, he again escaped from their custody, which surely must have established a local record. For the third time, Robert ("George") Hinson, notorious Confederate guerrilla and escape artist, disappeared into the Stewart County wilderness and returned to his unit to lead it until his violent death three months later.

The fifth sergeant's report to his hometown newspaper also reflects the hunker-in-the-bunker defensive thinking of the Federal command at Fort Donelson that summer of 1863. He reported, as good news, that they were "troubled but little" by the Confederates. In spite of his disparaging characterization of Robert's Confederates as "shotgun cavalry," he expressed relief that they hadn't done them even more harm than they actually had. He reported that the fort was being improved; was occupied by the Thirteenth Wisconsin in addition to his own Seventy-first Ohio Regiment, plus two batteries of artillery; heavy guns were being added; and preparations were being made "*to resist* any force that is likely to be brought against us" [emphasis added]. The Federals were thinking defensively, and the initiative belonged to Hinson's Raiders and the other Confederate units in the area.[27]

Killing Again

More and more, that summer, Jack was out and about on his big saddle mare, keeping his customary rounds, supervising the work in the fields, exchanging news and country wisdom on the courthouse square in Dover, maintaining contact with sympathetic informants, and observing the Union patrols. It was on one such occasion that he made the second kill.

With the lieutenant who had overseen the killing of his sons dead, Jack's mind often returned to one of his soldiers: the one who had arrived that day with the bloody burlap sack and placed the boys' heads on his gateposts. When he allowed his mind to return to that painful day, he could still see the sack and the blood-smeared hands that pulled the heads out by their matted, bloody hair and placed them on the posts. He could still see the look of sadistic satisfaction on the soldier's face as he did it. Jack didn't know his name, but he would always remember that face. Even years later, long after the war, it would sometimes sneer at him, out of the mists of troubled dreams.

On a particularly warm summer morning, Jack rode out to

check his corn, which would soon be too tall to cultivate and
would be laid by. Finding it satisfactory, he continued eastward
into the woods, following Lick Creek downstream. As he often
did, he was combining the oversight of his farm with meandering,
visiting with neighbors, and the observing of the Union patrols.

Passing onto Dr. Smith's land, he continued along the creek,
enjoying the cooler air in the creek bottom and the pleasant aroma
of the creek itself. He loved the way creeks smelled, except for some
times in the dog days when the water was low, pooled, and stagnant.
That day the fresh, watery smell of life filled the creek bottom, and
the shade combined with the cool water to moderate the summer
heat. It was a pleasant, peaceful interlude, riding easily downstream,
ducking at times, brushed by the willows and overhanging red
maples, his mare's hooves splashing in the clear, shallow water,
sending minnows and crayfish scurrying for shelter under rocks.

Passing Hay Ford, he continued lazily downstream as the creek
became deeper. Near Charlotte Road, the peace of the morning was
invaded by the growing sound of horses' hooves and the familiar
clanking and rattling of a Yankee patrol. Their vexing, unwelcome
presence seemed to be everywhere, invading every aspect of his
life, even the soothing solitude of the Lick Creek bottom. Moving
up and out of the creek, he dismounted and approached on foot
until he could see the road clearly without being seen. Without
moving, Jack watched the lead soldier appear, with the others
following. As usual, they seemed relaxed, settled into a long,
easy ride. This patrol was outbound, on a route he had watched
before; he knew the extent of their route, and he knew about
what time they would be returning. It seemed a waste of time
to watch them again—they were so entirely predictable—until,
examining each passing face, Jack saw *him*. As that face came
before him, something powerful stirred down deep in Jack; in his
mind, he could again see that leering face and the bloody hands,
placing the heads on his gateposts. Steady gray eyes locked onto
that face, studied the rest of the man, and hardened to the density
of Tennessee flint. He would have a surprise for that man on the
return leg of his patrol, and with that settled, Jack returned home

the long way, with a leisurely stop in Dover to visit, to observe, and—especially—to be seen.

Crossing the Rubicon

Toward the softening end of that long, hot day, cool gray eyes watched Charlotte Road near Smith Ford. It was quiet, and Jack was remembering the February day when Forrest had led one thousand freezing soldiers across that flooded ford to safety. The murmur of the creek, running unusually full and fresh for midsummer, played soft background music for the songbirds. Their melodies were pierced from time to time by the sudden discordant squawk of a kingfisher watching for unsuspecting minnows. It was a very pleasant time of day in a very pleasant place, but the quiet of that peaceful scene would soon be shattered by the crash of a large-bore rifle.

Jack hid behind a moss-covered log, watching the road, listening. When the first sounds of the approaching soldiers reached his ear, he smiled inwardly and reached for his rifle, lying beside him. He checked the load, checked the cap, and eased the hammer down. As the sounds of the returning patrol grew closer, he slid the barrel of the rifle across the soft surface of the mossy log and looked over the sights at the stretch of the road below him that constituted his kill zone. It was a restricted area, not as wide as he might have wished, but the spot was ideal in every other way. It provided almost perfect concealment from the road. A rising bank at the roadside would delay the Yankees should they attempt a direct assault, and there was a largely concealed draw that he could return to, to reach his mare, and a dense forest into which they could disappear once he was mounted.

As the patrol neared, he heard considerable conversation and some laughter. On the return leg, the minds of many were already back at the fort, thinking of pleasant things. They shouldn't have been.

Jack adjusted his sight picture and brought the bead to an aiming point across the road. That aiming point, a fork in a small tree, was chest high to a mounted soldier. With his rifle already aimed there when his man appeared before him, it would require only a slight adjustment of his aim to match the man—if any at all. As he waited, the only things moving were his eyes, waiting for the head of the lead rider's horse to appear.

Remembering the position of the man in the column, Jack cocked the set trigger, and pressed his trigger finger lightly forward, against the trigger guard, so as not to touch the trigger too soon. As he saw the patrol leader appear before him, he took a deep breath, let half of it out and held it; *his* man should be next. As his man appeared and moved into his sights, with the shiny silver front sight bead at the level of his upper arm, the man was speaking over his shoulder to the man behind him, laughing. His face was turned toward the place where Jack lay, with his upper body half turned toward him. The bead was on his left suspender buckle when Jack touched the trigger.

The road was so close that the crack of the rifle and the big, spinning bullet arrived simultaneously. The impact drove the man to his right, and he disappeared behind his horse, with his laughter interrupted. Forever.

As the horse jumped and whirled with the dead soldier's right foot still entangled in the stirrup, confusion, for a short period, reigned on the road as Jack rose to his knees. With his rifle in his left hand and his dragoon pistol, cocked, in his right, he turned, crouching, and disappeared into the draw behind him. Once mounted, he moved quickly westward and was swallowed by the darkening forest. It was done.

He had not waited to see if the man was dead, but he had seen the strike of the large .50-caliber bullet. There was no way that a man could survive such a wound. Anyway, he would hear soon, for such news moved quickly from the fort to Dover thence out through the county. He would know.

With darkness falling and assured that he was not being pursued, he headed straight for Bubbling Springs, stowed his rifle and kit in the barn, and tended to his mare. As the moon rose, big, full, and friendly, Jack pondered his situation.

Was it all now finished? He didn't know. Maybe he had gone too far to stop now. All his preparation and planning had been to avenge the murder of his two sons. Now he had done that. To make it perfect, he had killed the two men most guilty. However, he wondered if he killed no more of them, would the Yankees allow him to go on with his life?

He had a feeling that the answer was "No." Robert's fighting, his third capture and escape, had indelibly branded the entire family as outlaws. Under Union occupation policies their property could at any time be confiscated, and the entire family subject to banishment, imprisonment, or execution. Now, he had killed two Union soldiers, both of whom had been involved in the killing of his sons. Surely, that fact would not go unnoticed at Fort Donelson.

Jack really wanted no more trouble; he would be satisfied to let the matter end there, in the gathering darkness of a summer night. He had his vengeance, and justice had been done. As long as the Yankees would allow it, he would try to go on with life as before. Yet, like Julius Caesar of old, he felt that he had crossed the Rubicon. Whatever the future held for him, there could be no turning back.

Chapter 6

Twilight at Bubbling Springs: The Last Summer and Autumn

"The dreamy, sun-washed days of that blessed summer and autumn would soon be followed by the darkest winter of their lives."

As the summer of 1863 settled into an endless succession of hot nights followed by still-hotter days, the occupation force looked upon the Hinsons with increasingly cold eyes. Aware of, but not intimidated by, the hostile attention from the occupation forces, the Hinson family, both black and white, went on with their work, following the timeless, seasonal rhythms of past years and past generations.

Colonel Lowe and the Fifth Iowa Cavalry Depart

On June 8, Colonel Lowe and his Fifth Iowa Cavalry left the Twin Rivers and decamped for Murfreesboro to become part of the First Brigade, Second Division, Fourteenth Corps and follow the war eastward. They would never return. Col. William P. Lyon assumed command at Fort Donelson, but the situation didn't improve. In fact, the situation was even more difficult for Colonel Lyon because the Thirteenth Wisconsin and the Seventy-first Ohio were infantry regiments, which made it almost impossible for him to react adequately to the fast-moving Confederate cavalry units and mounted bands of guerrillas such as Robert Hinson's Raiders. The Confederates in the area continued to strike and with more freedom than before.[1]

In June, the early apples ripened and were a welcome treat in any form: raw, soft and juicy, cooked into applesauce and pies, or fried with sugar and sausage. June apples were good in any form, but their applesauce was best.

June also brought haying time—the cutting and housing of the early hay. The hay was mowed with scythes, and the mowing entrusted only to the older, experienced men. They moved across the field, side by side but staggered, rear to front so as not to cut one another, with each cutting his own swath, the sharpened blades swinging smoothly, rhythmically, with long-practiced efficiency and economy of motion. Behind the mowers, and after the hay was sufficiently cured in the swath, came the sweeps. The hay was raked into windrows with a "sweep" made of a long log, from which slender, long poles, pointed on the tips, projected forward perpendicularly like the teeth of a giant comb. With a mule hitched to each end of the log, the sweep would slide under the mown hay and accumulate it in long windrows, backing out from under each portion as that row grew to go get some more. When the hay was further cured, the wagons followed. The hands walked beside the wagons, forking the hay from the windrows onto the wagons, where it was carefully arranged so that the load could be built high without falling off the wagon. At the barn, it was forked into the loft to become the basic supply of feed, laid up to sustain the stock through the coming winter.

Through the summer, they cultivated corn, "bustin' the middles" to control the grass and weeds; what the cultivator couldn't get, the scraping hoes did. Their patch of cotton received the same care.

And Hinson's Guerrillas Were Having Their Way

As summer progressed, Robert Hinson and his mounted band of raiders grew steadily stronger, better organized, disciplined, and armed, and they operated throughout the area with growing freedom. As they improved in organization and discipline, they increasingly evolved from the status of a guerrilla band to that of legitimate partisan rangers on the order of Virginia's John Singleton Mosby and Kentucky's Adam "Stovepipe" Johnson. They began to be referred to as "Hinson's Command," significant terminology, normally reserved for legitimate military units. Robert seems to have had an inherent talent for leadership and an untutored genius for fast-moving cavalry tactics. At least a small part of his heredity seems to have been dipped from the same gene pool that produced Nathan Bedford Forrest. In short, the man was a natural; he seemed to have been born for what he was doing.

As Robert's band grew in strength, he boldly took on Union units of greater size. On July 29, Colonel Lyon, vexed with the ceaseless guerrilla activity, reported that, again, his telegraph line had been cut and that his repair party, although strengthened by a cavalry unit of forty men, had been attacked and scattered, taking casualties and fleeing for their lives. The Confederates were "supposed to be Hinson's Guerrillas," he said, and he complained that it happened regularly ("three or four times a week") and in the same area ("usually about fifteen miles from here"). In exasperation, he reported his belief that Hinson's Guerrillas had their headquarters near Waverly and were supplied and supported "by the whole community." Colonel Lyon's estimate of the situation was accurate; the situation as it existed was out of control, and he was fed up! He even went so far as to officially recommend Waverly be completely destroyed! And he meant it. The guerrilla problem in the area was maddening, and the Hinson family was definitely on his mind.[2]

Robert's band was giving the Federals fits. Smaller-than-company-size Union units could not travel outside their fortifications with safety let alone with confidence. Robert struck with regularity against Union patrols, supply wagons, telegraph lines, and the repair parties sent out to mend the broken lines. He and his men might appear anywhere, from Smithland to Eddyville to Pine Bluff, from Dover to Waverly. Their base of operations, however, their "Sherwood Forest," was the area between Hurricane Creek and Waverly.

That "Sherwood Forrest" of Robert's was described in detail by Lt. Ira B. Dutton of the Thirteenth Wisconsin Volunteer Infantry as being an area of beautiful, clear streams, dense forest, and high bluffs. The area, he observed, was one where "natural defenses abound." They even found a guerrilla hospital operating there. Dutton and his Thirteenth Wisconsin traversed the area from Fort Donelson to Waverly in late August 1863. Although they were in regimental strength and included mounted infantry, they were attacked by guerrillas several times in skirmishes and suffered sniper casualties along the way. They arrived at Waverly in awesome force, and "entered the village with [martial] music and colors flying" but failed to intimidate the citizens. As they turned back toward Fort Donelson, they lost one man to a sniper a short distance north of Waverly and left another, too badly wounded to travel, in the farm home of a widow. In complete agreement with Colonel Lyon's opinion of the citizens of the area, Dutton described them as "violent rebels." The Wisconsin soldiers arrived back at Dover in early September, leaving the guerrilla stronghold much as they had found it.[3]

Robert's "Sherwood Forest" would become the family's new home after the war. As the Thirteenth Wisconsin traveled between White Oak Creek and Waverly, they took note of the mill that would be purchased and operated by Jack Hinson after the war. In 1863, the property was known as Wilson's Mill. They also traveled through the land that would become Jack and Elisabeth's final home, Magnolia Hill.

William Comes Home

Early honey was taken from the bee gums, and the watermelons cooling in the spring were sweet. The sweetest thing about that summer by far, however, was the return of William from the war. In late May, he had been placed on furlough by his regiment and sent home from Virginia. He arrived in June, and it was almost too good to be true. He had been taken prisoner the previous September in the bloody Battle at Antietam Creek in Maryland, had subsequently been paroled, and made it back to his unit in Virginia. Sick with chronic bronchitis since his return, William was near death and had been placed on sick leave. He was so thin and looked so much older, but he was home, and that was where he needed to be. Nothing would give Elisabeth more pleasure than to nurse her William back to health. Sarah hovered over him like a protective mother hen. All of the Hinsons rejoiced, but the rejoicing was mixed with renewed grieving as William learned of the death of his brothers, George and John.[4]

With work on the farm progressing normally, Jack continued to make the rounds, visiting friends, doing business, hearing the news and courthouse gossip in Dover, keeping up with the war news, and scouting. With fall nearing, it was increasingly healthy for him not to be at home when Union patrols came by.

In early August, before the corn was too tall to be straddled by the cultivator, it was cultivated for weed control one last time, and then it was "laid by." Except for hoeing, if the grass and weeds recovered enough to require it, there was nothing else to do to the corn until time to cut and pick it. The same was true of the cotton patch. Until picking time, the work would be done by the crops themselves, growing and maturing. In the heat of August, they did grow; the corn grew taller than Jack, and the cotton was waist high.

Hinson's Guerrillas Strike Again (and with Style)

As the corn grew and the tobacco leaves matured in the August heat, Robert boldly took the battle to the enemy on his own ground. On August 6, with only seven men, he attacked in the very heart of the Union's stronghold. Identified in a contemporary newspaper account as a detachment of "Hinson's Command," they seized the telegraph station at Fort Henry and captured the station master Mr. C. E. Bush, "his clothing, watch, and $100 in money." As reported in the newspaper, they took away the telegraph equipment, plus "horses and mules, the property of Mr. Phillips, and made both gentlemen leave with them. They paroled and liberated Mr. B in the woods after carrying him thirty miles, and he was compelled to make his way, barefoot, to Fort Donelson, where he arrived safely, though much fatigued."[5]

This was Robert Hinson's most audacious and spectacular victory over the Union forces of which records have been found, and it took place not in the relative security of his "Sherwood Forest" on White Oak Creek, but right at the enemy commanding officer's headquarters. Robert was definitely bearding the lion in his den. He operated with exceptional boldness, courage, and what one can only call "style." It is regrettable that we know so little about him for he was an interesting, extraordinary man. We can only wonder what he might have done had he lived longer. With his ability to think under pressure, his coolness under interrogation, his genius for escape, his natural talent for leadership and cavalry warfare, plus what was called in that war "dash," he might have been remembered in the same category with such bold dragoons as John Hunt Morgan and John Singleton Mosby.

And here is further evidence that Hinson's Command was a disciplined military unit and not just a band of criminals. The criminals never observed such conventional civilities and protocols as "paroling" their captives. Almost always, they simply took what they wanted, then shot them. Robert, of course, couldn't know it, but this would also be his last significant victory.[6]

After a brief and frustrating tenure at Fort Donelson, Colonel Lyon was relieved and replaced with Col. A. A. Smith. Colonel Smith was better able to deal with the guerrillas for he had more mounted troops, but the problem continued and not much changed.

In August, as guerrilla warfare grew hotter between the rivers, there also came the hot, hard work of cutting and housing the tobacco. This was an all-hands effort, and everything else at Bubbling Springs revolved around it until it was completed. Like haying, the success of the entire crop depended on cutting and housing it successfully and at the right time. Everyone, except for the women and small children, worked at it. The most experienced hands did the cutting and "sticking" (arranging the stalks on slender, hickory sticks); everyone else could join in the physical labor of stacking the tobacco on wagons. They received a brief rest riding with the load from the field to the barn if they could find a place to ride. Afterwards, there came the hot, hard, and dangerous work of passing the sticks of tobacco upward from one man to the one above him, all the way to the top of the tall, narrow log barn. There, the sticks were carefully arranged, hanging across tier poles for curing. With the barn thus filled, from the top down, fires were started and tended in fire pits dug into the dirt floor of the barn, and the barn was closed. The workers tended the fires to produce smoke but not flames, and the smoke slowly cured the tobacco. It was, as always, a time of relief and satisfaction when the crop was safely housed and curing.

Word of Jack's Activities Was Getting Around

As Union forces moved ever-farther southward, several Southern newspapers, including the *Memphis Appeal,* the *Huntsville Confederate,* and the *Chattanooga Rebel,* became "newspapers on the run," moving ever more deeply into the South in order to publish without Union interference. During the years 1862 to 1865, the *Memphis Appeal* was published from Memphis; Grenada, Mississippi; Jackson, Mississippi; Atlanta; Montgomery, Alabama; and Columbus, Georgia. There was little actual news in those papers. They were largely filled with poems; jokes; instructions for knitting, weaving, and making dyes with homegrown materials; patriotic essays; substitutes for coffee; and ideas for other homemade supplies. They frequently reprinted old articles from other newspapers, including those in the North, when they could be obtained. They were very similar to the paper traditionally sold in rural America today called *Grit.*

On September 10, as the tobacco cured peacefully in the smoky barn, a story about the Hinsons appeared in the *Memphis Appeal.* At the time, the *Appeal* was "on the run," a newspaper without a home, publishing at this point in Atlanta. Amid the usual poems, jokes, and personal ads of soldiers seeking wives, there was an article praising the patriotic efforts of John "Captain Jack" Hinson of Stewart and Humphreys Counties in Tennessee. The article was a third-generation story, copied from the *Huntsville Confederate* (another newspaper "on the run"), attributed originally to an anonymous source and published in a newspaper four hundred miles from the scene with no verification. It attributed to Jack some elements of his own story; some elements of Robert's story; the story of Jack Hinson's nearest neighbors, Albert and Rebecca Rougement, whose plantation home had been commandeered as the Union hospital during the battle; and some parts that were simply fiction. Although the article had suffered much from the retelling, blending of stories, and badly distorted rumor, it does reinforce the important fact that by September 10, 1863, word of the Hinsons was getting around in the South.[7]

Robert (George) Falls in Battle

Eight days after the dateline on the garbled story, violent death again visited Bubbling Springs. On the eighteenth, a Confederate partisan unit, passing through Stewart County near Fort Donelson, encountered a Union patrol escorting wagons. It appears that neither unit expected to encounter the other, and the men at the heads of both columns immediately opened fire. Neither unit made a determined attack. After a few confused and violent moments, the skirmish ended. Both Confederate and Union soldiers, uncertain of the strength of the other, broke contact and withdrew. In the brief encounter, two soldiers and two guerrillas were killed, and the dead, for the moment, were left where they fell. Back at Fort Donelson, Colonel Smith reported the skirmish and the casualties. With a note of triumph, he identified one of the Confederate dead as "the notorious guerrilla, George Hinson."

It is a virtual certainty that "the notorious guerrilla" who died that day was Robert Hinson, using his dead brother's name, riding at the head of his company, dying, as John Rainey would later describe the scene, "with pistol in hand," a casualty of the opening volley of Union fire. In September 1863, the real George Hinson had been dead for nearly a year, and Robert is the only son of Jack Hinson whose death is not otherwise accounted for. There is no other guerrilla named George Hinson in the surviving war records of the area and certainly not one "notorious" as a guerrilla leader.[8]

According to the statement of one John Rainey, a contemporary source, the guerrilla killed in that skirmish was Jack Hinson's son. In 1906 he declared, "Captain Jack's son, [illegible first name] Hinson, was also a Southern guerrilla. He was killed about two miles from Fort Donelson by [a] Yankee bullet in [his] head. [He] fell with pistol in hand."[9]

According to Rainey, this man was such a prized trophy for the Union soldiers that they "tied him to [a] horse's tail, and dragged him all around in Fort Donelson." It is unfortunate that the first name of this son of Jack Hinson was illegible in the handwritten transcript of the interview. However, John Rainey's account is in complete harmony with the Fort Donelson provost marshal's charge sheet and Colonel Smith's report and is confirmation of the conclusion that the son of Jack Hinson who was killed that day was Robert. According to one Yankee soldier who saw the body, even in death his appearance was arresting. He wrote that his dead countenance "spoke of a reckless spirit [but one] engaged in a bad cause." Robert was indeed a bold dragoon. His star had blazed briefly but spectacularly in the skies above the Twin Rivers.[10]

Always an elusive, mysterious figure during the war years, Robert, at that point, disappeared completely from the records into a fog of secrecy, confusion, and doubtful wartime record keeping, leaving questions about his actions and ultimate fate that linger to this day. One thing, however, is clear. When "the notorious guerrilla George Hinson" was killed in September 1863, Robert A. Hinson disappeared completely from the records, and he left behind a wife and two daughters, who never saw or heard from him again. In 1871, Robert's two children, Delia and Ann Eliza, were provided for in their grandmother Elisabeth's will as orphans ("the heirs of Robert A. Hinson, Dec'd"). It is not known when or how their mother died, but many mothers died young in those days, often in childbirth. This common cause of death in nineteenth-century records is often listed as "childbed." The place and nature of Robert's burial are unknown.[11]

Lacking any other evidence, it would seem illogical to conclude anything other than the "notorious guerrilla" killed September 18, 1863, was Robert A. Hinson.

Pillow's Final Appeal: Invoking the Name of Hinson

As October came on and the corn and cotton matured in the fields, visits from the Union patrols became more frequent, and their behavior increasingly hostile. They were looking for any pretense at Bubbling Springs to declare the Hinsons enemies of the Union. Actually, they already had cause to do so under the policy that when a man (such as Robert) was known to be a guerrilla, then his family and neighbors were considered equally guilty. To this point, Colonel Lowe, Colonel Lyon, and Colonel Smith, in succession, had not been willing to invoke this policy in the case of the Hinsons. Their reluctance to do so was probably based upon three factors: the loss of the two Hinson sons the year before and the brutal treatment of the family; the fact that Robert's base of operations was far to the south of Bubbling Springs, near Waverly; and the Hinsons' friendly, if brief, acquaintance with General Grant. At any rate, no matter how attended by extenuation and mitigation, the Hinsons' status as legitimate, loyal citizens was becoming increasingly unsubstantial.

Although the surrender of Fort Donelson was by then more than a year and a half in the past, the controversy over who was responsible for the disaster dragged on, having taken on a life of its own. It persisted primarily because General Pillow continued his relentless campaign to justify himself. General Floyd, the Fort Donelson commander who was relieved in disgrace with Pillow, had returned to Virginia, where he served briefly with Virginia militia forces and had died on August 26, 1863. Pillow, now carrying the burden of disgrace alone, continued his campaign of self-justification.

On October 1, 1863, he wrote a letter directly to Pres. Jefferson Davis. With General Floyd dead and Buckner and Forrest busy fighting the war, Pillow had managed to redefine the debate. He had by then assumed the role of one who had opposed the surrender, rather than having been one of its befuddled authors. In this interesting and somewhat confused letter, Pillow, although an officer on active duty in Georgia, wrote the "unofficial" letter as a private citizen. In it, he shamelessly reminded Davis that he, Pillow, had been Davis's "personal and political friend for the last fifteen years." But it seems, in spite of his well-connected political friends and high-ranking officer acquaintances, Pillow invoked only four honorable and credible witnesses in his ultimate appeal to the president; the first was Jack Hinson. He wrote,

> I have also taken the sworn testimony of four other witnesses, to wit: Captain Hinson, Dr. Moore, Captain Newberry, and Lieutenant Hollister, all of whom testify that the enemy had not reinvested our position or army on the night of 15th February, as was then supposed, and never did reinvest, and that the army was surrendered under a delusion, and that our army could have marched out on the night of the 15th or morning of the 16th February without any obstacle or opposition.[12]

By this time, Jack Hinson had testified in Columbia as to the conditions surrounding the unnecessary surrender of Fort Donelson, and he executed a sworn affidavit to that effect (the affidavit is reproduced in facsimile in Appendix E). Pillow had redefined the argument, placing himself on the "we shouldn't have done it" side. This is the earliest known example of Jack Hinson's being called "Captain" Hinson in official communication. It was not unusual in that day for a man in a position of leadership, in business or community, to be called "Captain." It is a fact that he was referred to as "Captain" during the war and by writers and witnesses after the war. However, there is no known record of his ever having been inducted or commissioned as an officer of the Confederate army. This appellation may also be the source of the belief by some that he led a band of guerrillas in the area, but the overwhelming evidence indicates that, except when scouting for Forrest, Jack Hinson operated alone and as a civilian.

At the time Captain Hinson was being presented to the president of the Confederacy as a man of honor and reputation by General Pillow, he was being increasingly viewed as a dastardly villain by Colonel Smith at Fort Donelson. In spite of Robert Hinson's death, his old band continued to give Smith fits in Stewart and Humphreys Counties, operating freely throughout the area, known still by Robert's name. Hinson was a prominent name in the reports of guerrilla activity in that summer and fall of 1863, and the family was more and more on Colonel Smith's mind.

The Last Autumn

In the fall of 1863, the work at Bubbling Springs continued.

Sweet, cold, and wet with dew, the late apples were gathered. Some were put through the old cider mill; the cider was stored in oak barrels, with plenty more to drink, fresh from the mill. Some of the apples were sliced and dried in flat trays on the roofs of the outbuildings, then gathered into bags for storage and winter use. And, of course, there were pies. Bushels more of the "keeping" varieties were sorted and stored in the cool of the root cellar.

Turnips, sweet potatoes, and late Irish potatoes were dug, brought in, washed, culled, and stored for winter use. The root cellar was well stocked, containing more than enough for the Hinsons and for guests. In spite of the war's disruptions, the stagecoaches continued to run. Travelers continued to stop at Bubbling Springs, leaving rested and well fed.

Picking the corn, like haying and cutting and housing the tobacco crop, was an all-hands operation. The wagons moved slowly through the fields, with hands walking along on both sides, snapping off the ears and throwing them into the wagons. Others followed, cutting the stalks with long corn knives and gathering them into shocks. Each full wagon traveled to the barn where the corn was shoveled into the corncrib, filling it higher and higher with that yellow gold, then returned to the field to get another load. The ride on the wagon to and from the barn was a welcome rest for the pickers, one that became more and more welcome as each day wore on. Except for the noon meal, it was the only rest they would get until the setting sun ended the long, hot day. As was the custom in such all-out work, the hands were well fed. At noon, cold milk and portable food were brought to the field or to the shade of the trees at the barn. Drinking water was always there in buckets, carried from the springs, and a dipper full of that cool, clear water was more to be desired when hot and thirsty than the finest wine. Those who could get to the springs behind the big house got the water, cold and clear, bubbling up out of the ground, and munched on the refreshing mint and watercress that grew around the edges of the stream. For men and boys tired and hot from hard work in the fields and barns, there was nothing more refreshing.

Corn picking was a time of hard work by everyone; even the small children helped by carrying water and food, catching chickens, or in any other way they could. It was also an exciting time, a mixture of ongoing hard work with a touch of celebratory feasting. It was both satisfying and comforting to know that barns, cribs, and cellars were filling with food and feed to last all winter. It was a time of fulfillment. Throughout the Hinson family, there was a pleasant, comfortable, sense of accomplishment, satisfaction, and security, but Robert's death dulled and muted it all.

As the tobacco continued to cure, the cotton patch was picked and the crop cleaned and combed, removing the seeds and collecting the fibers for quilting and spinning.

It seemed that, in spite of the war, life for them would go on this way forever, but it seemed that way simply because life always had. They had no way of knowing that their peace and security had but a short time to live. The greatest trial of their lives was only weeks away.

The Union occupation forces had never known with certainty how to relate to the people of southwestern and south-central Kentucky, and West and Middle Tennessee. There were a few staunch Unionist families scattered throughout the area, but the vast majority of the populace was strongly Confederate in sympathy and, when the opportunity arose, in deeds.

By February 1863, the problems with irregular Confederate activities throughout the area had become so serious that Maj. Gen. George H. Thomas, commanding the Fourteenth Army Corps, headquartered in Murfreesboro, Tennessee, summarized the situation for the War Department and other concerned agencies in Washington. He concluded that the conciliatory approach to the citizens in the area had not worked and suggested a punitive approach to the problem was required. Summarizing his opinion of the bulk of the population, General Thomas reported, "Secessionism has so degraded their sense of honor that it is next to impossible to find one tinctured with it who can be trusted."[13]

He recommended depopulating the area of all people who were pro-Confederate—actually driving them out, an idea so radical that it had been attempted only once in American history. In that atrocity, under the Indian Removal Act of 1830, implemented by Andrew Jackson, the Cherokee Indians were driven from their homes in the Appalachian Mountains of the Southeast to relocate in what is now Oklahoma. Thousands died along the way, and the event is known as the Trail of Tears.

Unabashed, General Thomas wrote, "This report exhibits a state of affairs by no means peculiar to Tennessee. The State

of Kentucky is in the same condition. . . . The conciliatory
has failed, and however much we may regret the necessity, we
shall be compelled to send disloyal people of all ages and sexes
to the south, or beyond our lines." General Grant, in January,
had announced his intention of doing the same thing to families
suspected of Confederate sympathies "whether they have taken
the oath of allegiance or not." In an unusual departure from his
normal, unemotional manner, he advocated sending ten such
families south for every raid made upon his railroads. He must
have been having an unusually bad day for he ended by writing,
"I wish to give this letter all the force of an order."[14]

The people Between the Rivers were almost exactly in the center
of the area General Thomas described as needing to be depopulated.
The increasingly hostile policy toward citizens with Confederate
sympathies, but who were otherwise innocent, was approaching
the boiling point, and the Hinsons of Bubbling Springs were in the
epicenter of the crisis. The family's name was already "notorious"
in the minds of the Union occupiers. When Colonel Smith and his
subordinate commanders thought of the guerrilla problem that so
vexed them, the name "Hinson" came to mind. The uneasy tolerance
the Hinsons had previously enjoyed couldn't last much longer.

In spite of the growing tensions, however, as the pleasant Indian
summer of 1863 turned the night air cool and sent color flaming
through the forest, the annual time of relative ease returned again
to Bubbling Springs. The turnips were thick and plump for the
picking in the kitchen garden. There were the usual maintenance
and repairs to houses, barns, machinery and harness, and
mattress ticks to be filled with fresh corn shucks. The hard work
was finished until time to strip the tobacco and pack it for market.
Autumn was easing pleasantly into a mild early winter.

The Last Winter: Farewell to William

There was time to hunt; deer, turkey, and an occasional wild
hog added to the plenty the Hinsons already enjoyed. As the
temperature dropped and cold winds began to blow down from
the north, they also began to enjoy rabbit. It was a wonderful time
of the year for them. They all enjoyed the cool air, the warm sun,
and the comforting sense of peace and plenty. William was recovering
well; he was walking more and more and riding over the farm, regaining

his strength. The time was approaching when he would have to make his way back to Virginia and rejoin his unit, but, for now, he prospered in the nurture and safety of his home. His family, black and white, enjoyed the prolonged pleasure of his presence.

This was the setting in the Twin Rivers area that beautiful autumn of 1863. They basked in the beautiful weather, the satisfaction of crops harvested and stored, and the pleasure of seeing William recovering his health. In spite of the pain brought by Robert's death in late summer, those were halcyon days for the Hinsons, a sweet and mellow autumn to be remembered.

The same cannot be said, however, for General Rosecrans. When he arrived in St. Louis that fall, it was the darkest time of his military career. The pleasant weather was no remedy for the general's unhappiness. The sunshine of Indian summer could not warm his heart, the cool breezes could not ease the burning pain of being relieved of his command and banished to the backwaters of the war, nor could the big harvest moon brighten the dark memories of the blood bath over which he had presided at Chickamauga. To make it all much worse, he was still vexed by the guerrilla problem. This was a season the Hinsons would always remember fondly, but one that General Rosecrans would wish to forget.

Yes, General Rosecrans' terrible autumn was a wonderful time for the Hinsons, almost making them forget the ache of the loss of three of their number. They could not know that the dreamy, sun-washed days of that blessed autumn would soon be followed by the darkest winter of their lives.

Nor could they know that they would never see William again.

The Last Christmas

Despite the absence of three of their sons, Christmas was all that Jack and Elisabeth could have asked for. At least, they did have their boy William, who had grown to be a man in the terrible trials of war, still at home. It was, in spite of the war and its attendant death, a wonderful Christmas at Bubbling Springs.

The air was cold and still; yet the combination of comforting fires in all fireplaces and the soft December sun made the cold seem almost friendly.

Cedar trees were cut and brought into every house to be decorated with homemade ornaments. As to not waste the cedar, after Christmas festivities, the cedar would be cut up and burned, sweetening each house and the air around it, however briefly, with the pleasant aroma of the cedar smoke. Special foods were prepared, and gifts, mostly homemade like the tree decorations, were wrapped with elaborate secrecy and hidden away.

There was pleasant conversation and laughter in the great house as cooking and baking progressed. More laughter drifted up from the servants' quarters down the lane as similar preparations went on. The best meat was taken from the big smokehouse. Apples, potatoes, carrots, yams, and turnips were brought up from the root cellar, and cider barrels were opened. Generous portions were taken to each of the servants' cabins. Pumpkins, buried in loose hay in the barn since October, were brought in and cut up for pies. There was a wonderful sense of plenty, of blessedness, of security. The preparations for Christmas were, in some ways, even more pleasant than was Christmas day itself.

As her thoughts returned to Christmases past, Christmas day arrived with a heaviness in Elisabeth's heart for her lost sons, but she concealed it well and found solace in the warm presence of the rest of her family. The others, in varying degrees, had the same unspoken thoughts, but the sense of loss was most acute in Elisabeth.

The Christmas story was read from the family Bible; songs were sung; stories of past Christmases were told; cider, both hot and cold, was enjoyed; and gifts emerged from hiding places to be exchanged before the large fireplace in the parlor. The black Hinsons arrived at the big house with smiles and their traditional Southern greeting, "Christmas gift, Christmas gift!" There were gifts for everyone. There was candy for the children, along with special foods, homemade toys, and even some "store bought" goods such as hats, gloves, and pocketknives.

Elisabeth had bought pots, pitchers, and other housekeeping items that she knew the married black Hinsons needed. For Sarah, mistress of the kitchen, there was a pretty gingham apron, made to fit her formidable form.

Everyone observed from time to time that it was as fine a Christmas as they could remember. Memories of that Christmas would, in the years to come, be made more dear by subsequent tragedy. That Christmas of 1863 would not have been nearly such a happy one had they known that there would never be another like it.

The New Year arrived clear and cold as winter asserted itself and took firm control of the weather. As preparations for hauling the tobacco to market began, William started to wind up his personal affairs and prepared to return to his regiment in Virginia. Although he had been at home for several months and had been visited by friends, relatives, and Dr. Smith, he had not been disturbed by the occupying Yankees. They knew that he was home on convalescent leave, and those were the days when "parole" was respected and considered a guarantee. William was honor-bound not to participate in any way in hostilities against the occupying Union forces while at home, and they were likewise honor-bound to leave him alone. Anyway, they knew that he had arrived home deathly sick and represented no threat; they had not disturbed him in any way. He had thought much about his friends in Company E. He had been away for so long. But once he rejoined the unit, after a few days of "catching up," it would seem as if he had never been away. It is that way with friendships forged in the shared hardships and dangers of war; they have perennial roots.[15]

As January days passed and the time for William's departure neared, the tobacco crop was hauled away to the landing in Dover to be shipped to market in Clarksville or Paducah, and the well established cycle of life at Bubbling Springs once more came full circle. Actually, it was difficult to know when the farm year began and ended for it really never stopped, with one process phasing into and overlapping the next. There was something to be done at every time of the year. With the crop shipped to market, it was time to begin to clear a spot of new ground, work it up for the tobacco bed, and gather the tops and brush for burning it. Then it would again be time to plant the seed for the new crop. Between the Rivers, winter was neither long nor particularly hard, as a rule, but growing tobacco in that place and time sometimes made it seem that, in terms of surcease from work, there hadn't really been one.

A Final Farewell to William

When the day came for William to leave, the family gathered to see him off. Elisabeth provided him with good, warm clothing, and his saddlebags were bulging with food for the trip. His blanket roll was wrapped in a new oilcloth sheet, which he could use for a ground cover when sleeping or a makeshift tent in rainy weather. A small Bible was packed, along with medicines, and Jack gave him a soft leather moneybag that he could hang around his neck and down his back, to give his money some protection from robbers. In the bag was plenty of money, in Yankee greenbacks and gold and silver coin. When his food ran out, he would be able to pay for food and lodging. It was the custom of the day for farm families to take in travelers overnight for there were usually no public inns between towns. The traveler was not expected to pay, but if he had money, the existing protocol called for him to leave something for his host. William would find shelter, one way or another, most nights along the way.

As added protection, Jack gave him a fine, heavy dragoon, a "horse pistol," in a saddle holster, with extra powder, patches, caps, and shot. He should have nothing to fear from most Union troops along the way, but outlaw Union soldiers and men who preyed on vulnerable travelers were on those roads. They had no respect for the laws of man or of God, but they would respect the large gun in his saddle holster.

There was nothing more to be accomplished; it was time for final hugs, kisses, and a prayer for William's safekeeping and health. The family stood at the front gate, the place where so many strangers found a welcome reception, where such horror had taken place and from which William had ridden away to war before. Trying to hide his own tears, William mounted the fine saddle mare Jack had given him, turned her head away from the gate, and headed northward down the lane toward Dover Road. As he passed by the slave quarters to the right of the lane, he stopped and waved silent goodbyes to the black Hinsons gathered there to bid their tearful farewell and pray their blessings upon him. Choking on his emotions, he nudged his mare into motion again and, waving last goodbyes to all, urged her into a steady trot, disappearing around the first bend in the lane.

In the still, clear, cold of that pale January morning, his family watched him vanish. No one spoke as even the softening sound of hoof beats faded into silence. They had nursed him back to health and were sending him back to the war as well provided for as he could possibly have been. Now they could only pray for him. Perhaps Elisabeth felt an inarticulate dread in the deep recesses of her heart, but none of them could know that they would never see William again. Nor, mercifully, could William know that even if he did survive the war, Bubbling Springs would not be there for his return.

Those soft, golden days, their soldier son, their bountiful farm and beautiful home would live only in the memories of the survivors.

Chapter 7

The End of Bubbling Springs

*"And woe unto them that are with child, and to them who give
suck in those days! But pray that your flight be not in the winter."*
—Matthew 24:19-20

Suspicion of the Hinsons Becomes Terminal

As William made his way back to Virginia, decisions were being
made at Fort Donelson. Guerrilla activity had not diminished with the
passing months, and Jack Hinson was under ever-increasing suspicion.
The killing of his sons was still fresh in the collective memory. His
travels in the area had not gone unnoticed by the occupation force,
and whenever they encountered him, there was something about
those cold, gray eyes that was unsettling. Two soldiers had been killed
on or near his property. Both had been involved in the 1862 death
of his two sons. Although there was no proof that he was involved in
their killing, he was definitely a suspect.

The policy for dealing with guerrillas was clear and understood
by all. The only aspect that wasn't clear was how it should be
applied to the Hinsons. They had been allowed to live, unmolested,
because there was no proof against them and because of the
community's sympathy toward them. On the other hand, Robert's
guerrilla activities before and the fact that his final, fatal skirmish
had occurred only a few miles from Bubbling Springs loomed
ever larger in the deliberations of Colonel Smith. The colonel was
the man who would make the decision concerning their enemy
status, hence the future of the Hinsons.

Also to be considered was the increasing pressure from General
Rosecrans and his staff in St. Louis to do something about the
guerrilla problem, to "exterminate the rascals" and burn them out.
Proof wasn't necessary in the case of supporting families, those aiders
and abettors of the bushwhacking guerrillas. All that was necessary,
in order to punish the relatives and to confiscate or destroy their

property, was to suspect that they were guilty. Colonel Smith had more than enough cause to suspect that Bubbling Springs was, at least, a support facility for guerrilla activity.

Maybe Colonel Smith's tolerance of the Hinsons was further strained because of the weather; it was terrible and growing worse. The freezing winter rain was breaking his telegraph wires. The muddy roads, slick with ice, were becoming virtually impassable. As the storm developed into a blizzard, the ice was followed by snow and high winds. There was no end in sight. At any rate, suspicion of the Hinsons as secessionist troublemakers had become terminal. At Fort Donelson, Colonel Smith made a decision. The Hinsons would no longer be tolerated; they were enemies and would be dealt with as such. They would be dealt with. And it would happen at first light the next day.

Exodus and Inferno: The End of Bubbling Springs

Such things can never be kept secret for long, and loose talk by soldiers quickly spread word of the decision into Dover, where the news flashed across the village with the speed of summer lightening. Jack's friends in Dover saw to it that the news of the decision was carried to Bubbling Springs as quickly as a horse could get there on the icy roads. Before the sun set on that miserable winter day, Jack knew that the soldiers would be coming and not only were his home and property in great danger, but also his family.

His friends urged him to flee immediately; if caught, he was almost certain to be hanged or shot. Jack knew only too well that that was true, but he also knew what Elisabeth and the children faced, and he wouldn't leave them until they were safely on their way to a place of refuge. Decisions were quickly reached and plans made. The family would go west, across the Tennessee River and into the Sulfur Wells community of Henry County, where they would find safe haven with relatives.

Preparations had to be made and fast. Jack quickly gathered the family and explained the situation. Then he assembled the leading men among the servants and explained it to them. He was going to have to leave—that night—and would depend on them to get his family safely across the river and to take care of the farm. Leaving so suddenly would have been a difficult challenge in good weather. The blizzard conditions made it much more difficult and dangerous. To make the desperate situation worse, Jack's two youngest children were extremely ill with measles, a frequently fatal disease in that time.[1]

It was decided that the large farm sled, kept in the equipment shed for those occasions when ice and snow made wagons impractical, would be used. The big sled held more than a farm wagon, and when rigged with side rails, it could hold still more. In addition, the sled would make less noise in case soldiers were near, and it functioned well overland, away from the patrolled roads.[2]

Jack decided what would be taken along and what to do with the items that would have to be left behind. The servants would be trusted to protect the house and furniture as well as they could. Food would be loaded, as much as they had room for, with blankets and pillows, plenty of warm clothes, medicine, money, and some whiskey. They would also load guns and ammunition. Money for the immediate future, plus guns and ammunition, would also be left for the servants. It was difficult to know exactly what to take along, and what to leave behind, and there was precious little time to decide.

The silver table service, pitcher, bowls, and other silver utensils were taken behind the house and buried under a large Maple tree. Large, flat rocks were placed over the spot and snow shoveled onto them. The wind and falling snow soon made the silver's hiding place unrecognizable. Of the servants, only Sarah took part in this and knew where the silver was buried.

The meat in the smokehouse and as much of the fruits and vegetables in the root cellar as could be handled were taken to the servants' cabins and hidden.

Sarah would stay behind to take care of her own family; they would move into the big house and keep it until the white Hinsons could return. Jack placed his leading servant, a wise, dependable man and the eldest, in charge of the other servants and the farm. He would act for Jack while he was gone; the money and the guns would be in his keeping.

Into the Storm

Two of the strongest and most dependable of the young black men would go along, at risk to their lives, to handle the mules, protect the family, and get them all safely to Sulfur Wells. Jack, for their sakes, would only make the first part of the trip with them.

Jack led the way on his saddle mare, with his old slouch hat pulled down over his eyes and a horse pistol in his saddle holster. (Drawing by Joe McCormick)

He would accompany them safely away toward Wynn's Ferry crossing. If the family should be caught by the Union soldiers with Jack present, they would be in even greater danger because of his newly acquired outlaw status.

With two of the best mules hitched to the sled, and two more tied on leads to the back of the sled in case they were needed, the family crawled in and arranged themselves in the loose hay. They and their belongings were covered with quilts and more hay from the barn loft. A tarp was then stretched over the hay and tied down. Viewed from the outside, it was just a load of hay.

After dark, in a driving snow, with weeping farewells, the driver whipped up the team and the sled moved off to the west. Jack led the way on his big saddle mare, with his old slouch hat pulled low over his eyes and a big horse pistol in his saddle holster. As snowflakes mixed with their tears, those staying behind watched the darkness and the swirling snow swallow the sled.

Jack would return, briefly, to gather his rifle and other belongings. He would now be on the run, a hunted outlaw. Elisabeth and their children would never return. Even if they had, there would be nothing there to which they could return. The house with all its furnishings, its comfort, its security, and its memories would be destroyed before another day passed. The springs would continue to run clear and cold, feeding Hinson Creek. The creek, the meadows, and the ridges would remain, timeless, but Bubbling Springs, their home, all that it had meant, as they had known it for so long, would live after this night only in their memories.

Their tragic forced exodus was by no means unique; across the South, thousands of families were driven away and their homes burned. An interesting parallel to the experience of the Hinsons was the treatment of an innocent farmwoman in Virginia. The late Lt. Gen. Lewis B. Puller, USMC, history's most decorated Marine, has told of his widowed grandmother's tragic death at the hands of Union soldiers. Her home was burned, and she was driven away in a snowstorm. Forced to walk ten miles through the snow seeking shelter, she died as a result. The rationale for burning her out? The soldiers found her dead husband's spurs hanging on the wall and declared her guilty of possessing war supplies.[3]

Up in Flames: The End of Bubbling Springs

When the strange caravan was about a mile west of the house, Jack halted the sled to check the rig. As well as he could in the darkness, he checked the harness, the mules, and the sled. He checked on the family and the load since they had traveled far enough for a little bit of a shakedown, made final adjustments, and told them he would see them soon in Sulfur Wells. He turned to the servants for a last reminder that he was depending on them to get the family safely across the river. They assured him that if it could be done, they would do it, and if necessary, they would protect Elisabeth and the children with their lives. Jack knew that they meant it; otherwise, he could not have left them. With a nod from Jack, the mules were urged into motion. The big sled moved on southwestward and disappeared into the snowy darkness. The driver would have only the wind direction and his instincts to guide him in the near-zero visibility, but he was keeping to the valleys and avoiding the road. They were somewhere south of Wynn's Ferry Road, and he could correct his heading when daylight came. By daylight, he would have put many miles between his precious load and Bubbling Springs. That was what mattered most just then. They were well on their way and had neither seen nor heard a sign of anyone or anything else. Even the wild animals were bedded down for the night, weathering the storm. It was time for Jack to leave them.

He turned his big mare back toward home and pulled his soft hat brim down over his left ear to break the cold north wind. That steady north wind, plus his knowledge of the terrain, would guide him on the back trail; the snow and wind had already erased the tracks they had just made. As he headed back, the snow blowing against his face was mixed with silent tears as he allowed his iron will to relax, but it was alright to cry. He was alone, and only God could see his tears.

His big mare moved steadily through the storm, and he was soon easing her down the last slope above Hinson Creek. Reaching the meadow, he crossed the creek and urged her into an easy gallop across the meadow and up the lane to the house.

A Last View of Home

Tying his mare behind the house, he entered through the kitchen door, as he had done so many times in the past, and hurriedly gathered blankets, a large oilcloth, extra clothes, matches, and food. To save precious time, Sarah helped him and gave advice as he moved quickly from place to place. With the blankets rolled and tied inside the oilcloth and other essentials in flour sacks, he went back outside, fastened the blanket roll behind his saddle, and hung the sacks across the mare's flanks with the strings secure between the cantle of the saddle and the blanket roll. It was the last time Jack would ever go out that familiar door. The pleasant and friendly aromas of the kitchen that followed him briefly, before being whisked away southward by the cold wind, would never again brush his nostrils.

His powder, caps and patches, and matches sealed in small fruit jars were in his saddle bags, along with gold and silver coins. His rifle was wrapped in oilcloth he had bought in Dover for that purpose. Jack remounted and turned to wave a last farewell to Sarah standing in the kitchen doorway. With "God keep you," he crossed the yard, climbing the slope east of the house. He paused there, briefly, and looked back at his beautiful, comfortable home. Although the view was only intermittent through the blowing snow, he was struck by how peaceful and secure it looked, with white wood smoke rising from the chimneys. It looked as if it would be there forever, solid and secure. Jack couldn't know it, but his home, which seemed like the essence of permanence, would actually exist for only about twelve more hours.

Again turning away, he topped the small ridge and rode on at an easy trot as the house, barns, and outbuildings disappeared into the snowy darkness behind him. He was traveling, generally, in the opposite direction from his fleeing family so that should he be spotted and reported to the Yankees, he would lead them far away from Elisabeth and the children. As he rode on through the icy darkness toward the Hundred Acre Field, most of the soldiers at Fort Donelson were sleeping.

Again navigating by means of his knowledge of the terrain and the steady north wind, Jack rode southeast through the night. He slept for a few hours at the home of a friend, departing long before any soldiers would be in that part of the county.

Sarah and her family moved into the big house, had supper, and settled in for the night. In the quarters, the rest of the servants did the same. The storm blew with reduced force during the night, with brilliant stars shining through occasional openings in the clouds. Their beauty went unnoticed by the sleeping Hinsons and the sleeping soldiers.

The Heavy Hand of Occupation Justice: On to Bubbling Springs

Reveille roused the soldiers before daylight; they mustered for morning formation, washed, ate breakfast, and prepared for the new day's duties. One patrol, ordered to leave the fort at first light, was headed for Bubbling Springs on serious business. They were being sent to deal with the Hinsons, once and for all. They would arrest Jack Hinson and such members of his family as the lieutenant deemed appropriate, and then burn them out. Because of Jack's prominence and connections, they were not to shoot him on the spot. They were to bring him to the fort, and then shoot him.

The patrol passed out through Donelson's gate, rode into Dover, and turned south past the courthouse square. The Hinson's sympathetic friends in town watched them ride through town and prayed that Jack and his family were safely away. The soldiers rode out Dover-Paris Landing Road at a slow, deliberate pace. The sun was just rising above the river bluffs to the southeast, and the icy footing was treacherous for the horses. So, believing that the Hinsons knew nothing of his intentions, the lieutenant took his careful time. The storm had not fully passed, and, at times, the snow was so thick that he couldn't see the road. He had to feel his way along, staying within the banks of the road cut and trying to stay out of the ditches on either side.

The patrol had the road to itself as it slowly clopped and clanked its way toward Bubbling Springs, with the horses bobbing their heads and snorting and the soldiers hunched against the wind, trying to find a way to stay warm in the saddle. As pale winter sunlight began to appear above the surrounding hills and touch the roadway through breaks in the clouds, they reached the junction with Hinson Hollow and turned southward past the Rougement home into Jack's lane. As they neared, the servants heard them first. One boy ran to warn Sarah at the big house, and the others shut themselves in their cabins and prayed.

The soldiers were at the gate as the boy again ran, unseen beyond the barns, back to his house. Preoccupied with their own discomfort and the blowing snow, the soldiers had seen no one. The lieutenant dismounted, rubbed his cold, gloved hands together, and shivered as he approached the front door. As he mounted the steps to the wide porch, he pulled off his right glove and drew and cocked his pistol. The patrol surrounded the house, carbines at the ready. The dogs barked wildly but kept their distance; the soldiers were almost as unsure of what was about to take place as were the dogs, but they were prepared for action.

Knocking loudly on the front door, the lieutenant demanded that the Hinsons open it. As Sarah opened the door, he announced roughly that he wanted Jack Hinson. and he wanted him immediately. Sarah, not at all intimidated by his manner, the pistol, or the soldiers with their carbines, informed him that Mr. Hinson was gone, and she didn't know where he was, which was the truth. When asked when he was to return she, again speaking the truth, said that she didn't know. The lieutenant, becoming irritated, demanded then to see Mrs. Hinson. Sarah, with an air of cool regality, gave him the same answers as before. Becoming hostile, the lieutenant announced he was going to search the house. Sarah, her considerable bulk filling the doorway, looked upon him with disapproving hauteur, as if she were weighing the matter in her mind. Then she stood back and told him he could search all he wanted, but he wouldn't find the Hinsons in the house. As an afterthought, she told him to hurry in and close the door for the cold wind was blowing into the house.

The lieutenant called over his shoulder for three men to come in to help him with the search; he ordered his sergeant to remain in place with the others and to shoot anyone who tried to escape. Sarah, still unimpressed with the lieutenant's authority, told him not to let his soldiers shoot toward the servants' quarters for all of her people were there, staying indoors. After that, she maintained an aloof silence, her manner dripping with disdain.

The four soldiers searched the house, overturning furniture, dumping trunks and chests, pulling out and throwing drawers on the floor, demanding to know what was in each room as it was reached. It didn't take them long to begin to see that Sarah and her children were alone in the house. They could not find anything incriminating, and this growing realization frustrated and angered them.

Returning to the front porch, the lieutenant ordered the

soldiers to search all outbuildings. This process was quick until they reached the hayloft, which they searched with pitchfork thrusts until satisfied that there were no Hinsons hiding in the hay. Finding no one in the outbuildings, the lieutenant ordered the soldiers to search the slave cabins and to shoot anyone who tried to run away. This search was done easily and quickly, producing only wailing from the terrified children and weeping pleas from their mothers to do their families no harm. The soldiers found many black Hinsons in the cabins but not a single white one.

Realizing that their expedition was going to be fruitless, and with curses for all within earshot, the soldiers reassembled at the big house, cold and frustrated, to render their negative reports. The lieutenant conceded that they would find no rebel bushwhackers there that day, but he said they would do the next best thing. They would burn them out.

Sarah, who had been watching and listening, wrapped in a bed quilt the soldiers had earlier thrown on the floor, stepped out among them and addressed them all, her manner now earnest and conciliatory. She announced that the white Hinsons were all gone and were not going to come back, not ever. She told them the big house was now hers—she and her family were going to live there. She had done the soldiers no harm; in fact, she reminded them, they were supposed to be there to protect her and all the other servants. She said that she could repair the damage they had done to the house and clean up the mess they had made, asking only that they please leave her and her people in peace. They were all free, not slaves anymore. They had been legally freed the summer before and could show them the papers. She told them they were going to have to find a way to live without their former masters.

Her valid and reasoned appeal fell on deaf ears. The lieutenant, unmoved, sent his sergeant to find the coal oil in the kitchen.

Inferno: The End of Bubbling Springs

Seeing that this was not just a bluff, Sarah begged them not to burn the house. It was now her home, she cried out, over and over, and she could show them her freedom papers. Her pleas and protests were carried away by the wind, without effect, as the blue-clad soldiers scattered to kindle fires. The house, and all that was in it, was going to burn.

Realizing that she could not stop the soldiers, she thought frantically of what she might be able to save from the flames. Running into the house, she hurried from room to room, her mind in a swirl, trying to think. She grabbed as many blankets, quilts, and pillows as she could carry and ran out into the yard. Aware of her impotence alone, she rushed through the snow toward the slave cabins, shouting for the others to come and help her. Many of them were afraid to come outside, fearing those hostile white soldiers, but as fires were already being kindled on all sides, accelerated by the burning coal oil, she took the bold ones who answered her cry and rushed back toward the house. Sarah and the others ran wildly through the house, looking for valuable things they could carry out, trying to establish priorities as they ran. As they rushed to save the flour, sugar, salt, and meal from the kitchen, the stove was already ablaze with the coal oil that had been sloshed over it. There wasn't much time left; the kitchen was beginning to burn.

As they ran through the house, dragging out what they could and throwing it into the snow-covered yard, the soldiers, strangely, did not hinder them. Rather, they seemed to enjoy the scene, amused at the desperation they were creating and its futility.

With the curtains blazing upward, igniting wallpaper and paint, Sarah screamed for all her people to get out of the house. The fire gathered strength, rising and roaring, feeding on its own fury. As the heat within began to break the windows, flames roared through them and began to reach up the clapboard siding, licking it into flame. The heat from the blazing house began to melt the snow around it in the yard, and the servants rushed about, snatching up the things they had rescued from the fire and thrown out of doors and windows. Clutching their treasures awkwardly, they backed slowly away from the growing fury of the fire, shocked, breathless, and still struggling with disbelief. Surely, something still cried out within them, this could not be real—it must be a terrible dream, a nightmare. With their eyes transfixed by the growing inferno before them, they began to moan and wail, wordlessly, as they backed slowly into the surrounding snow, unable to take their eyes from the roaring nightmare before them.

Sarah, strong and tall, stood in the front yard, backing slowly toward the front gate, taking it all in and silently calling down on those Yankees every wretched curse she could remember from her distant African ancestry. This was her home; it had been her home in a very special way since the day she had grown old enough to proudly help in the Hinson kitchen, long before she had become its mistress and overseer of the household servants. The night before, she had begun to move in, actually to live there with her family, until the white Hinsons could someday return. Now she was watching it be consumed by the rising crescendo of the flames. She was seeing, in those flames, all the years, happy, warm times. She also saw in those flames the sad times. She saw the Christmases, the Thanksgivings, the Fourth of July celebrations, weddings, spring times, summers, and autumns, with all the living, birthing, and laughter. She remembered the sadness and the pain, watching the boys go out early to hunt and seeing their heads returned by the soldiers. She stood, imposing, strong and silent, watching, remembering, and weeping within, but she would never allow those Yankee foreigners to see her cry. Never!

The soldiers, themselves somewhat awed by the magnitude of what they had done, were also backing slowly into the snow, watching the growing inferno and giving little thought to the absent Hinsons, or the circle of weeping servants with their pathetic treasures.

Suddenly, smoke hissed from an opening where a chimney met the roof, the crack widened, and in an explosion of sparks, the fire erupted through the roof. The flames consumed the wooden shingles as if in a feeding frenzy. As rafters burned, cracked, and popped, the roof, some of it still intact, sagged, groaned, and collapsed into the flames with a deafening roar. The walls seemed to implode, melting, collapsing into the center of the inferno with thunderclaps of exploding sparks, sending burning firebrands flying in all directions into the yard. Both soldiers and victims involuntarily jumped backward and ran for a few steps, farther away from the fire, avoiding the incendiary missiles. The fearful sight was overwhelming, hypnotic, an irresistible thing that had sprung into existence before their eyes. It had taken on a life of its own and now seemed to grip them all with its primal power.

As time seemed to stand still, the thing before them roared

skyward. From time to time, unknown objects within what was left of the house exploded, sending new showers of sparks in all directions. As they watched, transfixed, the flaming, exploding mass finally reached its peak and began slowly to subside into an angry, red-white mass of intense, hissing heat. Leaping tongues of flame erupted randomly all over its white-hot surface and shot skyward in curls of white, yellow, red, green, and blue, fascinating the stunned onlookers. It was the nearest thing to hell that any of them had ever seen.

A dense snow shower came swirling out of the clouds, with the snow melting into raindrops in the rising heat, above what had been the house, and vaporizing as they touched the coals without effect, as if they had never existed.

The two stark, blackened chimneys stood, looking awkwardly down upon it all, with its four fireplace openings like absurd, blackened, gaping mouths. From time to time, shards were blown from chimney stones like shrapnel as their surfaces exploded in the blast furnace heat.

The lieutenant, still somewhat subdued by the awesomeness of what he had just seen and done, said it was time for the barns. The sergeant, himself somewhat distracted, began to assemble the men.

Next, the Barns

"Burn the barns?" Sarah thought, "No—they mustn't burn the barns, for her people would need them; they would need them to go on living there." There, at Bubbling Springs, was where they had to stay; it was their home. It was all they had, all they had ever known, and they had no place to go.

Some of the women standing by ran to their own cabins to call their husbands. Sarah told the rest to do the same thing. They would all have to gather; they had to make the soldiers see that they needed the barns and outbuildings; they had destroyed too much already.

As the soldiers were organizing for the burning of the barns, the servants gathered around them, their numbers growing until all the black Hinsons, except for the smallest children, were there in the snow, looking at them silently with beseeching eyes. Many were weeping. The white-haired ruling elder spoke for them all, his old hat clutched in his hands, saying that to burn the barns would not hurt Jack Hinson for he would never return. It would only hurt them; they needed the barns in order to live. One by one, the slaves pleaded for the barns and sheds to be spared. They said that the white Hinsons couldn't ever come back anyway, and now they would have to fend for themselves. They could take care of themselves if left alone but not without the barns.

Some of the soldiers wanted to hurry up and set the barns ablaze so they could start back to the fort. The sergeant stood ready to obey whatever the lieutenant commanded. He told the men to shut up and stand at ease.

The "Contraband" Problem and Shameful Neglect of Wounded Black Soldiers

As the lieutenant stood in the snow, all eyes upon him, he looked at the earnest black faces before him, then at the barns, then back over his shoulder at the blazing remains of the house. More and more of the women began to weep, and some began to wail, swaying back and forth in the blowing snow. The children, who understood only that there was big trouble with these white soldiers, cried with deeply felt distress and unfocused fears. Some of the men, with tears spilling down their faces, fell to their knees, pleading for mercy and invoking the name of "Mistah Linkum." As tensions approached critical mass, the snow continued to swirl about the strange, agonized gathering, the cold wind rising, whipping garments and the bed covers in which the women wrapped themselves. The soldiers stood, silently, waiting for a command. The lieutenant, like a solitary statue in the blowing snow, stood, looking at the rest, silent, intense, trying to think. With the sun occasionally breaking through the swirling snow, he moved only to turn his head side to side, surveying the scene and thinking. He was aware of the ongoing problem with the "contraband," the large numbers of unwanted, homeless, bewildered blacks arriving at the fort from all directions, expecting to be cared for. Even the Union generals had found no solution for the problem, and many resented them as human (if not subhuman) debris. The "contraband" problem never went away. The week of September 1, 1864, the Fort Donelson provost marshal reported eight civilian prisoners in custody and "412 negroes in camp, 350 without skills or assignments, 13 [serving as] officers' servants."

In one of the most shameful aspects of that war, even the wounded black soldiers could not be given adequate medical care there for they were not permitted in the army hospital with white soldiers. As the post surgeon at Fort Donelson put it, in a request on October 12, 1864, to move them to Paducah, "We have no Contraband [or Col] Hospital to take care of them."[4]

With all that innocent human misery before him, with the morning wind rising and making the cold worse, he made a decision: if these people could take care of themselves, let them do it.

"Mount up," he said quietly.

The soldiers, cold and no longer zealous for more burning or anything else out in that wind, were stirred with thoughts of warmth and hot coffee back at Fort Donelson. They moved silently toward their horses. At first, only Sarah understood what was happening. Then, one after another, the others realized that the barns had been spared and began to thank the soldiers. Falling on their knees, many cried out to God with prayers of thanksgiving. Some, not yet understanding, continued to weep and wail. Fathers stood, wiping tears from their faces. Some of them started back toward their cabins, arms around their wives and children. Slowly, the comprehension spread through the crowd that the ordeal was over. Very slowly, still subdued by the trauma, they all began, by ones, twos, and threes, to move quietly back toward their own cabins. Behind them the ruins of the big house were hissing, crackling, and popping in their death rattle.

The main house was gone. Their masters were gone. Life as they had always known it had come to a sudden, violent, and painful end, and they would have to work out their future. But, at that moment, they needed to calm the children and try to help them to understand.

They would work out the future later.

Into the Wilderness

As Elisabeth, the children, and their protectors made their way westward to Sulfur Wells, and as Jack circled around to the southeast, none of them had any idea of what was to happen to their home. On the sled, minds were occupied with thoughts of getting safely away, staying warm, the critical sickness of the two small children with measles, and of the uncertain future they all faced.

Jack's mind was occupied with the necessity of moving unseen and with finding his friend's home in the snowy darkness. The cold north wind drove at his back and whipped his mare's long tail against his legs. He worried about Elisabeth and the children and wished he could have gone with them all the way. He knew and trusted the men into whose strong hands he had placed them, but it is an exceptional man who feels that his loved ones are as safe with someone else as they would be with him. With that option not open to him, with his collar turned up against the wind and his old black slouch hat pulled down tightly on his head, he rode on through the swirling gray whiteness that seemed to fill the world. Easing his big mare along in the deepening snow, there was almost complete silence around him, broken only by the soft thudding of her hooves, her occasional snorting, and the whipping of the wind in the bare trees. As he rode along, he gave some thought to his immediate future on the run as a hunted outlaw. He worried about his family, both white and black, and he prayed.

He was going to have to adjust quickly to an entirely new and extremely difficult way of living. In a matter of just a few hours on that snowy night, the control of the safety and welfare of his family, and his own, had slipped largely out of his own work-hardened hands and into the hands of God. Only God knew how long it would last and how it would end.

Before daylight, rested and warmed after a few hours sleep at the home of a friend, and with a hot breakfast of sausage, biscuits, and gravy, Jack mounted his mare and turned her head southwest toward the area of Danville Crossing. He was well out of sight of the house before sunrise and was glad that his approaching tracks had been buried by the snow that had fallen overnight. The tracks he was making as he departed were already being erased by the snow that continued to fall. To bring down the wrath of the occupation force upon his friends would be poor thanks indeed for protecting and feeding him, and to avoid bringing such trouble upon friends would be a guiding principle in his actions for the rest of the war.

As he rode on to the southwest, the wind shifted, blowing first from one direction, then from another as the front passed over. The snow became intermittent, and the overcast began to thin. Although the pale sun did not yet reach the gray-brown forest to warm him, its morning twilight was growing in the southeast and that brightened his spirits. As he rode, deliberately and easily, through the pale early morning, tension slowly began to leave him. A comforting assurance grew within him that, at least for now, things were going to work out. He was deeply troubled about the condition of the two sick children, but everything else seemed to be alright. He knew they would get the best of care once they were safely with family at Sulfur Wells. Mercifully, he could not know, as he rode on through the snow, that his home was burning.

At Bubbling Springs: The First Day of a New Life

Back at Bubbling Springs, the black Hinsons welcomed the clearing weather. It would make facing the aftermath of the horror much easier; somehow, sunny weather, even with cold air and snow on the ground, makes painful things a little easier to bear.

After a delayed and troubled breakfast, they moved quite naturally, singly out of their warm cabins and up toward what remained of the big house. It lay there, still burning, curls of smoke climbing indifferently into the intermittent, cold sunlight, watched over by the blackened chimneys, so tall, gaunt, and looking strangely naked.

As the people gathered, they coalesced slowly into a group as if drawn by an unspoken desire for mutual comfort and support. They stood mute, looking upon the dying remains of a structure they had always held in awe, thinking it would last forever. The only sounds were the sporadic cracking, popping, and hissing from the deep bed of embers, and the sighing of the breeze. They needed no leader to tell them to be silent; they were all innately subdued by the sobering magnitude and finality of what they beheld as if they were standing before the open grave of a slain loved one.

With the rising sun warming the scene, Sarah spoke softly, almost reverently, and said they should all look over the yard to recover any rescued items dropped or overlooked in their haste. They spread out and walked over the yard, looking down into the snow for Hinson possessions. The things they picked up were taken to the tobacco barn, now emptied of its crop and containing only the sad accumulation of the other household effects rescued from the fire. As the day warmed, it would be necessary to sort it all, wash the items that had been soiled and store them properly in barrels to await Jack and Elisabeth's return. This job would be done by the house servants, under Sarah's watchful eye. All of this was going to require a lot of adjustment, in their lives and in their thinking.

On, Toward Danville Crossing

As the servants began to bring order to the chaos at Bubbling Springs, Jack rode steadily toward the southwest as the overcast began to break up. The sun climbed above the bare trees and its spreading light, reflected from the snow, made the morning brilliant and caused the forest to sparkle.

As he rode carefully and deliberately along, he had much to contemplate: his family was across the Tennessee River in Sulfur Wells, his entire farm and its related business ventures were now in the hands of his servants, and he had just become a wanted man, a fugitive from brutal wartime justice. His first consideration was to avoid being captured—or even seen—by Yankee soldiers, but he must also conceive a plan, he must think ahead—at least for the immediate future. For now, he needed to find a place to stay, a shelter where he could survive the weather and would be relatively safe from Union patrols. The Danville Crossing area, from Leatherwood Creek southward to White Oak Creek and Magnolia, was familiar to him, heavily wooded, and the people in the area were strongly pro-Confederate. Robert's guerrilla band still operated there, with strong local support and relative freedom of movement. Jack had friends and relatives in that area, and there, at the mouth of Hurricane Creek, was a high ridge and its bluff, overlooking the river. He had visited the bluff before, and it had remained high on his mental list of vantage points. With its caves, the bluff could provide ready-made shelter.

Two miles south of that bluff, at the mouth of Cane Creek and in the center of this hospitable area, was Danville Crossing. Danville Crossing had its origins in 1860, when engineers, foremen, Irish laborers, black slaves, and materials had been brought there for the construction of the railroad bridge across the Tennessee River. Although in future years Danville would become an important town, in 1863 it hardly qualified as a village. A cluster of families lived around the landing, brought there by the operation of the bridge, the steamboat landing, and the brick hotel. The nearest post office was across the river in Benton County; the next nearest was seven

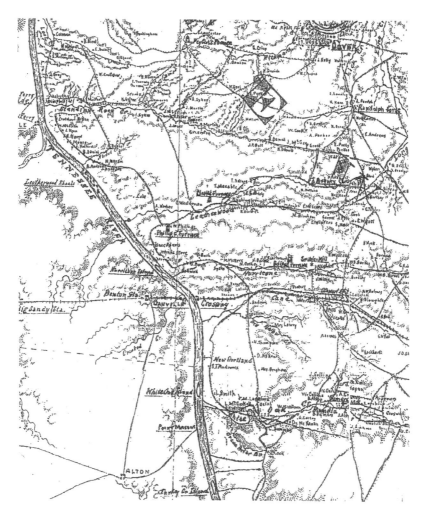

Southwestern Stewart County and adjacent Benton and Henry Counties, portion, from map of middle Tennessee, Department of the Cumberland, 1865. (Courtesy the U.S. National Archives and Records Administration)

miles to the southeast at Magnolia. At the time of the occupation by Federal troops two years earlier, all local food supplies had been confiscated by them, and the one general store, operated by S. W. Kelley, had been forced to close. There survives in the memory of one of the oldest living residents, whose grandparents operated the railroad commissary at the crossing, the story of one courageous man who risked his life to take cornmeal to the women, children, and elderly who were still living there, their own food having been seized by the Union soldiers.[5]

The two-story Outlaw Hotel, opulent by the standards of the time and area, was a strange contradiction to its wilderness setting. It stood there, an unlikely anomaly, fine, solid, and stately, with its solid-brick walls, its high windows, and its broad veranda overlooking the railroad and its small telegraph station. Built as an investment by Seth Outlaw in 1860 to house bridge personnel and transients from the river boats, trains, and stagecoaches, it had become a hospital. Ever since the first Confederate soldiers had arrived there in January of 1862 to defend the river landing and the bridge, the hotel had been used as a hospital for soldiers—briefly by the Confederates and subsequently by the Federals. Although no major battles were fought there and ongoing skirmishes in the area produced relatively few battlefield casualties, there were at all times many casualties to disease, which caused three times as many deaths during the war as did actual combat. It had the appearance of a building that had been constructed for a large town but had been set down in the wilderness by mistake. In 1861, an officer of the first Confederate unit assigned there described the crossing as a fine hotel surrounded by mud.[6]

Of interest to Jack was that, with its small garrison of Union soldiers from Fort Donelson and its telegraph terminal, Danville Crossing was a major source of news and information. People in the Danville area were generally better informed about current events than were others anywhere else in the county outside Dover, and Jack would need a source of information.

As he rode steadily on, his plan for the immediate future began to take form. He would stay north of Danville Crossing, cross the Dividing Ridge to the headwaters of Hurricane Creek, and follow it downstream to the bluff.

A Home in the Wilderness

A plan for the immediate future became clear. For the time being, the area from Leatherwood Creek southward to Humphreys County would be his home area, and the big ridge overlooking Hurricane Island would be his fox's den. To stay with relatives or friends, even in one of their barns, would place them in too much danger. For now, he would make himself as comfortable as possible high up on the bluff. In time, he would develop a system of scattered refuges throughout the area where he could hide briefly when necessary; his immediate future, however, seemed to be tied to that high ridge and its commanding bluff.

In the late afternoon, he rode into the widening valley along Hurricane Creek. The creek slowed and grew wider as it flowed toward its mouth at the river, and even in the chilly air, he caught the smell unique to rivers and large creeks. When the weather warmed, that earthy, aquatic aroma would fill the hollow. Nevertheless, on that chilly afternoon, it was there, unmistakable. He would have known he was riding near a big creek, even had he been blindfolded.

As Jack progressed downstream, avoiding houses, he smelled wood smoke, which the west wind was sweeping up the hollow. He liked the smell of wood smoke in cold weather; it spoke to him with wordless whispers of comfort and security. The aroma would have been more pleasant had it been coming from his own chimneys or from the home of a friend, but it was comforting still, in a primal way.

Nearing the mouth of the creek, he turned up to his right, before the ridge became too steep for his mare to climb. Following streambeds, he made his way to the top of the ridge. It was narrow at the top and densely wooded. He carefully made his way westward to the edge of the bluff. He dismounted, tied his mare, unpacked his gear, and looked the place over.

With little daylight remaining in the short winter day, he made his way down the steep front of the bluff to a small cave, built a fire, and arranged his essential possessions. He knew that there was a much larger cave near the bottom of the bluff, but it was easily accessible from the valley below and was visible from the river road and the river itself. It could provide shelter but neither concealment nor safety. The upper cave would be his place for the present.

Climbing back to the top he walked his mare down the ridge to the nearest pocket of rainwater and snowmelt, watered her, filled his cooking pan, and walked her back to the bluff. He brushed her, loosened the cinch, leaving the saddle and blanket on her, fed her, and left her for the night.

The upper cave was inconvenient. There was a steep climb down from the bluff, with only a small, fairly level surface in front of it before the hill dropped off steeply again, but it was otherwise perfect. The opening was narrow and low, requiring crawling to enter, but from only a small distance away, it was virtually invisible in its rocky setting. Inside, it immediately widened into a nice room. In the rock floor across the back wall of the room was a ledge, a step up about four inches above the floor and relatively flat. It ran north-south, crossing the "T" of the length of the room, and would become his bed. A fire built just inside the entrance would vent most of the smoke through the entrance, except in a west wind; would keep all wild animals out while he slept; and warm the cave comfortably. Even without a fire, the subterranean rock from which nature had built the small shelter would keep the temperature at the back of the room entirely survivable at about sixty degrees. It was ideal, almost as if it had been made for him. From the outside, one making the difficult climb up the face of the bluff would hardly notice the entrance, and even if noticed, a stranger would have to crawl inside to see what it was.[7]

At the End of the First Day

Late on that long day, with Elisabeth and the children safely across the Tennessee River with relatives at Sulfur Wells, the two black Hinson men turned around and headed back toward their homes at Bubbling Springs, unaware of the horror, the challenges, and the adjustments awaiting them there. Under clearing skies, the subsiding wind turned and blew from the west as they drove the mules at an easy pace over the snow. Rested, warmed, and fed, they pushed eastward toward the river and waited for the ferry. Going back, with only hay on the sled, they could take the road.

Behind them, Elisabeth and the children began to adjust to their new life at Sulfur Wells. Of immediate concern to Elisabeth

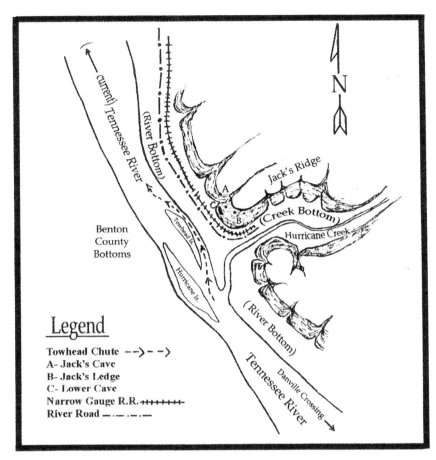

Jack's ridge and vicinity, 1861-1865

were the two sick children, who seemed to be weakening in spite of receiving the best medical care available there.

On the bluff, Jack watched the Tennessee River running bank full below him as the sun in its low orbit sank into the valley of the Big Sandy River, in Benton County to the west. He could see miles of the river and its valley from there, yet from the valley, he was invisible. With his fire stoked and with that thought triggering others in his weary mind, he reclined on the rock ledge to sleep.

He slept restlessly that first night on the stone floor of the cave and woke cold, stiff, and aching to the raucous cries of crows. He thought of the contrast between that and waking in his warm bed at Bubbling Springs to the morning call of Hinson roosters and the inviting aromas of boiling coffee and frying bacon rising pleasantly from Sarah's warm kitchen. In his cave, there was no Sarah, no breakfast, no pleasant aromas, and no coffee.

Eventually, he would adjust to sleeping on the cold ground, and in time, he would make his wilderness shelter much more comfortable, but he would never be able to rest well until he knew that Elisabeth and the children were safe in Sulfur Wells. On that first morning in the snowy forest, he had no means of communicating with them.

Building up his fire, he warmed himself as well as he could and set water to boil for coffee. While the coffee water heated, he fed his mare and rubbed her legs, enhancing circulation in them and in his cold hands. With the water brought to a full rolling boil, he added the coffee, removed the water from the fire, and watched it for a few minutes, enjoying the aroma. Anxious for a sip, he dipped out a little, set the cup aside, and commenced to prepare his breakfast. As the steaming tin cup cooled, he sliced bacon off with his knife, laid it in the small skillet, and set the skillet on the fire. Sipping his coffee warmed and comforted him, and he pondered his immediate future as the bacon began to sizzle, filling his cave with its singular perfume.

Jack tried to think about plans for the future, but his mind kept returning to the questions for which he had no answers. Did Elisabeth and the children make it safely across the river to Sulfur Wells? How were the two ill children? Did his servants make it back to Bubbling Springs without being harmed by thieves, or being seized with their mules, sled, and hay by Union soldiers? This "pressing" of slaves, livestock, wagons, and feed was a common practice, and they were usually never heard from again. He would have given a lot to be able to speak with Elisabeth and with his head man at home.

After he finished his simple breakfast, he had a last cup of coffee, smoked his pipe, and cleaned his skillet as well as he could with snow and leaf mulch. On the ridge top, the sun was up, and he looked down on the river and its wide valley, mostly still in shadow. He could see for miles upstream, past Danville Bridge all the way to White Oak Island. Downstream he could see past the mouth of Leatherwood Creek. The day was beginning clear and relatively still. A hawk was circling slowly, rising on the warming

"C. S. Hinson 1863" was carved into the "name" rock on Jack's ridge. (Courtesy Joe McCormick)

air over the river without a sound, looking for *his* breakfast. Jack felt a certain kinship with that hawk.

Evaluating the Terrain

Jack spent the morning checking out the western end of the ridge and its approaches from below and locating the best water sources near the bluff. To the west, below the bluff, the hill was so steep as to challenge a mountain goat; it would be impossible for a horse to climb. Even dismounted soldiers, in order to get up to the bluff, would have to crawl at times, pulling themselves up from tree to tree. If they should attempt to attack the bluff by climbing that hillside, their progress would be so slow that he would have plenty of time to get away to the east, or to shoot them, long before they could reach the top.

At the foot of the bluff, a small wagon road ran along the river bank, paralleled by a narrow-gauge railroad track built to haul iron ore and cast iron "pigs" between ore deposits, the furnaces, and the railroad at Danville Crossing. Branches of the wagon road turned up Leatherwood Creek to the north and up Hurricane Creek to the south as did the narrow-gauge tracks. He would avoid the river bottom at the foot of the ridge, at least in daylight. For down there, he would be visible from river traffic, at risk of encountering Union patrols on the river road, and the home of Isaac Adams was facing the road. No, that would be too dangerous, and he could see all of that from his vantage points on the bluff without being seen.

At the south side of the narrow bluff, about twenty feet down its steep face, there was a vertical, smooth wall of soft limestone, with a narrow, level ledge at its base. He climbed down to it and stood, looking at the hundreds of names and dates carved into it, some put there in the previous century. That of his son Charles was large and conspicuous: "C. S. HINSON 1863." Charles had done the carving the summer before, while waiting for his father, on one of his scouting trips to the area. He smiled, noting that although Charles had carved the letters carefully and in rather elegant, classic style, he had reversed the letter "S" both times. He had been only nine at the time, and there had been little school for him since the coming of the war, two years before that.

Just below the wall with its many carved names and dates, there was a horizontal stone ledge large enough for a man and his weapon and surrounded by small trees. The ledge provided a perfect overview of the river, and the surrounding small trees and bushes made it virtually invisible from below. That ledge would become Jack's favorite firing point.[8]

The ridge, with its steep bluff, was not only an ideal place for observation and for firing on the river traffic, but it also constituted a natural fortress for Jack. The steep, rugged slopes made it unassailable on three sides. Except by expert woodsmen, he could not be attacked effectively from those directions, and those trail-bound Yankee cavalrymen were not expert woodsmen. Even the one avenue of approach open to attackers, along the ridge from the east, would not be easy. The ridge was narrow, rough, densely wooded, and there was a healthy population of copperheads and rattlesnakes on the ridge and its slopes, enough of them that they alone would give most pursuers pause.

There were other effective and relatively safe places should he wish to continue making his one-man strikes against the enemy, and in time, he would use them, on both sides of the Dividing Ridge, from Trigg County, Kentucky, to the north all the way south to the Waverly area. He would also operate across the river, in Henry and Benton Counties and in Calloway and Marshall Counties in Kentucky, but for now, he just needed a safe place to hole up, and this bluff seemed perfect—as if it had been made for him. With a steady stream of troops and supplies flowing up and down the river, there would be no end to the opportunities if he later chose to attack them. For the immediate future, it was an adequate shelter, and he was almost completely safe.

In the afternoon, he worked at improving his living conditions, beginning with his "mattress." Pine and cedar branches piled on the rock of the cave floor would at least keep his back an inch or two above the rock. It wasn't luxury, but it was an improvement over bare rock. When the snow melted, he could pile leaf mulch on top of the pine and cedar, and begin to create a real sleeping surface.

With that done, he set out on his mare to scout the ridge and its various approaches. He needed to know the ways that he could get up onto the ridge, and down into the valleys on each side; equally important was to learn the approaches that Union soldiers would be able to use if they chose to pursue or attack him from the creeks below.

Riding down into the Hurricane Creek bottom, he turned east. Slowly and methodically, he progressed upstream, avoiding Eclipse Furnace and the homes along the creek, until the slopes became so gradual that they could be ascended easily, almost anywhere. Then he crossed over the ridge and repeated the process, downstream, along Leatherwood Creek, in the perpetual winter shadow of the ridge. Nearing the mouth of the creek, he turned around and made the climb back up to his bluff. It had been a long, hard ride for his mare, but he now knew much more about his citadel above the river.[9]

Back at the bluff, he tied her to a sapling, let her blow, fed her a little grain, and walked around the narrow ridge looking down the slopes and thinking. It had been more than two days now since he had seen his family off toward Henry County. Just before dark,

he would take one of the easier trails he had found down into
Hurricane Creek bottom to visit a friend. Maybe there would be
some news.

The News Is Bad—Very Bad

As evening twilight began to yield to the invading darkness, he
mounted, headed eastward down the ridge, turned down to the
creek, and followed it to the farm home of a friend to inquire.
By way of the telegraph terminal, the news had reached Danville
Crossing; from there, by the conduit of talkative, boasting soldiers,
it had reached the people around the landing. Then, the grapevine,
that invisible telegraph, had flashed news of the tragedy at Bubbling
Springs through hills and hollows like sheet lightning, and everyone
in the area knew that the Hinsons had been branded enemies, were
on the run, and had been burned out the day after they left. Jack
was a wanted man with a price on his head.

Jack took the news silently, with his customary restraint, thanked
his friend, and asked leave to take a walk. Outside, he walked
toward the creek, trying to take in the awful news. He couldn't
imagine his house—his beautiful home—gone. He wondered if any
of the servants had died in the fire. Or had they been lynched by
the soldiers? Had their houses been burned also? Were the barns
gone? What would become of the servants? How could they live?
What kind of barbarians would do this to people who had done
them no harm? And do it to women and children? Maybe in their
Yankee eyes he had it coming himself, but not his wife and children,
and not the servants. They had harmed no one.

Now there was a price on his head. Was there also a price on
the heads of his wife and children? What was to become of them?
These questions swirled in his mind without the satisfaction of
theories to answer them.

He hadn't wanted it this way—he had never wanted the war
in the first place, but now, since they wanted war, then war it
would be—all-out war—and he would take down as many of
those foreign invaders as he could. He walked along the creek
with a swirl of rising emotions threatening to choke him. He
could not yet think through the future; however, it seemed that if
it was to be all-out war, for the present, he was in the right place.
He thanked his friend and promised to avoid diligently doing

anything that might make trouble for him. With his newfound burden of bad news, he made his way up the slope to the bluff.

He slept little that night and woke with the same troubling thoughts that had filled his night.

Chapter 8

All-Out War

"He . . . rechecked his sight picture, and touched the trigger. Before the sound of the exploding powder reached the boat, the large, spinning lead projectile struck the captain in the left center of his chest."

Alone at the Top of the World

The morning dawned gray and cold, and Jack was already awake, stiff and sore, with his bones again complaining about his mattress of limestone, pine, and cedar branches. From the smoldering coals of his fire, deep in the ashes, he kindled it anew and soon had it crackling with welcome warmth. As he stretched, his thoughts focused on improving his sleeping arrangements. The forest leaf mulch was wet, but he could bring some into his cave and let it dry during the day, a little at a time. Each time he added padding between himself and the rock floor, it was an improvement, but he had a long way to go. Finding or making a real mattress of corn shucks or straw was fast becoming a priority.

With water heating for coffee, he turned his attention to his mare. She was also cold and stiff from the long night but not so much as he. She was young, in good flesh, her hide and hair were thick, and she was accustomed to it. Jack was not a novice at sleeping outdoors, but it would require some adjusting, and he was no longer young. In his fifty-seventh year, he was, by the standards of the day, an old man. He rubbed and brushed her down, which helped to warm and loosen her, and again helped to warm and loosen him. One starts slowly after a cold night in the wilderness, but each motion makes the next one easier. Beginning to feel a little better himself, he fed her and then took a look around. "Feed your stock before you feed yourself" is the rule in the country, "and that way you will never forget to feed your stock." This valid rule was as old as human history, and Jack thought it was pleasing to God for he charges us with responsibility for the welfare of our animals. In his uncertain future, it was particularly important; his life might well depend on his mare and her condition.

The sky was clear, the wind was still, and the air promised a slight warming. There would probably be considerable melting of the snow, more leaf mulch would be exposed, and the freshets on the hillsides would be running with clear, cold water. Below him, the river ran full and swift beneath a blanket of rising mist, which told him that the water was warmer than the air above it. From somewhere across the river a rooster crowed, and the sound, with nothing to impede or muffle it, carried directly to his ear as if it were there with him on his bluff. Feeling alone in the world and, in a way, on top of it and free of any immediate danger, he turned, without further thought of weightier matters, to the preparation of his breakfast.

With the coffee boiling and set in the ashes at the edge of the fire, he put bacon on to fry and dipped out half a cup of steaming coffee. The tin cup was hot enough to blister his lips so he set it on the stone floor to cool while he turned the thick bacon in the skillet and decided to make some cornbread. The pleasant aroma of the coffee alone was almost enough to justify its existence on such a morning, and he inhaled it as the steam rose from the surface, taking careful hot sips. That coffee was something to thank God for on such a morning, and he did.

While the bacon fried, making its own grease, Jack mixed cornmeal, water, and salt on his tin plate and molded it all into a ball. With the bacon removed from the skillet and onto his tin plate, he pressed the ball of wet cornbread dough into the skillet, as it erupted in hundreds of tiny explosions, reacting with the hot grease. He mashed the ball down into a thick, round pone and listened with satisfaction as it crackled, popped, and spit. He cooked it slowly, turning it with his knife when brown. That cornbread would last him all day, and the bacon grease in it would provide the fuel his body needed.

With his breakfast finished, as the morning twilight slowly brightened into a new day, he thought of Elisabeth, the children, the servants, and the burning of his home. He unwrapped his rifle. After three days in snowy weather, it was still clean. Before leaving home, he had rubbed it down with a light coat of oil and wrapped it in its waterproof, oilcloth table covering.

Now that the Yankees had declared war on him, he decided
that it would begin that day if a suitable target should present
itself on the river below him. He measured one hundred grains of
powder, poured it down the muzzle, and followed it with a patch
and a Minié ball. With light tamping, the charge was set, and with
a cap on the nipple and the hammer let gently down, the rifle was
ready. Climbing across and up to the limestone ledge, he smoked
his pipe and studied the scene below.

A Deadly Gauntlet: The Towhead Chute

The thing that made his firing point perfect there was the
location of the river's channel. On the far side of the river, there
was a large island called Hurricane Island. A second, smaller
island, near the east bank, was called Towhead or Towhead Island.
The channel, which the big boats had to follow in order to avoid
running aground, turned in toward the bluff and ran between
Towhead and the bank. The passage was narrow, close in, and the
current was both swift and powerful. At that point, much of the
power of the great river was concentrated, forced through that
narrow passage, which was called Towhead Chute. Northbound
boats, going downstream, were rushed through the chute at
breathtaking speeds, thus the name "chute." For southbound
boats, the opposite was true. When the river was running full, as
it did in winter and spring, the current in the chute was almost
more than they could overcome. As a result, southbound boats not
only had to pass right under Jack's bluff, but they moved through
the chute so slowly as to be almost stationary targets. For Jack,
it was perfect. For those on the boats, it was perfectly awful—a
deadly gauntlet that they were forced to pass through at very low
speed for a very long time. There were other chutes, including
the difficult one at White Oak Island, the next one to the south;
however, Towhead Chute was notoriously difficult.[1]

Seated and kneeling, he tested different positions for firing
down onto the river. He chose branches of the small trees around
the ledge for resting his rifle, and he cut away vegetation that was
in his way, taking care to remove only what was necessary. With
these things done, and with no sight or sound of a target, he set
his rifle and kit on the ledge, climbed back up to the bluff, and

walked his mare down to a freshet on the hillside to water her, drink himself, and to replenish his supply of water. He was quickly falling into a functional routine for living there on the bluff.

As the sun climbed in its low orbit into the pale sky above the ridge, peace prevailed. Jack gathered leaf mulch, spread it out to dry in the cave, climbed back over to the ledge, and sat down to smoke his pipe and think.

Before he finished his pipe, the boat appeared.

Death from Above in the Towhead Chute

She was downstream near Leatherwood Creek, apparently heavy laden, riding low in the water, and traveling at six or seven knots. The paddle wheels thrashed against the current, and her stacks belched out great clouds of black smoke into the still, cold air as she came slowly, steadily on.

He studied the boat and its cargo deliberately. He was under no constraints of time, and the choices were entirely his. As the big boat drew nearer, he could see that it was a United States Navy gunboat carrying a load of some kind of cargo, which seemed to be stacked everywhere that there was an open horizontal surface. There were sailors lounging around the deck guns; others seemed to be resting in the sun, in places out of the wind.

As the helmsman steered slowly toward the near bank, following the channel into Towhead Chute, Jack watched. Resting the rifle on a tree limb below him, he adjusted his position to kneeling on the ledge, and looked over the barrel of his rifle at the river below. He moved the muzzle slowly back and forth, watching his sight picture, aiming generally at the chute and adjusting his body position. As the boat struck the swift current coming down the chute, it slowed as suddenly as if it had thrown out two anchors astern. It was straining to make steerageway, barely making progress.[2]

Jack swept the boat with his sights. There was plenty of time to select a target. Even with her engines straining at full capacity, the boat was almost standing still. Although all navy commands in the region had been warned to expect small Confederate units to fire at boats on the rivers, sometimes with artillery pieces, the crew seemed completely relaxed. On the quarterdeck, the helmsman concentrated on keeping the bow straight ahead in the narrow channel, and the captain was totally focused on maintaining sufficient speed to make it through the chute. Below, in the engine room, the chief engineer was pushing his boilers to a point near their limits, trying to make that possible.[3]

On deck, a few of the sailors looked up toward the bluff, shielding their eyes from the glare of the sun, and enjoyed the scenery. Although they were looking directly toward Jack's ledge, they didn't see him, but his cool gray eyes saw them. He studied each one. As his eyes slowly swept the boat, from fantail to bow, he settled on the quarterdeck. The captain and his executive officer stood there, the sunlight reflecting off their brass buttons. He felt more inclined to choose an officer than a common sailor; after all, sailors only followed orders. It had been an officer, Colonel Lowe, who had ordered the killing of his boys, and it had been that cruel lieutenant who had supervised the executions, the mutilation of their bodies, and the brutalizing of his family. Yes, he thought, it would be an officer. In this case, he had the best view of the one he took to be the captain.

As the boat approached the place in the chute directly below Jack's ledge, he swung the sights onto the captain and watched him as he turned his head, searching ahead and to port and starboard. The man was turned slightly to his left, exposing about half his chest. There were two vertical rows of brass buttons on his coat, and the ones on his left shined brightly in the sunlight. Jack adjusted his sight picture, with the polished German silver bead snug in the "V" notch of the rear sight, and on the third button from the top. Then he lowered the bead to the fourth button for he knew he tended to shoot a little high when firing downhill. There was no wind; the range was about six hundred yards. He cocked the hammer and pressed the cap firmly down on the nipple. Cocking the set trigger, he pressed his trigger finger forward, against the trigger guard, to avoid touching the trigger prematurely. He took a deep breath and slowly let it out. Taking another deep, easy breath, he let it half out and held it. With a mental command to his shoulders and arms to relax, he checked his sight picture once again, saw the silver bead on the fourth button, and touched the trigger.

Before the report of the rifle reached the boat, the captain was slammed to his knees. Then he toppled over onto his right side, blood leaping from the .50-caliber hole in his left chest and the one under his right arm. The shock of the impact had instantly rendered him semiconscious, and he looked, blankly, up at his executive officer as if bewildered by the unexpected event. The executive officer, himself momentarily immobilized with shock, stared dumbly back down at the captain, trying to comprehend it all. Time seemed to stand still. As the captain's blood spread over the clean quarterdeck, the crew heard the heavy report of the rifle and looked upward, searching for the source. Still unaware of what was happening on the quarterdeck, they searched the bluff above them and saw, far up, near the top, a small puff of white smoke, which was quickly disappearing into the warming air.

As the executive officer's mind grappled with the reality of what had just happened, he opened his mouth to call for help but only whispered. On his second attempt, he regained his voice, called for the medical orderly, and shouted for bandages.

The commanding officer heard none of that; he did not see any of it either. His heart, along with part of a lung and several arteries, had been ripped away, and there was no blood reaching his brain. The shock alone of such a grievous wound would have been enough to kill him, but shock was not needed to snuff out his life. It was gone. The executive officer knelt on the bloody deck and held the captain's head in his trembling, bloody hands; he felt like vomiting but choked it down and wept instead. The medical orderly cut off the captain's coat and shirt and stuffed bandages into the wounds, but he knew that he was applying emergency aid to a dead man. As knowledge of what had happened spread to the crew, they stood around, staring. Some of them wept; others looked back up at the bluff, anger rising within them toward that unseen rifleman. They could only shake their fists in impotent anger and frustration, shouting curses only sailors know for their rifles were stowed below. Even if they had loaded rifles in their hands, they didn't know where to shoot. As these thoughts and emotions surged through the crew, the boat continued its struggling way up the chute. The executive officer gently laid the captain's lifeless head on the bloody deck, stood up, and looked around at the crew. Still dazed, he rose to the occasion, announced that he was now in command, and ordered the helmsman to proceed as before. When the boat finally reached the south end of the chute and began to turn out, away from the shore, he called down to the chief engineer to back off on the steam. In thirty more minutes, still puffing great clouds of black smoke and blowing sparks from her stacks, the boat passed from sight, southward, beyond Danville Crossing.

Jack watched the scene below from his ledge without moving or making a sound. He was, of course, farther removed from what had just happened, both physically and emotionally, than were the men on the boat. Nevertheless, as he looked down upon the scene, watching the boat until it passed from sight, things not entirely pleasant stirred within him, and he gave those feelings their freedom. He needed to face what he had just done, honestly, and he thought about it.

Yes, he realized that officer was human, and he probably had a wife and children just as Jack did. The man had done nothing to harm Jack or his family personally, as Colonel Lowe and his cruel lieutenant had done. In fact, that naval officer had presented no direct threat to Jack or his family. Had Jack allowed him to live, they probably would never have met.

Yet that officer was commanding a ship of war armed with guns, guns that had probably killed Confederate soldiers, sailors, and, perhaps, civilians and would do it again. The man and his ship were committed to the destruction of the Confederate forces of which Robert had been a part, and of which William still was. He and his ship were part of the Yankee force structure that had already killed his friends and neighbors and would continue to do so. They were part of the same force structure that had driven him and his family from their home, and then burned it to the ground.

He took no pleasure in what he had just done. In fact, both Jack and the dead captain were caught up in something vastly larger than either of them, swept along by events that gave neither one much choice. Both were part of opposing forces, committed to destroying one another. So, for men like Jack and the captain, the killing couldn't stop. Although Jack was only a lone rifleman and the captain had been in command of a mighty gunship with an armed crew, their situations had been essentially the same. They would kill until they themselves were killed or disabled, or until this dreadful war ends, whether they enjoy it or not. Turning back was not an option for they were both honorable and patriotic men.

For Jack, who never approached life on superficial levels, it was an occasion for thought and for prayer. There was plenty of time for both.

Civilian Packets Were Safe

The leaves he had brought into the cave were about dry so he gathered another load. The noonday sunshine was melting the snow, exposing more of the deep, brown mulch, and drying the top layer. This time he piled a large amount of the leaf mulch on a blanket and returned to his cave to dry it, taking care to keep the leaves safely away from the fire.

With these chores done, he stoked his pipe, made his way over to the firing ledge, and sat down. As he enjoyed his pipe and the warm sunshine, smoke appeared downstream to the north; another boat was coming.

This one came into view more quickly than had the other one, and as it approached Towhead Chute, he saw that it was smaller, riding higher in the water, and making better speed. He had plenty of time to get his rifle from the cave if he chose to, but as the boat came nearer, he saw that this one was only a small packet, probably the mail packet from Paducah headed for Danville Crossing or places farther south. On deck he saw only two men. One appeared to be the captain, standing in front of the wheel house, watching the channel, and turning often to speak to the helmsman in the wheelhouse. The other man stood aft, relaxing, apparently a deck hand with no immediate responsibilities. Neither man was in uniform. Jack could see no guns. This was just a civilian boat captain trying to make a living carrying mail and passengers in spite of the war that made his life difficult. Neither the captain nor his crew had anything to fear from Jack—not that day or on any other day.[4]

Jack refilled his pipe, watched as the packet cleared the chute, followed the channel back out into the stream, and headed for Danville Crossing. He finished his pipe and looked down on the river. Some coffee seemed like a good idea. With the coffee reheating on the fire, he climbed back up on the bluff to check on his mare. He untied her and walked with her eastward along the ridge. After walking about a furlong, he watered her at a clear, fresh rivulet, and then drank of the cold water himself. By the time he walked back with her, his coffee was ready and he felt better; the walk had been good for them both.

Feeling relaxed, he moved over to his ledge and sat down. Leaning back against the steeply sloping ground behind it, Jack put his old slouch hat under his head and closed his eyes. The sunshine penetrating the leafless trees around him felt good, and he dozed there a while.

Another Kill in the Towhead Chute

Waking and feeling rested, although the slope on which he was leaning was cold and damp, he sat up, stretched, looked around, and saw smoke.

Downstream, past Leatherwood Creek, black smoke was rising, climbing easily above the hills that still obscured its source. Another boat was coming. Without actually posing the question to himself, a decision arose clearly and firmly and declared itself in his mind. He stood up, stretched again, and made his way over to the cave to get his rifle. There was plenty of time, and he checked his fire, moved the coffee away to cool, and fluffed the drying leaf mulch.

As the black smoke moved nearer, Jack picked up his rifle and shot bag, and made his way back over to the ledge. Seated on the ledge, he opened the shot bag, laid out what he needed, and waited. The midwinter sun was slipping lower into the southwestern sky when the boat came into sight, working against the full-running river, coming steadily on. This was a big one but not as low in the water as the first boat, and it was making slightly better speed. As the boat came into full view, belching black columns of smoke, he saw that she was a transport traveling at maximum speed. As she drew still nearer, he saw that there was no heavy cargo piled on her broad decks. This transport was carrying a different kind of cargo: embarked troops, perhaps a company of infantry—maybe more. In addition, the soldiers were armed with rifles.

Jack turned his attention to loading his rifle and tapped the load to make it snug. With a percussion cap on the nipple and the hammer eased down upon it, his rifle was ready.

As the boat approached, he saw the embarked soldiers lounging in various ways, as such soldiers always do. They were making themselves as comfortable as possible, making the best of an essentially uncomfortable situation. Some stood along the rails, talking, smoking, and looking at the scenery; some were playing cards. Others, who could find a place for it, slept in the afternoon sunshine. The visible crew, except for the helmsman and the officers on the quarterdeck, appeared to be "standing down" and were as relaxed as were the embarked soldiers.

With his rifle again rested on its tree limb and the afternoon sun slipping lower in the sky to his left front, it occurred to him that at no time of day would the sun be a problem for him from that spot. In the morning, it would be behind him, in his enemies' eyes, and ideal for his purposes. Overhead at noon, it would illuminate his target but not shine in his own eyes. In the afternoon, even in midsummer, with the sun shining directly into his face, it would not be in his eyes for he would always be looking downward at the river. There, he realized, was still another virtue of his chosen bluff; having realized this, he filed it away in his orderly mind.

As the boat and its men came into increasingly clear view, Jack looked over the sights and slowly scanned the deck. In addition to the naval officers on the quarterdeck, there were a few who appeared to be army officers. Although their uniforms were also blue, they were distinguishable from the naval officers' uniforms, and they stood apart from the naval officers, who were engaged in the operation of the boat. These were undoubtedly the officers of the embarked troops. They appeared to be as relaxed as their troops were if less informal in their postures.

Jack concentrated on the army officers. They all wore their rank insignia on their shoulders and wore no gold stripes on their sleeves. Looking over the sights, he scrutinized them, one by one, and settled on the one who appeared to be the commanding officer. He was smoking a pipe, and the others were gathered loosely around him, appearing to listen to what he was saying, treating him with some deference. With the boat nearing, he cocked the hammer and pushed the percussion cap down on the nipple with his thumb.

As the boat arrived below him, he took aim at his man; as he tightened his sight picture, the man turned until he was almost facing toward Jack, pointing to something on the hillside, his pipe clenched in his teeth. Silently thanking the man for turning toward him and presenting a better target, Jack aligned the German silver bead of the front sight snugly into the rear sight "V" and moved it to the center of the man's chest. Like the navy captain's coat, this one had two vertical rows of brass buttons, and Jack chose the third one from the top on the captain's left. There was a gentle south wind blowing from Jack's left. With the boat almost directly below him, he moved the bead a little to the left of the button and slightly below it to allow for the wind, the boat's motion, and the downhill shot. He cocked the set trigger. Holding his sight picture, and with the tree limb bearing the entire weight of the rifle, he inhaled easily, let half of it out, rechecked his sight picture, and touched the trigger.

Before the sound of the exploding powder reached the boat, the large, spinning, lead projectile struck the captain in the left-center of his chest, driving him backward off his feet, carrying him and the lieutenant behind him forcefully onto the deck. The captain's pipe fell from his mouth as the impact caused the muscles in his jaws to release their grip. The pipe seemed to hang briefly, suspended in air and strangely alone, before falling to the deck in a shower of sparks. The immense bullet tore through the captain's chest, ripped through his heart, exited from a large hole in his lower back, and, largely spent, buried itself in the lieutenant's leg.

The captain, with a spreading dark stain on his blue coat front, his chest cavity filling with blood, and shocked into unconsciousness, lay sprawled on his back, his eyes wide, looking surprised, seeing nothing. Beneath the captain the lieutenant, dazed but conscious, was drenched in the captain's blood and some of his own. Still not feeling pain, he struggled to comprehend the situation. The others stood, transfixed, looking down on the two bloody, prostrate forms, speechless. As the widening pool of blood reached their shoes, they began, one by one, to cry out, calling reflexively on God, then calling for human help.

As the naval officers realized what had happened, the captain sent his orderly for the surgeon. The dead captain was lifted off his lieutenant and placed beside him. The wounded lieutenant tried instinctively to get up but was unable, his hands finding no purchase on the blood-slick deck. As word spread through the crew and the embarked infantrymen, some began to shout in self-compounding confusion; others tried to find cover from imagined

Confederate attackers along the riverbank. Sailors ran to their battle stations, waiting for orders, as the big boat continued its slow struggle up the chute. When the surgeon arrived, he saw immediately that the captain was dead, turned his attention to the wounded and shocked lieutenant, and ordered him carried below to the sick bay.

By the time the soldiers found their rifles and cartridge boxes and prepared to fire, searching the river bank and the steep ridge above them, the small white cloud of smoke from Jack's exploding powder had disappeared into the breeze, and they found no target. A few fired blindly, furiously, and impotently into the riverbank and hillside. Their sergeants, realizing that they were taking no more fire from the shore, restored order as the boat labored toward the upstream end of the Towhead.

As Jack watched, motionless and silent, the big boat finally cleared the Towhead, increased speed, and turned out into the river, away from the bank. They had run the gauntlet, had come through the valley of the shadow of death, and the boat was steaming southward at full speed, with black smoke, sparks, and flame blowing from her stacks.

Jack watched, feeling no elation, as the sun slipped downward toward the hills of Benton County across the river, and the boat slowly disappeared into its brightness, passing under Danville Bridge and beyond. He felt no inclination to move, and so he sat, again allowing his emotions their freedom, and mused.

As the pale sun brushed the low hilltops beyond the river with softest gold and darkness flooded the valley below, the chilly air reminded him that it was time to tend to his mare. The darkness that had filled the valley below was flooding steadily upward. Before it reached his bluff, he needed to feed and water his mare, tend his fire, and see to his own supper.

With his mare settled for the night, he stoked his fire, went back up to the bluff and listened. There were no sounds of pursuers, no hint of danger in the cold, clear night. There was only the sound of the breeze, and the voices of two owls exchanging earnest comments in the valley below. It seemed as if he were alone at the top of the world.

With the remaining coffee heating on the fire, he added the newly dried leaf mulch to his bed. He wasn't very hungry, but he made a satisfactory supper of the rest of the cornbread, with dried apples he had brought from home. Then he cleaned his rifle, reloaded, and wrapped it in its oilcloth cover.

With his fire set for the night, Jack wrapped himself in blankets. His crude bed still left much to be desired, but progress was being made. He wondered about his family, both white and black, and wished that he could have news of them. Maybe he could go to them if he would be very careful. With such thoughts growing increasingly disorganized and dim in his mind, he drifted into sleep.

It had been quite a day.

Settling in on the Ridge

Jack woke feeling less abused by his bed than he had the morning before and vowed to continue to improve his "mattress." Outside the cave, he stood slowly and stretched. The air was noticeably warmer. The wind was out of the south, and gentle. He was accustomed to periodic warm spells in winter, and he knew very well their fickle nature. Although living in the wilderness and not yet fully equipped for it or fully adjusted to it, he indulged himself in a bit of optimism. Spring, he thought, may be coming a little early this year.

Much of the snow had disappeared from the bluff, except where the shade of the trees, stumps, rock outcrops, and deadfall logs left predictable white remnants beyond them on the ground. The "snow shadows" of the standing trees were like compass needles. They were the width of the trunk at the base, becoming progressively narrower where the morning and afternoon sunshine had trimmed them to slender tips pointing due north.

There was still neither sight nor sound of anyone else on his ridge, other than the wild animals that lived there and his mare above him, pawing the ground and nickering softly to remind him that it was time for her breakfast. Although a little restless from being confined, she was in fine form. While she ate, Jack returned to the cave to check the fire and fetch his kettle. The next time he was in a place where he could, he was thinking, he would get a coffee pot, so he could have coffee heating while he took his kettle to get the day's supply of water; and he made a mental note to do just that.

Again, he walked the mare the furlong's distance to water. They both drank their fill, and he filled his kettle and canteen. On the walk back, he thought about the fact that in late summer and early autumn, these wet weather streams, high up on the ridge, would dry up. During those months, he would have to find a permanent spring somewhere on the ridge, or go down into the valleys for water.

After breakfast, he grabbed a cup of coffee and his pipe and climbed over to the ledge to plan for the day. Satisfied from his breakfast, comforted by the fairing weather prospects, and enjoying his pipe, Jack thought on the events of the day before and wondered if yesterday's boats had stopped somewhere to report what he had done. Even if they hadn't, he knew that the incidents would be reported and soon. He also knew that he would not be able to continue that way indefinitely without drawing some kind of intrusion by the Union forces. Each new day that he was there would require increased watchfulness.

It appeared that there was not as yet any general alarm concerning the dangers to boats passing below Jack's bluff, because on every boat that had passed, the men aboard seemed relaxed. But that would change. In time, both navy and army personnel on passing boats, especially those boats laboring to pass southward through the chute, would come to know it as a deadly gauntlet, a passage to be dreaded, a valley where the shadow of death hung darkly over them as long as they were in it. Towhead Chute would become a notorious killing field, remembered by those who passed through it and survived for the rest of their lives.

Eventually, elements of nine regiments would be sent against that one old man and his deadly rifle. There would even be an amphibious task force, made up of specially trained and equipped Marines and sailors, sent against him, but that was in the future. Just now, although he was wanted, with a reward for the one who could kill or capture him, it seemed that Jack was in no immediate danger up there on the ridge.

As the sun climbed higher and its warming rays reached the top of the ridge, he went back up on the bluff and gathered more leaf mulch for his bed. With that spread out in his cave to dry, he carried in selected rocks to improve his fire pit and its cooking surfaces, with flat rocks to hold his kettle and skillet above the fire. There was a plentiful supply of rocks.

Jack was establishing an increasingly sufficient wilderness home. Nevertheless, he was also feeling, ever more strongly, the desire to have news of his family. He was thinking of ways to contact them when black smoke, rising above the hills to the north, announced the approach of another boat.

Death Again in the Gauntlet

He made his unhurried way, with his rifle and kit, over to the ledge. It was steep, but he was beginning to tread a narrow, fairly level pathway from the cave to the ledge, making it an easier climb.

The smoke was down near the mouth of Leatherwood Creek, and the boat would soon appear. Kneeling on the ledge, he checked his rifle, tapped the load snugly against the powder, and laid the ramrod beside him on the ledge. With a cap on the nipple and the hammer down, he was ready. With his thumb, he rubbed the German silver of the front sight blade, and it shined brightly in the sunlight. It was the only reflective surface on that otherwise dull, businesslike weapon.

With his rifle resting across his knee, he watched as the boat came into view, laboring against the current. It appeared to be another transport carrying supplies southward to the railhead at Johnsonville. As it followed the channel toward the entrance to the chute, he rested the rifle across the tree limb and waited.

Entering the racing current of the chute, the big boat slowed until it was barely making steerageway, and Jack examined the men on the quarterdeck. The officers in their blue uniforms were easily recognizable by their caps and the gold stripes on their cuffs, and this time there were three of them. One, whom Jack took to be the captain, was intently watching the narrow channel ahead of him and giving orders to the helmsman. Looking over the sights, Jack studied the man. He adjusted his sight picture, bringing the silver front sight bead to rest on the man at the level of his chest. He cocked the hammer, seated the cap firmly on the nipple, and cocked the set trigger. With his sight picture tight, Jack eased the bead slightly lower. As he took the second breath and let half of it out, the officer pointed at something ahead and turned to his right. As Jack touched the trigger, the captain faced away, turning his back toward Jack.

The big, spinning, supersonic projectile struck the captain

between his shoulders, driving him to his knees as his face struck the wheelhouse wall. As before, the others aboard the boat first saw the captain go down, suddenly and violently, and then they heard the report from high up on the bluff above them. They stood, staring in disbelief at a scene not readily accepted by the unprepared mind. It wasn't until they saw the dark, wet spot between his shoulders, already spreading on the back of his coat, that their stunned minds connected the three bits of data: his sudden fall, the report, and the blood. Their captain had been shot.

As the boat continued in its slow progress southward, those around him called for help, cried out to God, and looked wildly around and up, as the small white cloud of smoke from Jack's rifle was dissipating into the warming air. With their attention divided between searching for the source and looking to their captain's needs, they really weren't sure what they had seen way up on the hill—or that they had seen anything at all.

The captain was still kneeling on the deck, slumped forward with his face and shoulders against the wheelhouse. His cap, knocked from his head, rested a few feet away. When they turned him onto his back and straightened his legs, they saw that the bullet had exited above his brass belt buckle. In deep shock, the captain's eyes expressed that awful combination of surprise and bewilderment; he sighed as if relieved, and was dead.

The helmsman continued to concentrate on keeping the boat in the channel, adjustments were made in the crew, and the boat continued slowly up the chute as the captain was carried below. Jack had time to kill several more, but he didn't. He just watched.

As the big boat cleared the south end of the Towhead and eased away from the bank, picking up speed, Jack sat motionless and silent, watching as the boat steamed upstream toward Danville Crossing. Finally passing from sight at White Oak Island, the boat left only black smoke, floating languidly above the brown river. Jack stood up, picked up his rifle and kit, and made the short climb to the top of the bluff. Walking over to where his mare stood tethered, he leaned his rifle against the tree and set his shot bag on the ground beside it. He had taken pleasure in killing the first two, that lieutenant and his sergeant. Perhaps it wasn't pleasure—maybe a sense of justice served—but it was different now. It wasn't personal.

With an arm loosely over the mare's neck, Jack stroked her

muzzle with the other hand and spoke to her, thinking aloud. "That makes five, old girl—and maybe that's enough. I take no pleasure in this. Let's take a walk." Slowly, deliberately, he tightened the cinch, mounted, turned her head around to the east, and rode off down the ridge at a slow walk. He guessed he could water her while they were out, but, mostly, he just felt the need to go somewhere. Anywhere.

As he made his way slowly through the woods along the ridge, he felt heavy. Birds filled the air with love songs, responding to the lengthening days, but he didn't hear them. Maybe he needed to get away for a few days. Where would he go? What would he take? What would he do? Inwardly, he posed the questions, but no answers came. He rode slowly down the ridge for a mile or two, dismounted, and walked her for a while. When he decided that he had gone far enough, he found a place to water the mare. He drank his fill also, remounted, and started back, walking her, with the low winter sun on his face. Midday had come and gone, and he failed to notice that he had not yet eaten that day.

Back at the bluff, he fed his mare and brushed her down. Smoke downstream told him that another boat was approaching the chute, but he paid it only scant, indifferent attention. He took one of his blankets, draped it over her, and tied it at her chest; she would be warmer now, and he would get by with one.

Jack cleaned his rifle, reloaded it, and fixed his supper. He ate apathetically, took his coffee to the ledge and sat, watching darkness fill the valley below. Firing up his pipe, he sat pensively as the last rays of the sun brushed his hilltop with fading gold. He watched the darkness flooding upward toward his ledge. He didn't know why, but he knew that it was time to leave his little fortress for a while. Something within him was making that increasingly clear. He would pack up in the morning and leave. Maybe he would go back home and check on the servants. Maybe not. He would know in the morning.

Just then, he felt very, very tired.

A Change of Scene

Jack slept better that night on his improved bed and woke early to the chorus of forest birds, filling the clear morning air with their optimistic declarations. Only they and God understood them, but Jack loved them. They brightened any day. He was cold and stiff, as usual, and some bruised parts of his back and legs were complaining about the lumps and ridges in his "mattress"; but he wasn't as sore as on the day before. Besides, the singing of the birds was soothing to his soul. It was chilly, but the mild weather was holding, and it looked like the moderate spell would last a little longer. His heart was lighter than when he had gone to bed, and as he got up, stepped outside, and stretched, he found himself looking forward to the day. "When I bed down tonight," he was thinking, "it will not be here."

With his fire rekindled, and his kettle of coffee water on to boil, he took note with pleasure that his new arrangement of cooking rocks was a decided improvement. He looked up and down the river below, with a detached lack of interest in the scene. He would be leaving today. He also felt sure that he would be returning, but he didn't know when. For the moment, that was enough for Jack. He knew he would be leaving for a while, and that realization was wrapped in peace.

The coffee boiled, dark and aromatic. Like bacon frying, the aroma of coffee as it cooked was almost as pleasant as the actual drinking of it. Dipping out a steaming cup, he climbed across to his ledge and sat down on the edge of it, with his legs hanging down. The coffee was still too hot to drink, but as it cooled on the cold rock ledge between his legs, he enjoyed the aroma, rising to his nostrils in a pleasant, fragrant mist. The river valley below him was still deep in darkness, but the morning sun was kissing the hilltops across the river with fresh promise. Yes, he thought, this was a beautiful morning, and things would be better today.

About that latter thought, he could not have been more wrong.

Across the River to Sulfur Wells

Jack brushed his mare, fed her, and enjoyed the furlong's walk with her, down to his watering place; and by the time he got back to the bluff, he was hungry. His usual breakfast was satisfying, and he cooked extra cornbread and bacon to take along, knowing that he might not find a place to cook before night.

Cleaning his plate and cooking utensils as well as he could, he packed them away, along with his supply of cornmeal, salt, bacon, and coffee. As he gathered his belongings and straightened up in his cave, it was remarkable to see how elaborate his home in the wilderness had become. He pushed the loose leaves back into his crude bed, pulled unburned wood out of the fire to save it for the next time, and left the coals to burn themselves out.

Jack dipped his cup into the remaining coffee and climbed over to his ledge. He sat there, considering his alternatives with an after-breakfast pipe. As one possibility, he could circle wide around Danville Crossing and head south into the area of White Oak Creek. He had family there, and he could probably find Robert's guerrilla band there. He could also go back home to see how things were. The servants could probably use some guidance and encouragement from him, and he worried about them. Most of all, though, he wanted to hear news from Elisabeth and the children, especially of the two sick ones; however, it seemed unlikely that word from them could have reached the home place so soon. In addition, he thought, there would most likely be Yankee patrols watching Bubbling Springs and all trails leading to it, looking for him.

An alternative would be to cross the river and go to Sulfur Wells. The best way to hear news from Elisabeth and the children would be to hear it directly from them; he missed them already. The largest obstacle would be the river: it was running full, too wide and swift for a horse to swim. He could easily get across in a boat, but he would have to leave his mare and walk the rest of the way. He would need to be mounted in Henry County in case of discovery and pursuit. There were the ferries at Danville Crossing, Wynn's Landing, and Paris Landing. Danville Crossing was always guarded by soldiers, and Paris Landing was often guarded. It appeared that his best course of action would be to scout out Wynn's Landing to learn if they were operating and the hours of operation. The best time to cross would be at the end of the day when pursuit of him would be less likely and more difficult. Once across the river, it would be but a short ride to reach his family. Once there, he would be among relatives. Camp Lowe and Fort Heiman, to the north on the Kentucky border, had been abandoned. Although Union troops occasionally used them as temporary patrol bases, and their patrol routes often included Sulfur Wells, there were no soldiers permanently stationed in that part of Henry County. Once across the river, the rest should be easy and relatively safe.[5]

With his decision made and a plan taking form in his mind, Jack set about breaking camp. He repacked his supplies, filled his canteen with the leftover coffee, and drank the remainder. With his big dragoon pistol in its saddle holster and his rifle loaded, he leaned his rifle against a tree and set about sanitizing the place, removing evidence that would identify him. Before mounting, he took a handful of brush and obscured the pathways he had created in the leaf mulch in the short time he had been there.

Slinging his shot bag across his chest and picking up his rifle, he mounted, took a long, last look at the bluff and the river, reigned his mare around, and headed eastward, along the ridge. The sun was above the hills along Hurricane Creek, warming the ridge. A steady breeze was blowing from the southeast as if guided by the rays of morning sunshine. He couldn't remember a more perfect morning, and his heart grew steadily lighter. God knew that he would need that emotional lift and a mellow day before he reached his family that night.

Turning north, Jack followed a small branch downhill, down toward the valley of Leatherwood Creek, keeping the mare to a slow walk and allowing her to pick her own way. Crossing the narrow-gauge railroad that served the mines and furnaces and easing down into the wide creek bottom, he noticed the familiar smell of the creek hanging in the morning air. As always, it was pleasant and somehow reassuring.

Staying wide of the Phillips place and the furnace, Jack crossed Leatherwood Creek and began the climb up to the ridge that ran northward, along the river. There were small farms all along the river there, fronting on the river road, but he could travel above and behind them, paralleling the river but staying high and in the woods. The river bottom was cleared and farmed, but the ridge behind the farmhouses and barns was wide and densely forested.

When he was near enough to see the ferry landing, he stopped and watched as the ferry made its way back and forth across the river, and the sun sank lower in the southwest. He saw nothing on either side of the river that would be a threat to him and, cautiously, he moved nearer. In the evening twilight, with the ferry on the Stewart County side and no one else waiting, he rode down to the landing and spoke to the operator. There would be one more crossing, and it appeared that Jack might be the only passenger. He led his mare onto the ferry, thanked the man, paid him five times the usual toll for a man and a horse, and asked him to go ahead and shove off. He also asked the man to forget that he had seen him.

The river was up, wide with winter runoff, and the trip across seemed long. The river also had a characteristic, sterile smell when running full and cold. Such things were woven so deeply into Jack's being that he was seldom conscious of these sensory perceptions. They were just a part of him, and of most anyone else who had grown up Between the Rivers.

On the far bank, the ferryman looped his chain around the big tree stump that served as a bollard, and held it while Jack led his mare off onto the Henry County bank. Jack thanked him again, reminded the man to forget that he had seen him, and the ferryman assured him that he would.

Forgetting that they had seen Jack Hinson was something at which many citizens of the Kentucky and Tennessee counties in the Twin Rivers would become expert, and this helped him considerably in staying alive.

He watched the ferry begin its last trip of the day back to Stewart County, waved again to the ferryman, mounted, and picked his way up the red clay and brown gravel of the riverbank into the last, pale twilight. The road to Sulfur Wells wound through familiar territory. He had relatives in the area, had bought and sold land in that part of the county, and had done other business there for upwards of thirty years. He could travel at an easy pace and reach his family after dark, making his arrival there safer for all concerned.[6]

It seemed that the day, which had begun so well and had gone so smoothly, was also going to end perfectly. His expectations were pleasant, thinking he would soon reunite with his family in a safe and comfortable place, relieving his anxiety about their welfare, particularly the welfare of the sick children. He was right about almost all of that.[7]

Fresh Heartbreak

Jack saw the lamplight from far down the road as if he had been expected, as if the yellow light from the kerosene lamps was there to greet him and guide him in. His emotions had been taken to their limits during the past six days, and they were stirring mightily within him as he approached the house. Could it really have been only six days? It had seemed like at least six months! So much had happened, with such radical and tragic changes. Now, after the six longest days of his life, he rode up to the house as dogs began to bark. They came out from their sleeping spots under the house and surrounded the front porch in a noisy semicircle, with each dog barking and pointing at Jack like compass needles. The door opened a cautious crack, and then opened wide, spilling light onto the porch. He removed his old hat and stepped in as the dogs ceased to bark and returned to their several places of comfort under the house.

As he walked into the soft light of the parlor and the door closed behind him, that other life, the life of a renegade guerrilla soldier, was, for the moment, left behind out there in the darkness.

The reunion was at first wordless, with emotions too compelling for talk. Jack looked around him, mentally calling the roll, and found the children short by two. He hoped that they were in bed safely sleeping for they were so young and so sick. Still no one spoke, but as he looked at Elisabeth, he saw the answer. Her eyes were aching pools of sadness. He held her as she sobbed wordlessly, her face buried in his coat. The old coat was dirty, saturated with wood smoke and dust, with bits of dry leaves clinging to it; but Elisabeth didn't notice. As he continued to hold her, and she continued to release her agony into his dirty coat, the younger children began also to cry. The older ones joined in the family embrace while the smaller ones clung to what they could reach of him and Elisabeth's skirt. He let them all cry. No words were necessary; they would not help anyway.

Amidst the grieving, Jack decided not to tell them that night what had happened to their home. They had been through enough emotional wringing already. Tomorrow, he would go out to visit the two small, new graves, and then he would tell them.

How hard it was for them all. How very hard, and how it hurt. But at least, Jack thought, they were together again, and his babies were buried among their kin.

After the children were off to bed, the rest sat before the fire for a long time and exchanged information. Pipes were smoked, and there was much silent gazing into the fire. Albert, whom they called Ab, now seventeen and the eldest son at home, was assuming the responsibilities of a man. He sat with them. They talked—of family matters, of the farm, of food supplies—of happy things. They didn't speak of the war, and Jack didn't tell them about the burning of their home or of the killings. He would tell them about the burning tomorrow; he might never tell them about the killings.

When they were sated with the exchange of news, the conversation slacked off gradually to silence, and Jack was asked if there were anything he would like before going to bed. "Yes," he said, knowing that they would have it, "I'd like some buttermilk and cornbread, please. And," he added slowly, "a bath."

Return to Bubbling Springs

Sleeping in a real bed was as good as Jack had thought it would be as was the special breakfast that followed. It would require no adjustment at all for him to return to normal living—if only he could.

After breakfast, he and Elisabeth visited the two new graves, and he held her as she wept. His weeping was internal, with his aching heart concealed behind his massive, clinched jaws. They spoke quietly of the future's uncertainties and agreed that if possible, when the war was over, they would take their dead babies back home and rebury them there.

Returning to the house, Jack gathered the family, prepared them for more bad news, and told them what the Union soldiers had done to their home. He said that he had no way of knowing what had been saved and what had perished until he could go there himself. He was concerned too, he told them, about the well-being of the servants, for only God knew what those Yankee soldiers might have done to them. It was his plan to go there as soon as he left them; he would make Bubbling Springs his next stop.

Family prayer laid the unknown and the uncontrollable in the hands of God and brought a measure of peace to them all. The day of reunion that followed was a pleasant one although clouded with sadness due to the deaths of the children and the knowledge that the setting sun would bring another separation, with Jack disappearing into an unknown and deadly future, perhaps never to return. They all made the most of the sunny day, trying not to think of the night to come.

There had been no one to come to the house all day, no visitors to notice Jack's presence. If he could avoid being seen as he left, a departure at dusk would mean he had brought no danger to the family.

As the sun slid downward behind the hills in the southwest, Jack said his goodbyes, mounted his mare, and headed back toward the ferry landing in the fading light. It was harder to leave his family this time than it had been the first time, a week before. He would be telling them goodbye again, many times, before the end of the war. It would become a little more difficult each time.

Returning to the ferry landing, he moved at an easy trot; he wanted to get there soon enough to watch it before boarding but didn't want to appear to be in a hurry. Halting before the ferry landing came into view, Jack dismounted and walked. Staying back in the trees, in what concealment he could find, he scanned the landing below him. Looking out across the river at the ferryboat on the far shore, he saw passengers debarking and others waiting to board. He saw no sign of soldiers on either side.

As the ferry made its way toward the west bank, Jack watched until it was nearing, remounted, and waited there as the bow ramp slid up on the wet clay bank and the ferryman looped his chain around the bollard and secured it. As the last rider debarked and started up the road, Jack rode out of the woods onto the riverbank, waving a greeting to the ferryman. He rode quickly aboard and dismounted as the chain was unwrapped, recovered, and the ferry cast off for the Stewart County side. Jack's timing had been perfect, and he was the only passenger on the final crossing of the day. When the ferry bumped and slid up the wet clay bank on the Stewart County side, Jack walked his mare off the ferry and remounted. Again, with generous payment and a reminder to forget seeing him, Jack rode up the bank and disappeared, heading northeast on Wynn's Ferry Road.

Turning off the road, he walked his mare a short distance into the woods and then proceeded northeastward again, parallel with the road, watching and listening. It seemed that the Yankee soldiers who patrolled the road had returned to Fort Henry and Fort Donelson and secured for the night. Nevertheless, he stayed in the woods, moving as silently as he could; even though the road seemed clear, he could not afford to take chances.

Heartsick Homecoming

About an hour after full dark, he rode past the Rougement Cemetery, down the slope to the meadow, and across the creek to his own lane. He turned up the lane, rode past the servants' quarters and stopped, taking in the awful scene. His eyes transmitted to his brain what he had known he would find, only with the awful finality of actually seeing it. In the deepening darkness, where his home had been, there was only charred, surreal emptiness. The fire-blackened desolation before him dropped from his brain and into his gut with sickening impact. He sat, choking on the dreadful reality, for what seemed a very long time, but it was actually only a minute or two. It is a terrible thing to have your home burn; it is very much like a death in the family.

Turning his mare back down the lane, he headed toward the servants' quarters; he would examine the charred remains of his home in the morning. His reunion with the servants was emotional for them all. There was much to tell, and there were many questions to be answered, amidst a mingling of smiles and tears. There was grieving at the news of the deaths of the little children.

The black Hinsons had heard nothing of Jack, Elisabeth, and the children since they left. At times, they had thought they might be left there at Bubbling Springs without them forever. They had plenty of food to last the winter, most of it hidden, but they didn't know what they would do if they were left there indefinitely. They feared that strangers would come to take possession of the place and drive them away. The soldiers had returned, they said, several times, looking for him but had done no further damage. They had, however, made threatening comments to Sarah concerning her belligerent resistance when the house was burned. She had fled, fearing for her life, and they did not expect her to return. If she did return, they said, it would not be until the war was over.[8]

The servants offered to give him a bed for the night, doubling up themselves, with the children sleeping on pallets on the floor. He declined. He would not place them in that much danger. He told them he would make his bed in the tobacco barn and do just fine. He would appreciate a mattress tick filled with dry corn shucks, however, and would gladly accept any invitation to breakfast.

Waking the next morning in his tobacco barn, Jack looked around at the barrels of clothing, pieces of furniture, and other items that had been rescued from the burning house. He was impacted anew by both the loss and the loyalty and courage of his servants. He would never be able to repay them, he thought, and he must never do anything that would unnecessarily draw them into the deadly danger in which he now lived.

Before daylight, he made his way, cautiously, to his breakfast appointment. On the way, he asked one of the boys to feed and water his mare in the tobacco barn. It was a wonderful breakfast—his second in so many mornings. Yet that yester morning at Sulfur Wells already seemed like a very long time ago. Jack told the servants to live, as well as they could manage it, as they had lived before. He told them to go ahead and burn the tobacco bed and plant it as always. He left them money with which to buy supplies. He promised to return as often as he could, and, always, he told them, he would come after dark and leave before first light.

After breakfast, feeling an urgency to leave, Jack asked if there was an extra coffee pot anywhere on the place. It need not be a nice one, he said, as long as it didn't leak. Before he made his final farewell, thanking them again for the breakfast, a child appeared, as if by magic, with a big smile and a serviceable porcelain pot. Holding it up to a lantern and seeing no light coming through the bottom, he thanked all concerned and pressed into a small, black hand enough money to buy several such coffee pots.

In the first gray morning twilight, he walked, circumspectly, to the barn, where he found his mare ready and a fresh supply of food in his sacks. Stopping in his blacksmith shop, Jack picked up a small hammer and a one-eighth-inch steel punch. He had decided to keep a record of his kills. If he didn't survive, those who cared would at least see what he had accomplished in his private war. With great care, he punched one circle on the rear of the top surface of the octagonal barrel, just forward of the barrel's tail-like tang. It represented the lieutenant, the first kill. Just forward of that one he made a row of three more, representing the sergeant and the first two on the boats. One more, forward of and centered on the three, represented the captain of the transport who had turned his back as Jack fired. With that done, he dropped the hammer and punch into a saddlebag.[9]

In the pale predawn light, Jack rode from the barn to the charred remains of his home, rode slowly around the blackened foundation beneath the charred old shade trees, taking it in, swallowing his reaction to what he saw. With no place special to go and no immediate plan in his mind, he decided to check the area around his home for signs of an enemy presence.

He circled to the southwest to Standing Rock Creek, followed it eastward for a while, and then rode northeast in a large arc, a careful reconnaissance of the area around Bubbling Springs. That done, he headed into the morning twilight toward the Hundred Acre Field. He didn't know it, but he had a rendezvous there with danger.

Encounter in the Hundred Acre Field

The Hundred Acre Field was a large open field, the largest cleared field in the area. It could hold one hundred modern football fields. It had been cleared, gradually, in the process of making charcoal, which was sold to the county's iron furnaces. Known as "coaling fields," such clearings quite naturally resulted when portions of the forest were clear-cut and the trees burned to

Jack saw them before they saw him. In one easy motion, he leaned over on the side of his horse opposite the soldiers, lowered his rifle into the tall broom sedge, and let go. (Drawing by Joe McCormick)

The Hundred Acre Field today.

make the charcoal. Surrounded by forest, the big field was grown up in grass and the winter's abundant growth of rank, golden brown broom sedge.[10]

Jack rode slowly through the silent forest. The only sound, other than his mare's breathing and muted hoof beats muffled in the deep leaf mulch, was the whispering of the rising breeze in the naked trees. The solitude was pleasant, but he was still sickened from the sight of his home's charred remains. He emerged from the woods and was about fifty yards out into the big field when he saw the soldiers.

They were riding out of the woods and into the far side of the open field. Jack saw them before they saw him, and he reacted instinctively. In one easy motion, he leaned over on the side of his horse opposite the soldiers, lowered his rifle into the tall broom sedge, and let go. It disappeared as if swallowed. Then he released the ties on his rolled shuck mattress and dropped it in the deep sedge with his sacks of food. These things done, he turned his mare and headed toward the soldiers. He wanted to meet them as far away from his rifle, food, and mattress as possible for those items would raise questions he did not want to answer.

There were two of them, definitely Union soldiers, and when they saw him, they immediately turned and came toward him at a trot. It was extremely unusual for only two soldiers to be on a legitimate patrol. These two fellows, he thought, were "freelancing," out on their own, after the reward. He looked down at his dragoon pistol, cocked it, and closed the holster flap over it. He didn't want to look as if he expected trouble, but he would be ready if trouble came.

Filling and lighting his pipe, he smoked it and watched them from under the brim of his old black hat as he rode slowly toward them. Near the middle of the field, the soldiers rode up to Jack and halted him with hands in the air; he raised his hand in greeting, with an air of passive indifference. Apparently suspecting nothing, they asked if he knew a man named Jack Hinson. He answered that, yes, he did know Jack Hinson. "We're looking for him." one of them said, and asked, "Have you seen him?" Jack knew what the next question would be, and in no more than a second or two, an idea took form in his mind. "Why, yes," answered Jack with a poker face, and speaking the truth, "in fact, he was back over yonder on the logging road, on Standing Rock Creek, not an hour ago." "Where on the logging road?" the other soldier asked, now definitely interested. Jack described the location, again speaking truthfully, and gave the soldiers directions to reach the spot but by a route longer than necessary. They thanked him, turned, and hurried off into the woods. Jack recovered his rifle and disappeared into the woods as well but in a different direction.

He would reach the designated spot before the soldiers and would be waiting there with a surprise when they arrived.

Hunters Become Prey on Standing Rock Creek

Although Jack was calm, he was experiencing the heightened alertness that occurs in such situations, his mind working at light speed, his body chemistry at battle stations, all senses functioning at their peaks. He was soon tying his horse in the forest above the road and walking down the slope to the spot he had thought of as the soldiers questioned him. It was one of his preselected firing positions, and the place was as he remembered it.

From behind the stump and root wad of a downed tree, further concealed by a thicket of buck bushes with their red-purple berries, he looked down slope, his gray eyes sweeping his carefully selected field of fire. He could see clearly, through a natural opening in the underbrush and large, bare trees, directly onto the logging road. At that spot, there was a small clearing; it was open to the morning sun and was cathedral quiet, in shafts of soft and slanting sunlight. There, where the logging road passed through the approximate center of the clearing, was his kill zone. From where he sat, he could see almost the entire clearing, and, from the road, he was virtually invisible.

Jack unwrapped his rifle, checked the load and the cap on the nipple, and eased the hammer down on it. Then he laid out powder and shot for two more rounds, with the powder measured and wrapped in paper, and he sat down behind the base of the stump. In case things really went sour, he placed his big dragoon pistol on the leaf mulch beside them. With the rifle laid across the mossy, horizontal stump, he looked over the sights and scanned his field of fire. It was considerable. They would be coming from his left, facing into the dazzling brilliance of the rising sun. The soldiers would be looking ahead, searching in the brightness for a rider, but that rider would not be ahead of them on the road. He would be looking directly down on them, over his sights. This was going to be a challenge more dangerous than the killing of any of the others for the hill was not steep, and in the bare forest, he would be clearly visible once he stood up. His route of escape, if pursued, would be straight behind him, up the hill to his mare. No, he thought, fleeing after the first shot, clearly visible and in a foot race with a Yankee horse, he would probably be run down and killed. He would need to kill them both.

Jack had figured he would arrive about ten minutes before the soldiers did; so he wasted no time in preparing. They, however, had pushed their horses and made the trip faster than he had expected. He had been ready for no more than two or three minutes when the first sounds of their approach reached him.

He heard the horses snort and blow as they slowed from a gallop to a brisk trot and then to a walk. The soldiers were looking ahead to the open area where they had been told Jack Hinson had been. Reigning back, they were speaking to their horses in quiet, reassuring tones and examining the hoof prints in the dirt road, left as Jack had passed through earlier.

The first one was going to be easy, Jack thought; however,

reloading fast enough to kill the second soldier before he could spot Jack and open fire was going to be a challenge. If the second soldier reacted by charging up the slope toward him, Jack would be in a very bad way. During the past year, he had practiced a rapid-reload technique until he could fire, reload, and fire again in six seconds. In less than a minute, his life would depend on doing it, under pressure, and doing it right.

He looked over his sights, slowly cocked the hammer, squeezed the set trigger, and aimed at the level where the first soldier should appear from his left. With his trigger finger pressed forward against the trigger guard to keep it clear of the sensitive trigger, he adjusted and tightened his sight picture. With the silver bead of the front sight blade centered snugly in the "V" of the rear sight, he took several full, easy breaths. His adrenalin levels were running high, and he needed to be calm. As the head of the first horse appeared from his left, he adjusted his aim upward to chest height, took another breath and let half of it out. As the Yankee rider appeared in his sights, Jack touched the trigger. His rifle cracked and the forest birds flew up in a flurried rush and then went silent, all but a flock of crows, which persisted in their flapping, complaining cacophony. The big lead projectile struck the soldier diagonally between his right shoulder and his breastbone, tearing through the top of his right lung and the great vessels just above his heart, driving him leftward, off his horse.

As the horse reared and wheeled to its left, with the soldier falling under its hooves, Jack jerked his rifle back under his armpit; tore the powder load open with his teeth; poured the powder down the muzzle; followed it quickly with the Minié ball, base down; picked up the ramrod; rammed the load home; pushed the rifle back over the stump; cocked the hammer; recapped; and set the trigger. He had done it flawlessly. While he was reloading, the second rider lunged forward, around the dead soldier and his frantic horse, and looked uphill toward the sound of the shot. Too late, he spotted the top of Jack's head and realized he was looking into the muzzle of the rifle. As the soldier cocked and raised his heavy dragoon pistol in hasty aim, Jack touched the trigger a second time, and the spinning projectile struck the second soldier in the center of his upper chest. He never heard the crack of the rifle. He was slammed backward, twisting in the saddle, and over the off side of his horse, his right boot still caught in the stirrup. His horse spun around and ran up the road a short distance, dragging the soldier by the stirrup leather, and stopped, out of sight.

Jack reloaded quickly and waited as his heart raced and his breathing tried to keep up. By the time his heartbeat and breathing had subsided to something near normal, the only sounds were from the muted forest returning to normal, and the stamping and nervous, heavy breathing of the horses on the road below. The soldiers' horses, both spattered with their masters' blood, knew they should stay where they were, but the frightening abnormality of their situation had them nervously pawing, stamping, and questioning one another with nervous nickering. The cries of the crows were growing faint in the distance as silence returned.

Leaving the rifle on the stump, Jack took his pistol and walked slowly and carefully down to the road. Reaching the first soldier, he eased up to the horse, speaking softly, and moved around it until he could see the soldier fully. He had been dead when he hit the ground. At least if he had lived another minute or two, he hadn't known it. Moving eastward up the road, staying in the edge of the woods, he reached the second horse. The soldier was still partly suspended by his right leg and stirrup leather, on the left side of his horse, with his head and shoulders on the road. Although he had seen Jack for a fraction of a second, the shock of the bullet's impact, coupled with the immediate loss of blood supply to his brain, caused his death to be essentially instantaneous. The bleeding rider, whom the horse had dragged a short distance up the road, had known nothing of that final bit of travel.

Jack stood briefly looking at the dead soldier. It didn't seem right to leave him that way, so he slowly took the reigns in one hand, close up to the horse's chin, and with the other hand freed the dead foot from the stirrup. Then he led the horse to a sapling tree, tied him, and dragged the soldier off the road. He positioned him face up, arms at his side. Even that early in the warming of the morning, flies were already finding him. Jack waved them away and covered the man's face with his blue campaign hat.

Moving back up the road to the first soldier, he tied the horse and turned the soldier on his back, just off the road. With the man's blue campaign hat, he waved the flies away and covered his face. As an afterthought, he collected their weapons and ammunition. There were men who could make good use of them. Then he released both horses, knowing that they would return to Fort Donelson. He started them on their way down the road and headed back up the slope. He would need to find a place to conceal the newly acquired weapons. He would come back for them later; he couldn't afford to be seen carrying them.[11]

Jack had taken no pleasure in killing those two men. They had families—maybe wives and children, as he had. But it seemed clear that they had come there seeking to kill him. Had they had the chance, he was certain they would have killed him without even questioning him, would have taken his body, triumphantly, back to Fort Donelson and claimed their reward. They had, in a very real sense, fallen victim to their own trap. Where, he wondered, was all this killing going to lead?[12]

Perhaps it was better not to know.

Chapter 9

Making Military History

"Slipping in the blood that was spreading over the quarterdeck, the orderly returned with the [white] tablecloth tied to the halyard and ran it to the top of the signal mast. Looking on in disbelief, Jack stopped firing."

Jack returned to the Hundred Acre Field, recovered his shuck mattress and his food and headed southeast toward Hurricane Creek. Those two horses with empty, bloodstained saddles would be getting back to Fort Donelson soon, and the Yankees would come boiling out of the fort after him like angry hornets. He needed to get as far away from that spot as he could, as fast as he could, and he urged his big mare into an easy, steady trot, a gait she could maintain for the rest of the day.

As he rode south, he avoided the furnaces, coaling floors, and iron mills, for the Yankee soldiers often used them for brief stopping points to refill canteens and to "press" food and coffee. They also used them for overnight points for the same reason. The hot coffee and fresh food available at the larger sites was preferred over the water in their canteens and the hard tack and cold bacon in their saddlebags. At Cumberland Mills, there was a full-fledged mess, often with better food than they had at Fort Donelson. All such places were to be avoided.

Riding far around Randolph Forge, off to his left, he climbed the ridge above Long Creek, made his way down the south slopes, and crossed the creek. Under ordinary circumstances once he got over Long Creek, he would feel reasonably safe. However, these weren't ordinary circumstances. He had just killed two soldiers who may have bragged to the others that they were going out to kill him. In addition to that, word would reach Danville Crossing by telegraph, much faster than he and his mare could travel, and all soldiers in the Danville area would be "on the qui vie," watching for him.[1]

It also occurred to him that the reward for killing him had probably just been increased. There were a few Union sympathizers in the area, and some of them might be sorely tempted to turn him in. He could afford no careless moment, and the sooner he got back up on his ridge, the better.[2]

By noon, he was at the upper reaches of Hurricane Creek, and he followed it downstream, staying in the woods above the creek bottom. As the ridge rose to his right, he turned up slope and began the climb. That ridge wasn't home, but it would be the nearest thing to home that he would have for more than a year to come.

Back on Graffenried Bluff

Once on the ridge, he headed west toward the river and the bluff. One hundred yards short of the bluff, he dismounted, tied his mare to a sapling, and approached cautiously on foot, moving from tree to tree, pistol in hand, listening. He was watching not only for the presence of anyone else up there, but also for evidence that anyone had been there while he was away. He found neither; only the wild animals and the wind had been up there during his absence.

He made his way down to the ledge and stood for a few minutes, watching the river below. The weather was holding mild, and the Tennessee was peaceful and copper colored, reflecting the afternoon sunlight. Relaxing progressively, and grateful to God that he had made it safely back to his bluff, he enjoyed the walk back down the ridge to get his mare. He took the occasion to water her, drink his own fill, fill his canteen and his kettle, and he walked her back to the bluff. It was a quiet, peaceful, postscript to what had been a highly stressful day.

With a fire started in his improved fire pit, Jack put water on to heat in his real coffee pot, smiled at it, and set about unpacking and moving back into his cave home. Animals, probably raccoons, had been scratching around in the fireplace and in his crude bed; but he easily put it all back in order and then unrolled his mattress, filled with corn shucks. He felt better already just looking at this small, but significant, improvement in his crude furnishings.

With his mare fed and covered, his hot coffee, bacon, and Bubbling Springs cornbread—real cornbread—made a fine supper, which he topped off with dried apples. A cup of coffee and a pipe on his ledge as the pale sun disappeared in the southwest was a pleasant way to end a long, hard day. It didn't seem possible that he had been over the river, reunited with his family, traveled back to Bubbling Springs, emerged safely from the deadly encounter with the two soldiers in the Hundred Acre Field, and returned to his ledge in only two days.

With his rifle cleaned and loaded; his mare fed, brushed down, and covered; and his dragoon pistol beside him, Jack rolled up in his blanket and fell asleep quickly. It had been a very long day.

Turning Point

He rose in the pale, gray, predawn light to find that the warm spell had ended, driven southward before a biting, chilly north wind, which had brought with it a solid, gray, overcast. His cave protected him from the direct effect of north winds, but the chilly air had made its way into the cave, causing a rekindled fire to rise, in his early-morning thinking, to priority number one. Priority number two was to put that coffee pot with the rest of last night's coffee on the fire to heat.

The addition of his new shuck mattress was a decided improvement. Despite the colder air, the complaining bruises in his back, shoulders, and hips were only a murmur compared to their outcries of those earlier mornings. In fact, he thought, the addition of more pine and cedar branches and another load or two of dry leaf mulch, with the cushion of the shuck mattress above them, would make his bed just about perfect.

The walk down the ridge with his mare wasn't as pleasant as before because of the gray morning and cold, biting wind; but the walk loosened them both, and the cold water in the branch was delicious. Returning to the bluff with his canteen and water kettle full, he fed the mare and turned to the fixing of his own breakfast.

After breakfast, he took his coffee and pipe, climbed over to his ledge, and sat down to think, his coat wrapped around him, his old slouch hat pulled down, and the collar turned up against the wind. He had banked his fire in ashes to preserve it and suppress the smoke it made, but there was little need to worry about smoke on that gray, blustery morning. It would have been essentially invisible from below had he left it to its own devices.

Jack had reached a turning point, a crossroad in his new life as a renegade, and he knew not which way to go. He was back on his bluff, better equipped than he had been before, with a good supply of food and tobacco, and was relatively safe up there. Nevertheless, he realized he didn't know what to do next. Of course, he could probably just stay up there, lying low, returning periodically to Bubbling Springs or visiting friends in the area, to replenish his supplies. As old as he was, just doing that successfully would be a fairly remarkable accomplishment. That thought did not sit well in his Hinson mind; he was not the kind to hide, doing nothing, for very long. There was a war, after all, one that had been forced upon him and his family. The war had already taken the lives of five of his children—maybe even six for he had no way of knowing whether William was still living or lying dead on a far-off Virginia battlefield.

The hot coffee and his warm pipe were comforting as he sat, thinking, on his cold, wind-whipped stone ledge. He needed a plan, but none came to him. As he looked pensively down upon the river, it just looked back at him, brown and indifferent, suggesting nothing.

Roosters were crowing, somewhere below, greeting the chilly, gray morning without enthusiasm. The sun rose behind him in the southeast, subdued and concealed by the overcast, doing little to brighten the gray day. As he sat, thinking long on his ledge, the sun broke through the overcast, touched the hilltops across the river, and gradually spread its light into the valley below him. As the sunlight grew brighter, he began to understand his future. He realized he would not be able to map out a plan for himself, not a complete one, anyway, but that was alright. As the warming, illuminating sunlight was coming first to the distant hills, he still sat in deep, chilly shadow planning. As the sunlight moved ever closer to where he sat, his plan developed. By high noon, with the sun at its zenith overhead, the gray overcast had dissipated, and the entire valley was flooded with light. Likewise, he would have to solidify his plan. He needed only to make long-range plans at first, but as the time for action approached, so would come the knowledge of what he should do next.

From there on his bluff, he could not only attack the boats below him on the river, but he also could move to the river bottoms to attack enemy patrols on the trails, or attack the boats from the riverbanks. He could cross the river, as he had just done in the past two days, and do the same things along the west bank. He could also cross over the Dividing Ridge, as he had just demonstrated, and strike along the Cumberland. But he would always return there, eventually, to his ridge, his bluff, his cave, and his rock ledge. It seemed that they had been created just for him and that violent hour.

Jack had a long-range plan, and he would make specific arrangements as each day arrived, letting the morrow, for the most part, take care of itself.

So it would be, until the nightmare ended.

Hailstones and Better Shelter

As Jack slept the next night, the wind shifted to the south, and the warmer air collided with the wintry air that had settled over the Tennessee Valley. Swirling winds, from changing directions, announced the collision. The mixing air mass gathered strength, boiling, building, and feeding on itself until, in the early morning, energized storm clouds erupted in lightning bolts and thunderclaps that sounded like an artillery exchange. He woke to the furious explosions that seemed to shake the ridge. Realizing that it was the first thunderstorm of the new year, he said, to himself, "That's winter's back breakin'." In a manner of speaking, it was. The heavy rain that followed was cold, and the last of it fell as ice, hailstones carried high into the heavens, frozen and compounded, and then hurled earthward like cosmic bullets. But thunderstorms always announced the beginning of the end of hard Winter. There would still be cold, gray spells of weather, but they wouldn't last long. There may be late snow, with its big, wet flakes, but the people, like the crocuses and daffodils, took the cold spells in stride, undaunted. Like the daffodils and crocuses, they endured them, outlasting them as the warming sunshine melted the frost and snow, and energized them anew. It wasn't the end of winter, but it was good to see the beginning of the end.

He was comfortable and safe in his cave, but his mare had only the protection of a blanket. He climbed to the bluff and led her to a larger tree. Although the tree was leafless, its many-branched form provided a measure of protection for her, resisting and slowing the hailstones before they hit her. He would have to find a better place for her to spend the nights up there, especially in bad weather. A big cedar tree would be perfect for her, but there was none near enough, and she needed to be kept nearby—for her safety and for his. Well, he thought, it would be a simple matter to rig a brush arbor for her, and he would have plenty of time and materials to take care of that.

The sky cleared and the sun appeared as if a gigantic gray curtain had been opened to reveal the light and life waiting behind it. The hailstones, silver-gray remnants of the violence, lay all about, spent and melting. The warming sun had prevailed, and the scene around Jack's bluff and the valley below seemed to be flooded with a dazzling brilliance. It was as if life had just begun anew, and bright light filled the world.

After the morning walk to water his mare and replenish his own water supply, Jack fed and brushed her. She was still jumpy from the hail, and he spent some extra time with her. After breakfast, he sat down with his coffee and his pipe, enjoying the glorious brilliance of the new day. A packet carrying mail and passengers passed downstream, rushed through the chute, and disappeared toward Paducah. A hawk circled, high above the river, screeching its mysterious declarations into the clear morning air. Yes, he thought, he would build a brush arbor for his mare, and he should do it right away. Thunderstorms would be an increasingly frequent possibility now until next December when cold weather returned. The arbor, covered with cedar branches now, with maple branches added later, would also give her shade from the hot summer sun and some protection from rain. Just then, however, both he and his mare were enjoying the sun, which was climbing above the hills between Hurricane Creek and Danville Crossing, warming the ridge.

With his last cup of coffee finished, he returned the cup to the cave and picked up his rifle, the punch, and the small hammer. Seated on his sunny ledge, he unwrapped his rifle, laid it across his lap, and examined the top surface of the octagonal barrel. Just forward of the breach plug and centered on the flat surface were the five one-eighth-inch circles. He centered the punch just forward of the one he had added last, tapped it, and then gave it one sharp blow. That circle, permanently indented in the soft iron of the barrel, represented the first of the soldiers from the Hundred Acre Field. The circle for the other soldier who had been hunting him there, made the beginning of a second row of three.

With the hammer and punch put away, he lighted his pipe and watched the valley below him. A transport appeared upstream, its thick smoke billowing overhead as the following breeze and the speed of the boat balanced one another. Apparently carrying little cargo, it was riding high in the water. Jack watched the boat follow the channel to starboard, ever closer to the near bank, and pick up speed as it caught the swift water pulling it toward the chute. The big boat raced down the chute at speeds it could never approach on its own, veered to port, followed the channel out away from the bank, and steamed away toward Paducah to pick up a load of supplies for the terminal at Johnsonville. It would be back.

Two More Circles

At midmorning, a gunboat appeared, way down toward Leatherwood Creek, slicing through the muddy water, heading south, its smoke trailing slightly behind it in the light breeze. As it steamed slowly nearer, Jack could see its deck guns, and some of the crew topside. It appeared to be a gunboat making good speed, but it would require at least a half hour to traverse the chute. As the big boat hit the first of the surging water coming out of the chute, it slowed abruptly, almost as if it had run onto a sand bar. It would be in the chute a good forty-five minutes. He would have plenty of time; in fact, he thought, he would have plenty of time to get off more than one shot. He was thinking of maybe two.

As the gunboat struggled to overcome the current in the chute, Jack checked the load already in his rifle, firmed it with a tap of his ramrod, checked the cap, and eased the hammer down. Then he laid out shot, powder, and caps for two more shots. He liked to be prepared for one more than he expected. He wrapped the powder, measured to one hundred grains, in oiled papers twisted at both ends like hand-rolled cigarettes.

With his rifle resting its weight on the tree limb, Jack looked over the sights and scanned the upper decks, moving the muzzle slowly, fore and aft. On the quarterdeck, there were three officers, Jack's targets of choice. He could not read the rank insignia at that distance, but he chose the one who appeared to be in command, focused his eyes on him, and cocked the hammer. Checking his sight picture, and holding the shiny silver bead of the front sight snug in the rear sight notch, he centered the bead on the man's chest, on the line of shiny brass buttons and cocked the set trigger. Taking a deep breath and letting half of it out, he moved the bead slightly lower and touched the trigger. As the man was driven backward off his feet, Jack jerked his rifle back and reloaded. Shoving the rifle back across the tree limb he cocked, recapped, and again looked over the sights at the quarterdeck. The other officers were staring impotently down at the motionless man on the deck. Moving the sights onto the back of one of them, Jack cocked the set trigger, tightened the sight picture, held the bead in the center of the blue back, eased it a little lower, and touched the trigger. He wondered, as he saw the second man hurled forward on top of the one already down, if he had remembered to breathe correctly. Actually, as he thought about it, he realized that, from the time he reaimed onto the quarterdeck, totally absorbed, he had forgotten to breathe at all. He mustn't do that again; he must always take time to do it all and do it deliberately.

Jack's rifle barrel, with part of the thirty-six "kill" circles.

He reloaded but sat back, his rifle on the ledge beside him, and watched the bloody scene below him as the one remaining officer on the deck took charge, and sailors rushed to help. Most of the sailors, not otherwise engaged, looked wildly around them, instinctively crouching, wondering where those deadly bullets were coming from. A few seized rifles, already loaded, and fired blindly into the riverbank and the bluff rising above it. Jack had plenty of time to fire again—several times—but felt no inclination to do so. He watched it all, and as the boat finally cleared the chute, he went to the cave for his hammer and punch. Seated again on the ledge, he added, very carefully, two more circles, completing a row of three. That brought his total to nine. He cleaned his rifle, reloaded it, put it away, and spent most of the rest of the day building the brush arbor shelter for his mare.

And so it went through the spring, and into the summer.

As weeks passed, he made occasional trips away for supplies, to visit his family across the river, or just to let the bluff cool off for a while. Sometimes he would stalk Yankee patrols in the forest, on both sides of the Dividing Ridge. Sometimes he crossed over the Ridge for a boat on the Cumberland. But, mostly, he stayed on his bluff, punishing the gunboats and transports that passed below his ledge. He knew of no other place like it. The number of tiny circles on his rifle barrel continued to grow in their orderly progression like tiny soldiers marching forward in small formations. They passed the rear sight and continued forward beyond it. Three of them represented kills at a distance of more than one thousand yards, all the way across the Tennessee River. And, as the little circles increased in number and marched steadily forward, so increased the fear on the Yankee boats—on both rivers—the fear of the unseen, deadly sniper.[3]

Making Military History

Many were the Yankee gunboats and transports, which passed through Jack's sight picture that spring and summer of 1864 and suffered losses; but one still stands out, unique in his war on the Union navy—unique, in fact, in the annals of naval warfare, anywhere in the World. Nothing like it in recorded history had ever happened before, nor has anything like it happened since.

In the "dog days" of late summer and early fall, the river levels slowly dropped and the currents diminished, making progress upstream less difficult. This improvement in southward travel on the river would continue until water levels dropped to the point at which through traffic would no longer be possible. After that, big boat traffic would not begin again until winter rains could raise river levels again. The current in the Towhead Chute still raced northward at a speed much greater than in the wider stretches of the river but was more easily navigable upstream, even for the heavily loaded transports. In fact, it was one of these heavily loaded, armed transports that, with Jack's assistance, made ignominious naval history.

This boat, heavily loaded with cargo for Grant's army, was also carrying a capacity load of soldiers to bolster his blue-clad legions. She was riding low in the water, and fairly bristled with soldiers, their packs, and their rifles, filling every available space topside. The soldiers were predictably hot, lethargic, and bored. Some blue coats hung open and many were off. Some passed the time

As Jack looked over the barrel of his rifle, he patiently scanned the exposed men on the boat looking for the rank insignia of an officer. (Drawing by Joe McCormick)

writing letters home, some found room to play cards as money changed hands, others smoked and watched the river flow by, and some found what comfort they could and drowsed. All expected to be in a battle within the next few days, but none expected to be in one in the next few minutes.

High above them, cool gray eyes scanned the boat and its cargo, and Jack estimated the time it would require to traverse the chute. In spite of the diminished velocity of the current, the large, overloaded, transport would require at least forty-five minutes to get out of his kill zone—maybe an hour. He had a lot of time and a concentrated target.

Aboard the boat, the naval officers and crew were not bored or lethargic; not a one of them was asleep. They had made these trips before, and all were aware of the dangers there. That narrow, difficult passage had become legendary among veterans of river service as a gauntlet to be feared. All the narrow chutes in the area had become known as dangerous when steaming south. Jack had created much of this awareness—on both rivers. This chute, however, below Jack's bluff, was known to be in a high-hazard class all its own.

The heavily laden boat was barely making steerageway. On the quarterdeck, the captain was watching the channel ahead, speaking corrections to the helmsman. All other naval eyes were scanning the Stewart County bank, the wide cornfields beyond it, and the big wooded hill rising steeply above it. The sailors not actively involved in moving the boat through the chute held rifles, loaded and ready. Gun crews were at battle stations, standing beside their naval guns, which were aimed at the shore.

As Jack observed all this, he laid out a quantity of loads beside him, checked the load already in his rifle, tapped it down, placed the ramrod beside him, and firmed the cap down on the nipple. He slid the barrel onto the small limb, its bark worn off on the top from repeated use, and scanned the quarterdeck over his sights.

As the first naval officer went down, slammed to the deck by the impact of Jack's Minié ball, the other officers stared at their friend's sudden motion, then heard the crack of the exploding powder in Jack's rifle and crouched reflexively. A navy rifle cracked in response, firing into the willow thickets along the bank, then others, firing blindly in the direction of the disappearing puff of white smoke on the hill. The crews of the deck cannon saw no targets but fired anyway into the green sameness of the cornfields and the rising slope beyond.

Another naval officer went down. More navy rifles fired blindly into uninhabited space along the shore and up on the hill as the boat struggled steadily up the chute. With blood spreading steadily over the quarterdeck, orders were being shouted amidst growing confusion. Some of the embarked soldiers loaded their rifles, clumsily, dropping things, getting in one another's way, shouting, cursing. Sporadically, some of the soldiers began to fire, as blindly as the sailors did; others began to search the green shore and point this way and that. Some began to pray.

The captain, frantic and feeling helpless, looked up the channel ahead of him and knew that he had a long time in that deadly gauntlet. Orders were now being shouted at the embarked soldiers. Officers and sergeants, trying to be heard over the din, added to the confusion, accomplishing little.

An army officer, his blue coat proper and buttoned with his shiny rank insignia on his epaulettes, waved his sword over his head, trying vainly to bring order to the chaos. He was driven suddenly to his knees, his upper body twisted violently to his left, with his sword appearing to hang briefly in the air before falling on the man next to him. As the sword fell, the crack of another shot from Jack's rifle went unnoticed among the crackling of futile musketry from the boat's crew and the embarked soldiers.

Jack's cool eyes saw another officer move into his sights, waving his sword and shouting orders that no one seemed to hear. That army officer went down and didn't move as the crowded soldiers around him first jumped back away from him, and then moved close, wanting to help but not knowing what to do.

There were officer targets aplenty on that ship, and as fast as he could reload, he found another blue coat with epaulettes or rank stripes on the sleeves. Officers continued to fall, knocked from their feet in midutterance by the shocking, tearing impact of the big, spinning, .50-caliber, lead projectiles. These were replacement troops not battle-hardened veterans. Although many continued to fire at the bank and the bluff above it, confusion began to give way to panic.

On the quarterdeck, the captain looked around on the carnage, saw the generalized confusion, and the creeping cold sensation of panic struggled against his judgment. Looking about him and seeing all his officers lying dead or wounded and not moving, watching the little cyclonic stirrings of panic around the dead and wounded army officers as they continued to fall, he realized that his boat would still be in that deadly gauntlet for at least another thirty minutes. Feeling that something must be done to stop the carnage, he made a decision. He gave orders to back the engines off and drop the two bow anchors. With that being done, he ordered the nearest petty officer to run up a white surrender flag; however, he was told there was no such flag aboard. The captain's orderly was sent below to the officers' wardroom and brought back a tablecloth. Slipping in the blood that was spreading over the quarterdeck, the orderly returned with the tablecloth, tied it to a halyard, and ran it to the top of the signal mast. Looking down on the scene in disbelief, Jack stopped firing.

As the big boat slowed and stopped, bow anchors down, and engines just balancing the flow of the current, the confusion began to diminish. Sporadic firing from the boat sputtered and stopped. Those who noticed the white tablecloth flying at the top of the mast stared up at it in bewilderment. As quiet once more prevailed, the captain looked about him, expecting at least a troop of Confederate cavalry to come riding down the riverbank toward him. There was only silence. No one came.

From high above, Jack Hinson wondered if his old eyes were playing tricks on him. Was he dreaming? No, he decided, the unbelievable really had taken place: the captain had surrendered his boat—to him. He had captured the boat, complete with cargo, deck guns, surviving crew, and the embarked infantry unit, weapons and all. Although the captain didn't realize it, he had placed his entire ship at the feet of one amazed old man.

The boat's commanding officer knew, in general terms, what was expected of him in such a situation and called for his sword; however, Jack Hinson, up on his bluff overlooking the bizarre scene below him, had not the foggiest idea of what to do next. It would be easy to kill the boat's captain or anyone else in view on the boat, but he couldn't do that, not with the boat and everyone aboard surrendered to him and under a white flag.

Aboard the boat, confusion gradually subsided, and except for activity around the dead and dying, the boat fell silent. Some of the sailors wept. As the realization grew that they were being surrendered to the rebels, some of the embarked soldiers wept also. Mostly, however, bewildered silence prevailed aboard the surrendered boat. The only constant sounds were those of the water, rushing and eddying past the stationary boat, and of the engines, turning the paddles slowly against the current.

Realizing the bizarre situation below him, Jack wished for Forrest to appear, or John Hunt Morgan, or Lyon, or Wheeler. However, no soldiers in Confederate gray appeared to take this great prize off his hands. In fact, there was not a Confederate soldier or even a genuine guerrilla anywhere around for miles in all directions. Old Jack Hinson was alone to meet this challenge, with his single-shot muzzleloader rifle and one dragoon pistol. And, the pistol was in the cave.

Seeming to stand still, time hung heavy in the hot air as the big boat's paddle wheels continued their slow, stationary churning. The armed sailors and soldiers aboard the big boat had dropped their rifles in surrender. The officers had done the same with their swords and pistols.

It was Jack's move, but he had no move to make. He couldn't fire on them any more, and there was simply no way for him to accept their surrender and then control them, alone. It was a uniquely bizarre situation.

After what seemed like an awkward eternity, the captain began to grasp the reality that no troops were coming, no Confederate hordes to swarm down onto the boat and take possession of it and the prisoners of war aboard. He began to think that none would come.

Jack didn't move or make a sound. Not knowing anything else to do, he just watched. Finally, restless murmurs began slowly to spread among the soldiers and the crew. Subdued shuffling and limited, random movement began to replace their frozen-in-place silence.

Simultaneously, the captain seemed to come to life. He looked around and saw the absurdity of the situation. Gaining his voice, he gave orders for the engines to go to all-ahead full and to weigh anchors. The big boat began to move again, making slow forward progress against the current. The captain ordered the tablecloth lowered and returned to the wardroom. Scattered cheers spread and grew into generalized rejoicing as the boat passed through the rest of the chute, steered to starboard with the channel, and picked up speed against the stream. She was free again to steam south toward Johnsonville.

The casualties began to receive organized care, but they were all beyond human help. There would be bodies to bury and letters to be written to next of kin. With cleanup underway, the liberated naval vessel steamed steadily upstream, beyond Danville Crossing and White Oak Island, and passed out of sight.

Jack sat on his ledge and loaded his pipe. Even though he was becoming increasingly hardened to the killing, it always left a lingering, subtle sadness stirring deep within him. He fired up his pipe and smoked it indifferently as he thought about it all. He had no idea that he had just made military and naval history; nor, I believe today, would he have cared had he known.

It was the only time in recorded history that a fully armed naval vessel with embarked combat troops ever surrendered to one man, and it was probably the shortest period of military confinement after being captured in combat.[4]

The record still stands.[5]

Dog Days Arrive and Joseph Goes Away

In the dog days of September 1864, Jack's sixteen-year-old son Joseph left Sulfur Wells and enlisted as a Confederate soldier. His term of enlistment was expressed simply as "War" and constituted a commitment to serve for the duration of the war, how ever long that might be. Unhappily for Joseph, the "duration," which would prove to be only seven months, would be a dismal and deadly time. He arrived in time for the cold and hungry winter of 1864 and 1865, the siege at Petersburg, and the final, hopeless, bloody spring of 1865. Joseph, so young, marched off to join Company F of the Fourteenth Tennessee Infantry in Virginia, William's company. The fact that the two brothers would be together brought some consolation to Jack and Elisabeth. William could look after his little brother.[6]

At the same time, water levels in the Cumberland River dropped until they approached the point at which large naval vessels could not ascend the river. On the Tennessee, there was less gunboat and transport traffic under Jack's bluff. Those that did pass upstream had an easier time with the reduced current. In addition, as Jack had expected, his water sources on the ridge were drying up, retreating progressively farther down the flanks of his ridge. He decided that it was time to move his base of operations until fall and winter rains again replenished the small streams higher up.

Operating on the West Bank

Soon, boat traffic on the Cumberland would have to stop for a month or two. In addition, his ridge "needed a rest" from him and his operations until Yankee attention was directed elsewhere.

Thoughts of Henry and Benton Counties across the river struck a responsive chord in his mind. Although he had been looking across the river and its valley almost every day for several months, he had seen few Yankee patrols along the river over there. There was plenty of concealment in the willow thickets and cane breaks along the river, and in the green forest that covered the rising bottomland and the hills to the west. There would also be abundant water there for him and his mare. An added consideration was the proximity of Elisabeth and his children; if he didn't get careless and overdo it, he could see them more often and replenish his supplies as well. He would not have a place to sleep and cook as nice as his cave under the bluff, but with the dry weather, he could sleep almost anywhere with relative comfort. By never staying in the same place for very long, he would be safe from all but the most determined Yankee pursuit. It would be hotter down along the river and mosquitoes more of a problem, but he could deal with both. Although there would be leeches in the streams, he could bathe as often as he liked. There would be good grazing for his mare down in the valley, and he would need less feed for her. Also to be considered were the increases through the spring and summer in the price on his head, and he was no longer wanted "dead or alive"—just dead.[7]

Moving across the river for a while made sense, and a plan was coming together. This plan would take him across the river where he would move, with freedom and liquidity, up and down the west bank, from abandoned Fort Heiman in Kentucky south to Benton County. The idea had a peaceful feel to it. So, he thought, why wait?

At noon, he ate, slowly and thoughtfully, then stretched out in the cool of his cave and slept through the heat of the day.

Waking, he cooked bacon and cornbread to last a few days, filled his canteen with the leftover black coffee, and packed his gear. He had plenty of powder and shot, matches, and the other essentials. Coffee and tobacco had become luxuries in his wilderness existence, but he had found ways to maintain supplies of both. He noted the extent to which he had "spread out and moved in" there on his ridge. It was striking for a man on the run to be so "established," but that would change now. He would be a moving target across the river, traveling light, never settling in, until late autumn.

In late afternoon, he took one last look around his hilltop home and mounted and rode off in the direction of Leatherwood Creek. That evening, in the lingering pastels of summer twilight, he led his mare off Wynn's Ferry and disappeared into the thickets of the mouth of Big Sandy above the riverbank.

Through the rest of late summer and into fall, Jack inhabited the river bottoms, swamps, and hills along the west bank of the Tennessee River and the mouth of the Big Sandy, moving almost constantly, from Benton County in Tennessee to Calloway County in Kentucky. He moved like a shadow from abandoned Fort Heiman and Camp Lowe southward to Cypress Creek Swamp and the forest ridges across the river from Johnsonville.

He found blue-uniformed targets on passing boats, firing down from the bluffs, and firing up from his duck blinds along the river. He also stalked the cavalry patrols, and the less frequent infantry sweeps, when they came through the area. To them he became a shadowy terror, a deadly phantom who seemed to be ever-present but was never seen. It was said in the area, long after the war, that many a Yankee soldier, conversing casually with his companions on patrol, "died in the middle of a sentence," torn out of his saddle by a .50-caliber bullet from Jack's rifle.[8]

Making Military History Again

On several occasions, because of his detailed knowledge of the terrain, the trails, and enemy activity, Jack acted as scout and guide in Nathan Bedford Forrest's disruptive, lightning attacks on Union forces in the area. The one for which both he and Forrest are best remembered was Forrest's raid on Johnsonville, Tennessee, the huge Union supply depot and shipping point on the east bank of the

Tennessee River. It was the last significant victory of the Confederacy in the west, and there, once more, Jack would make military and naval history in a unique accomplishment never achieved before, or since. This time, however, he would not be alone.[9]

Johnsonville was in Humphreys County, twelve miles west of Waverly. Like Danville Crossing, Johnsonville was a transportation hub for supplying the Union armies fighting in East Tennessee and Georgia. Food, weapons, ammunition, clothing, and even hay for the horses were shipped from there to Nashville, thence to Chattanooga, and ultimately to Sherman, as he pressed the battle toward Atlanta. Like Danville Crossing, in addition to the river landing, there was a railroad terminal at Johnsonville, but there was no bridge. Unlike Danville Crossing, there was also a very large supply depot there with warehouses, massive amounts of food, uniforms, weapons, and other supplies for Sherman's army. Union navy boats were frequently moored there, offloading supplies. To protect the vital supply center from Confederate attack there was a thirty-gun fortress on the bluff above it, plus varying numbers of Union gunboats that operated from Johnsonville Landing to defend it.

Forrest had decided to do something about that, and he would need Jack Hinson's help.[10] In late October 1864, Forrest rode northeastward out of Jackson, Tennessee, toward a rendezvous with Jack Hinson—and with history. His mission was to disrupt Yankee supply lines on the river between Paducah and Johnsonville, and on October 28, Jack met the lead elements of Forrest's force on the sand road west of Paris Landing. It was Gen. Abraham Buford with Forrest's artillery, and Jack led them directly to Fort Heiman.[11]

Fort Heiman was an empty, brooding presence looking down on the river below. Built by the Confederates in late 1861, it had been abandoned in February 1862 upon the fall of Fort Henry across the river. After that time, it had been occupied as an operating base by Colonel Lowe and his Fifth Iowa Cavalry, until Lowe had abandoned it in March of 1863 and moved across the river to Fort Henry. Since abandonment by Lowe, Heiman had been used from time to time as a temporary base camp by Union units, including the Third Minnesota Infantry Regiment, patrolling in the area. In recent weeks, however, one lone Confederate sniper had occupied it. It was one of Jack's regular haunts, and he knew with precision the channel that the Yankee boats would be forced to follow in passing below it.[12]

Jack advised General Buford as he placed his guns in the old Confederate earthworks; included in the newly arrived Confederate artillery were two six-inch Parrott rifles, lovingly operated by Capt. E.S. Walton's battery of General Lyon's Kentuckians.

About three hundred yards to the north of Fort Heiman, Capt. John W. Morton's battery was set up on the west bank. Between Morton's Battery and Walton's Battery at Fort Heiman, the artillerymen had established a kill zone for Yankee boats. Five miles to the south, more of Morton's guns were set in at Paris Landing. If a Yankee boat escaped one battery, there were others waiting.

With the Confederate guns in place, situated with Jack's advice, and plenty of daylight left, two big Union transports appeared upstream making good speed with the current, headed for Paducah. General Buford ordered the gunners to hold their fire. The boats were empty, and they would wait for transports on their way to Johnsonville loaded with supplies. Although no one there could have imagined it, when loaded transports appeared, Forrest's initiative would cause military and naval history to be made.

The next morning their patience was rewarded. Early on the twenty-ninth, a boat appeared, headed south. As predicted, it was heavily loaded with supplies for Sherman. In addition, she was pulling a loaded barge behind her. She was the *Mazeppa,* built in Cincinnati and newly arrived in the war zone. As she steamed into the kill zone between Morton's Battery and Walton's big guns at Fort Heiman, the Confederates opened fire and *Mazeppa* was immediately hit and disabled. The rebels' cheers quickly turned to groans, however, as the disabled boat, with its cornucopia of food, uniforms, and other supplies, drifted aground on the far bank beyond their reach. Most of the Yankee crew leapt ashore and disappeared into Stewart County.

Capt. Frank P. Gracey swam to the crippled *Mazeppa,* took the captain's surrender, and rigged a way to drag the boat to the west bank. Having heard the firing, three gunboats from upstream came steaming onto the scene and opened fire, but accurate, heavy fire from the Confederates drove them back toward Johnsonville. The *Mazeppa* was unloaded, and her brief naval career ended. She was burned to the waterline and sank.

The next day, the thirtieth, two more Union transports appeared, steaming casually upstream, apparently unaware of the new Confederate presence at Fort Heiman. In the lead was the *Anna*. Hit immediately but not disabled, she ran up a white flag and slowed to a stop. It was a ruse. As soon as the Confederate gunners left their guns and ran, cheering, down to the riverbank to seize their prize, the ship went to full power and steamed away, flame and sparks spewing from her stacks. Remanning their guns, the cannoneers quickly disabled the *Anna,* and she drifted helplessly downstream toward Paducah.

Next appeared the transport *Venus* pulling two loaded barges, and escorted by the gunboat *Undine*. Behind them came another Yankee boat, the *J. W. Cheeseman*; they all seemed unaware of the trap. Once all three were in the kill zone, both batteries opened fire, and within minutes, the *Cheeseman* was disabled and run aground, the *Undine* had been run aground across the river, and the *Venus,* carrying an armed infantry unit, had surrendered.

After being built by Confederates and abandoned without a fight, then occupied by Colonel Lowe's Federals for more than a year and again abandoned, Fort Heiman's first real battle, and its last, was an audacious, resounding Confederate victory.

At this point, looking upon the scene, Forrest's eyes sparkled. An unorthodox idea was occurring to that uneducated military genius. Turning to Captain Morton, he asked, "John—how'd you like to put your guns aboard those boats out there and become a commodore?" Morton, demurred, pleading ignorance of boats, but he recommended Captain Gracey, hero of the seizure of the *Mazeppa* the day before since "he used to be a steamboat man."[13]

And so it was that Captain Gracey, of Forrest's horse artillery, became commanding officer, *pro tempore,* of the captured Union gunboat *Undine*.

Forrest's Improvised Navy

There was still one Yankee boat available, the *Mazeppa* and *Cheeseman* having already been unloaded and burned. Turning next to Lt. Col. W. A. Dawson, Forrest ordered him to put howitzers aboard the *Venus,* embark his troops with horses, and take command of the Yankee transport, newly become Confederate gunboat. Like Captain Morton, the colonel pleaded ignorance of things nautical, but Forrest insisted, saying if things went sour, Colonel Dawson was to run her aground, recover what he could, and burn her.

Then Forrest decided to go aboard the *Undine* himself, and he walked with considerable difficulty aboard. Although he tried to conceal it, Forrest was suffering from a recent, severe abdominal wound. Most of his men had never seen him dismounted, and they were shocked at his difficulty in walking. With Forrest aboard, "steamboat man" Captain Gracey shoved off, and Forrest's little flotilla took a cruise from Paris Landing down to Fort Heiman and back to Paris Landing. Colonel Dawson and the *Venus* followed along on the brief, bizarre, shakedown cruise. Having had his moment of naval command, Forrest wished Captain Gracey well and went ashore where he belonged.

This odd cruising on the Tennessee was seen and reported to Union commanders. From Donelson, Lt. Col. E. C. Brott reported to Colonel Smith at Clarksville, "They have two transports [sic] in running order, and run them up and down the river at [their] pleasure."[14]

On the way to Johnsonville, Jack confers with Nathan Bedford Forrest near Paris Landing. (Drawing by Joe McCormick)

With his army/navy task force organized, Forrest issued his orders and, with Jack Hinson scouting ahead, turned south toward Johnsonville on November 1.

Jack led Forrest's command through the often-muddy river bottom forest, choosing pathways he knew well, keeping them out of sight but near the riverbank in case they needed to rush to the support of their amateur navy. The leaves were taking on autumn coloration, and the air was cool, making the task a little easier for the sweating, straining horses pulling artillery pieces and caissons through the mud. As Forrest's "navy" with embarked "horse Marines" sailed upstream toward Johnsonville, Yankee gunboats appeared upstream and immediately took *Venus* under fire. Colonel Dawson returned fire with his Parrot guns but presented a large target to the smaller gunboats and took several hits. With greatly reduced power, he ran *Venus* aground, burned her, and moved out to rejoin Forrest with his guns.

Aboard the *Undine,* Captain Gracey, much more able at using his boat, tried to lure the Yankee gunboats into range of Captain Morton's batteries ashore. The gunboats, however, refused the bait and withdrew. The next day, with their longer-range guns, they stayed at a distance and crippled *Undine.* With his brief naval command at an end, Captain Gracey ran *Undine* aground on the west bank, put his men ashore, and set fire to the boat's powder magazine. She was blown to pieces as he swam ashore. He and his crew set out up the bank to rejoin Forrest.[15]

It was during a halt on the move toward Johnsonville that Maj. Charles W. Anderson, Forrest's adjutant general, had occasion to converse with Jack about his campaign as a sniper. Anderson knew Jack from two previous expeditions when Jack had served as a guide for Forrest. Major Anderson's recollection of that conversation, in later years, has given us the only known record of an informal statement by Jack. As Anderson asked him about his increasingly notorious one-man war against the Union, and the growing price on his head, Jack replied, "They murdered my boys, and may yet kill me; but the marks on the barrel of my gun will show that I am a long way ahead in the game now, and am not done yet."[16]

Major Anderson's memories also provide us with the most complete physical description of him known to exist. He recalled,

"Hinson's clear, gray eyes, compressed lips and massive jaws, clearly indicated that, under no circumstances, was he a man to be trifled with or aroused; and, under the great bereavement inflicted upon him by the wanton slaughter of his sons, he kept his oath until the close of the war."[17]

The Flaming End of Sherman's Johnsonville

During the night of November 3, Forrest's command, now without its "navy" but with Jack Hinson leading the way, crossed Cypress Creek Swamp and arrived undetected across the river from Johnsonville. They quietly went into firing positions that night, and the Union commander at Johnsonville was not aware of any threat, thinking that the neutralization of *Venus* and *Undine* had eliminated the enemy unit that had been causing the trouble downriver. He could not have been more wrong.

He also felt secure with his fifty-gun fortification facing the river and navy gunboats tied up at the landing below. It seemed that he had nothing to fear from the river or from the west bank. He was wrong again.

As the sun rose on November 4, Forrest's troops and guns were deployed for attack, but Captain Morton wanted to place a section of his guns farther upstream to bracket the target, and Forrest agreed. After hours of work making a roadway and struggling through the muddy forest without being seen, Morton's guns were in place and camouflaged with bushes. By that time, the Union commander knew that there were Confederates on the west bank. Since he thought it was only a scouting party, he did not send anyone across the river to investigate. His failure to do so cost him a major defeat and a logistics disaster.

At 2:00 in the afternoon, Forrest's guns in unison opened fire on the warehouses, giant piles of supplies in the open, the railroad terminal above the boat landing, and the gunboats and transports along the shore. The Confederate fire was accurate and devastating. Explosions and fires erupted at the depot and huge amounts of hay, clothing, meat, and other supplies began to be consumed in roaring mountains of flame and smoke.

Federal commanders quickly got their guns in action also, and they blazed away in impotent fury. Johnsonville was on the bluff side of the river, and its fort was on the bluff. The fifty guns in the fort could not be depressed enough to hit Forrest's howitzers, and their shots screamed harmlessly over the heads of his gunners. The gunboats had the same problem but in reverse. Their guns couldn't be elevated enough, and their shots fell short, plowing into the muddy bank as Forrest's gunners continued to wreak havoc on Sherman's supplies, the boats, and the facilities around them.

Elements of four Union regiments at Johnsonville blazed away with their rifles. Union artillery fire, although ineffective, was so heavy that Forrest described it as a "storm of shell" and reported that some of his gun crews were nearly buried in the flying dirt.[18]

Forrest himself was having the time of his life. Forgetting the pain of his wound, he manned a gun himself. He was serving as a cannoneer, firing away at Johnsonville and shouting in erroneous terms, "Elevate the breech a little lower, boys—elevate the breech a little lower!"[19] Each time he fired and the recoil rolled the gun back, the generals Abraham Buford and Tyree Bell repositioned the gun. It was undoubtedly the highest-ranking gun crew in all of military history. The real cannoneers stood back, laughing and shouting, enjoying the three-general performance. They would have stories to tell their children and grandchildren as long as they lived. At one point, Forrest looked around at Captain Morton and shouted, "We'd wipe old Sherman off the earth, John, if they'd give me enough men and you enough guns!"[20] He was probably right, but it was far too late for that, and the Davis government had neither guns nor men to give them.

Johnsonville, its depot, rail terminal, and supplies were going up in flames, the Union transports and gunboats were destroyed and sinking, and the hungry, exhausted Confederates, while rejoicing in the victory, were being tormented by the smell of burning bacon, coffee, and exploding barrels of whiskey filling the air with their fragrance. They would have given a lot to have some of the good items they were destroying, but they were out of reach across the river. Forrest later reported to General Taylor that on November 4, the warehouses, supplies at the landing, transports, and gunboats burned as a continuous sheet of flame for a mile along the river that afternoon and all night.

On the morning of the fifth, the cannoneers shelled the burning wreckage one last time and pulled out. Seeing them departing, black Union troops rushed down to the Johnsonville landing, leaping, shaking their fists, and hurling curses at Forrest's rear guard. The weary Confederates paused and opened fire with rifles, killing some and scattering the rest, then turned again and, with Jack Hinson leading, disappeared into the forest. The remarkable battle of Johnsonville was over.

Those ragged Confederates would go on being tired, hungry, and cold most of the time during the remaining five months of the war. They would go on winning small victories, would suffer in the futile carnage at Franklin and Nashville, and would be the last Confederate command to surrender. Nevertheless, the survivors could look back with satisfaction to Johnsonville, one last decisive victory gained in enemy-held territory. Moreover, not the least of their accomplishments was that they were able, with Jack Hinson's expert guidance, to march with artillery all the way from Fort Heiman to Johnsonville, thirty-five miles, in less than three days, stopping along the way to destroy, capture, and use enemy naval vessels, and arrive and dig in their guns without being detected. They had destroyed the Union fleet on the Tennessee River, destroyed Sherman's principal supply depot, and at least six million dollars worth of supplies.

The supply depot and rail terminal at Johnsonville would never function again during the war. Forrest's losses were two killed and nine wounded.[21]

Grudging Praise from Sherman

General Sherman, writing about it later, called it "a feat of arms which, I must confess, excited my admiration."[22] This was rare praise by Sherman of a Confederate leader's accomplishment for he despised all things Confederate. In fact, while Sherman was fully occupied with the Atlanta campaign, Forrest, although far away in west and middle Tennessee, was still on his mind. He wrote to Secretary of War Stanton, calling Forrest "the very devil" and asking for his death "even if it cost 10,000 lives and breaks the treasury." In Sherman's troubled mind, this estimation of a valid price for Forrest's death was probably not hyperbolic.[23]

What Forrest had done still stands unique in the history of warfare. Never before, or since, has a land army commander captured naval vessels, manned them, and then used them in further combat against that enemy. In addition, never before, or since, has a field artillery piece been manned in combat by an all-general-officer crew.

For the second time in his one-man war against the Union army and navy, Jack Hinson had made military history, but this time he was not alone. This time he was part of a team—an exceptional team—led by his friend Nathan Bedford Forrest.

Epilogue to Johnsonville

In the fall of 1925, the Tennessee River was so low that the sunken Union vessels were exposed. People came from far and wide to see the things that the local river people had known were there all along. In the boats were found bags of beans, coffee beans, cases of canned goods and whiskey, pencils, pen points, penstocks, ink, hardtack, biscuits, burned and twisted rifles, and artillery ammunition. Some of the wrecks in deeper water could be seen but could not be searched.[24]

Chapter 10

The Last Campaign

"To everything there is a season . . . a time to kill, and a time to heal . . . a time of war, and a time of peace."
—Ecclesiastes 3:1, 3, 8

The Final Autumn

After Forrest departed the area, Jack traveled to Sulfur Wells to see Elisabeth and the children and to replenish his supplies. With that done, he crossed the river and returned to Stewart County. It was mid-November, the weather was pleasant, the forest was in its brilliant autumn colors, and increasing rains had water levels rising in the creeks. Riding slowly across Leatherwood Creek and up the slope toward his ridge, he noticed water in the branches farther up the slope than when he had left in late summer.

Joseph had been reunited with William in Virginia, but the war news from there was not encouraging. They were with Lee, defending Petersburg and Richmond, the fighting was at times fierce and all supplies were scarce, including food.

At Fort Donelson, Fort Henry, and Clarksville, units came and went, commands were redesignated, and commanders continued to change. In the fall and winter of 1864 total effective strength at Fort Donelson was averaging only about 230 men, including two batteries of artillery. At times, Fort Donelson was temporarily commanded by a Capt. James P. Flood, who was also commanding officer of Battery C of the Second Illinois Light Artillery. In October, the post was commanded by Lt. Col. T. R. Weaver and manned by elements of his 119th Colored Infantry Regiment. Other units cycled through the Henry-Donelson-Clarksville command that fall and winter included the Forty-second Missouri Volunteer Infantry and Virgil Earp's Eighty-third Illinois Volunteer Infantry.[1]

Other news of the war was ominous. Gen. J. E. B. "Jeb" Stuart, Lee's eyes and ears, who had been with Lee at Harper's Ferry and was like a son to him, had been mortally wounded at Yellow Tavern and died a few days later in Richmond. Kentucky's dashing Gen. John Hunt Morgan, "the Thunderbolt of the Confederacy," had been betrayed by a local citizen in Greenville, Tennessee, and shot dead. Jack hoped that what Forrest had accomplished from Fort Heiman to Johnsonville would hinder Sherman's further progress. However, Atlanta had fallen. Sherman was burning Atlanta and beginning his brutal march to the sea. Mercifully, Jack could not know these things.

Back up on his ridge, he found little change. Raccoons had scattered his rustic bed and the ashes in his fireplace, but it would all be easy to restore. His mare's brush arbor had likewise suffered from wind and neglect, but that also would be simple to repair. He was thinking of adding a wall on the north side to protect her from the coldest winter winds. Except for a deepening layer of autumn leaves, his ledge was as he left it.

It was good to be back. Although at first it had been only a refuge, a means of survival, his ridge had become a home to him. Even in his latter years, after the war, he thought from time to time about the ridge, the bluff, the cave, and the ledge with a poignant, bittersweet affection.

Boat traffic past the bluff was heavy that winter, and tiny circles continued to be added to the record on the barrel of his rifle. He descended from the ridge from time to time and attacked Union patrols, foraging parties, and "press" parties that were seizing horses, mules, meat, and other things from the local farmers. Patrols continued to look for him, but none ever returned with the old man's head. Instead, they often returned to Fort Donelson with one of their soldiers tied across his bloody saddle, with one less "present or accounted for" at the next day's reveille.

Ellet's Marine Brigade

Added to the array of military power deployed against guerrillas had been the Mississippi Marine Brigade, a special amphibious force of Marines on specially equipped boats. The unit came to be called "Ellet's Brigade" for its commander, Brig. Gen. Alfred Ellet. The brigade had its own fleet of seven steamers, specially equipped to carry horses and ramps that could be quickly run out onto the bank for the "horse Marines" to gallop ashore. Each of Ellet's boats carried 125 mounted Marines, who could come galloping down the ramp and onto the beach, and 250 infantrymen to support them on foot. They even had light, horse-drawn artillery pieces. In a way, the boats were a nineteenth-century version of the LST (Landing Ship, Tank) of World War II, Korea, and Vietnam, which could be run up on a beach and its bow doors opened to disgorge amphibian tractors, tanks, and fighting troops. Theoretically, Ellet's Marines could deal with threats from the riverbanks in seven different places at the same time.

The theory was good and not unlike the amphibious concepts developed by Marines in the Banana Wars of the 1920s and 1930s in the Caribbean and Central America. However, their independent status and Ellet's independent attitudes created problems almost from the beginning, and the outworking of the theory in the river country of the Western Theater was not pretty. Ellet and his men developed a generally arrogant, autonomous attitude, discipline was lax, and the brigade became one of the most disreputable organizations in the Federal service. They acquired a reputation as undisciplined looters, taking advantage of their independent status to enrich themselves. They looted tons of cotton from Mississippi plantations and sold it. They were even accused of selling military supplies to the Confederates. General Ellet was rebellious, with a reputation for ignoring orders from superiors and doing as he pleased. His flag steamboat was appropriately named the *Autocrat*. Although the brigade attempted some operations along Jack's stretch of the Tennessee River, from the Duck River to Paducah, they accomplished little and left a nineteenth-century blemish on the term "Marine." Grant wanted them disbanded, and even Lincoln became personally involved in the problem. The amphibious task force was never a serious threat to Jack Hinson. Catching him would have been, for Ellet, like catching the wind in his fist.[2]

Added "Luxuries"

During November, he continued to make improvements in his living arrangements, including some elaboration of his rustic fireplace. He acquired a piece of an old tarpaulin with which he made a better "blanket" for his mare and a closeable entrance, inside his cave, not visible from the outside. He also added to his staple supplies a lard bucket full of salt, a gracious gift from one of his friends in the area, for he had ideas of supplementing his steady diet of smokehouse bacon with some fresh meat. He also acquired a lard can with a tight lid and filled it with dried beans, black-eyed peas, butter beans, and several other kinds of dried beans and peas available in the area.

In the river bottom near the big lower cave, there was a grove of chestnut trees, where he gathered a large supply of chestnuts for roasting. His living conditions, and his diet, were considerably improved during that last fall and winter on the ridge.

As the sun ran its course, lower and lower in the southern sky, and the air grew colder, he borrowed a small-bore rifle, some shot for it, and hunted. He had lost track of days, but about the end of November, he killed a wild turkey hen and reckoned her as his Thanksgiving turkey. He picked it as well as he could without a scalding pot and roasted it over his improved fireplace. With a pot of pork-seasoned beans and peas, cornbread, and dried apples, the turkey made a veritable Thanksgiving feast.

In early December, with its alternating cold and warm spells, he shot only rabbits, bypassing the deer. Later in the month, he shot a small deer, cut it up, and salted it, providing meat for weeks to come. He visited friends in the valley from time to time to hear the news and to find out the date. He had invitations to Christmas dinner, but he declined them rather than bring more danger to his friends. Instead, he prepared his own celebratory dinner at the end of December, with another wild turkey, mixed beans and peas, roasted chestnuts, and a rustic pudding he made with stewed dried apples, sugar, and broken-up cornbread. A jug of cider, also a gift from a thoughtful friend, coffee, and his pipe made it a memorable Christmas dinner for a man living alone in the wilderness.

The Final Winter

Through that dismal, miserable winter of 1864 and 1865, many Confederate soldiers, poorly clothed and chronically hungry, were sleeping on frozen ground with only one thin blanket—some had neither shoes nor blankets. The remnant of John Hunt Morgan's Kentucky Brigade was wintering in southwestern Virginia, where Capt. Edward O. Guerrant, who had been with Morgan throughout the war, described that Christmas: "We washed our faces in snow, and ate our breakfast off a piece of cold corn beef." They found the heads of some butchered hogs, left behind at an abandoned Federal camp, roasted them, "and made a jubilee over the feast!" On New Year's day 1865, he wrote in his journal, "The old year froze to death last night. . . . Many of our bravest boys have no shoes." There was very little sand left in the Confederacy's hourglass that winter, and that rapidly disappearing sand was a parallel to the dwindling, pitiful, supplies of food, clothing, medicine—and men.[3]

In Jack's one-man war, however, the opposite was true; his conditions grew steadily better. He was staying warm and was well fed, and the scales of battlefield success were tipping decidedly in his favor. The changes in his little theater of the war were all for the better, and the columns of one-eighth-inch circles continued to march, slowly but steadily forward, on the barrel of his rifle.

Between the Rivers, the Confederates Were Having Their Way

During that last fall and winter, as the dwindling Confederate forces in the east fought an increasingly hopeless retrograde battle with the growing Union juggernaut, Union forces in Tennessee were unable to control the occupied areas, and the Confederate guerrillas were increasingly bold. At times, they even held public auctions to sell weapons, saddles, horses, and other things they had captured from the Yankees.[4]

Between the Rivers, the Federals had completely lost control. They nervously speculated about the possibility of again losing Clarksville, and even Fort Donelson. They felt insecure within their own strongholds. In stark contrast with the sputtering Confederate war machine elsewhere, its forces, regular and guerrilla, virtually owned the Twin Rivers area, and the Confederate regulars there were having things their way. Union message traffic was often panicky due to local commanders nervously reporting the presence of threatening Confederate forces and anticipating Confederate attacks, first in one place, then in another. On November 1, as Jack, with Forrest's Brigade, was starting the move south toward Johnsonville, Capt. I. P. Williams at Clarksville reported that guerrillas had ambushed and burned the transport *Dave Hughes* loaded with supplies and towing a full barge, fifteen miles upstream on the Cumberland. In early December, General Thomas was apparently considering giving up Clarksville to the Confederates and evacuating its supplies.

Gen. Hylan Lyon and his Kentuckians were haunting the

Union commanders' dreams. On December 7, Col. A. A. Smith reported from Clarksville that "rebel General Lyon *is between the rivers somewhere,* with from 900 to 2,000 men" [emphasis added]. On December 8, General Lyon rode boldly up to the gate at Fort Donelson, as if he expected arrival honors, and demanded the surrender of a Union soldier whom he charged with killing a helpless Confederate prisoner. The commanding officer at Donelson seemed relieved that Lyon was only there to demand the turning over of the soldier and not to attack the fort. On the ninth, General Lyon captured the transport *Thomas E. Tutt* between Fort Donelson and Clarksville, used it to ferry his command across the river, and burned it. During that week, he captured another boat at Cumberland City, and he detained the *Ben South* on the tenth. Confederate domination of the Cumberland was so intimidating to General Thomas that he forbade all Union boats to go farther south than Smithland. On the eleventh, Lyon was nervously reported to be encamped at Danville Crossing with one thousand men and artillery "building boats." On the same day, Colonel Smith at Clarksville reported to Brigadier General Whipple, "My scouts have just been driven in by Lyon's men." He stated that his position was "threatened," but he added, hopefully, that he didn't believe Lyon would try to capture Clarksville.[5] As the Confederate armies in the east struggled on in the cold with little hope, hungry, and often barefooted, Confederate cavalry units and guerrillas were prospering and succeeding in the Twin Rivers country. December 22, Col. William Forbes, in command at Fort Donelson, wrote rather sardonically to Colonel Smith at Clarksville. He stated, "Guerrillaism seems to be quite popular . . . in this particular locality . . . *and safe"* [emphasis added].[6]

In the Twin Rivers area that winter, the Confederates had seized the initiative, and they were definitely having their way.

Back to Bubbling Springs

The New Year had arrived on Jack's ridge, clear and cold, and he was glad that he had made his mare's crude shelter more comfortable by adding a north wall. When warmer, moist air moved back in from the south, heavy, wet snow fell, and he made his way, circuitously and carefully, back to Bubbling Springs, with the falling snow and reduced visibility providing a measure of protection for him, covering his tracks as they were being made.

He found things there going as well as could be expected. The elder to whom he had entrusted the money had been a faithful steward and had managed it well, keeping it safely hidden when not needed and maintaining a careful account. The black Hinsons had made their crops and gardens and stocked food for the winter. Albert had returned and managed to sell the tobacco crop and pay the taxes. Sickness had taken some of the children in spite of Dr. Smith's best efforts, and some new arrivals had been born. The Yankee soldiers still came occasionally to ask about Jack. They were consistently hostile and sometimes threatened to shoot them all, but they had done them no real harm. The black Hinsons had always told the soldiers that they believed "Marse Jack" to be dead, didn't expect any of his family ever to come back, and were just trying to carry on with their lives and feed their families, all of which was essentially true. Each time Jack left them, they had no assurance that they would ever see him again, except, perhaps, as a corpse on public display in Dover.

They had received some visits from jayhawkers and guerrillas, of the thieves-and-murderers class, but they had their own rifles and shotguns, plus the rifles and pistols Jack had left with them, which they kept loaded. The thugs didn't victimize armed folks; they preferred the defenseless. The Hinson servants had complained to the Yankee soldiers about the roving thugs, but they had been told it was their problem. They were dealing with the problem in a very adequate way.

The servants were preparing to clear a tobacco bed in new ground, burn it, and sow seed for another crop. On Valentine's Day, following tradition, they would plant their early vegetable gardens, still moving in the normal rhythm of the farm year. Jack looked around and praised them for the way they were carrying on. After a good night's sleep in his tobacco barn, with his mare's hooves trimmed and reshod, and with a good breakfast warming his stomach, he prepared to leave. He told them that it looked like the war couldn't last much longer, and he really couldn't say what the future would hold for him, Elisabeth, and the children. Even after the war ends, he told them, it would not be safe for them to return any time soon. He had no way of knowing how long he would be hunted. He would, he promised, continue to come back from time to time to see them, advise them, and replenish their cash reserves. And he did the latter, just before leaving.

He reminded them that they were legally free. If he should be allowed to return, rebuild his home, and live there as before, they could go right on working and living there. He would provide for them like before and pay them a salary. If he should never be allowed to return, he assured them, he would find a way to take care of them. Of course, he pointed out with a twinkle in his eyes, that would depend on his staying alive and free, so perhaps they should be keeping him in their prayers. They would, they assured him, most surely do that.

With that assurance, thanks to them for the way they were carrying on without him, and with a number of patches on his coat and trousers and missing buttons replaced, he disappeared into the same curtain of soft, white snow from which he had emerged the night before.

Death Comes to the Family Again

On January 13, Jack's son William was severely wounded in his left leg at Petersburg. At the Confederacy's Chimbarozo Hospital in Richmond, the shattered leg was amputated by weary surgeons, and he died the next day. Jack would not know about it for some time, a merciful aspect, perhaps, of the almost nonexistent Confederate communication system.[7]

As winter began to give way to spring, Jack continued his private war but with a decreasing sense of urgency. He didn't expect the war to last much longer, but he would keep up the fight in his own small theater of operations. For him, there could, as yet, be no ceasing.

Therefore, he continued his one-man war that spring from his ledge above the Towhead Chute, from his blinds along the swollen rivers, and from his trailside ambush points. He moved and fought with a strange deceleration, an inclination to ease back, and look well to his own safety. This is a natural and universal reaction in soldiers when they sense that a war is near its end. No one wants the honor of being the last name on the monument in the courthouse square.

There were other guerrillas operating in his area. Some of them were legitimate Confederate partisans, but there were those others whom he knew to be just opportunistic criminals, victimizing isolated, defenseless farm families. They preyed upon

Jack's rifle muzzle containing the "extra" kill record. (Courtesy Joe McCormick)

the "Secesh" families as readily as they did the few pro-Union families there; the thugs did not discriminate.[8]

Jack identified some of the worst of the criminals, and they began to disappear. He didn't add them to his record of legitimate kills; he considered those victimizers of defenseless women, children, and old men decidedly unworthy of being included in the record with real soldiers. As he removed some of the rapacious criminals who roamed the countryside, he earned the appreciation of both pro-Confederate and pro-Union families.[9]

As the last soft, wet snows melted and the air warmed, May apples pierced the brown leaf mulch with their unfolding green umbrellas. Purple trillium and Dutchman's breeches dappled the forest floor with splashes of welcome color. Around old home sites, both the occupied and the abandoned, daffodils burst forth, indomitable and optimistic, in spreading carpets of green and brilliant yellow. It was a soft and pleasant time of the year in the Stewart County forest and, compared with the previous three springtimes, strangely, almost subliminally, peaceful.

Rising water levels in the river and the rushing currents made the dreaded gauntlet below Jack's bluff ever more deadly. He continued to take out selected targets below his ledge, and he continued to punish Yankee land patrols but with a steadily waning zeal. In the last week of March and the first week of April, that declining fervor became a growing reluctance. He didn't know it, but his William was dead, and the Confederate government was itself on the run, rapidly disintegrating into nonexistence, never notifying the family of William's death. Jack also had no way to know that Richmond and Petersburg had fallen, or that Gen. Robert E. Lee, whose Army of Northern Virginia was only a tattered, hungry remnant, was retreating southward through Virginia, trying to link up with what remained of Gen. Joseph Johnston's Army of Tennessee in North Carolina. Grant, whose Army of the Potomac was growing larger and stronger daily, was pressing relentlessly after Lee while Sherman had turned north from Savannah and was closing in on Johnston from the south. The Confederacy was in its death throes.

The war continued between the rivers but in sharp contrast with the war in the east. With the bulk of Union assets and most of Union attention concentrated in the Eastern Theater, the Confederates definitely retained the initiative Between the Rivers. On the last day of March 1865, guerrillas attacked the harried Federals at Magnolia and attacked them again on White Oak Creek on April 1. Although Robert was dead, Hinson's Raiders were still going strong and were on the offensive in the closing days of the war.[10]

Lee's Surrender and the War's Final Chapter

Joseph, who had joined Lee's army in September and fought through the battles around Petersburg and Richmond, fought on in Lee's futile move south and was with him until the very end. On April 9, outside Appomattox Courthouse, Lee's "poor boys" turned and attacked, temporarily routing Grant's advancing juggernaut one last time. Joseph was part of that final, small, and meaningless victory. When Lee, later that day, ended the hopeless bloodshed in surrender, Joseph stood with his weeping, hungry, exhausted, bloodstained comrades in one final salute to their beloved "Marse Robert."

On the afternoon of the ninth, after the surrender was signed at the McLean House, a very great honor was bestowed on a Confederate warrior. A reporter asked General Lee who had been the greatest of all his subordinate commanders. Lee replied, "A man I have never seen, sir; his name is Forrest." With that, a circle was somehow closed, and the neglected war in the west was finally recognized in the east; however, it was too late to matter.

Within less than six days, Lincoln was dead, shot from behind in Ford's Theater in Washington. Eleven days after Lincoln's death, Joseph Johnston surrendered to Sherman near Durham, North Carolina.

But Joseph Hinson was still far from home. At Appomattox, with some of his fellow soldiers from the Fourteenth Tennessee, Joseph began the long walk back to Stewart County. Without money and deprived of their weapons, they had to find food and run the gauntlet of guerrilla thugs, plus a growing number of surrendered-soldiers-turned-highwaymen, who chose to rob and kill their fellow veterans for the pitiful little they might possess. Staying together, Joseph's group from Company F pressed homeward.

News of Lee's surrender, flashed across the nation by telegraph, reached the Union contingent at Danville Crossing within hours. Via the "green telegraph" of the backcountry grapevine, the news reached Jack as Joseph was beginning his journey home.

Still, Forrest fought on, unaware of events at Appomattox and Durham. He was getting no direction from the Confederate government for it no longer existed. He didn't know it, but his was the last significant Confederate force still in the field. Suffering from unhealed wounds but unconquered, he gathered his few hundred survivors and fought his last battle near Selma, Alabama, on May 9, a full month after Appomattox. Learning, then, of the surrenders of Lee and Johnston, Forrest called an end to the useless bloodshed, disbanded his command, and sent his men home. He was unaware of the great honor that Lee had conferred upon him.

After nearly a month on the road, Joseph reached Dover and was paroled at Fort Donelson on May 6. His brief, brutal time as a soldier was finished. His parole document listed his age as seventeen, but in mind and body, he was much, much older. Gaunt but wearily hopeful, he set out to find his family. He looked first at Bubbling Springs, saw the desolation there, and had a muted reunion with the servants. He finally found the remnants of his family at Sulfur Wells, bringing with him the heartbreaking news of William's death.[11]

Standing Down

Now Jack understood his waning inclination to continue his private war. He was not a die-hard, ideological fanatic and further killing in the war's final hours would accomplish nothing but additional heartbreak. There had been too much of that, he knew so well, already. Looking down at his rifle, he counted the tiny circles; there were thirty-six of them. There would never be a thirty-seventh. It was time to stop.

Actually, there had been a great many more than thirty-six kills, probably more than a hundred. Jack never knew the actual number of kills. When he was firing many shots in one encounter only to break contact and withdraw, as he had on troop ships and contingents of soldiers, he couldn't know the death toll. He did not count the guerrilla criminals he had killed. Only God knows why he chose to record only those thirty-six men; for us the answer is lost in misty yesterdays.[12]

He took his rifle to the rock ledge and sat, looking down on the river, running springtime full and brown, through its valley clothed in tender new green. All around him were the sights, sounds, and scents of new life. It was a soft and pleasant, pensive moment. An armed transport was passing through the Towhead Chute, headed south, struggling ahead with black smoke and sparks erupting from her stacks. Jack looked down upon the officers in their blue uniforms with a strange and dreamy indifference. He definitely would not fire on that boat or on any other boat, but conflicting emotions stirred in disorder within him. This readjustment to peace was not going to occur overnight.

Smoking his pipe contemplatively, Jack sat on his ledge over the Towhead Chute and enjoyed the beautiful May day for a long time, and in that peaceful, dreamy afternoon, time made no demands on him. He watched the western sky turn soft as the sun descended over Benton and Henry Counties. There, not long before, he had stalked Union soldiers, and they had searched in vain for him. He had lain in wait for army and navy officers on Union boats and had participated in Forrest's operations.

But that was then.

As the sun disappeared behind the far hills, the sky became a vapor canvas lightly brushed with blended pastels of pink, yellow, and the palest blue. As the sunset's softness spread over the western sky, a growing peace spread over Jack Hinson, the legendary Confederate sniper, and he heaved a long, involuntary sigh.

The reluctant warrior could lay his special rifle down. His one-man war with Grant's army and navy was finally over.

Chapter 11

The Twilight Years

"And they shall beat their swords into plowshares, and their spears into pruning hooks. . . . Neither shall they learn war anymore. But they shall sit every man under his vine and under his fig tree."

—Micah 4:3-4

Jack Hinson's shooting war had come to an end, but he would stay in his hilltop citadel until things settled down and his status as a fugitive could be resolved. That, he realized, might take some time. Meanwhile, he contacted Elisabeth and the children. He still didn't know whether his boys with Lee's army were alive or dead. And, although he didn't know it, the war wasn't really over. The conflict would continue but under new rules and with a different cast of characters.

Reconstruction: The Conflict Continues

In that agonized spring of 1865, the war was over, and yet it wasn't. The South lay in ruins with so many of her men dead or disabled, her resources ravaged, her people in poverty, and her currency worthless—literally not worth the paper it was printed on. In many places, her structure for law and order was largely collapsed, replaced by the rule of force with the weak preyed upon by the strong, and her economy reduced to a barter system, a situation resembling the Dark Ages. The struggle there was to survive, pick up the pieces, and try to go on with life. Moreover, unknown to most of those who had fought the war and experienced its hardships and its horrors, at home or away, a new kind of war was just beginning in Washington, D.C.

The new war had been building, and battle lines had been drawn, before the shooting war had ended. The new war would be a political one between those who wanted to punish the South with a crushing, retaliatory Reconstruction, and those who favored Lincoln's plan for a conciliatory, healing Reconstruction. At the head of the faction determined to punish the South was Lincoln's strong-willed, arrogant, autocratic secretary of war, Edwin M. Stanton. Although Stanton was only a cabinet officer serving at the pleasure of Lincoln as president, he was notorious for doing what he pleased, with or without Lincoln's approval. He privately looked upon Lincoln as an inferior, crude, country bumpkin from the Illinois prairie, referring to him as "imbecilic" and an "original gorilla."[1]

This conflict was already finding form during the closing months of the shooting war. Lincoln had even been feeling its pressure in a cabinet meeting on the very last day of his life, and in the meeting, he had seemed to be gaining some support for his gentle approach. But a few hours after that cabinet meeting on Good Friday in 1865, with things looking good for a healing Reconstruction, a bullet was fired into the back of his head as he sat in the state box at Ford's Theater. Early the next morning, he breathed his last breath and died without regaining consciousness. Lincoln's body had hardly cooled before that second war got hot.[2]

Nineteenth-century writer Herman Melville, author of *Moby Dick*, brilliantly summarized, in four crystalline lines in his poem "The Martyr," the political result of Lincoln's murder:

> *He lieth in his blood—*
> *The Father in his face;*
> *They have killed him, the Forgiver—*
> *The Avenger takes his place*[3]

At the head of the opposition to Stanton's vengeful policy was Andrew Johnson of Tennessee, the new president of the United States. He had inherited not only Lincoln's office as president, but also his policy for a helpful, healing Reconstruction. This conflict over Reconstruction policy, one which Stanton and the Radical Republicans would win, would lead to Johnson's being impeached by the House of Representatives for firing Stanton and would produce political confusion, unprecedented political corruption, and a twelve-year-long nightmare for the South. It would also, eventually, contribute to retaliatory Jim Crow laws across the South, beginning in Kentucky, which would create a segregated South for another century.

This was a chaotic, tumultuous time of confusion, disorientation, and passion in the South, with massive Union forces in place, many of them still hostile toward Southern people, and Union commanders still following wartime policies, which had not been revoked. Kentucky, although its Frankfort government had not been able to secede, was treated like a conquered foe, with a Union army of occupation. Many citizens, prominent and obscure, were arrested and imprisoned without trial. Punished with arbitrary emancipation of all slaves without compensation, Kentucky refused to ratify the Thirteenth and Fourteenth Amendments, was denied representation in Congress, and subjected to full-force Reconstruction. Although the South was no longer at war with the North, the North was still attacking the South with a vindictive Reconstruction that would be more divisive in many ways than the four-year war itself. There were certainly other factors at work contributing to the creation of Jim Crow laws in the South, but Stanton, the Radical Republicans, and their determination to punish the South were central. The turning of the culture upside-down by Reconstruction policies and creating black legislatures, judicial systems, and police forces of men still totally unprepared for such responsibilities contributed powerfully to radical countermeasures by the remaining white establishment. Eventually, it all led to a counterrevolution and the virtual resubjugation of blacks in the South after occupation forces left. Jim Crow laws were a conspicuous part of that counterrevolution, and they remained in effect for one hundred years.[4]

In this setting, with vengeance dominating Union attitudes in all of his home area, Jack Hinson was still very much a wanted man with a price on his head. He had to find his place and very carefully make his way into an extremely volatile and uncertain future.

The Danger Remains: Keeping a Low Profile

Soldiers in blue still patrolled the backcountry from Paducah and Smithland to Waverly and Columbia; they still occupied Forts Henry and Donelson; and they manned outposts like the one at Danville Crossing. In addition, predatory hoodlums, no longer with even the pretense of serving the Confederacy or the Union, still roamed the backcountry, robbing, raping, and murdering the defenseless. Except for the influx of emaciated Confederate soldiers in faded, tattered uniforms making their weary way home, there in the Kentucky and Tennessee counties Between the Rivers little had changed in the spring and summer of 1865.

It was a time, Jack realized, for him to maintain a low profile and do what he could do to help his family and his neighbors while remaining as inconspicuous as possible. He could see that it was going to take some time for things to return to peacetime normality, and for himself, as a fugitive, the outlook was even more grim than that of his neighbors and friends. But he was well established on his ridge, and no one seemed interested in coming up there after him at the moment, so he enjoyed the Tennessee springtime as he pondered long-range plans.

He didn't think that he could go back to Bubbling Springs, rebuild the house, and go on as before. Right there, on the main road between Forts Henry and Donelson, he would be too close, inviting attention, intervention, and trouble. He wasn't even sure that he wanted to go back to Bubbling Springs for it was the scene of so many painful memories. He had freed his slaves during the war, and with some help from him, they could take care of themselves. No, it seemed increasingly clear that he and the family would not return to their home place. After all the tragedy, they could use a fresh start somewhere else.

He thought he would resettle what was left of his family away from Dover—away, in fact, from any town of its size. The arm of the law, while long, was never as energetic in the backcountry as it was in and near population centers.

As he pondered the matter of resettlement, complicated by the fact that he was still a fugitive from Yankee justice, it became ever more clear that a good place to resettle would be there—right where he was. Not on the ridge, he thought, but in the area—somewhere between the valley of Cane Creek and Humphreys County, Robert's old Sherwood Forest. He and Elisabeth had family in that region, as well as good friends who had helped him during the war years. Therefore, his thoughts turned southward, and he began to be attracted to the beautiful valley of White Oak Creek.

Post-War Adjustments: At Fort Donelson and in the Hinson Family

The garrison at Fort Donelson was also adjusting to the new

situation. Many of the soldiers did not understand why they couldn't leave and go home now that the war was over, and this presented an additional leadership challenge to officers, sergeants, and corporals. Patrolling continued but with much less to motivate them; drilling and work details occupied more and more of their time.

Units represented at Donelson on June 13, 1865, were portions of the Seventy-first Ohio Infantry, the Eighty-third Illinois Infantry, and the Thirteenth Wisconsin Infantry. Females reported at Fort Donelson on that date reflect the class system of the day: "Ladies—61, Laundress—1." There were forty-eight children reported on the post. Effective strength (strength, less those sick, on leave, or otherwise not available for duty) of the complement at Fort Donelson reported on June 26, 1865, was 153 (8 officers and 145 enlisted men).[5]

Jack and his family were also making adjustments that spring and summer. Clandestine visits to Elisabeth, across the river in Henry County, and to Bubbling Springs to check on things there, all the while evading Yankee patrols, occupied much of Jack's time and effort during the warmer months of 1865. From time to time, he had the opportunity to put some of the predatory thugs who roamed the countryside out of business.

Albert (whom the family called "Ab") had been Jack and Elisabeth's right arm during the exile period, watching over the family at Sulfur Wells and taking care of business matters at Bubbling Springs. During the difficult period immediately following the war, he continued to play this vital role by acting for his father, caring for his mother and the younger children, and standing in as "the man" of the family.

It seems that a boy becomes a man when a man is needed, and Ab had risen admirably to that challenge. By the end of the war, he was a mature, responsible, young man in his nineteenth year. He began to visit the Danville Crossing area soon after the war ended, seeing friends and relatives and serving as Jack's eyes and ears. In time, he found himself also attending to his own interests. He was paying court to Sarah Cummings of Danville Crossing. Sarah was the ward of Mr. Seth Outlaw, patriarch of the Cane Creek area, who had provided the land for what became Danville Crossing, the steamboat landing, and, later, the town of Danville.

He had built and owned the Outlaw Hotel, and he was one of the most wealthy and influential men in the entire region. In light of his wealth and position in the area, it is safe to assume that he was protective of Sarah and he suffered Ab's presence and courtship only after close and careful scrutiny.[6]

A New Home on White Oak Creek

In 1867, Jack and Elisabeth chose the village of Magnolia, on White Oak Creek as the place to live out the rest of their lives. Magnolia was a thriving little community with a post office, stores, churches, a school, and two physicians. Jack and Elisabeth purchased, from Jarman Jackson, 294 acres of land along White Oak Creek for $3,100. It was a beautiful, well-watered valley with two smaller streams that flowed into White Oak Creek. On the property, there was an excellent water-driven mill known as Wilson's Mill, as well as two dwellings. They called their lush new farm Magnolia Hill. It would be their home until they died.[7]

Jack Hinson in old age, the only photograph of him known to exist. (From Bromfield L. Ridley's Battles and Sketches of the Army of Tennessee, *1906)*

Except for brief visits, the Hinsons never returned to Bubbling Springs. In December of 1867, Jack deeded the Bubbling Springs property to Ab. A month later, on January 12, 1868, Ab and Sarah were married and moved into the second dwelling on the White Oak Mill property. They were both twenty-one.

In February 1868, a month after he and Sarah were married, Ab sold the Bubbling Springs house site for his father, along with 182.5 acres, to George Dougherty. The slave cabins and the surrounding acreage were reserved for the Hinson's former slaves. Those homes became the nucleus of the community Hinson Town, one which grew eastward, merging with the southwest part of Dover, and continued to exist by that name into the mid-twentieth century.[8]

Jack and Elisabeth, with increasing help from Ab, operated Magnolia Mill (referred to in some records as Hinson's Mill), the adjacent shops and store, and the farm on White Oak Creek. In spite of the threat of retribution that persisted like a dark cloud over Jack's life, it was a happy time. The mill, reputed to be one of the very finest in Tennessee, prospered, as did the other businesses and the farm. Charles and Thomas were still at home, helping with the work. The daughters, Mary and Sarah Margaret, were away in school, and a girl named Annie Cornelia, taken into the home in her teens, was living with them and helping Elisabeth keep the house. It was a peaceful, happy time.

Jack and Elisabeth's son Joseph seems to have died very soon after the war. In Elisabeth's 1871 will, he is not mentioned nor are any children attributed to him. There is no mention of him in public records or the few postwar letters that survive. He apparently died as a result of the stresses of the war, leaving no heirs. Ab named his first child after him.

On November 21, 1868, Ab and Sarah's first child, Joseph James Hinson, was born in their White Oak Creek home. A year and a half later, on July 23, 1870, a second son, Robert Edgar Hinson, was born, named for Ab's older brother, the dashing Confederate partisan and escape artist, killed in the war.[9]

Living in a New County Without Moving

On January 21, 1871, Houston County was formed from southern Stewart County, northern Humphreys County, and a corner of Dickson County. From that day on, although they didn't move an inch, the Hinsons were citizens of Houston County. The new county line was established about one hundred yards north of Jack's ridge above Towhead Chute, placing his old wilderness home and citadel in the extreme northwestern corner of their new county.

With the formation of the new county and transfer of records from Dover to the new county seat of Erin, there was predictable confusion resulting in some loss of county records. In light of this, and probably because of Jack's precarious position under

Reconstruction law, the Magnolia property was kept in Elisabeth's name. Eleven months after the formation of the new county, Elisabeth wrote a will, as sole owner of the property, executed on November 4, 1871.[10]

Life Goes On: Business, Birth, and Death on White Oak Creek

In addition to operating the mill and its related enterprises, Jack operated a store dealing in general merchandise. One of his steady customers, Henry R. Atkinson of Magnolia, seems to have kept a written record of all his business transactions, even the most minute of them. Although his spelling was inconsistent, Atkinson's journal gives us an interesting glimpse into Jack's last years, and it is clear that he was still active. On August 27, 1872, Atkinson recorded, "Bought of John Hintson [sic] 3 lbs coffee [for] 1.00, one plug tobacco .25, 3 bales snuff .25, five cts worth candy, one plug tobacco [apparently a different quality] .10, one quart whiskey 1.00." Whiskey was a common item of general merchandise in country stores of that day; the concept of a "liquor store" had not yet been born.[11]

Jack also attended estate sales in that small community for business purposes and as pleasant social outings. When Henry R. Atkinson's father, Thomas Atkinson, died, Jack attended the estate sale and bought chickens and guinea fowl ("2 Doz. fowl") for the interesting price of $4.13. Such sales were an important part of community life on White Oak Creek.[12]

In early January 1873, death and life visited Ab and Sarah's home, on consecutive days. On January 8, their two-year-old son, Robert, died. The next day, their third child, Thetis, was born. Three days later, on the twelfth, they observed the fifth anniversary of their marriage. Their young family was already smitten by the pain of death.[13]

Still Refusing to Die

On March 1, 1873, there was a report of Jack's death published in the *Jackson Whig and Tribune* (quoting the *Nashville Union and American*). It announced, "Hinson, Captain Jack, died 7 Feb., aged 80 years, on White Oak Creek. 'It is said that he killed about 80 federal soldiers during the late unpleasantness.'" Their reporting of his age was way off; in March 1873, he was in his sixty-sixth year. The year of his birth is variously published, but the consensus of records indicates that he was born in July 1807. The day of his birth is not known.[14]

As was the case with Mark Twain, later, the report of Jack's death was "greatly exaggerated" for he was still alive. Two days later, on March 3, the *Nashville Union and American* quoted a story in the *Dover Record* of February 27: "[D]eath of Captain Jack Hinson, died on 7th, is mistake and that he is alive."[15]

It is significant that "Captain Jack" was prominent enough that, even eight years after the close of the war, his reported death was an item of news interest in the Reconstruction newspaper in far-off Nashville, and the error, once discovered, was considered worthy of correction.

At the time of those speculative reports concerning his death, Jack had only a year to live, and even that final year would not be a peaceful one.

In June of 1873, a process was set in motion to bring Jack before a Reconstruction military tribunal and execute him for his wartime activities. The *Clarksville Tobacco Leaf* published a news and opinion article about Jack, who was sufficiently well known that he was identified simply as "Captain Jack." The article read,

> Captain Jack is said to be tried by a military commission, but the peace men propose to get a writ of habeas corpus. Captain Jack is a brave man, a rude, untutored hero, a thief and a scoundrel no doubt when viewed through the social ideas we have, but a hero nevertheless. His execution would serve no good purpose, while it would be a crowning act of infamy. [16]

By 1873, whoever wrote this item for the Clarksville newspaper was blending fact with popular fiction, perhaps deliberately. We should remember that the reporter was writing under Reconstruction scrutiny, thus he was at risk in writing anything favorable about this old man who was about to be drummed through a military tribunal and hanged. No matter what "prism" through which we view Jack Hinson, the preponderance of the evidence bears testimony to his having been a literate, responsible man of substance; a prominent community leader; and a man of honor and integrity. Men like John

Bell, Nathan Bedford Forest, and Gideon Pillow would not have associated with, nor would Pillow have invoked in his own defense the name of, "a rude, untutored . . . thief and a scoundrel." Likewise Seth Outlaw would never have allowed a daughter or ward of his to marry the son of such a man.[17]

Apparently, Jack's friends were successful in their efforts to save him from a Yankee noose. If he was indeed tried by such a tribunal, he was not executed. He died peacefully at home thirteen months later. However, he lived under this hanging sword of Damocles, the constant threat of Yankee retribution, until he died.[18]

Although the stresses of the military tribunal and other threats continued through 1873, Jack largely ignored them, tending to his life at Magnolia Hill, still the active businessman. The meticulous Henry R. Atkinson recorded in his journal, "August 22nd 1873, bought of Jack Hintson [sic] one bushel meal. Paid .75." On September 8, he recorded, "Bought of John Hintson [sic] one bushel meal. Paid .75." Again, on September 22, he recorded, "Bought of John Hinson one bushel of meal. Paid .75." Someone at the Atkinson home was using a lot of corn meal, but the price was consistent.[19]

In the closing years of his life, Jack enjoyed one thing that was

The Twilight Years: Jack and his friend, Patrick Henry Bateman, in a rifle marksmanship competition. (Drawing by Joe McCormick)

definitely reminiscent of the war years: he participated in turkey shoots and other forms of competition in rifle marksmanship. His vision was still keen, his hands were still steady, and his aim still true. In these matches, he was the grand old man, a living legend, the region's elder statesman of rifle marksmanship. He also enjoyed the company of his old friend Patrick Henry Bateman, of the nearby Yellow Creek community. Bateman was a Confederate veteran of the war, and they enjoyed visiting and talking of old times, a bittersweet pleasure for them both in the twilight of their lives. Bateman was also another keen-eyed rifle sharpshooter, and he and Jack enjoyed participating together in the rifle competition.[20]

The Final Year

The year of Jack's death, 1874, was a year of severe storms and flooding along the Tennessee River. Johnsonville had been rebuilt after the riverfront area was demolished in 1864 by Forrest's artillery and the resultant fires. However, in 1874, the rampaging river flooded the town, bringing fresh ruin. The current was so strong that some buildings were not just inundated, but were torn from their foundations. When Jack heard of the fresh devastation at Johnsonville, his mind returned to the raid with Forrest ten years earlier in 1864. At times, that raid seemed like only yesterday, but at other times, when he was very weary, it seemed a lifetime ago.[21]

Jack was in his sixty-seventh year, an old man for the time. His sixty-seven years had not all been gentle years. In addition to the stresses of the war years, the physical dangers, and the hardship of staying on the move and living outdoors in all types of weather, there was the stress of living under the threat of public execution after the war. For most of the warriors, the spring of 1865 had brought peace—at least a measure of it. Although many of the Confederate veterans who survived had lost homes and savings, most of them had been able to go on with life in some way, leaving the threat of violent death behind them. This was not so for Jack Hinson. Even in the closing months of his life, the threatening shadow of retaliatory execution hung over him like a relentless, dark presence. His wife and children also lived with that dread, the ever-present threat, although it was seldom given voice.

He remained active at the mill, the shops, in the store, and on the farm. He consulted with and advised Ab, visited in the community, exchanged visits with Patrick Henry Bateman, and watched his grandchildren grow. Despite his activity, he was feeling his age, and the pains in his body reminded him daily of what he had put it through.

Jack also lived with his private memories, as old men do. There was so much to remember—many happy times and some very painful ones. There were so many dead faces—some beloved, some despicable, most anony-mous. It seems the lot of a man in his latter years is to remember both the pleasant and the painful.

Summer came on hot in 1874, as it always did. In July, the month of his sixty-seventh birthday, Jack's weary heart finally

Confederate veteran Patrick Henry Bateman. (Courtesy Mrs. Cheryl J. Smith)

sputtered and stopped. As the blood supply to his brain failed, his piercing gray eyes peered into the far distance, softened, and closed, and with one final sigh, he slipped into eternity.[22]

Old man Hinson, Captain Jack, the reluctant warrior, legendary sniper, the avenging phantom of the Twin Rivers area, courageous as a lion and tough as whet leather, passed from a weary, troubled present into the shadowy past, from loving husband, father, and grandfather into legend—a community treasure of a proud people. His weary, one-man war with the Union colossus was finally over.[23]

In the Years that Followed

"One Ab Hinson was waylaid by two young men named Wiggins and shot and killed. Later Joe Hinson, a son of the murdered man, killed one of the Wiggins boys with a knife and cut his heart entirely out of his body."

Jack's Simple Possessions Were Sold

On July 20, 1874, Jack Hinson's few possessions were sold at auction in an estate sale, as was the custom. The items sold, including debts owed him, filled less than one ledger page. Itemized thereon are the very ordinary possessions of one most extraordinary man. The highest priced item that sold that July day was his farm wagon; it sold for $40.00. The second highest price paid was for a mule. His son Charles, who had carved his name in the soft rock wall above Jack's ledge in 1863, bought the mule for $39.00. A cow with calf sold for $11.50. They must have been Jack's pets. Old men who have lived on farms love to have at least one farm animal to care for in their twilight years. More than half the items in the sale sold for less than a dollar, and the total paid that July day for all of Jack Hinson's disposable earthly possessions was $208.80.[1]

Once the last item was sold and recorded in the ledger and the last of the buyers put his purchases in his buggy or farm wagon, tipped his hat, and drove away from Magnolia Hill, it was all over. John W. Hinson, the legendary Confederate sniper, was history.

Jack left behind more than just those extremely meager possessions that were auctioned off to the highest bidder on that July day in 1874. He left a family and an example of personal integrity and courage. He left all his slaves free, with homes of their own and, in the process, established a small community that has borne his name for more than one hundred years. He founded a family line of proud, honorable, and productive people who have served their communities and their country into the fifth generation as this is being written.

Old Captain Jack also bequeathed a dark side to the legacy, one of revenge and violence, one passed down through his family bearing the bitter fruit of tragedy, as subsequent events were to prove.

Elisabeth's Final Years

A year after Jack's death, life at White Oak Mill and Magnolia Hill Farm was brightened by the birth of a daughter to Ab and Sarah. Thula Hinson was born the last day of July in 1875. The happy little girl especially brightened Elisabeth's outlook. With baby Thula there, the beautiful valley of White Oak Creek seemed greener that summer.

In that same year, Danville reached a milestone on its way to becoming a town: the little crossroad community got its first post office. No longer was it necessary to cross the river on the ferry to Benton County or make the seven-mile trip to White Oak Post Office to send and receive mail; Danville had its own. The post office was a thing of not only convenience, but also a matter of pride. It put Danville on the map, literally, and was a distinctive sign of growing up, like a boy's first pair of long trousers.

Danville grew quickly after the war, becoming an increasingly prosperous little village. It grew and prospered after the war for the same reason that Confederate and Union leaders considered it to be of strategic value during the war: its junction of railroad and river landing. The Outlaw Hotel, of course, had been there since 1860, standing in unlikely elegance with no town, but after the war, the town rose up around it. The hotel had ceased to be used as a military hospital after the war and returned to keeping riverboat and railroad crews, workmen, and overseers. Soon it became an overnight refuge for travelers from riverboats, stagecoaches, and the trains, fulfilling its ultimate purpose.

The Hinson enclave on White Oak Creek, with its gristmill, sawmill, blacksmith shop, and general store, continued to prosper. The mill's reputation for excellence spread in ever-widening circles, and White Oak Mill was becoming something of a celebrity in its own right.

In late December of 1876, two and a half years after Jack's death, Elisabeth died. She was only fifty-nine, but she had suffered much and fought hard. The war years, the death of at least seven of her children, the loss of her Bubbling Springs home, and Jack's death had taken their toll.

The End of a Home: The Sale of Elisabeth's Possessions

Elisabeth's estate sale inventory also tells a muted, sad story of finality; it was obviously the end of something. There were beds, tables, chairs, a candle stand, clock, and other furniture. There was a wash kettle, a Charter Oak Cook Stove, a second stove, harness, and farm equipment. There were also Elisabeth's gray saddle horse and her sidesaddle.[2]

The inventory declared, for anyone who cared to hear the message, that the end of a long trail had been reached. The lifetime home, begun when young Jack Hinson with his serious, gray eyes asked for permission to marry the daughter of John and Agnes James, had reached its end. That home, established more than forty years before, had known prosperity, prominence, devastation, and fugitive status. It had risen from the ashes of wartime disaster to shake off the past, reestablish itself, live, and prosper again. That home had survived a terrible war and produced at least twelve children, of whom only five survived their parents. Now, it had ceased to exist. Elisabeth's sale on June 13, 1877, had written "finis" on a remarkable saga of joy, heartbreak, accomplishment, tragedy, and survival.[3]

Carrying On: The Second Generation

In that ongoing cycle of life and death in the Hinson family, a daughter was born to Ab and Sarah on August 30, 1877, eight months after Elisabeth's death. They named her Stella. The following August, Thetis died. She was only five and one-half years old. Little Stella lived only fourteen months and died on October 8, 1878, when Sarah was great with the next child.

Four months after baby Stella died, on February 8, 1879, another daughter was born to Ab and Sarah, and they named her Bettie. The following year, in April 1880, Sarah gave birth to a son. They named him John Stewart, for Ab's father. He was appropriately named for that little acorn didn't fall very far from the Jack Hinson tree. Young John S. Hinson would grow up proving to have many of his namesake's characteristics, both physical and attitudinal, in his long and eventful life.

Four months after John's birth, little Bettie died at age one and a half.[4]

Two years later, in May of 1882, Jack's son Thomas was qualified by the court as legal guardian of his niece, Annie Hinson. Annie was the minor daughter of his older brother, Robert, the bold and notorious guerrilla killed during the war. Thomas took her into his home as his own daughter. It appears that Robert Hinson's wife had died by this time, and their older daughter, Delia, had a home of her own. No record has been found of the circumstances of the death or place of burial of either of Robert's daughters.[5]

The Jesse James Connection

There is a fascinating sidelight to the already amazing Hinson story. From 1878 to 1879, Jesse James lived with his family on a rented farm in adjacent Humphreys County, not far from Johnsonville, the scene of Forrest's great victory, together with Jack Hinson. During this time, Jesse lived under the alias J. D. Howard. He was an expert in the judging and handling of horses, and in Humphreys County, he raised, trained, traded, and sold fine horses. There is evidence to support the family belief that Jesse was a cousin to Elisabeth (James) Hinson, and during the time that the James family lived in Humphreys County, Jesse twice visited the Hinsons in neighboring Houston County. In 1878, twin boys were born to Jesse's wife, Zee. They were either stillborn or lived only briefly. They were buried on the farm, and the graves with their single marker can be seen there today. The marker, handmade from a single piece of native stone, read, "Gould and Monty, Sons of Jessie [sic] James, B 1878 D 1878" (he sometimes spelled his name with an "i"). One may wonder why Jesse (Jessie), hiding from law enforcement authorities and living under an alias, would put his real name on the grave marker. Actually, it was perfectly in character. After the death of the twins, the "Howards" did not receive visitors at their farm, other than close friends and relatives; and they soon moved away, accompanied by a Mr. B. J. Woodson (Frank James). After moving away, the marker would have been a characteristic calling card for Jesse. It was also in character for Jesse to refuse to leave his babies in unmarked graves. Perhaps their deaths and this resulting revelation of his true identity were what forced their leaving.[6]

There is a Hinson family tradition to the effect that after Jesse James was murdered by Robert "Bob" Ford in 1882. Ab Hinson traveled to Missouri, in search of Ford, to avenge Jesse's death.

The handmade grave marker of Gould and Montgomery James, twin boys of Jesse and Zee James, Humphreys County, Tennessee.

If true, reason prevailed, and he eventually returned to White Oak without Ford's blood on his hands. This part of the story was strongly believed by Ab's grandson, John S. Hinson, Jr. Other family members question it, but vengeance would definitely have been a characteristic reaction on the part of Jack Hinson's son. In little more than a decade, Ab himself would become the victim of vengeance and the cause for further vengeance.

Elisabeth's Interesting Will

Elisabeth's will was finally probated on May 27, 1882, five years after her death. The will has a vitality and story of its own. From the faded and yellowed ledger pages, her personality, her beliefs, and her intentions emerge to speak with clarity to the reader.

A refreshing aspect of the will is that it was, as every other aspect of public life then, solidly and obviously rooted in the principles and language of the Bible. Exactly as in the Mayflower Compact, Elisabeth's will begins with the declaration, "In the name of God, amen"; and it is dated, "this 4th day of November in the year of our Lord one thousand eight hundred and seventy one." People of that time were very much aware of their own mortality and were certain about God's position in the universe. Their worldview was unclouded, rooted in eternal absolutes, and they lived with no philosophical confusion or uncertainty about life and death.

Instead of the predictable, terse, and sterile "being of sound mind and body" of today's wills, this nineteenth-century document elaborates with a philosophical observation on the fleeting, uncertain nature of life: "Considering the uncertainty of this frail and transitory life, I do therefore make, ordain and declare this to be my last will and testament."

The will also reveals that, at the time of its execution, just three years before her death, only five of Jack and Elisabeth's twelve children were still living. She decreed that the Magnolia Mill and farm property be sold and the proceeds equally divided among her "beloved children, (viz) Ab F. Hinson, Chas. S., Thos. W., Mary E. and Sarah M. Hinson." She decreed that one full share be divided equally between the orphaned daughters of her late son, "Robert A. Hinson, dec'd, Delia and Ann Eliza Hinson."[7]

A high priority of Elisabeth's, expressed in her will, was the education of her two daughters. The only direct cash bequests in the will provided for each daughter "two hundred dollars in gold, which I wish appropriated for their clothing and education." This, plus the very fact that they could buy the property on White Oak Creek, prior to the selling of the Bubbling Springs property, reveals that Jack, ever the solid businessman, kept as much of his money as possible in gold and silver coin, not Confederate currency, which had become worthless by 1865."[8]

On June 15, 1882, the Magnolia Mill and farm were sold at auction by Ab, as executor of Elisabeth's will. It was the final step in closing out Elisabeth's estate. Such was the reputation of the mill that, seven years later, although it had been sold to others, it was still known as Hinson's Mill. County Road Orders for 1889 assigned "Hinson's Mill hands" responsibility for maintaining a section of road on White Oak Creek.[9]

There is a chronological mystery here, unresolved as of this writing. In Elisabeth's will, she directed that the mill and farm property be sold within one year after her death. Yet it was five years after her death that the Magnolia Mill and farm property were sold at auction, and the estate finally settled. It may mean that there were claims filed against the estate that required several years to resolve, or that there were other compelling reasons to delay the sale. This delay by Ab was perfectly legal.

On February 20, 1884, Sarah presented Ab with a daughter whom they named Florence.

Moving Away from Magnolia

With the sale of the Magnolia Mill and farm, Ab and Sarah moved their family to the growing little village of Danville, where Ab would engage in a number of business ventures through the years. They purchased acreage on the north side of McKinnon Road, land that would come to be called Hinson Hollow, as it is known today. There, in January 1886, their last child was born. Little George Franklin lived only six months and died in July.

In 1886, Danville's population reached one hundred, and in August of that year, Charles Hinson and John Wiggins were selected as delegates and traveled to the Democratic Convention

Albert Hinson and family in Danville, 1889. Left to right: John Stewart (8), Albert (43), Joseph (20), Sarah (43), Thula (14), and Florence (5). (Courtesy Mrs. Frances Hinson)

in Erin, where the party declared for Grover Cleveland in the coming presidential election. Ab operated Hinson Brothers' Saloon, in partnership at times with his brothers Charles and Thomas. Another early business in the growing little village was the Dry Goods and Groceries store of their friend John Wiggins. Twelve years later, Ab's family and the family of John Wiggins would become inseparably connected in Danville history.[10]

On January 12, 1891, death again called at the Ab Hinson home when their daughter, Thula, died at age fifteen. Ab and Sarah's three remaining children were Joseph, age twenty-two; John, age ten; and Florence, not quite seven.

In the mid-1890s, Ab and Sarah moved to Clarksville where Ab was licensed to operate a "tippling house," a quaint nineteenth-century name for a saloon. They lived at 548 Greenwood Avenue, and their two youngest children, John and Florence, attended Clarksville Academy, a private school.[11]

Trouble in Danville: An Ominous Warning

In the late 1890s, Ab and Sarah, with their surviving children, Joseph, John, and Florence, moved back to Danville and resettled in Hinson Hollow. Fresh tragedy awaited them there.

Ab and John Wiggins had been friends for many years. Both were early residents of Danville and both were prominent businessmen there. John Wiggins and the Hinson brothers had also been active together in Democratic Party politics. But by the time Ab and his family moved back to Danville, John Wiggins had died, and a personal conflict arose between the Hinsons and John's grown sons, Dave and John Wiggins, Jr. During that period, Thomas Hinson moved to Alabama for reasons now unknown, but apparently, he feared for his life. On August 8, 1898, he wrote a fascinating letter to his niece, Florence.

In the letter, he thanked her for the letter she had written to him, spoke of pleasant family topics, and referred to the new railroad bridge being built at Danville. Then his letter became mysterious, ominous, and, as later events would reveal, prophetic. He called Danville "the last place on earth" for him, telling his fourteen-year-old niece that he plans never to be there again for any length of time. He asks Florence to deliver a somewhat cryptic message to her father, warning him to leave Danville: "Tell your papa I think a change of country would agree with him, and I would certainly leave there if I had to walk away." Even more mysteriously, he adds, "and don't let anyone know where I am [staying]." He goes on to ask who the present postmaster at Danville was, apparently concerned about who might see the postmark on his letter. The last statement in the letter, other than brief family news and salutations, was pregnant with future significance. He asked the whereabouts of John and Dave Wiggins. The mysterious parts of the letter were explained, and their prophetic nature revealed when, the following month, John and Dave Wiggins shot Ab Hinson from ambush.[12]

The Law of Vengeance: The Second Generation

There were only two roads into and out of Danville: one ran eastward, away from the river, toward McKinnon and Stewart, roughly paralleling the railroad; the other ran southward, across Cane Creek, toward Magnolia. Magnolia Road intersected with McKinnon Road where it crossed the railroad, adjacent to the railroad station. This was the very heart of Danville. As Ab, returning to Danville on Magnolia Road in his buggy, crossed over the railroad, a shot was fired, and he was severely wounded. He was treated by local physicians, and Sarah nursed him at home, assisted by her neighbor and friend Emma Hilmus. He lingered in pain for a month, and at 8:00 A.M. on Monday, September 26, 1898, Ab Hinson, the son on whom Jack and Elisabeth had so depended during and after the war, died. He was fifty-two.

Secrets can't be kept for very long in such places, and the identity of the killers was soon common knowledge in the Danville area. They were Dave and John Wiggins, and the shooter was Dave. Like his grandfather, Old Jack Hinson, Ab's son, Joseph, who was then twenty-nine, buried his father and immediately set out to avenge him. The *Bakerville Review* published what was known of the grim and tragic events.

> A TRAGEDY. We have heard a great deal of unreliable news about a terrible tragedy that took place at Danville, Tenn. One Ab Hinson was waylaid by two young men named Wiggins and shot and killed. Later Joe Hinson, a son of the murdered man, killed one of the Wiggins boys with a knife and cut his heart entirely out of his body. We have not heard all of the particulars of the double

crime except that it originated from an old family feud. We have been very much interested in this affair from the fact that we knew the Wiggins' father when he was our preceptor, and we also knew the father of Ab Hinson, the redoubtable Capt. Jack Hinson.[13]

One thing not included in the *Bakerville Review* story is the fact that Joseph not only cut out Dave Wiggins' heart, but, in a remarkable public statement, he hung the heart on the railroad crossing sign, at the spot where his father had been when he was shot—in the very heart of Danville.

Joseph seems never to have been charged in the killing of Dave Wiggins, nor is John Wiggins known to have been charged in the murder of Ab. It seems that, as things were often done during the war, justice served, whether legal or not, was allowed to suffice. Joseph did, however, move to Canton, across the Cumberland River in Trigg County, Kentucky. He lived there with relatives, corresponded with his family in Danville, married, and died four years later of tuberculosis, on October 21, 1902.[14]

Jack and Elisabeth's Other Children

Charles Hinson moved to Jackson, Tennessee, where, according to historian Clement A. Evans, he became "an influential citizen." He was engaged in several businesses. He, his wife Frances Weis Hinson, and their children lived at 335 South Royal Street. He died in 1919 and was buried in Calvary Cemetery not far from his home and St. Mary's Church.[15]

True to the sentiments Thomas Hinson expressed in that fascinating 1898 letter to Florence, he never returned to Danville to live. He lived out the latter years of his life in Ocala, Florida, and died in Florence, Alabama. He wrote a letter on August 5, 1920, in which he said, "I am getting old, will be 66 next October." Thomas Hinson didn't live to celebrate that sixty-sixth birthday. He went to bed after writing the letter, awoke later in pain, and died that very night.[16] He was the last of Jack and Elisabeth's sons.

No further record of Jack and Elisabeth's daughters is known. They, like their parents, passed into obscurity. Ah, but Ab's son, John S., a veritable chip off his grandfather's block, carried on in Old Jack's tradition and, one might say, spectacularly.

Carrying On: The Third Generation

On September 9, 1899, eleven months after his father's death, John S. Hinson enlisted in the army for the Spanish-American War at age nineteen and served with Company G of the Thirty-eighth U.S. Volunteer Infantry in the Philippines. He was discharged on June 30, 1904; was declared to be in good health, with "Character: Good"; and returned to Danville.[17]

On February 12, 1914, Sarah Hinson died. She was sixty-eight, survived only by John and Florence, who had by then married and established her own home (as Florence Hinson Bell). Florence died in 1959 and is buried in Colorado Springs, Colorado.

On June 20, 1918, John S. Hinson rode the packet boat to Paducah and volunteered again for service in World War I; he was thirty-eight years old. Because of his age, he was assigned to guard duty and was not allowed to go overseas. On January 17, 1919, John was discharged at Camp Pike, Arkansas, his character was declared to be excellent, and he returned to Danville with sixty dollars in mustering-out pay.[18]

By 1919, John, age thirty-nine and veteran of two wars, was ready to settle down. He paid court to Miss Ollie Richardson, child of a prominent Houston County family. Ollie was twenty-six and Danville's respected schoolmistress. They were married on December 6, 1919, in Clarksville and made their home in Danville, on a hillside north of Stewart Road.

Like his grandfather and namesake, Captain Jack, and like most men of that family line, John was not physically large. He was only five feet and five inches tall but tough as a pine knot, and like Old Jack, John had unusually long, strong arms. In addition, like his grandfather and his father, he was a gentleman, whose manners were courtly for that time and place. He was courteous, soft spoken, and deferential to ladies.

Also like his grandfather, John was a fighter. He never initiated strife, but when strife occurred, he was already "loaded and cocked." On one occasion, he was deliberately insulted and attacked in Danville by two men much larger than he, who were looking for trouble. They found it. He thoroughly whipped them both, at the same time. Most men, at least thinking men, either befriended him or left him alone. It was the sensible way to relate to Hinsons.

John S. Hinson at age thirty-eight, a veteran of the Spanish-American War, enlists in World War I. (Courtesy Mrs. Frances Hinson)

Ollie Richardson Hinson and her six children, Jack Hinson's great-grandchildren, circa 1968. Rear, left to right: Charles Dudley, Henry, George; front, left to right, John Stewart, Ollie, Helen, Betty Jo. (Courtesy Mrs. Frances Hinson)

A son, John Stewart, Jr., was born to John and Ollie on September 6, 1920. In January 1922, a daughter, Betty Jo, was born to them. Two years later, on January 28, 1924, Ollie gave birth to a boy; they named him Charles Dudley. On March 6, 1925, Henry Lorin was born. Ollie had a baby girl, Helen Jean, on June 5, 1927, and, finally, on February 16, 1934, their last child, George Emmitt, was born. All of their six children grew up in Danville.

At the outset of World War II, John Hinson, ever the patriot and warrior, tried to enlist in his third war. By then, however, he was sixty-two, and to his great disappointment, he was rejected. All his sons who were old enough, however, volunteered, and the family tradition remained intact.

After they were displaced by the flooding of Kentucky Lake during World War II, John and Ollie bought one of the houses destined to be flooded and moved it to a large lot on the road to McKinnon, close to the Methodist church, where she was as much of a fixture as was the piano she played there. In that home, they lived out the rest of their lives. John Hinson, "the little acorn that fell not far from the Jack Hinson tree," died in April 1963, three weeks after his eighty-third birthday. He was buried in Fort Donelson National Cemetery. Ollie Hinson died in February 1988 in her ninety-fifth year, and she was buried in Cane Creek Cemetery.

She was the last of the nineteenth-century Hinsons.

Appendix A

Scenes in the Story, Then and Now (What Remains Today?)

Bubbling Springs

The grassy meadow where the Hinson home stood is much the same today, peaceful and picturesque, by Hinson Creek. The old Keel home that now stands there, surrounded by ancient maples and outbuildings, was built about 1890, probably on the foundation of the burned Hinson home. One can make the short half-mile drive to the site from U.S. Highway 79. Stopping by the house, near the bridge now spanning Hinson Creek, one can almost hear the laughter of Hinson children, black and white, at play; the nickering of saddle horses tied at the old front gate; and seem to catch the aroma of good foods, floating on the breeze from Sarah's kitchen. The springs are still bubbling in clear, cold profusion, feeding Hinson Creek, which still runs through its meadow as it did when the Hinson children played and fished in it. On cold, clear days, one can almost hear the weeping over two fresh graves, out beyond the kitchen garden.

The lane from the house place to Dover Road is now paved and called Keel Hollow Road. The old wagon road back to the slave cabins has had a new house built across the site. The Hundred Acre field can still be seen, and is today part of vast land holdings of the WestVaco Timber Company.

In February 1868, Ab, acting for his father, sold the Bubbling Springs house site and 182.5 acres to George Dougherty; seven months later, in September 1868, George transferred it to William A. Dougherty. In November 1889, it was sold to W. S. Scarboro, who sold it to J. M. Riggins two years later, in December 1891. In 1897, R. E. Keel bought the place, and the Keel family lived there for the next three generations. It passed to Lucien D. Keel in 1919 and to Bob Keel in 1967. In recent years, since the death of Bob Keel, the property has been divided, but the house place and its setting remain essentially the same.

Hinson Town

Remnants of the Hinson Town community still exist, but today it is known by that name only to the older citizens. Originally consisting only of the Hinson servants' cabins and outbuildings, it grew into a suburban black community. As Dover grew westward, Hinson Town became a part of it and, with the passing of time, black/white lines faded away. The slave cabins are gone, and today it has largely become a charming, shady, upper-middle-class area of southwest Dover.

Sarah, the faithful and formidable queen of the kitchen and mistress of the house servants, who fled the wrath of the Union soldiers, returned to Hinson Town many years later to visit. She searched for the silver and other valuables buried so hastily the night the family fled in the snow storm but found nothing. Either the treasure had been recovered and liquidated during the war or someone beat her to it—probably the former.

On May 13, 1892, the *Stewart Courier* reported the death of Anderson Gray "at his home in Hinson Town." He had been a slave, an ironworker owned by Jack Hinson, who had leased his services to Woods Yeatman Company at Cumberland Mills. His obituary calls him a "skilled forageman" (this is almost certainly a printer's error, meant to read "forgeman"). Anderson and Sarah are the only two of the Hinson slaves whose names are known today.

Fort Donelson and Dover

Much of the Fort Donelson battlefield is preserved as a National Battlefield Park, and the park acreage is being expanded to include more of the battlefield. One can still stand in the earthworks of the Confederate right flank, look down into the steep ravine, and almost see and hear the soldiers of the Second Iowa, fighting their way uphill through snow, mud, and a storm of shot as Buckner's few Kentuckians and Tennesseeans defended, with their shotguns and flintlock muskets. The cold, the mud, the blood, the aching exhaustion, the cries of the wounded, and the desperate courage so generously expended on both sides still linger in the air there.

Some streets in Dover, although bearing the same names, have been relocated since 1862, making identifications confusing and difficult; most of them in the center of town, however, are still as they were then. The west end of Wynn's Ferry Road is the same, except for the pavement. The spot where Lew Wallace set up his hasty defenses at midday on Saturday, stopped the Confederates, and saved everything for Grant is well marked and little changed.

What was the courthouse square, which, during the occupation, featured the formidable naval siege gun, is now just a very wide spot on Main Street, at its intersection with Spring Street (Charlotte Road/River Road). But one can still walk up Petty Street ("Generals' Row") from the river landing, past the Dover Inn and the sites of the Major Rice home and the Robertson Hotel, to Spring Street. Turn right there (as Private Cunningham expressed it, "at the perpendicular"), walk uphill toward what was then the courthouse square, and imagine what it was like for the Confederate replacements who marched up that street through direct, canister artillery fire from their left flank. One can also walk up Spring Street today and imagine the tumult and the carnage as Forrest's men attacked uphill toward the big gun in the courthouse square in the second battle, but maybe not—maybe the slaughter then was too great for most of us even to imagine today.

The Dover Inn above the boat landing, Buckner's quarters, then briefly his headquarters, and then Grant's Headquarters and the place where Jack Hinson probably spent Friday and Saturday nights during the battle, is still there, beautifully preserved as the Surrender House. The stone foundations of Major Rice's home and the Robertson Hotel can be seen, up the hill toward Spring Street, at the southwest corner of Petty and what is now called Pillow Street. The stately brick home of kindly, courageous Dr. J. W. Smith still stands on the east side of Main Street. It is painted white and, with an addition built on the front, is now a funeral home. Much of Dover was destroyed in the second battle; the old Smith home on Main Street may have been built after the war. Dr. Smith's medical office, a crumbling, small, brick building, still stands, just around the corner to the east, on the south side of Church Street.

Charlotte Road (River Road), now Tennessee Route 49, out which Forrest led his command and hundreds of others on Sunday morning, and up which he reluctantly attacked in the ill-fated battle a year later, is much the same, except for the pavement. One can drive out, southeast, along the river (which is now the upper reaches of Lake Barkley) past Bear Spring Furnace and, except for the pavement, see it essentially as Forrest did. It is easy to believe that many of the houses and barns were there in 1862 and 1863; some probably were. Smith Ford, which Forrest crossed as he led his contingent to freedom, is under water. It and lower Lick Creek are now a small neck of Lake Barkley.

The old cemetery, across which General Wharton's brigade attacked, broke the Union defenses and captured some of the Union artillery in the tragic battle for Dover in February 1863, is still there, and the graves of Elisabeth Hinson's parents may still be seen there. The church, on the north side of the cemetery, is the approximate location of the point where Wharton's attack stopped for lack of ammunition.

The Widow Crisp

Martha Crisp, unable to rebuild burned fences and operate the farm on Hickman Creek by herself, moved in with her brother, Dave Jones on the Cumberland, north of Dover. She later remarried, died in 1918 at age eighty-one, and is buried in the cemetery at Trinity Methodist Church on the east side of State Route 49 (old Model Road, which becomes the Trace), about a mile north of U.S. Highway 79. Her gravestone simply identifies her as Martha Kernel and gives no hint of her brief and tragic moment in history.

The Place of Execution of Jack's Sons

The spot where George and John Hinson were executed is on the north side of U.S. Highway 79, exactly two-tenths of a mile east of the junction with Tennessee Highway 49 (old Model Road). The old Joe Martin Company building stands there now.

Jack's High Bluff

Jack's ridge, with its bluff, caves, "name rock," and ledge, became the secluded home of Bart Stephenson and is virtually unchanged. The name and year that young Charles Hinson carved in the rock wall in 1863 are still clearly visible, but one must know where to look among many hundreds of names and dates. The upper cave is essentially unchanged. The ceiling is lower now due to the raising of the floor by 140 years' accumulation of organic matter. There is still a fire pit, just inside the entrance. An earthquake collapsed the larger cave, near the bottom of the bluff, in November 1969, but the remains are visible slightly above lake level.

Hurricane Island, Towhead, and the Towhead Chute

In the postwar years both islands became Graffenried property and were farmed, although the margins remained fringed with trees and cane, a local source of fishing poles. Until the formation of Kentucky Lake, Hurricane Island was also a popular place for whiskey making, relatively safe from the sheriffs on both sides of the river. Today, both islands are under water, and the current no longer rages down the Towhead Chute.

Sulfur Wells, Fort Heiman, and Camp Lowe

The Sulfur Wells community of Henry County, where Elisabeth and the children found refuge after being driven from their home, is now submerged under a relatively shallow part of Kentucky Lake; fishermen on that part of the lake sometimes report bubbles rising from the sulfur wells below. Local highway signs still point to the Sulfur Wells area, south of U.S. Highway 79 near Paris Landing. Fort Heiman and Camp Lowe are privately owned, accessible, and little changed, although local knowledge is required for finding them, especially Camp Lowe. Most of Camp Lowe is now the home of Mr. Jack Smith, who intends to protect and preserve it. Camp Lowe functioned only as a satellite facility of Fort Heiman, a base camp for patrolling. The only battle ever fought there was between the author and hundreds of seed ticks; the seed ticks won. At the time of publication, a program was underway to restore Fort Heiman, vastly enlarge National Park Service land holdings around Fort Henry and Fort Donelson, and combine them as one national battlefield park.

Fort Henry, Pine Bluff, and Johnsonville

Fort Henry and Pine Bluff are now in the Land Between the Lakes National Recreation Area. The lower parts of Fort Henry, which stood in muddy floodwater during the battle, are now submerged under Kentucky Lake water. The Pine Bluff site, occupied alternately by Confederate soldiers, Union soldiers, and guerrillas is largely unchanged and can be reached from the trace by a combination of driving and walking. Most of Johnsonville is under Kentucky Lake, as are the opposite banks from which Forrest attacked. The sunken gunboats, transports, and barges are still there, only under deeper water.

Danville

Kentucky Lake took most of Danville. The boat landing, site of the hotel, train station, and most of the town are under lake water, including the spot where Ab was shot from ambush as he crossed the railroad track. Nevertheless, Hinson Hollow and a few other landmarks can still be seen. Home and church sites that were on the hillside rising to the north of the road to McKinnon and Stewart, and the railroad levee, can still be identified. The open freight elevator, which transferred cargo of all kinds between boats, trains, and the town was not demolished, and the upper part is still visible above the water. A railroad bridge functioned there continuously from 1861 until demolished between 1980 and 1982. The near section of the most recent bridge remains there, where the railroad levee meets the lake. The last mail postmarked Danville, Tennessee, left

Danville on a train, November 15, 1943. The higher part of Danville remains, and some of the former residents are building new homes there. A project is underway to erect a marker to identify the site and commemorate the part of Danville that is gone.

The house where John and Ollie lived out their latter years still stands on Danville-Stewart Road, the first residence west of Ollie's Methodist church, in McKinnon. Former Danville residents return for reunions annually, usually in early October.

Magnolia and White Oak Mill

The site of Jack and Elisabeth's mill at Magnolia was altered in 1943 by the building of a concrete bridge over White Oak Creek, but a small remnant of the mill race can still be seen on the bank of McIntosh Branch, just above White Oak Creek and below an abandoned house on the lower slope of Magnolia Hill. Charles Dudley Hinson remembered his father taking him as a small boy in the early 1930s to see the mill site. The water wheel was still there at the time. Both the branch and the creek are still fresh, clear, and beautiful. If one ignores the bridge with its graffiti and the inevitable discarded trash, one can see, hear, feel, and smell them, just the way Jack and Elisabeth Hinson did and as Charles, Thomas, Ab, Sarah, and the children did. Although one of the oldest houses was recently torn down, remnants of the once-thriving village of Magnolia can still be seen if one knows where to look. A large sign, installed at the top of Magnolia Hill, identifies the location and presents a summary of its history.

The Hinson Graves

Jack Hinson was buried in the oldest part of Cane Creek Cemetery, between Magnolia and Danville, on a high bluff that overlooks the Tennessee River (Kentucky Lake) and the mouth of Cane Creek. The site and the view there are similar to those at Jack's old citadel over Towhead Chute, two miles upstream. It is a virtual certainty that Elisabeth is buried beside him. The graves were unmarked until recent years, apparently for fear of desecration, a part of the price they paid for the war years. That curse clung to them long after their deaths. In 1993, their great-grandson, John Stewart Hinson, had markers installed at the approximate site of their graves; all available evidence supports his location within a possible variance of a few feet. John Stewart was probably correct about the approximate location, but the inscription, "Captain, Confederate Infantry," is incorrect and unfortunate. Although sometimes referred to as "Captain Jack," it was not his rank. He was never in the Confederate Army. Both the birth and death years are wrong. Jack was born in 1807, and he died in 1874.

Ab, Sarah, and six of their nine children are buried next to Jack and Elisabeth; the graves are centered on a large Hinson family monument in the form of an obelisk that Ab had installed in 1896, two years before he was murdered. Milton Sykes (1883-1976) told in later years of having been hired by Ab Hinson to haul the obelisk up to the hilltop cemetery in 1896 on a cart pulled by a yoke of oxen.

Appendix B

The Fourth Generation
(World War II and the Death of Danville)

World War II and the Death of Danville

During World War II, Danville was demolished. Some structures were moved, and the rest of the area was flooded by the Tennessee Valley Authority to create Kentucky Lake. Since John Jr., Charles Dudley, and Betty Jo's husband, whom she followed, volunteered for the war, only Henry, Helen, and George were at home to witness the death of Danville. When the rest came back from the war, their home was gone. Unlike Joseph, who returned in 1865 to find his Bubbling Springs home gone, when they returned, their town was gone. It was gone—just not there. Even the river was gone. Hurricane Island and the Towhead, where they went to cut cane for fishing poles, were gone—submerged under the new lake. The creeks where they had played, fished, and swum were gone. Those creeks, so real in their memories, had become unrecognizable bays and sloughs of giant Kentucky Lake. For them, it was like the end of Bubbling Springs again, eighty years later—only worse.[1]

Interesting Family Connections: Hinson, Ross, Bateman, and Lewis

The vine of the Jack Hinson story lives on, and its branches continue to intertwine in interesting ways. Captain Reuben Ross, the hero of the river batteries during the battle for Fort Donelson, went on to become a brigadier general. In 1865, after surviving imprisonment and parole, numerous savage battles, capture, and a daring escape, he was returning home, near Hopkinsville, Kentucky, when he was set upon by two Union soldiers. As he fought with one, the other bludgeoned him from behind with his rifle butt; he is buried near Guthrie, Kentucky. However, like Jack Hinson, his hereditary line grows on. Ross's descendant, historian and journalist David Ross, is now a newspaper editor in Dover and Erin and was of significant assistance in the research for this book. Evelyn Ross, another descendant, married Jack Hinson's great-great-grandson, Charles Hinson; she died in April 2000.

Perhaps the most interesting connection in the story is the union, eighty years after Old Jack's war, of Charles Dudley Hinson and Frances Lewis. Frances grew up at Magnolia, on White Oak Creek, just up the hill from the site of Magnolia Mill, and walked past the mill site many times, going to and from the creek. She actually lived on part of Magnolia Hill, the old Jack Hinson farm, up the hill above the millrace but was completely unaware, either of him or his story. In school, she met, and later married, Charles Dudley Hinson, Jack Hinson's great-grandson, and developed a close relationship with Dudley's father, John.

She met John, while engaged to marry Dudley, and came to know and love him while Dudley was overseas in World War II; she called him "Dad." Frances had grown up on Jack Hinson's Magnolia Hill land and had gone through Danville each day to and from school. She had lived in the scene of much of the story and had married into the family, but she didn't become aware of the story until long after "Dad" Hinson was dead. Now a meticulous, relentless researcher, she has pursued the story, and has been the gracious linchpin of the project to produce this book.

The little log schoolhouse where Ollie Richardson Hinson conducted her early teaching was moved by her son, Dudley, to his country home near Clarksville. His wife's grandfather, John Nolan, originally built it two-and-a-half generations before Frances ever heard the name "Hinson." She now uses it as an arts and crafts studio and marvels at the way her life was already connected to the Hinsons long before she knew them.

There is one more interesting nexus in this amazing story, only recently discovered. Patrick Henry Bateman, Jack Hinson's friend and fellow marksmanship competitor in the twilight of his life at Magnolia, is also an ancestor of John S. Hinson's children, through their mother, Ollie. Only Betty Jo and Helen lived to know that their maternal ancestor Patrick Henry Bateman was a friend and companion of their paternal ancestor Jack Hinson.

In Recent Times

When I met Dudley and Frances in 1993, they were active in the Houston County Historical Society, and Frances was part of the team writing the history of Danville. American history, especially the history of Houston, Stewart, and Humphreys Counties, is a quiet passion to which she has dedicated the remaining years of her life. In the process, she has rescued the history of the village of Magnolia in an excellent, privately published book.

Death has continued to take its toll. All four of John and Ollie's sons have died: George in 1987, Henry in 1990, Charles Dudley in 1995, and John Stewart in 1997. As of the time of this writing, Betty Jo Hinson Dortch of Victor, Montana, and Helen Hinson Edmondson of Clarksville, Tennessee, are the only known living great-grandchildren of Captain Jack Hinson, the legendary Confederate sniper.

Appendix C

Jack Hinson's Rifle, Chain of Possession

The identity of the rifle that Jack Hinson commissioned and used in his private war with the Union is certain. The rifle's chain of possession has been established. There is only one point of dispute in the rifle's history: how it came into the possession of Maj. Charles W. Anderson, Confederate States Army of Murfreesboro, Tennessee, whence it was passed down through his descendants.

The Bromfield Ridley Version

One version, often repeated in local histories, dates from Bromfield Ridley's 1906 book *Battles and Sketches of the Army of Tennessee.* On page 596, Ridley wrote,

> After the war and the death of its owner, this rifle was presented to Major Anderson by Captain Clint Winfrey of Johnsonville, Tenn., whose letter of presentation was accompanied by certificates identifying it, as the rifle owned and used by Old Jack Hinson in avenging the death of his two sons, who were captured by Colonel Lowe's Federal cavalry, and after being captured were taken out and shot to death charged as Bushwhackers.

According to Ridley, Major Anderson's "nephew," Mr. W. T. Love of Murfreesboro, was in possession of the rifle at the time of Ridley's writing.

In one certain error, the venerable Bromfield Ridley was wrong about W. T. Love being Major Anderson's nephew. William T. Love was Major Anderson's brother-in-law, the brother of Major Anderson's wife, Martha Love Anderson, not his nephew.[2]

The Anderson/McFarlin Family Tradition

The second version of the story is that after the war Jack Hinson gave the rifle to General Forrest, who subsequently gave it to his adjutant general and friend, Major Anderson. Major Anderson, who had no children, then passed it on to his brother-in-law, W. T. Love. This account is strongly attested by the Anderson/McFarlin family tradition, and tradition in such a family is formidable evidence, for they are, and have been, a proud and distinguished family to whom such tradition is almost sacred.

The family knows nothing of a letter of presentation or accompanying certificates of authenticity. If they ever existed, they would have to have been discarded by Major Anderson before giving the rifle to W. T. Love, and reason cries out against this thought.

Concerning Clint Winfrey, I have been unable to find any record of his existence outside Bromfield Ridley's book, and the several local histories that have repeated Ridley's account. No record has been found of a Confederate captain named Clint Winfrey, or of such a soldier of any rank with that name, or of anyone by that name in Humphreys County history, Confederate soldier or otherwise. It may be that he was one of those men who, like Jack Hinson, came to be called "Captain" although a civilian. If he existed, his connection with Jack Hinson's rifle appears to be apocryphal.

Therefore, the following is the actual chain of possession of Jack Hinson's legendary rifle, as clearly as I can determine.

The Rifle's Chain of Possession:

1. After the war, Jack Hinson gave the rifle to his friend, Gen. Nathan Bedford Forrest.

2. General Forrest gave the rifle to his adjutant general and friend Maj. Charles W. Anderson of Murfreesboro, Tennessee.

3. Major Anderson, who had no children, while still living, gave the rifle to his brother-in-law, Mr. William T. Love (1857-1916).

4. Mr. Love died in 1916 at the family home Bridgeview, overlooking the Murfreesboro/Stone's River battlefield. He passed the rifle to his daughter, Frances Virginia Love (1885-1976), who knew Major Anderson as "Uncle Charlie." She married and became Frances Virginia Love Black.

5. Frances Virginia Love Black left the rifle to her daughter, Gene Marie Black McFarlin, with written instructions attached to the rifle to give it to her grandson ("the gun goes to Bennie"), Eugenie McFarlin's son, Judge Ben Hall McFarlin of Murfreesboro.

6. The rifle is now in the possession of Judge Ben Hall McFarlin of Murfreesboro, Tennessee.

John W. "Jack" Hinson Genealogy (Partial)

Notes for the Reader

1. Because of the suppression of the Jack Hinson story after the war years and the loss of his family Bible and family papers in the burning of his home, even fragmentary information concerning his genealogy has been rare and difficult to find. Except for census records and the family Bible of Ab and Sarah Hinson, practically nothing about Jack Hinson's ancestry and his descendants was known prior to the research for this book. Genealogical information is valuable, so that not only his living descendants can know something of their ancestry, but also to find possible leads to letters, Bibles, and other documents that could fill in gaps in the historical record of this remarkable man and those associated with him.

2. The identity of the father of John and Thomas Hinson is uncertain. Available evidence strongly indicates that their father was Jacob Hinson (Henson) of Little Richland Creek in Humphreys County. In the Stewart County Courthouse records, he is recorded as having purchased a tract of land on Little Richland Creek from William Murray, "a tract where Hinson now lives," on July 26, 1819, recorded on February 10, 1820.

3. In the censuses prior to 1850, the only name recorded was that of the head of the household; all others were listed only by age (within spans of time—not specific ages) and sex.

4. Years so marked (*) are derived from census records, thus may be off by one year, depending on the month in which the census was taken. And, at least in the 1870 census, it appears that ages were rounded off upward to the next year of age (Joseph, Ab's son, is listed as age two in August, yet he wasn't two until November).

The First Tennessee Generation:

Jacob Hinson (Henson) of Humphreys County, Tennessee (b. North Carolina, circa 1785)

Married, date of marriage unknown, name unknown (b. North Carolina, circa 1785)

Children:

John W. (b. North Carolina, July 1807)

Thomas (b. North Carolina, probably 1810 [he was listed as forty in 1850 census])

Two other sons, younger, names unknown

One daughter, name unknown (b. 1811 to 1820)

Second Tennessee Generation (John W. Hinson Line):

John W. Hinson (b. North Carolina, July 1807; d. Houston County, Tennessee, July 1874)

Married, circa 1835, to Elisabeth James (b. Tennessee 1817*; d. Houston County, Tennessee, December 1876)

Children:

Robert A. (b. 1837*; d. circa September 18, 1863)

George (b. 1839*; d. 1862)

William (b. 1841*; d. January 14, 1865)

John (b. 1844*; d. 1862)

Albert Franklin (b. July 31, 1846; d. September 26, 1898)

Joseph S. (b. 1846*; d. between 1865 and 1871, probably summer/fall 1865)

Charles S. (b. 1853?*; d. 1919)

Thomas W. (b. October 1854; d. August 5, 1920)

Mary Evelyn (b. 1857*; d. ?)

Sarah Margaret (b. 1858*; d. ?)

Two children who died in the forced exodus from Bubbling Springs; names, sex, and birth years unknown

Other children, born and died between census enumerations, number and sex unknown

Third Tennessee Generation (John W. Hinson Line):

Albert Franklin Hinson (b. Stewart County, Tennessee, July 31, 1846; d. Houston County, Tennessee, September 26, 1898)

Married, January 12, 1868, to Sarah Cummings, ward of Seth Outlaw (b. August 15, 1846; d. February 12, 1914, Houston County, Tennessee)

Children:

Joseph James (b. Nov 21, 1868; d. October 21, 1902)

Robert Edgar (July 23, 1870; d. January 8, 1873)

Thetis (b. January 9, 1873; d. July 16, 1878)

Thula (b. July 31, 1875; d. January 12, 1891)

Stella (b. August 30, 1877; d. October 8, 1878)

Bettie (b. February 8, 1879; d. August 16, 1880)

John Stewart, Jr. (b. April 8, 1880; d. April 30, 1963)

Florence (b. February 20, 1884; d. June 30, 1959)

George Franklin (b. January 12, 1886; d. July 28, 1886)

Fourth Tennessee Generation (John W. Hinson Line):

John Stewart Hinson (b. April 8, 1880, Stewart County, Tennessee; d. April 30, 1963, Houston County, Tennessee)

Married, December 6, 1919, to Ollie Richardson, Houston County, Tennessee (b. April 29, 1893; d. February 7, 1988)

Children:

John Stewart (b. September 6, 1920; d. September 3, 1997)

Betty Jo (b. January 11, 1922)

Charles Dudley (b. January 28, 1924; d. September 6, 1995)
Henry Lorin (b. March 6, 1925; d. March 2, 1990)
Helen Jean (b. June 5, 1927)
George Emmit (b. February 16, 1934; d. October 14, 1987)

Second Tennessee Generation (Thomas Hinson Line):

Thomas Hinson (b. North Carolian, 1809 to 1810*)
   Married, February 14, 1833, to Eliza Stanfil (b. ?; d. ?)
      Children:
            Frances Missouri Hinson (b? d ?)
            Married to Joseph Collins Gold
            Child: Eliza Thomas "Tommie" Gold (b. ?; d. ?)

Third Tennessee Generation (Thomas Hinson Line):

Eliza Thomas "Tommie" Gold
   Married to John William Smith
      Children:
            Hallie Smith (b. ?; d. ?)

Appendix E

Documents
(Facsimile)

<u>Sworn Statement of John Hinson</u>

I was in Dover in the morning of the 16th February 1862, when the Fort Donelson army was surrendered. I live in two miles of the Fort. On that morning I left Dover after the surrender, and passed out up the bottom to the rear of the river Batteries. In about one mile I met the Federal forces and fell in with Genl Grant. I told General Grant that I was just out from Dover and that the white flag was up. Some of the officers with General Grant expressed the opinion that it was a "trick". Some of the officers present asked me if I would ride through their lines and let the fact of the white flag being up be known. I consented to do so. I accordingly rode along the line to the extreme right of their line. I found the extreme East of the Enemy's line to be right on the Winn's Ferry road, near where their Battery was on the previous day; They had no forces East of that road on Sunday morning 16th Feby. After leaving the Federal army I passed out over the Battlefield of the previous day and over the ground the Enemys line had occupied and found no Rebel force any where East of the Winn's Ferry road, I know there were no forces East of that road. When I met the Enemy's force on the

1. Jack Hinson affidavit of February 2, 1863, page 1.

much that morning, it was about two hours by sun, and at that time the Enemy's cavalry were returning to re-occupy the ground from which he had been driven the previous day. From the Head of the Enemy's Column on the Winn's Ferry road, it is about one mile and a half East to the Charlotte road, and about two miles to the River Bluff. I know that the whole of the intervening space was open and free from Federal troops, Sunday morning, and that there was nothing to have prevented our forces marching out, and retreating towards Charlotte or Nashville.

I am a citizen, and am in the 58th year of my age, I was on the Battle field with our forces on Saturday, made a report, and gave information to Genl. Pillow – and heard Genl. Pillow direct our forces to be withdrawn, saying that we were out of ammunition and could not meet Smith's fresh forces of Twenty Thousand men.

(Signed) John Hinson

Sworn to and subscribed before me acting justice of the Peace for Maury County Tennessee, This July 2nd 1863.

(Signed) James H. Wilkes, J. P.
for Maury County

2. Jack Hinson Affidavit, page 2.

In the name of God Amen I Elizabeth
Hinson of the County of Houston and State
of Tennessee, being of sound mind and
memory, Considering the uncertainty of
this frail and transitory life, do
Therefore make ordain and declare
this to be my last will and testament,
That is to say, after my burial expenses
are paid and discharged, the residue
of my estate both real and personal I
give bequeath and dispose of as follows
towit, The Farm and mill property on
which I now resides deeded to me by
Jarman Jackson I want sold within
one year from the time of my death, and
the proceeds of said property equally
divided between my beloved children
(viz) Ab. F. Hinson Chas. S. Thos W. Mary E.
and Sarah M. Hinson and one share
to be equally divided between the
heirs of Robt A Hinson dec'd Delia
and Ann Eliza Hinson;
And to my two daughters Mary E. and
Sarah M. Hinson I give two hundred
dollars in gold, which I wish appropriated
for their Clothing and education
I give bequeath and devise all the
rest residue and remainder of my
real and personal estate (should
there be any omitted in this will) to my
Children now living or to their heirs
who may be living at the time of my death
to be equally divided between them share
and share alike,
        I further make and appoint my
Cousin Joel Boyd Guardian of all my children who are minors at the time of my death
        Likewise I make constitute and appo-
int my own Son. Ab F Hinson and my
Cousin Joel Boyd to be Executors of this
my last will and testament hereby revo

3. Elisabeth Hinson's will, November 4, 1871, page 1.

In witness whereof I have hereunto subscribed my name and affixed my seal this
the 4th day of November in the year of our
lord one thousand eight hundred and
seventy one.

                Elizabeth X Hinson (seal)
                        mark

The above written instrument was
subscribed by the Said Elizabeth Hinson
in our presents and acknowledged by
her to each of us, and she at the same
time declared the above instrument so
subscribed to be her last will and
testament and we at the testators
request and in her presents have signed
our names as witnesses hereto, and written
of our own names our respective places
of residence

N M Hinson   Magnolia Po Sum
J A Bonner   D Hinson   Sum

4. Elisabeth Hinson's will, page 2.

Inventory and account of Sales of the Estate
of John Hinson dec'd July 20th 1874

1	Pr Hames	H. McKinnon		30
1	Auger	D. O. Ackens		55
1	4 Gal Jug	J. S. Floid		50
1	Sprinkler	W. J. Wilson		30
1	Pr Buck Gloves	A. M. Eckles		55
1	" "	F. B. Holmes		75
4	" Cotton "	John Hansel		35
3	" "	P. P. Brigham		20
2	" "	W. J. Wilson		10
1	Lot Buttons & Needles	James Baker		35
1	Pr Butts & Screws	S. D. Holmes		50
2	Brass Collars	S. Lankford		10
1	Lot trim	S. W. French		10
1	Hair Brush	P. P. Brigham		30
1	" "	S. W. French		30
1	Vest	A. Holmes	1	40
1	" "	C. C. Wilson	1	45
1	Hat	James Baker	1	55
1	" "	" "	1	20
1	" Ginger	S. W. French		40
1	Saw	W. J. Wilson	1	05
1	Gun Rifle	H. Busby	10	00
1	" "	A. Hinson	6	00
1	" Shot	H. J. McKinnon	12	00
1	" Rifle	C. D. Hinson	15	00
1	Waggon	Henry Dudley	40	00
1	Mule	C. D. Hinson	39	00
1	Cow & Calf	W. J. Wilson	11	50
	Accounts			
1	a/c on W. Wynns (good)		4	50
1	" " John Patterson (")		12	26
1	note " Wm Obarr (doubtful)		2	90
1	a/c " Miles Dennis (good)		2	20
1	Note " Bart Braville (")		7	00
1	a/c " W. J. Wilson "		10	25
1	" " Wm Hall (doubtful)		6	10
1	" " S. A. Patterson (good)		8	10
1	" " Christena Dennis (doubtful)		6	10
1	" " Joseph Duffel (")		5	00
			8	208 80

5. Jack Hinson Estate Sale Record of July 20, 1874.

Inventory and account of Sales of the Personal Property belonging to the Estate of Elisabeth Hinson

	Item	Buyer		
1	Stand & Bed	Miss M. E. Hinson	5	00
1	Lounge complete	A. F. Hinson	2	00
1	Stead and bed	J. H. Hinson	2	00
1	Clock	C. S. Hinson		50
1	Candle Stand	A. F. Hinson		50
1	Bureau	J. W. Hinson		25
1	Stead & Bed	C. S. Hinson	5	00
1	Small Table	" " "		50
1	Trunk		1	00
1	other Small table	" " "		50
1	Bureau	" " "	2	00
½	Dog Chain	A. F. Hinson	2	70
3	Chairs	C. S. Hinson		50
1	Table & Bureau cover	Miss M. E. Hinson	2	00
1	Desk	J. W. Hinson		35
1	Safe	C. S. Hinson	1	50
1	Side Saddle	W. T. Wilson	7	00
1	Mowing blade	C. S. Hinson		10
2	Tongue Plows & Stocks	J. W. Wilson	1	00
1	pr Padded Hames	W. T. Wilson	1	00
1	Drawing Knife	C. S. Hinson		35
1	⅞ Auger			35
1	Frow	J. Pitt		25
1	Sythe Blade	J. A. Outlaw		30
1	Single Tree	Wm Carthey		05
1	Fore Plane	L. D. McGraham		50
1	Smoothing "			85
1	No 8 Cast Plow	C. S. Hinson		30
1	Cutting Knife	W. B. Scott		10
1	Capstick Waggon	C. S. Hinson	2	70
1	Cow & Calf white	W. J. Outlaw	20	25
1	Cow & Calf Brindle	J. W. Hinson	16	25
3	1st Choice hogs	C. S. Hinson	10	00
4	2nd " "	A. F. Hinson	9	30
3	3rd " "	J. W. Hinson	4	50
1	the Chance of Sow	" " "	3	00
1	Gray horse	A. F. Hinson	50	00
1	Watch Hattle	" " "	4	65
1	Charter Oak Cook Stove	J. W. Hinson	18	00
1	Kansas Cook Stove	B. P. Summers	10	20
1	Falling leaf Table	C. S. Hinson	2	15

6. Elisabeth Hinson Estate Sale Record of January 18, 1877, page 1.

Continued

	Amt forward			
1	Log Chain	B S Summers		55
1	Dr. Auggers	A McKinnon	1	10
1	Livestock	F S Summers	1	00
1	Crop Cut Saw	J H O'Quin	3	70
1	Water Cask	A S Hinson	2	75
1	Set Old Irons	R S Hinson	1	20
1	Shovel	" " "		50
1	Grinding Rock	J H O'Quin	3	00
1	pr. Saddle bags	R S Hinson	2	25
1	Pr. Ballance	" "	1	20
	Land & House Rent	James Buck	40	00

7. Elisabeth Hinson Estate Sale Record, page 2.

Notes

Chapter 1

1. In the latter eighteenth and early nineteenth centuries, in large areas of Scotland, the English aristocracy summarily drove the people from their farms to establish vast estates and hunting preserves for themselves. Many of these dispossessed Scots migrated to the Southern colonies in America and moved westward into the mountains and beyond. This mass deportation from Scotland came to be called the Highland Clearances.

2. Sgt. Maj. Eugene Marshall, Brackett's Battalion, Minnesota Cavalry diaries, with 1912 typescript by his daughter, Rare Book, Manuscript, and Special Collections Library, Duke University, Durham, North Carolina (hereafter cited as Marshall).

3. Betty Joe Wallace, *Between the Rivers* (Clarksville, TN: Austin Peay State University, 1992), 41.

4. Cheryl Jameson Smith, interview by author, Waverly, Tennessee, 30 September 2000, and 4 September 2002. She is the granddaughter of the source (1895-1998) whose family knew Jack Hinson well (hereafter cited as Cheryl Smith).

5. Bromfield Ridley, *Battles and Sketches of the Army of Tennessee* (Mexico, MO: Missouri Printing and Publishing Company, 1906), 596-598 (hereafter cited as Ridley).

6. (a) Jill Knight Garrett, *A History of Humphreys County, Tennessee* (Columbia, TN: self-published, 1963), 102 (hereafter cited as Garrett, Humphreys County). Interview with Mrs. Mildred Sullivan Gambill of Waverly, Tennessee, n.d. (b) Jack Hinson's partial genealogy may be seen in Appendix D.

7. Tennessee Land Grant No. 18447 dated 14 May 1847.

8. "Nineteenth Century Road Orders, Stewart County Tennessee." Reprinted in Nina Finley, *In the Beginning: An Early History of White Oak, Cane and Hurricane Creeks* (Erin, TN: Friends of the Houston County Library, n.d.), 10.

9. Betty Jo Hinson Dortch, letter to the author, 10 November 1993, quoting her father, Jack Hinson's grandson John S. Hinson.

10. Jill K. Garrett, ed., *River Counties Quarterly* 8, no. 1 (January 1979): 20.

11. Stephen Vincent Benét, *John Brown's Body* (New York: Rinehart and Company, 1954), 71.

12. Map of the State of Kentucky with the Adjoining Territories, 1795 (western portion), Austin Peay State University Library.

13. (a) Stephen B. Oates, *With Malice Toward None: A Life of Abraham*

Lincoln (New York: Harper & Row, 1977), 70,197, 200-201, 218 (hereafter cited as Oates). (b) Carl Sandburg, *Abraham Lincoln: The War Years,* vol. 1 (New York: Harcourt, Brace & Company, 1939), 126-27.

14. (a) Walter Isaacson, *Benjamin Franklin: An American Life* (New York: Simon & Schuster, 2004), 152, 463-64. (b) Thomas Fleming, *Duel: Alexander Hamilton, Aaron Burr, and the Future of America* (New York: Basic Books, 1999), 318-19 (hereafter cited as Fleming).

15. (a) Jay Coughtry, *The Notorious Triangle: Rhode Island and the African Slave Trade, 1700-1807* (Philadelphia: Temple University Press, 1981), 5-6, 8, 25, 110, 190. (b) Underground Railroad Essays, Vermont Historical Society, http://www.vermonthistory.org/educate/urass. (c) Venture Smith, *A Narrative of the Life and Adventures of Venture, a Native of Africa, but Resident above Sixty Years in the United States of America, Related by Himself* (New London: C. Holt, at the Bee-Office, 1798; Electronic edition, Academic Affairs Library, University of North Carolina at Chapel Hill).

16. (a) B. F. Cooling, *Forts Henry and Donelson: The Key to the Confederate Heartland* (Knoxville: University of Tennessee Press, 1987), 248 (hereafter cited as Cooling). (b) U.S. War Department. *War of the Rebellion: A Compilation of the Official Records of the Union and Confederate Armies,* ser. 1, vol. 23/2, 41-42 (hereafter cited as ORA). (c) Jim Bishop, *The Day Lincoln Was Shot* (1955; reprint, New York: Gramercy, 1983), 13 (hereafter cited as Bishop).

17. (a) Ben Kinchlow, *Black Yellowdogs: The Most Dangerous Citizen Is Not Armed, but Uninformed* (Garden City, New York: Morgan James Publishing, 2008), 7. (b) Larry Koger, *Black Slaveowners; Free Black Slave Masters in South Carolina, 1790-1860* (Columbia: University of South Carolina Press, 1995), xiii, 20-21.

18. It was Burr's involvement in these discussions (he was the likely one to be president of any such Northern Confederation) and Hamilton's passionate opposition to such breaking up of the Union that prompted Hamilton to say and write things about Burr that led to the duel that took Hamilton's life and effectively ended Burr's political career.

19. (a) Joseph J. Ellis, *Founding Brothers: The Revolutionary Generation* (New York: Alfred A. Knopf, 2001), 44 (hereafter cited as Ellis). (b) Fleming, 50, 67, 147, 179, 196-203, 256, 265, 288, 304, 313, 317, 352, 358, 375, 400-401.

20. (a) James M. Banner, Jr., *To the Hartford Convention: The Federalists and the Origins of Party Politics in Massachusetts, 1789-1815* (New York: Random House, 1970), ix. (b) Claude G. Bowers, *Jefferson in Power: The Death Struggle of the Federalists* (Boston: Houghton Mifflin Company, 1936), 220-253. (c) Josh Cracraft, *SparkNote on Alexander Hamilton,* 22 June 2005, <http://www.sparknotes.com/biography/hamilton>. (d) Ellis. (e) Fleming. (f) David Gordon, ed., *Secession, State & Liberty* (New Brunswick, NJ and London: Transaction Publishers, 1998), 135-143. (g) John Remington Graham, *A Constitutional History of Secession* (Gretna, LA: Pelican Publishing Company, 2002), 129-144.

21. Some records, including his burial record, have the year of Charles' birth as 1853.

22. J. Winston Coleman, Jr., ed., *Kentucky, A Pictorial History* (Lexington: University Press of Kentucky, 1971), 46-48.

23. Lowell H. Harrison, *The Civil War in Kentucky* (Lexington: University Press of Kentucky, 1975), 31 (hereafter cited as Harrison).

24. Cooling, 2.

Chapter 2

1. Diary of J. W. McGaughey of Christian County, Kentucky, privately published by R. H. McGaughey as *Life with Grandfather,* (Murray, Kentucky: Murray State University, 1981), 113; entry for 31 August 1861 (hereafter cited as McGaughey).

2. Company Muster Roll, Company E, Fourteenth Tennessee Infantry, November/December 1862.

3. Evert A. Duyckinck, *National History of the War for the Union, Civil, Military and Naval: Founded on Official and Other Authentic Documents,* vol. 2 (New York: Johnson, Fry and Company, n.d.), 83-86.

4. McGaughey, 14 September 1861, 114.

5. Ibid., 2 May 1861, 112.

6. Ibid., 22 November 1861, 115.

7. Cooling, 57-58.

8. Ibid., 51.

9. McGaughey, 116.

10. Ibid., 117.

11. Cooling, 111.

12. Kendall D. Gotte, *Where the South Lost the War: An Analysis of the Fort Henry-Fort Donelson Campaign, February 1862,* (Mechanicsburg, Pennsylvania: Stackpole Books, 2003) (hereafter cited as Gotte).

13. David R. Logsdon, ed., *Eyewitnesses at the Battle of Fort Donelson* (Nashville: Kettle Mills Press, 1998), 1 (hereafter cited as Logsdon).

14. Cooling, 126.

15. Stewart County, Tennessee Deed Book #27, 595. The deed states that J. W. Rice sold to G. C. Robertson, lot No. 109, on the southeast corner of Petty St. and what is now called Pillow St., "joining on the north the hotel now kept by G. C. Robertson, it being the lot upon which J. E. Rice resided up to February 16th 1862." Obviously, Mr. Robertson was buying the vacant lot next to his hotel. Since the lot was vacant by 1879, the Rice house was almost certainly destroyed later in the war. There is a lovely old home in Dover, southwest of the courthouse, called the Rice House. This was the home of a "General Rice" after the war, causing many to believe that it was Pillow's headquarters. However, this man was a former attorney general of Tennessee and was addressed as "General." The deed record has clarified the confusion over names and settled the controversy.

16. (a) Interviews with Mrs. Willouise Crisp Williams, granddaughter of Hiram Crisp, who told her of his and his mother's experiences. Interview by author, Dover, Tennessee, 3 September and 15 October 2002 (hereafter cited as Crisp Williams). (b) Mrs. Williams possesses a beautiful, heirloom-quality cherry sideboard, inherited from Martha Crisp.

17. The author has seen a beautiful, heirloom-quality cherry sideboard that

belonged to Martha Crisp. It is very definitely **not** the kind of furniture that one would find in a home of "the white trash" variety.

18. Logsdon, 8. The first night Grant slept upstairs, but, because of the cold, a bed was moved into the kitchen for him, where it was warm.

19. Ibid.

20. Ibid., 6.

21. Ibid., 9.

22. Ibid., 10.

23. Journal of Captain (later brigadier general) Reuben R. Ross, 29 March 1862, Ross family papers, published in the *Maury Democrat* 14, 21, and 28 January and 4, 11, and 18 February 1897 (hereafter cited as Ross).

24. (a) Stewart County Tax Records, 1852-1860. (b) Stuart County Deed Books 15, 16, 17. (c) Stewart County Marriage Record, Albert Rougement and Rebecca Wells, 1 November 1847. (d) Interview with George Wallace. Interview by author, Dover, Tennessee, 15 June 2005. Neighbors reported that during the battle, wagon loads of amputated limbs were hauled away from the house at night, so as not to demoralize the soldiers.

25. Logsdon, 14-17.

26. General Clement A. Evans, *Confederate Military History* (Athens, GA: Confederate Publishing Company, 1899), 540 (hereafter cited as Evans).

27. McGaughey, 16 March 1861, 111.

28. Logsdon, 18-19, 21.

29. Ibid., 18-21.

30. (a) Ibid., 28. (b) Cooling, 155. (c) Ross.

31. (a) John A. Wyeth, M.D., *Life of General Nathan Bedford Forrest* (New York: Harper & Bros., 1899), 47 (hereafter cited as Wyeth). (b) Cooling, 156.

32. (a) U.S. Navy Department. *Official Records of the Union and Confederate Navies in the War of the Rebellion,* (Washington, D.C.: 1894-1927), series 1, vol. 22, 585-597 (hereafter cited as ORN). (b) Logsdon, 33-34.

33. (a) Gene Smith, *Lee and Grant, a Dual Biography* (New York: Promontory Press, 1984), 67-72 (hereafter cited as Smith). (b) Logsdon, 34

34. Logsdon, 39.

35. (a) Ibid., 51. (b) Robert Underwood Johnson and Clarence Clough Buel, eds., *Battles and Leaders of the Civil War,* vol. 1 (New York: Century Company, 1887-1888), 422 (hereafter cited as Battles and Leaders). (c) Cooling, 182-83.

36. Logsdon, 49-50.

37. John Hinson affidavit of 22 February 1863, Columbia, Tennessee, copy in the possession of the author (hereafter cited as Hinson).

38. Logsdon, 59.

39. Ibid.

40. Ibid., 64-65.

41. (a) Cooling, 195, 198. (b) Battles and Leaders, 424-25.

42. Isaiah 9:5 King James Version.

43. Cooling, 201.

44. Logsdon, 70.

45. Dr. J. W. Smith affidavit of 1 January 1897, quoted in Wyeth, 63-65.

46. (a) Logsdon, 72. (b) Cooling, 203-4.

47. (a) Ibid. (b) Stephen Ambrose, *The Campaigns for Fort Donelson* (Conshocken, PA: Eastern Acorn Press, 1992), unnumbered page (hereafter cited as Ambrose).

48. (a) Logsdon, 73-75. (b) Battles and Leaders, 426. (c) Cooling, 203-4

49. (a) Cooling, 207-8. (b) Logsdon, 76-78.

50. Charles A. Johnson, *Wise County, Virginia* (Norton, VA: The Norton Press, Inc., 1938), 331 (hereafter cited as Johnson, Wise County).

51. (a) ORA, ser. 1, vol. 7, 386-87. (b). Logsdon, 75-95.

52. (a) Logsdon, 79. (b) Frank H. Smith, *History of Maury County, Tennessee* (Columbia, TN: Maury County Historical Society, 1969), interview with Major N. F. Cheairs in 1904, recorded in Book 1, 1-3 (hereafter cited as Frank Smith).

53. (a) Logsdon, 79. (b) Lieutenant Richard Channing, Thirteenth Missouri Volunteer Infantry, journal and letter of 21 February 1862, Special Collections Library, Filson Historical Society, Louisville, Kentucky.

54. (a) Cooling, 205-7. (b) Wyeth, 65. (c) Johnson, Wise County, 331.

55. Logsdon, 80.

56. Ibid.

57. (a) Bearss and Jones, "Dover Hotel; Historic Structures Report," 10, 13, 23; letter, Louise Runyon to C. L. Johnson, 13 March 1934, Fort Donelson National Military Park Library. (b) Cooling, 211.

58. (a) Hinson. (b) Frank Smith, 3.

59. Hinson.

60. Smith, 113-14.

61. (a) Cooling, 212. (b) Smith, 113-14, op cit.

62. (a). Ambrose, unnumbered page. (b) Smith, 114.

63. Crisp Williams.

64. (a) Ambrose, unnumbered page. (b) Smith, 114.

65. (a) ORA, ser. 1, vol. 7, 679-684. (b) James J. Hamilton, *The Battle of Fort Donelson* (New York and Cranbury, NJ: Thomas Yoseloff, 1968), 338.

66. Clint Johnson, *Bull's-Eyes and Misfires: 50 People Whose Obscure Efforts Shaped the American Civil War* (Nashville: Rutledge Hill Press, 2002), 13-17 (hereafter cited as Clint Johnson).

67. Gotte.

Chapter 3

1. Logsdon, 90-92.

2. Ibid., 91.

3. Ibid., 93.

4. Ibid., 92

5. (a) Ibid., 93. (b) Ambrose, unnumbered page.

6. (a) Goodspeed Publishing Company, *Goodspeed's History of Tennessee, 1886* (Columbia, TN: Woodward & Stinson Printing Company, 1972), 913, 1303-04 (hereafter cited as Goodspeed). (b) Cooling, 124. (c) *Frank Leslie's Illustrated Newspaper,* 15 March 1862.

7. (a) Cooling, 215. (b) Wyeth, 60.

8. Cooling, 217.

9. Smith, 114.

10. (a) Ibid., 114-117. (b) Cooling, 245-250. (c) Stephen W. Sears, *George B. McClellan: The Young Napoleon* (New York: Ticknor & Fields, 1988), 103, 132.

11. (a) Flag Officer Andrew H. Foote, letter of 20 February 1862, to the secretary of the navy (hereafter cited as Foote), copy in possession of the author. (b) ORA, ser. 1, vol. 7, 644-45. (c) Ibid., 679-80. (d) Ibid., 682-684. (e) Ibid., vol. 10/2, 30.

12. (a) Ibid., vol. 7, 649. (b) Cooling, 245-46. (c) Flag Officer Andrew H. Foote, proclamation to the citizens of Clarksville, 20 February 1862, copy in possession of the author.

13. John Metzger, Seventy-sixth Ohio Volunteers, letter of 4 March 1862.

14. (a) Cooling, 245-46. (b) Foote.

15. Cooling, 251.

16. (a) Anthony James Joes, *America and Guerrilla Warfare* (Lexington: University Press of Kentucky, 2000), 52. (b) Stephen V. Ash, *When the Yankees Came: Conflict and Chaos in the Occupied South, 1861-1865* (Chapel Hill: The University of North Carolina Press, 1995), 47-49 (hereafter cited as Ash, Yankees Came).

17. Jill Knight Garrett, historian, interview by author, Columbia, Tennessee, 14 September 1993. Concerning her Grandmother's experiences in Stewart County during the war years.

18. (a) Donald Davidson, Rivers of America Series: The Tennessee, vol. 2, *The New River: Civil War to TVA* (New York: Rinehart and Company, 1948), 77-85 (hereafter cited as Davidson). (b) ORN, ser. 1, vol. 23, 421. (c) Letter from acting rear admiral C.H. Davis concerning the problem of guerrilla attacks from the riverbanks, Squadron Letters, NARA.

19. Ibid., vol. 23/2, 5.

20. Ibid., vol. 31/3, 459-60.

21. Daniel E. Sutherland, ed., *Guerrillas, Unionists, and Violence on the Confederate Home Front* (Fayetteville: University of Arkansas Press, 1999).

22. Flavius Josephus, first century A.D. historian. *Life of Flavius Josephus,* 7: 67.

23. ORA, ser. 1, vol. 23/1, 353.

24. Ash, Yankees Came, 64-65.

25. ORA, ser. 1, vol. 23/2, 10.

26. Ibid., ser. 1, vol. 34/3, 216, 232, 366.

27. Ibid., ser. 1, vol. 34/4, 182, 202, 525.

28. Ibid., ser. 1, vol. 41/2, 719.

29. Ibid., ser. 1, vol. 48/1, 485.

30. (a) Hazel Shaw, whose father knew and worked for Phillip Redd, interview by author, Cadiz, Kentucky, 8 August 1993. (b) Hall Allen, *Center of Conflict* (Paducah, KY: Paducah Sun-Democrat, 1961), 134-136 (hereafter cited as Allen). (c) J. Milton Henry, *The Land Between the Rivers* (Clarksville, TN: Written under contract between Austin Peay State University and the Tennessee Valley Authority, Taylor Publishing Company, n.d.), 122 (hereafter cited as Henry). (d) Provost Marshall's return of oaths of allegiance administered at Fort Henry in

the month of September 1862, copy in the possession of the author (NARA).

31. (a) Henry, 122. (b) Barry Craig, "Thousands of Civil War Soldiers Died Near Their Homes", the *Paducah Sun,* 16 April 1995, p. 11A. (c) Interviews with Golden Pond natives, interview by author, Golden Pond Reunion, Golden Pond, Land Between the Lakes National Recreation Area, August 1994.

32. (a) Iris Hopkins McClain, *A History of Stewart County, Tennessee* (Columbia, TN: Iris Hopkins McClain, 1965), 64 (hereafter cited as McClain, Stewart County). (b) Goodspeed, 913, 1303-4.

33. (a) Interview with Doug Mitchell, grandson of Almary Barnes, who told him of the event many times, interview by author, Waverly, Tennessee, 30 September 2000. (b) Garrett, Humphreys County, 101.

34. Jill Knight Garrett, "Guerrillas and Bushwhackers in Middle Tennessee during the Civil War" (manuscript, Tennessee State Archives, Manuscript Division, AC Number 69-338, n.d.), 75, quoting the *Stewart County Times,* 18 September 1931 (hereafter cited as Garrett, Guerrillas).

35. (a) ORA, ser. 1, vol. 31/3, 459-60, op cit. (b) John M. Gibson, *Those 163 Days: A Southern Account of Sherman's March from Atlanta to Raleigh* (New York: Bramhall, 1961). (c) Harvey Reid, Twenty-second Wisconsin Volunteer Regiment, letter of 28 March 1865. (d) Mark Grimsley, *The Hard Hand of War: Union Military Policy Toward Southern Civilians, 1861-1865* (New York: Cambridge University Press, 1995).

36. James L. Head, *The Atonement of John Brooks: The Story of the True Johnny "Reb" Who Did Not Come Marching Home* (Geneva, FL: Heritage Press, 2001), 117-125.

37. Emma Inman Williams, *Historic Madison, The Story of Jackson and Madison County Tennessee, From the Prehistoric Mound Builders to 1917* (Jackson, TN: Jackson Service League, 1972), 169-180.

38. ORA, ser. 1, vol. 32/3, 117-119.

39. (a) Kevin D. McCann, *Hurst's Wurst: Colonel Fielding Hurst and the Sixth Tennessee Cavalry U.S.A.* (Dickson, TN: Three Star Press, 2000), 6, 9, 23-25, 31-33, 35-37. (b) ORA, ser. 1, vol. 32/3, 118-19.

40. (a) McClain, Stewart County, 65. (b) Goodspeed, 990.

Chapter 4

1. (a) Record of Events, Equipment and Ordnance, Fifth Iowa Cavalry, 1-17 (hereafter cited as Record of Events). (b) Marshall, 2 December 1861.

2. Charles C. Nott, Fifth Iowa Cavalry. *Sketches of the War: A Series of Letters to the North Moore Street School of New York* (New York: Charles T. Evans, 1863; reprinted in E. McLeod Johnson, *A History of Henry County, Tennessee,* vol. 1 (Paris, TN, E. McLeod Johnson, 1958), 90-107.

3. (a) Record of Events, 23 February 1862. (b) ORA, ser. 1, vol. 10/2, 74. (c) Marshall, 13, 20, and 24 February 1862.

4. (a) ORA, ser. 1, vol. 7, 679-80, 682-684. (b) Ibid., vol. 10/2, 30. (c) Smith, 62-65.

5. ORA, ser. 1, vol. 10/2, 30, Grant to Lowe.

6. Marshall, 4-7 April 1862.

7. (a) John Hinson Parole dated 19 March 1862. (b) *St. Louis Democrat*, n.d.; republished in the *Indianapolis Daily Journal* as "Civilians Taken at Fort Donelson," 28 February 1862.

8. (a) Kurt D. Bergemann, *Brackett's Battalion: Minnesota Cavalry in the Civil War and Dakota War* (St. Paul: Borealis Books, 2004), 34-38 (hereafter cited as Bergemann). (b) ORA, ser. 1, vol. 10/1, 879-883.

9. Ibid.

10. Marshall, 22 November 1862.

11. (a) Record of Events, 20 February, 17 July, 18 August 1862. (b) Morning Reports, Fifth Iowa Cavalry, 1862-1863 (hereafter cited as Morning Reports). (c) Fifth Iowa Cavalry Special Order 63, 22 August 1862 (hereafter cited as Special Order 63).

12. Marshall, August 1862.

13. H. A. Revelle, Thirty-fourth New Jersey Volunteer Infantry, letter of 14 December 1864.

14. ORA, vol. 17/2, 126.

15. The freeing of the Hinson slaves is a Hinson family tradition supported by a letter to this effect from John S. Hinson, Jack Hinson's great-grandson, to the author, 11 November 1995.

16. (a) ORA, vol. 16/1, 862-868. (b) Ibid., vol. 17/2, 181.

17. Ibid., vol. 31/3, 459-60.

18. Ibid., vol. 17/1, 36.

19. Ibid., vol. 17/1, 37-38.

20. Ibid., 38-39.

21. Ibid., vol. 16/1, 955-56.

22. Ibid., vol. 17/1, 39.

23. (a) Ibid., 150. (b) Morning Reports, September to December 1862.

24. ORA, ser. 1, vol. 17/2, 730-31.

25. Ibid., 730-732.

26. (a) Ibid., 303-4. (b) Ibid., vol. 20/2, 100. (c) Morning Reports, 20-24 October 1862.

27. Clark G. Reynolds, "The Civil War and Indian War Diaries of Eugene Marshall, Minnesota Volunteer" (master's thesis, Duke University, 1963), 248.

28. (a) Noel C. Fisher, *War at Every Door: Partisan Politics and Guerrilla Violence in East Tennessee, 1860-1869* (Chapel Hill: University of North Carolina Press, 1997), 62-95. (b) Sean Michael O'Brien, *Mountain Partisans: Guerrilla Warfare in the Southern Appalachians, 1861-1865* (Westport, CT: Praeger Publishers, 1999), 5-13.

29. (a) The place where the Hinson sons were killed is today the location of the old Joe Martin Company building, two-tenths of a mile east of the present junction of U.S. Highway 79 and the Trace (Tennessee Highway 49). What is now Tennessee Highway 49 was then called the Model Road. (b) Interviews with David Ross, interview by author, Dover, Tennessee. Ross is a newspaper editor and battle historian, who read the original report at Fort Donelson National Battlefield while an intern on staff there in the fall of 1980. (c) Henry, 121. (d) Garrett, Guerrillas, part 1, 79.

30. (a) Proverbs 18:19 KJV. (b) Zechariah 13:6 KJV.

31. (a) Wyeth, 63-65. (b) Logsdon, 93 ("a doctor's office"). (c) ORA, ser. 1, vol. 39/1, 857.

32. Cheryl Smith.

33. Series of interviews with the Black-McFarlin family, interview by author, Murfreesboro, Tennessee, August 1993.

34. This bluff and the surrounding area was later part of the Graffenried (in time, spelling evolved to Graffreid) plantation called Riverside Farm, and the bluff became known as Graffenried Bluff. Today, it still towers above Kentucky Lake at the mouth of Hurricane Creek and is known to recent generations as Name Rock Hill.

Chapter 5

1. Record of Events, 7 January 1863.

2. There were six Earp brothers; Newton, the eldest; Virgil; James; and Francis served as Union soldiers. Virgil and Francis served throughout the war in the Eighty-third Illinois (Francis until medically discharged in September 1864—Virgil served until the regiment was disbanded in 1865). James served in the Seventeeth Illinois Infantry, was severely wounded in 1861, and was later discharged for disability. Due to the confused nature of Earp family records, Francis may have been Virgil's cousin, rather than his brother, but they were both born in Morgantown, Ohio County, Kentucky, and they enlisted together in Monmouth, Illinois.

3. (a) Frank Waters, *The Earp Brothers of Tombstone: The Story of Mrs. Virgil Earp* (New York: Bramhall House, 1960), 28, 154-160, 185. (b) Frederick H Dyer, *A Compendium of the War of the Rebellion* (Dayton: OH: The Press of Morningside Bookshop, 1978), 1082. (c) The U.S. National Archives and Records Administration, Union Records, Union soldiers from Illinois, general index. (d) Muster Rolls, Company B, Eighty-third Illinois Volunteer Infantry, 21 August 1862 to 26 June 1865 (hereafter cited as Muster Rolls). (e) Muster Rolls, Company C, 21 August 1862 to 26 June 1865. (f) Stuart N. Lake, *Wyatt Earp: Frontier Marshall* (Boston and New York: Pocket Books, 1931), 283-300.

4. Pillow had been directed to submit an explanation of his behavior to the president immediately after the surrender. By March 4, his report still had not been received, but Pillow had given his story to the press. In Paducah, General Sherman had read Pillow's account of the surrender in the *Memphis Appeal* of February 26, ten days after the surrender, and forwarded it to General Halleck. The Union commanders had already read Pillow's account, yet President Davis had seen nothing of it. Davis was not pleased.

5. (a) ORA, ser. 1, vol. 7, 677-78. (b) Ibid., 917. (c) Ibid., 278-300.

6. Clint Johnson, 180.

7. (a) Cooling, 265. (b) ORA, ser. 1, vol. 7, 917.

8. Hinson (His entire sworn affidavit may be read, reproduced in facsimile, as Appendix E).

9. (a) Morning Reports, 4 February 1863. (b) Bergemann, 52. (c) Ambrose, unnumbered page.

10. Since there was never a threat of Confederate attack on Donelson from

the river, the cannon of the water batteries, including the huge Columbiad, were removed for use elsewhere.

11. Since there were only minutes—an hour or less—to prepare for the hasty defense of Dover, not nearly enough time to dismount the huge siege gun at the river batteries, move it to the courthouse square, and mount it there on its pivot track, it was obviously already mounted there, probably by Major Hart, Harding's predecessor in command at Dover.

12. (a) Returns, Eighty-third Illinois Volunteer Infantry, April to June 1863. (b) Muster Rolls, July/August 1863.

13. (a) ORA, ser. 1, vol. 23/1, 34-39. (b) Ambrose, unnumbered page.

14. Oath of Allegiance, John Hinson, dated 21 February 1863.

15. (a) Morning Reports, 8 March 1863. (b) ORA, ser. 1, vol. 23/1, 353-54. (c) Bergemann, 54.

16. John S. Hinson, letter to the author dated 20 January 1995, with recollections of his mother, Mrs. Ollie Richardson Hinson, widow of John S. Hinson, Jack Hinson's grandson, in 1963.

17. Ann Wyley, Waverly, Tennessee, letter to her sister, Mary Wyly Lankford, dated 7 April 1863, copy in author's collection.

18. (a) Morning Reports, 7-10 April 1863. (b) This could have been a clerk's error, intended to be "83rd" Illinois, but it could have been the Eightieth. From 7-19 April, the Eightieth Illinois was in transit from Nashville, down the Cumberland River, and up the Tennessee, passing Fort Donelson and Stewart County on both sides.

19. (a) Capture Record, Roll of Prisoners of War, Fort Donelson, Tennessee, May1863. (b) It is probable that Robert Hinson was never actually a Confederate soldier. Although Cross's history of the Fourteenth Tennessee Infantry, *Ordeal by Fire,* and the Civil War Centennial Commission's *Tennesseans in the Civil War* list Robert as a member of the Fourteenth Tennessee Infantry, those compilations appear to be based upon the surviving Federal capture documents, which are, themselves, based only upon what Robert told his captors and wanted them to believe. No record of his enlistment or discharge exists in Confederate records, nor is there a single unit muster roll or payroll concerning him known to exist.

20. James M. Wells, "Union Prisoners of War Break Out of Libby Prison," *McClure's Magazine,* January 1904; republished in *Old News,* vol. 12, no. 6, March 2001, 9.

21. Register of Prisoners of War, Department of the Cumberland, Nashville, May 1863.

22. Charge Sheet (rough/worksheet), Fort Donelson, case of George F. Hinson, County of Stewart, State of Tennessee, unsigned, n.d.

23. "From the Seventy First," the *Troy (Ohio) Times,* 25 June 1863 (hereafter cited as *Troy Times).*

24. Bergemann, 74-77.

25. (a) ORA, ser. 1, vol. 23/1, 346-47. (b) Marshall, 23 May 1862.

26. *Troy Times.*

27. *Troy Times.*

Chapter 6

1. (a) Special Order No. 1, Thirteenth Wisconsin Infantry, assumption of command at Fort Donelson, 8 June 1863. (b) Record of Events, 13 June 1863. (c) *Troy Times.*

2. Lt. Ira B. Dutton, journal with maps, August to September 1863, 43-45.

3. ORA, ser. 1, vol. 23/1, 844.

4. (a) Regimental Return, Fourteenth Tennessee Infantry, for the month of October 1862. (b) Parole of Prisoner of War, Office of the Provost Marshall General, Army of the Potomac, 30 September 1862. (c) Regimental Return, Fourteenth Tennessee Infantry, for the month of November 1862. (d) Company Muster Rolls, Company H, Fourteenth Tennessee Infantry, September/October 1863 and November/December 1863.

5. (a) Garrett, Guerrillas, 74, quoting the *Nashville Union,* 25 August 1863. (b) ORA, ser. 1, vol. 23/2, 595.

6. (a) Garrett, Guerrillas, 74, quoting the *Nashville Union,* 25 August 1863. (b) ORA, ser. 1, vol. 23/2, 595.

7. *Memphis Daily Appeal* (published in Atlanta), 13 September 1863; reprinted from the *Huntsville Confederate.*

8. ORA, ser. 1, vol. 30/3, 730.

9. (a) Garrett, Guerrillas; interview with John F. Rainey, part 2, unnumbered page, 31 July 1906. (b) Frank Smith, 115.

10. (a) Garrett, Guerrillas; interview with John F. Rainey, part 2, unnumbered page, 31 July 1906. (b) Frank Smith, 115.

11. William H. Doris, Eighty-third Illinois, letter to wife.

12. Will of Elizabeth Hinson, 4 November 1871, witnessed by N. M. McKinnon, Magnolia Post Office, Tennessee, and J. A. Bomar, Danville, Tennessee, "Houston County Wills," 274-75 (hereafter cited as Will) (Note: Although in the earliest documents her name was spelled with an "s" in the British style, in later documents, including this will, her name is spelled with a "z" as it is here.)

13. ORA, ser. 1, vol. 7, 325-26.

14. (a) Ibid., ser. 1, vol. 23/2, 57. (b) Ibid., ser. 1, vol. 17/2, 525.

15. After spending his first two years in Company E, he would be reassigned to Company F upon his return, but casualties had made the regiment and its companies so much smaller that it would involve little change for him.

Chapter 7

1. Because of the ten-year time lapse between the 1860 census and the 1870 census, the identities of the sick children are unknown; they were born, lived briefly, and died in the family's exodus. The story has survived the passage of time in family memory, but the family Bible, with its records of names and dates of births and deaths, has never been found. It apparently burned with the house the next day, along with family photographs and letters.

2. Betty Jo Hinson Dortch, letter 11 October 1993.

3. (a) Burke Davis, *The Civil War: Strange and Fascinating Facts* (New York: Fairfax Press, 1982). (b) General Puller, interviewed by author, Saluda, Virginia, 1966.

4. Post Surgeon William S. Cuthbert, Eighty-third Illinois Volunteer Infantry Regiment, letter to post commander, Fort Donelson, 12 October 1864.

5. Marcella (Mrs. Terry H.) Stigal, Memphis, Tennessee, granddaughter of Frank and Mary Creney, operators of the railroad commissary for the workers at Danville Crossing in the early 1860s, letter dated 31 July 1996, copy in the author's collection.

6. Iris Hopkins McClain, *A History of Houston County, Tennessee* (Columbia, TN: Iris Hopkins McClain, 1966), 26. War diary of Capt. Andrew Jackson Campbell, Company F, Forty-eighth Tennessee Infantry, 1861-1863 (hereafter cited as McClain, Houston County).

7. The author has carefully examined the cave and spent time in it. It is exactly as described here.

8. Rev. Mr. Roy West, Clarksville, Tennessee, interview by author, 3 October and 14 December 1993. A Danville native, West, as a boy, was told the stories of Jack Hinson and Graffenried Bluff by one who lived there in the nineteenth century (hereafter cited as West Interviews).

9. Some researchers assign the name "Eclipse" to another furnace, on the south side of Leatherwood Creek, operated by Phillips.

Chapter 8

1. (a) Interview with Frank Cherry, Danville native and area river boatman, interview by author, 27 July 2002 (hereafter cited as Cherry interviews). (b) West interviews. (c) Letter, report of Lt. Comdr. LeRoy Fitch, commander Tenth District Mississippi Squadron, "Tennessee River," 9 November 1864. In it he describes the difficulty of traversing the chute at White Oak Island, upstream (hereafter cited as Fitch letter).

2. (a) Towhead Chute was notoriously difficult and remained a challenge for boats even after steam power was replaced by diesel. (b) Cherry interviews.

3. (a) Cherry interviews. (b) West interviews. (c) Fitch letter.

4. (a) ORN, ser. 1, vol. 23, 406. (b) Interviews with John Stewart Hinson and Charles Dudley Hinson, interview by author, 3 October 1993 (hereafter cited as Hinson interviews). (c) All sources found have been consistent in saying that Jack's targets were uniform coats of blue and his targets of preference were officers. Concerning boat targets, Donald Davidson, *Rivers of America Series: The Tennessee*, vol. 2, *The New River: Civil War to TVA*, states about Hinson, "He specialized in gunboats, and in officers and crew members of gunboats" (p 90). There has been found no record of Hinson ever targeting civilians or civilian boats. ORN, ser. 1, vol. 23, 406.

5. ORA, ser. 1, vol. 23/1, 353-54.

6. The earliest record known to the author of Jack Hinson's doing business in Henry County is that of the estate sale of George Gibson in 1835.

7. (a) Hinson family tradition. (b) Letter from Betty Jo Hinson Dortch to the author dated 11 October 1993.

8. Sarah did return after the war. She checked to see if the buried silver service was still there; it wasn't.

9. Personal observation of the special rifle by the author; the orderly arrangement of small circles is still clearly visible.

10. (a) The Hundred Acre Field still exists and today is part of vast acreage belonging to WestVaco, a West Virginia timber company. (b) The controlled burning, which created the charcoal, was done on prepared, clay "coaling hearths." The remains of these coaling hearths can still be found in Stewart County, recognizable by the abundant black charcoal residue in the soil at, or near, the surface.

11. One version of the story has it that there was a larger number of soldiers involved in the incident, and Jack escaped in a hail of Yankee bullets. The bulk of the evidence, however, indicates that it occurred as written here.

12. (a) Hinson interviews (b) Garrett, Guerrillas, Book 1, 79-80; citing *Stewart-Houston Times,* 15 November 1967.

Chapter 9

1. "On the qui vie" was an expression commonly used in that war. It meant to be watchful and alert. It means "long live who?" and was borrowed from the French, who used it as a challenge for pickets and sentries.

2. It is significant and revealing that, in spite of the increasing rewards offered, the great poverty of many of the people in the area, and the fact that among them were Union sympathizers, there is no record that anyone ever betrayed his presence to the occupation forces—not even a remnant of a rumor. He was respected there, even by the pro-Union families.

3. (a) McClain, Stewart County, 66. (b) Garrett, Guerrillas, Book 1, 78-79. (c) Garrett, Humphreys County, 102, interview with Mrs. Mildred Sullivan Gambill, Waverly, Tennessee, n.d. (d) Davidson, 89-90.

4. (a) Evans, 540-41. (b) Letter from Porter, acting rear admiral David D., to Secretary of the Navy Gideon Welles, dated 3 January 1862, concerning the surrender of a navy boat to guerrillas after being fired on from the riverbank, copy in possession of the author (NARA) (hereafter cited as Porter to Welles).

5. (a) Porter to Welles. (b) Davidson, 86-87. (c) The Navy Official Record for the war has no record of the abortive surrender, but there are many documents missing from the Official Record. Also, any thinking commanding officer would be likely to omit that embarrassing detail, which was, after all, never consummated from his log book. It would have been, at best, the ignominious end of his career. Multiple-sources document and narrative history substantiates the story as recorded here. At least two other navy boats in the region surrendered to guerrillas but not to a single man as in this case. One of the captains who surrendered faced the threat of hanging for surrendering his boat. Another boat, an armed transport with a contingent of Ohio infantry aboard, ran aground in the Tennessee River, was subjected to a hail of gunfire from the bank, and the captain surrendered to a large guerrilla band by waving a white bed sheet on a broomstick. The guerrillas floated the boat, used it, and then burned it.

6. Department of the Cumberland, Descriptive List (Confederate), Parole of Joseph S. Hinson, private, Company F, Fourteenth Regiment, Tennessee Infantry, dated 6 May 1865.

7. Garrett, Guerrillas, Book 1, 78.

8. McClain, Stewart County, 66.

9. *Nashville Banner,* 14 October 1955 (hereafter cited as *Banner).*

10. It is not known today how Forrest was able to contact Jack for he certainly had no home address during those months on the run. One can only make the reasonable assumption that there were people in the area, trusted by both Forrest and by Jack, who acted as message centers.

11. (a) Charles Moss, "Forgotten Fort Heiman: 'Land of Late Victory,'" 5 parts, part 3, *Nashville Banner,* 1957, p. 5 (hereafter cited as Moss). (b) Davidson, 89-103.

12. (a) Ibid., 5-6. (b) ORA, ser. 1, vol. 23/1, 353-54.

13. (a) Moss, part 3, 7. (b) Allen.

14. Ibid., vol. 39/3, 608-9.

15. Moss, part 3, 8.

16. His affidavit concerning the surrender of Fort Donelson survives as well as many title deeds and other legal documents, but this brief statement, recalled by Major Anderson, represents the only informal utterance of Hinson's, spoken or written, of which any record has been found.

17. (a) Ridley, 596-598. (b) Major Anderson lived out the rest of his life in Murfreesboro, Tennessee. It seems fitting that Jack's rifle, which was presented by Forrest to Major Anderson after the war, has remained in his family and still resides in Murfreesboro, in the possession of Major Anderson's descendant, Judge Ben Hall McFarlin.

18. (a) Col. Donald H. Steenburn, *Silent Echoes of Johnsonville: Rebel Cavalry and Yankee Gunboats* (Meridianville, AL: Elk River Press, 1994), 74-82 (hereafter cited as Steenburn). (b) ORA, ser. 1, vol. 39/1, 871-72. (c) Garrett, Humphreys County, 103-8. (d) Davidson, 92-103.

19. (a) Allen, 145-6.(b) Moss, part 3, 7; part 4, 8-9. (c) Davidson, 102-4. (d) Steenburn, 76.

20. (a) Allen, 145-6. (b) Moss, part 3, 7; part 4, 8-9. (c) Davidson, 102-4. (d) Steenburn, 76.

21. (a) Wyeth, 520-533. (b) Steenburn, 83-84. (c) ORA, ser. 1, vol. 39/1, 858-875. (d) Davidson, 102-4.

22. (a) ORA, ser. 1, vol. 39/2, 517. (b) Ibid., vol. 38, 480. (c) Evans, vol. 1, Forrest Biography. (d) Davidson, p 93.

23. (a) ORA, ser. 1, vol. 39/2, 517. (b) Ibid., vol. 38/4, 480. (c) Evans, vol. 1, Forrest biography. (d) Sherman hated all things Confederate but pragmatically admired military excellence. He wrote of Forrest, in official correspondence, "I take it for granted that Forrest will cut our road. . . . His cavalry will travel a hundred miles in less time than ours will ten. . . . I can whip his infantry, but his cavalry is to be feared." Davidson, 93.

24. (a) Garrett, Humphreys County, 107. (b) *Banner,* 19 March 1958.

Chapter 10

1. Loose Records, Fort Donelson, Tennessee, Part 5, Box 413, Record Group 393, NARA (hereafter cited as Loose Records).

2. (a) ORA, ser. 1, vol. 32/3, 624. (b) Ibid., vol. 24/3, 181-82. (c) Ibid., vol. 30/3, 24. (d) Ibid., vol. 17/2, 323. (e) Davidson, 82.

3. J. Gray McAllister and Grace Owings Guerrant, *Edward O. Guerrant: Apostle to the Southern Highlanders* (Richmond, VA: Richmond Press, 1950), 52.

4. Ash, Yankees Came, 49.

5. ORA, ser.1, vol. 45/2, 153.

6. (a) Ibid., 92. (b) Ibid., 138. (c) Ibid., 152-154. (d) Col. William Forbes, Fort Donelson commanding officer, letter to Col. A. A. Smith at Clarksville dated 22 December 1864, copy in the possession of the author (NARA).

7. (a) Confederate Archives, chapter 6, File No. 68, 82. (b) Curiously, the record surviving in Confederate Archives states that his leg was amputated on 13 January 1865, and that he was "retired" the next day. This, of course, means that he died the next day. Even in the threadbare medical system available in the Confederacy's final weeks, no surgeon would amputate a wounded soldier's leg one day and "send him home" the next day, on his own, with shock, infection, and a bleeding stump. That would constitute killing the patient. (c) At the time, Richmond's Chimborazo Hospital was the largest hospital in the world.

8. (a) Harrison, 75. (b) Champ Clark, Kentucky lawyer turned Missouri newspaper editor and congressman, later described the problem and the sort of men who did such things as he remembered them: "The land swarmed with cutthroats, robbers, thieves, firebugs, and malefactors of every degree and kind, who preyed upon the old, the infirm, the helpless, and committed thousands of brutal and heinous crimes—in the name of the Union, or of the Southern Confederacy." One old Kentucky man told his family to kill them if they got the chance for "they are not fit for no place but Hell."

9. (a) There is a series of small notches, on the right edge of the top surface of the barrel, forward of the front sight. It is the author's belief that they are the record of such criminals killed, separated on his barrel as far as possible from the record of real soldiers and sailors who fell, with honor, under his sights. (b) It is only fair to point out that the late J. Milton Henry, of Austin Peay State University, wrote that Jack Hinson robbed and terrorized pro-Union families in the area. However, his one supporting reference, a little boy's memory of "how the old man's hand shook as he held the candle while he looked for valuables," flies in the face of all other known evidence, narrative or otherwise, concerning Jack Hinson. It could well be that some unscrupulous old man with shaky hands went about robbing people, claiming to be Hinson to frighten them into submission. However, it would be irrational to accept this one, unsubstantiated, family tradition and ignore the mass of evidence to the contrary. All other evidence establishes him as a wealthy, respected, courageous man of integrity, not a petty thief. The many Union soldiers and sailors who became his targets would shout in unison that his hands were definitely not shaky (Henry, 122, endnote 129).

10. McClain, Houston County, 40.

11. Parole of Joseph S. Hinson, 6 May 1865, Fort Donelson, Tennessee.

12. Jill Knight Garrett, *Obituaries from Tennessee Newspapers* (Easley, SC: Southern Historical Press, 1980), 168; quoting the *Whig and Tribune* of

Jackson, Tennessee, 1 March 1873; quoting the *Nashville Union and American* (hereafter cited as Garrett, Obituaries).

Chapter 11

1. Oates, 103, 278.
2. Bishop, 121-127.
3. Herman Melville, "The Martyr," originally published in his *Battle-Pieces and Aspects of the War* (New York: Harper & Brothers, 1866).
4. The wounds were very long in healing; Kentucky did not ratify the Thirteenth Amendment (Emancipation) until 1976.
5. (a) Loose Records, 13 June 1863. (b) Ibid., Weekly Report of Effective Force, Fort Donelson, Tennessee, 26 June 1865.
6. As is so often the case, different records are not consistent in the spelling of her name, sometimes spelling it, as it was pronounced, "Cummins."
7. (a) Some in later years have spelled his name "German" Jackson, the way it came to be pronounced. (b) Although there is one source suggesting the contrary, it seems clear that the Magnolia property was put in Elisabeth's name when purchased. In her will, executed three years before Jack's death, she bequeaths the property as her own and states specifically that it had been "deeded **to me** by Jarman Jackson." This, the fact that Jack died without a will, and the meagerness of his personal possessions at his death, support the belief that all postwar property was protected by having it in either Elisabeth's or Ab's name.
8. (a) For the chain of ownership of the house site and its surrounding acreage see Appendix A. The rest of the 1,200-plus acres of the Bubbling Springs property was apparently sold at about the time the White Oak Creek property was purchased; the records have not been found. (b) Garrett, Guerrillas, 79. (c) McClain, Stewart County, 66.
9. Albert and Sarah Hinson family Bible (hereafter cited as Family Bible).
10. Will.
11. H. R. Atkinson, Magnolia, Tennessee, Journal, entries for 27 August 1872 and 22 August and 8 and 22 September 1873, in possession of Mrs. Frances Hinson, Clarksville, Tennessee (hereafter cited as Atkinson, Journal).
12. Nina Finley, *Houston County Wills and Inventory, 1871-1881* (Erin, TN: Houston County Public Library, 1997), 4.
13. Family Bible.
14. (a) Garrett, Obituaries, 168. (b) *River Counties Quarterlies,* vol. 3, #1234, 11.
15. Ibid.
16. Garrett, Obituaries, 168; quoting the *Clarksville (Tennessee) Tobacco Leaf,* 18 June 18 1873.
17. Ibid.
18. Ibid.
19. Atkinson, Journal, op cit.
20. Cheryl Smith.
21. Steenburn, 105.

22. Jim Carpenter and Daniel Schaffer, project directors. *Tennessee's Iron Industry Revisited: The Stewart County Story,* Land between the Lakes Association, n.d.(booklet), 39.

23. (a) Sale Record, inventory and account of sales of the estate of John Hinson, dec'd, 20 July 1874 (hereafter cited as John Hinson Sale). (b) The day of Jack's death is uncertain. In the record of the sale of his personal effects, the heading reads "Inventory and Account of the Sales of the Estate of John Hinson, Dec'd July 20th 1874." July 20 could be the date of his death, or the date of the sale, but it is most likely the latter.

Epilogue

1. (a) John Hinson Sale. (b) To the end, Jack was a meticulous businessman; the items sold included several debts, owed to Jack at his death, to be collected by the buyers. The complete record of the sale of his simple possessions can be seen in Appendix E.

2. This wash kettle, bought at the sale by Ab, has stayed in the Hinson family and has seen service in recent times as a deep fryer at family fish fries.

3. Sale Record, "Inventory and account of sales of the personal property belonging to the Estate of Elizabeth Hinson, Dec'd, Rep'ted by A.F. Hinson", dated 13 January 1877.

4. Family Bible.

5. *Erin Review,* Erin, Tennessee, 6 May 1882, Action of the Houston County Court.

6. (a) Steenburn, 104-109. (b) T. J. Stiles, *Jesse James: Last Rebel of the Civil War* (New York: Alfred A. Knopf, 2002), 351-356. (c) Robert L. Dyer, *Jesse James and the Civil War in Missouri* (Columbia: University of Missouri Press, 1994), 61. (d) Hinson interviews.

7. There were at least twelve children born to Jack and Elisabeth, but the total is unknown for babies were born and subsequently died during the ten-year periods between census enumerations. The mortality rate of small children was particularly high between the 1860 and 1870 censuses because of the war.

8. Will.

9. Nina Finley, *Roads of Houston County (1871-1899) and Maps of Houston County (1795-1938)* (Erin, TN: Friends of the Houston County Public Library, n.d.), 31.

10. (a) Circuit Court Proceedings, Houston County, Tennessee, 7 August 1886. (b) Annie Marie Fowler, *An Introduction to Danville History (Danville, Tennessee)* (Clarksville, TN: privately published, 2001), 8.

11. (a) Zorn's (City) Directory, Clarksville, Tennessee, 1895-96, 35. (b) State of Tennessee, Montgomery County, "License to Keep a Tippling House in Clarksville," dated 7 November 1894.

12. Thomas Hinson, Alsboro, Alabama, letter to Miss Florence Hinson, Danville, Tennessee, postmarked 8 August 1898, copy in possession of the author.

13. (a) Garrett, Obituaries, 168; quoting the *Bakerville, Tennessee Review,* 3 September 1898. (b) According to census records, Dave and John Wiggins were twenty-five and twenty-three, respectively, at the time of the killing.

14. In the early 1930s, Joseph's widow, then living in Louisville, Kentucky, visited the Hinsons in Danville; many years later, her nephew John Stewart Hinson recalled that during that visit "Aunt Lizzie mended my jumper [denim work jacket]." Only her first name, Elizabeth, is known.

15. (a) Evans, vol. 10, 541. (b) City Directories, Jackson, Tennessee, 1896, 1900, 1901, 1906, 1910. (c) Burial Record, Saint Mary's Catholic Church, Jackson, Tennessee, 4 March 1919.

16. Thomas Hinson, Florence, Alabama, letter to John S. Hinson dated 5 August 1920, in the possession of Betty Jo Hinson Dortch.

17. (a) Discharge (replacement), John S. Hinson, private, Company G, Thirty-eighth Regiment, United States Volunteer Infantry, dated 13 October 1961. (b) One document summarizing his Spanish-American War service states the discharge year as 1901.

18. Certified copy of discharge, John S. Hinson, Ser. No. 5, 236, 310, private, U.S. Army, Camp Pike, Arkansas, 17 January 1919.

Appendices

1. The Hinsons were still a volunteering, fighting family. Stewart, who was already in the navy, was at Pearl Harbor when attacked, and made the navy a career. Dudley served in the Pacific on a battleship and a destroyer. Henry volunteered but was rejected; a few years later, he served in Korea where he was decorated for bravery. George, too young for Korea, served after the Korean War.

2. Martha Love Anderson and William Thomas Love were the children of Thomas Bonner Love (1823-1917).

Bibliography

Books

Allen, Hall. *Center of Conflict.* Paducah, KY: Paducah Sun-Democrat, 1961.

Ash, Stephen. *Middle Tennessee Transformed 1860-1870.* Baton Rouge: Louisiana State University Press, 1988.

———. *When the Yankees Came: Conflict and Chaos in the Occupied South, 1861-1865.* Chapel Hill: University of North Carolina Press, 1995.

Banner, James M., Jr. *To the Hartford Convention: The Federalists and the Origins of Party Politics in Massachusetts, 1789-1815.* New York: Alfred A. Knopf, 1970.

Batterson, Tia, et al. *Danville, Tennessee, Gone . . . But Not Forgotten, History of Danville, Tennessee 1861-1993.* Erin, TN: Houston County Historical Society, 1993.

Benét, Stephen Vincent. *John Brown's Body.* New York: Rinehart and Company, 1927, 1928, 1954.

Bergemann, Kurt. *Brackett's Battalion: Minnesota Cavalry in the Civil War and the Dakota War.* St. Paul: Borealis Books, 2004.

Bishop, Jim. *The Day Lincoln Was Shot: An Hour-By-Hour Account of What Really Happened on April 14, 1865.* New York: Gramercy Books, 1984.

Bowers, Claude G. *Jefferson in Power; The Death Struggle of the Federalists.* Boston: Houghton Mifflin Company, 1936.

Brownlee, Richard S. *Gray Ghosts of the Confederacy: Guerrilla Warfare in the West, 1861-1865.* Baton Rouge: Louisiana State University Press, 1958.

Coleman, J. Winston, Jr., ed. *Kentucky: A Pictorial History.* Lexington: University Press of Kentucky, 1971.

Cooling, Benjamin Franklin. *Forts Henry and Donelson: The Key to the Confederate Heartland.* Knoxville: University of Tennessee Press, 1987.

———. *Fort Donelson's Legacy: War and Society in Kentucky and Tennessee, 1862-1863.* Knoxville: University of Tennessee Press, 1997.

Coughtry, Jay. *The Notorious Triangle: Rhode Island and the African Slave Trade, 1700-1807.* Philadelphia: Temple University Press, 1981.

Cross, C. Wallace, Jr. *Ordeal By Fire: A History of the Fourteenth Tennessee Volunteer Infantry Regiment, CSA.* Clarksville, TN: The Clarksville-Montgomery County Museum, 1990.

Davidson, Donald. *The Tennessee.* Vol. 2 New York: Rinehart and Company, 1948.

Davis, Burke. *The Civil War: Strange and Fascinating Facts.* New York: The Fairfax Press, 1982.

Davis, William C. *Breckinridge: Statesman, Soldier, Symbol.* Baton Rouge: Louisiana State University Press, 1974.

————, ed. *Diary of a Confederate Soldier: John S. Jackman of the Orphan Brigade.* Columbia: University of South Carolina Press, 1990.

Duyckinck, Evert A. *National History of the War for the Union, Civil, Military, and Naval, Founded on Official and Other Authentic Documents.* 3 vols. New York: Johnson, Fry and Company, post-1865, n.d.

Dyer, Frederick H. *A Compendium of the War of the Rebellion.* Dayton: The Press of Morningside Bookshop, 1978.

Dyer, Robert L. *Jesse James and the Civil War in Missouri.* Columbia: University of Missouri Press, 1994.

Ellis, B. G. *The Moving Appeal: Mr. McClanahan, Mrs. Dill, and the Civil War's Great Newspaper Run.* Macon: Mercer University Press, 2003.

Ellis, Joseph J. *Founding Brothers: The Revolutionary Generation.* New York: Alfred A. Knopf, 2001.

Evans, Gen. Clement A. *Confederate Military History.* Athens, GA: Confederate Publishing Company, 1899.

Fellman, Michael. *Inside War: The Guerrilla Conflict in Missouri During the American Civil War.* New York: Oxford University Press, 1989.

Finley, Nina, et al. *World War II Years Remembered by Houston County Citizens.* Erin, TN: Houston County Historical Society, 2002.

Fisher, Noel C. *War at Every Door: Partisan Politics and Guerrilla Violence in East Tennessee, 1860-1869.* Chapel Hill University of North Carolina Press, 1997.

Fleming, Thomas. *Duel: Alexander Hamilton, Aaron Burr, and the Future of America.* New York: Basic Books, 1999.

Fowler, Annie Marie. *An Introduction to Danville History: Danville, Tennessee.* Mena, AR: Annie Marie Fowler, 2001.

Garrett, Jill Knight. *A History of Humphreys County, Tennessee.* Columbia, TN: Jill Knight Garrett, 1963.

————. *Obituaries from Tennessee Newspapers.* Easley, SC: Southern Historical Press, 1980.

Gibson, John M. *Those 163 Days: A Southern Account of Sherman's March from Atlanta to Raleigh.* New York: Bramhall, 1961.

The Goodspeed Histories of Montgomery, Robertson, Humphreys, Stewart, Dickson, Cheatham, Houston Counties of Tennessee. Reprint, from Goodspeed Publishing Company, *Goodspeed's History of Tennessee, 1886.* Columbia, TN: Woodward & Stinson Printing Company, 1972.

Gordon, David, ed. *Secession, State & Liberty.* New Brunswick, NJ and London: Transaction Publishers, 1998.

Gosnell, H. Allen. *Guns on the Western Waters: The Story of River Gunboats in the Civil War.* 1890. Reprint, Baton Rouge: Louisiana State University Press, 1949.

Gotte, Kendall G. *Where the South Lost the War: An Analysis of the Fort Henry-Fort Donelson Campaign, February 1862.* Mechanicsburg, PA: Stackpole Books, 2003.

Graham, John Remington. *A Constitutional History of Secession.* Gretna, LA: Pelican Publishing Company, 2002.

Grimsley, Mark. *The Hard Hand of War: Union Military Policy Toward Southern Civilians, 1861-1865.* New York: Cambridge University Press, 1995.

Hamilton, James J. *The Battle of Fort Donelson.* New York and Cranbury, NJ: Thomas Yoseloff, 1968.

Harrison, Lowell H. *The Civil War in Kentucky.* Lexington: University Press of Kentucky, 1975.

Head, James L. *The Atonement of John Brooks.* Geneva, FL: Heritage Press, 2001.

Henry, J. Milton. *The Land Between the Rivers.* Clarksville, TN: Taylor Publishing Company, n.d.

Hicks, John D. *The Federal Union: A History of the United States to 1877.* Cambridge: The Riverside Press, 1957.

Hinson, Frances Lewis. *Magnolia: A History of Magnolia, Tennessee.* Clarksville, TN: Frances Lewis Hinson, 2001.

Isaacson, Walter. *Benjamin Franklin: An American Life.* New York: Simon & Schuster, 2004.

Joes, Anthony James. *America and Guerrilla Warfare.* Lexington: University Press of Kentucky, 2000.

Johnson, Charles A. *Wise County, Virginia.* Norton, VA: The Norton Press, Inc., 1938.

Johnson, E. McLeod. *A History of Henry County, Tennessee: Descriptive, Pictorial Reproductions of Old Papers and Manuscripts.* 2 vols. Paris, TN: E. McLeod Johnson, 1958.

Johnson, Robert Underwood, and Clarence Clough Buel, eds. *Battles and Leaders of the Civil War.* 4 vols. New York: Century Magazine, 1887-1888.

Jones, Virgil Carrington. *Gray Ghosts and Rebel Raiders.* McLean, VA: EPM Publications, 1956, 1984.

Josephus, Flavius. *The Life of Flavius Josephus.* Translated by William Whiston in *Josephus, the Complete Works.* Nashville: Thomas Nelson, 1998.

Koger, Larry. *Black Slaveowners: Free Black Slave Masters in South Carolina, 1790-1860.* Columbia, SC: University of South Carolina Press, 1995.

Lake, Stuart N. *Wyatt Earp: Frontier Marshall.* Boston and New York: Pocket Books, 1931.

Logsdon, David R., ed. *Eyewitnesses at the Battle of Fort Donelson.* Nashville: Kettle Mills Press, 1988.

Lyon, Clyde. *A Country Boy From Owl Hollow.* Nashville: Country Life Publishers, 1994.

Martin, Destine. *Cemetery Records of Stewart County, Tennessee.* Dover, TN: The Stewart County Historical Society, 1983.

McAllister, J. Gray, and Grace Owings Guerrant. *Edward O. Guerrant: Apostle to the Southern Highlanders.* Richmond, VA: Richmond Press, 1950.

McCann, Kevin D. *Hurst's Wurst: Colonel Fielding Hurst and the Sixth Tennessee Cavalry U.S.A.* Dickson, TN: Three Star Press, 2000.

McClain, Iris Hopkins. *A History of Stewart County, Tennessee.* Columbia, TN: Iris Hopkins McClain, 1965.

———. *A History of Houston County, Tennessee.* Columbia, TN: Iris Hopkins McClain, 1966.

McClellan, George Brinton. *The Civil War Papers of George B. McClellan, Selected Correspondence.* New York: Ticknor and Fields, 1989.

Nott, Capt. Charles C. *Sketches of the War, A Series of Letters to the North Moore Street School of New York.* New York: Charles T. Evans, 1863.

Oates, Stephen B. *With Malice Toward None: The Life of Abraham Lincoln.* New York: Harper & Row, 1977.

O'Brien, Sean Michael. *Mountain Partisans: Guerrilla Warfare in the Southern Appalachians, 1861-1865.* Westport, CT: Praegar, 1999.

Paludan, Phillip S. *Victims: A True Story of the Civil War.* Knoxville: University of Tennessee Press, 1981.

Ridley, Bromfield L. *Battles and Sketches of the Army of Tennessee.* Mexico, MO: Missouri Printing and Publishing Company, 1906.

Sandburg, Carl. *Abraham Lincoln: The War Years.* 4 vols. New York: Harcourt, Brace & Company, 1939.

Sears, Stephen W. *George B. McClellan: The Young Napoleon.* New York: Ticknor and Fields, 1988.

Sensing, Thurman. *Champ Ferguson: Confederate Guerrilla.* Nashville: Vanderbilt University Press, 1942.

Simmons, Don. *Marriage Records, Stewart County, Tennessee (From 1834).* 4 vols. Dover, TN: Stewart County Library, n.d.

Smith, Frank H. *History of Maury County, Tennessee.* Columbia, TN: Maury County Historical Society, 1969.

Smith, Gene. *Lee and Grant: A Dual Biography.* New York: Promontory Press, 1988.

Smith, S. D., C. P. Stripling, and J. M. Brannon. *A Cultural Resource Survey of Tennessee's Western Highland Rim Iron Industry, 1790s-1930s.* Nashville: Tennessee Department of Conservation, Division of Archeology, Research Series No. 8, 1988.

Smith, Venture. *A Narrative of the Life and Adventures of Venture, a Native of Africa, but Resident above Sixty Years in the United States of America. Related by Himself.* New London: C. Holt, at the Bee-Office, 1798. Electronic edition Academic Affairs Library, University of North Carolina at Chapel Hill, 2000.

Steenburn, Col. Donald H. *Silent Echoes of Johnsonville: Rebel Cavalry and Yankee Gunboats.* Rogersville, AL: Elk River Press, 1994.

Stiles, T. J. *Jesse James: Last Rebel of the Civil War.* New York: Alfred A. Knopf, 2002.

Sutherland, Daniel E., ed. *Guerrillas, Unionists, and Violence on the Confederate Home Front.* Fayetteville: University of Arkansas Press, 1999.

Tennesseans in the Civil War: A Military History of Confederate and Union Units with Available Rosters of Personnel, in Two Parts. Nashville: The Civil War Centennial Commission, 1965.

Wallace, Betty Joe. *Between The Rivers: History of the Land Between the Lakes.* Clarksville, TN: Austin Peay State University, 1992.

Waters, Frank. *The Earp Brothers of Tombstone: The Story of Mrs. Virgil Earp.* New York: Bramhall House, 1960.

Watkins, Sam. *"Co. Aytch," Maury Grays, First Tennessee Regiment; Or, a Side Show of the Big Show.* 1882. Reprint, Wilmington, NC: Broadfoot, 1990.

Williams, Emma Inman. *Historic Madison, the Story of Jackson and Madison*

County, Tennessee, from the Prehistoric Mound Builders to 1917. Jackson,
    TN: Jackson Service League, 1972.
Wyeth, John A., M.D. *The Life of General Nathan Bedford Forrest.* New York:
    Harper & Brothers, 1899.
Zorn's (City) Directory. Clarksville, TN: n.p., 1895-1896.

Booklets
Ambrose, Stephen. *The Campaigns for Fort Donelson.* Conshocton, PA: Eastern
    Acorn Press, 1992.
Carpenter, Jim, and Daniel Schaffer. *Tennessee's Iron Industry Revisited: The Stewart
    County Story.* Golden Pond, KY: Land Between the Lakes Association, n.d.
Cooling, Benjamin Franklin. *National Parks Civil War Series: The Campaign
    for Fort Donelson.* Eastern National, 1999.
Finley, Nina. *Roads of Houston County (1795-1938) & Maps of Houston County
    (1795-1938).* Erin, TN: Houston County Public Library, n.d.
———. *In The Beginning: An Early History Of White Oak, Cane & Hurricane Creeks.*
    Erin, TN: Houston County Public Library, n.d.
———. *Houston County Review & Erin Review, 1878-1882.* Erin,TN: Houston
    County Public Library, n.d.
———. *Historical Lists, Houston County (1871-1900).* 2 vols, Erin, TN: Houston
    County Public Library, 1983.
———. *Houston County Wills and Inventory (1871-1881).* Erin, TN: Houston
    County Public Library, 1997.

Journals and Diaries
Atkinson, H. R. Journal. In possession of Mrs. Frances Hinson, Clarksville,
    Tennessee.
Campbell, Capt. Andrew Jackson War Diary. Company F, Forty-eighth Tennessee
    Infantry, CSA; quoted in McClain, Iris Hopkins, *History of Houston County,*
    op cit.
Cannon, J.P., M.D. "The Daily Life of a Private in the Confederate Army, with
    Illustrations." *The National Tribune* (1900).
Channing, Lt. Richard. Company F, Thirteenth Missouri Volunteer Infantry, with
    Channing's table of contents. Special Collections Library, Filson Historical
    Society, Louisville, KY.
Haycraft, Samuel Jr. Hardin County, Kentucky, 1849-1878. Special Collections
    Library, Filson Historical Society, Louisville, KY.
Kirwan, Albert D., ed. *Johnny Green of the Orphan Brigade: The Journal of a
    Confederate Soldier:* Lexington, The University of Kentucky Press, 1956.
Marshall, Eugene. Diaries, with 1912 typescript by his daughter. Rare Book,
    Manuscript, and Special Collections Library, Duke University.
McGaughey, J.W. Diary, 1852-1905. Privately published by R. H. McGaughey,
    ed., Murray State University, as *Life with Grandfather,* 1981.
Ross, Brig. Gen. Reuben R. CSA, West Point Journal, Jan. 1851-Jan. 1853. 2
    vols. War Journal of 29 March 1862. In possession of Ross descendant Walter
    M. Silvey, Clarksville, TN.

Unpublished Manuscripts and Theses

Garrett, Jill Knight. "Guerrillas and Bushwhackers in Middle Tennessee During the Civil War." Tennessee State Archives, Manuscript Division, AC Number 69-338. Nashville, 25 August 1963.

Marshall, Eugene. Diaries, typescript by Marshall's daughter. Rare Book, Manuscript, and Special Collections Library, Duke University, 1912.

Reynolds, Clark G. "The Civil and Indian War Diaries of Eugene Marshall, Minnesota Volunteer." Master's thesis, Duke University, 1963.

Letters

Baker, John. Ninety-sixth Illinois Volunteer Infantry, Baker Family Letters. Special Collections Library, Filson Historical Society, Louisville, KY.

Channing, Lt. Richard. Company F, Thirteenth Missouri Volunteer Infantry, 21 February 1862. Special Collections Library, Filson Historical Society, Louisville, KY.

Cuthbert, William S. Post Surgeon, Fort Donelson letter to post commander dated 12 October 1864. Copy in possession of the author.

Davis, Acting Rear Adm. C. H. Letter to secretary of the navy, 2 October 1862, concerning guerrillas operating from the banks of the Tennessee River. Copy in possession of the author.

Dortch, Betty Jo Hinson. Letters and notes to the author and others. In author's collection.

Fitch, Lt. Comdr. LeRoy. Commander Tenth District, Mississippi Squadron, aboard U.S. Steamer Moore. "Tennessee River Nov 9 1864." Letter describing the difficulty of traversing the chute at White Oak Island upstream. Copy in possession of the author.

Foote, Flag Officer Andrew H. Letter to secretary of the navy, 20 February 1862. Copy in possession of the author.

Forbes, Col. William. Commanding Officer, Fort Donelson, letter to Col. A. A. Smith at Clarksville, Tennessee, dated 22 December 1864. Copy in possession of the author.

Fortiner, Pvt. James. Second Illinois Cavalry, 8 December 1862(?). Special Collections Library, Filson Historical Society, Louisville, KY.

Hinson, John S. Letters to the author, January to December 1995.

Hinson, Thomas. Letter to Ms. Florence Hinson, 8 August 1898. Copy in author's collection.

Metzger, John. Seventy-sixth Ohio Volunteer Regiment, 12-13 and 22 February and 4 and 11 March 1862. Southern Historical Collection, Manuscripts Department, Wilson Library, University of North Carolina, Chapel Hill, NC.

Porter, Acting Rear Adm. David D. Letter to Secretary of the Navy Gideon Welles dated 3 January 1862. Copy in author's collection.

Pusard, Pvt. James. Company H, Forty-second Illinois Volunteers, 9 September 1862. Special Collections Library, Filson Historical Society, Louisville, KY.

Reid, Harvey. Twenty-second Wisconsin Volunteer Regiment, 28 March 1865. Southern Historical Collection, Manuscripts Department, Wilson Library, University of North Carolina, Chapel Hill, NC.

Revelle, Sgt. H. A. Thirty-fourth New Jersey Volunteer Infantry, 14 December 1864. Special Collections Library, Filson Historical Society, Louisville, KY.

Runyon, Louise. Letter to C. L. Johnson, 14 March 1934. Fort Donelson National Military Park Library.

Stigal, Marcella (Mrs. Terry H.). Letter. Memphis, Tennessee, 31 July 1996. Copy in author's collection.

Weston, John Burton. Massachusetts Volunteer Militia (1861) and First Massachusetts Cavalry (1862 to his death 27 November 1863), letters of. Published in Frost, Robert W., and Nancy D. Frost, ed. *Picket Pins and Sabers: The Civil War Letters of John Burden Weston.* Ashland, KY: Robert W. Frost and Nancy D. Frost, 1971.

Wyley, Ann. Waverly, Tennessee, letter to her sister, Mary (Wyley) Lankford, dated 7 April 1863, provided by Tennessee state representative Joe F. Fowlkes on 20 November 1993. Copy in author's collection.

Affidavits, Deeds, Land Grants, Wills, and Other Public Records

Hinson, Charles S. Burial Record. St. Mary's Catholic Church, Jackson, Tennessee, 4 March 1919.

Hinson, Elizabeth. Will. Magnolia Post Office, Tennessee, 4 November 1871.

———. Estate Sale Record, dated 13 January 1877.

Hinson, John. Affidavit of 2 February 1863. Columbia, Tennessee. Copy in author's collection.

———. Estate Sale Record, dated 20 July 1874.

———. Tennessee Land Grant No. 18447, dated 14 May 1847.

Smith, J. W., M.D. Affidavit of 1 January 1897; quoted in Wyeth. *The Life of General Nathan Bedford Forrest,* op cit.

Stewart County, Tennessee, Deed Book Number 27, 595.

———, Deed Book 15, 370.

———, Deed Book 16, 316.

———, Deed Book 16, 154.

———, Deed Book 16, 157.

———, Deed Book 16, 161.

———, Deed Book 17, 95.

———, Marriage Record. Albert Rougement to Rebecca Wells, 1 November 1847.

———, Tax Records. Albert Rougement, 1852, 1853, 1855, 1860.

———, Census 1860. Albert and Rebecca Rougement.

———, Marriage Record. John Mather (of Sweden) to Rebecca Rougement, 26 May 1865.

Military Records, USA

Casualty Sheet. Pvt. James C. Earp, Company B, Seventeenth Illinois Volunteer Infantry, 21 October 1861.

Certificate of Disability for Discharge. Pvt. James C. Earp, Company B, Seventeeth Illinois Volunteer Infantry, 22 March 1863.

Charges and Specifications (rough/worksheet). Provost Marshall, Fort Donelson,

Tennessee, case of George F. Hinson. Period February 1862 to May 1863, unsigned, n.d.

Company Muster-Out Roll. Company B, Eighty-third Illinois Infantry, Case of Pvt. Francis M. Earp, 26 June 1865 (effective 30 September 1864).

Company Muster Rolls. Company B, Eighty-third Illinois Volunteer Infantry, 21 August 1862 to 26 June 1865.

Company Muster Rolls. Company C, Eighty-third Illinois Volunteer Infantry, 21 August 1862 to 26 June 1865.

Discharge (Certified Copy). John S. Hinson, private, U.S. Army, Camp Pike, Arkansas, 17 January 1919. Copy in author's collection.

Morning Reports. Fifth Iowa Cavalry, 1862-1863.

Parole of John Hinson. Fort Donelson, Tennessee, 19 March 1862.

Parole of Joseph S. Hinson. Private, Company F, Fourteenth Regiment, Tennessee Infantry. Department of the Cumberland, Descriptive List (Confederate), 6 May 1865.

Parole of Prisoner of War. Office of the Provost Marshall General, Army of the Potomac, camp near Sharpsburg, MD, 26 September 1862. (William Hinson capture.)

Parole of Prisoner of War. Office of the Provost Marshall General, Army of the Potomac, 30 September 1862. (William Hinson capture.)

Parole (verbatim) of Private William Hinson. Fourteenth Tennessee Regiment, "with letter of transmittal dated Headqrs, Winchester (Va), Oct. 4 1862."

Provost Marshall's Record of Oaths of Allegiance Administered. Fort Donelson, Tennessee, December 1862 to February 1863.

Provost Marshall's Return of Oaths of Allegiance Administered. Fort Henry, Tennessee, month of September 1862.

Record of Events, Equipment and Ordnance. Fifth Iowa Cavalry.

Register of Prisoners of War (R. A. Hinson). Department of the Cumberland, Nashville, dated 8 May 1863.

Roll of Prisoners of War. Fort Donelson, Tennessee, n.d. (Robert A. Hinson capture.)

Special Order 63. Fifth Iowa Cavalry, 22 August 1862.

Union Soldiers General Index. Illinois National Archives and Records Administration.

U.S. Navy Department. *Official Records of the Union and Confederate Navies in the War of the Rebellion.* 30 vols. Washington, D.C., 1894-1927.

U.S. War Department. *War of the Rebellion, Official Records of the Union and Confederate Armies.* 129 vols. Washington, D.C., 1880-1901.

Weekly Report of Effective Force. Fort Donelson, Tennessee, 26 June 1865.

Military Records, CSA

Company Muster Roll. Company H, Fourteenth Tennessee Infantry, September/ October 1863.

———, November/December 1863.

Confederate Archives, Chapter 6, File Number 68, 82.

Regimental Return. Fourteenth Tennessee Infantry, October 1862.

Regimental Return. Fourteenth Tennessee Infantry, November 1862.

Periodicals

Bakerville (Tennessee) Review, 3 September 1898.

Clarksville (Tennessee) Tobacco Leaf, 18 June 1873.

Confederate Veteran, S. A. Cunningham, ed., monthly, 1893-1932.

Craig, Barry. "Thousands of Civil War Soldiers Died Near Their Homes." *Paducah Sun,* 16 April 1995.

Erin (Tennessee) Review, "Houston County Court Action," 6 May 1882.

———, "Circuit Court Proceedings," Houston County, Tennessee, 7 August 1886.

"From the Seventy First." *Troy Times,* 25 June 1863. Report from fifth sergeant, Seventy-first Ohio Volunteer Infantry Regiment.

Gilmore, J. R. Review of *Sketches of the War,* by Capt. Charles C. Nott. *Continental Monthly* 3, no. 4 (April 1863): 502.

Jackson (Tennessee) Whig and Tribune, 1 March 1873.

Memphis Daily Appeal (Atlanta), 13 September 1863.

Moss, Charles. "Forgotten Fort Heiman: 'Land of Late Victory.'" 5 parts. *Nashville Banner,* 1957.

Nashville Banner, "Sunken Union boats at Johnsonville, Tennessee exposed in low water" (originally published fall 1925), 19 March 1958.

Nashville (Tennessee) Union and American, 3 March 1873.

River Counties Quarterlies. Written, edited, and published by Iris Hopkins McClain and Jill Knight Garrett, Columbia, Tennessee, 1972-1978.

Ross, Dan. "The Other Reuben Ross." Parts 1-5. *Cumberland Lore.* Edited by Charles Waters. Published in *Clarksville Leaf Chronicle* (September-December 1989).

Ross, David, et al. "Bugle Echoes from Fort Donelson." Series. *Stewart-Houston Times.*

Stewart County Times, 28 October 1927.

———, 18 September 1931.

Wells, James M. "Union Prisoners Break Out of Libby Prison." *McClure's Magazine* (January 1904). Reprinted. *Old News* 12, no. 6 (March 2001).

Internet Sources

Cracraft, Josh. *SparkNote on Alexander Hamilton.* 22 June 2005. <http://www.sparknotes.com/biography/hamilton>.

Underground Railroad Essays. Vermont Historical Society. <http://www.vermonthistory.org/educate/urass.htm>.

Unpublished National Park Service Studies, Fort Donelson National Military Park Files

Bearss, Edwin C. "The Dover Hotel, Historic Structures Report, Part I." December 1959.

Index